A LETTER

ON

NATIONAL CURRENCY,

ADDRESSED TO

The Secretary of the Treasury,

BY

ELEAZAR LORD.

NEW-YORK:

A. D. F. RANDOLPH, No. 683 BROADWAY.

1861.

Frontispiece: One of several specific plans for a uniform currency submitted to Secretary Chase in 1861 was that of New York businessman Eleazar Lord.

THE COMPTROLLER AND BANK SUPERVISION

A Historical Appraisal

ROSS M. ROBERTSON
Indiana University
Visiting Scholar in the Office of
the Comptroller of the Currency

Assisted by Abby L. Gilbert

The Office of the Comptroller of the Currency
Washington, D. C.

SOURCES OF ILLUSTRATIONS

Frontispiece: The Library of Congress, Toner Collection, Rare Book Room.

CHAPTER 2   **13:** The Chase Manhattan Bank Money Museum. **14:** Robert Friedberg, *Paper Money of the United States.* **17:** United States Treasury Department. **18:** United States Treasury Department. **20:** The Historical Society of Pennsylvania. **22:** Robert Friedberg, *Paper Money of the United States.* **24:** United States Treasury Department. **30:** *American Banker.*

CHAPTER 3   **35:** Robert Friedberg, *Paper Money of the United States.* **38:** United States Treasury Department. **39:** Robert Friedberg, *Paper Money of the United States.* **41:** *American Banker.* **43:** United States Treasury Department. **46:** Office of the Comptroller of the Currency. **48:** Office of the Comptroller of the Currency. **50:** Office of the Comptroller of the Currency. **52:** Robert Friedberg, *Paper Money of the United States.*

CHAPTER 4   **56:** *Frank Leslie's Illustrated Newspaper,* March 10, 1888. **58:** National Archives. **60:** Library of Congress. **62:** Robert Friedberg, *Paper Money of the United States.* **65:** Office of the Comptroller of the Currency. **68:** *Harper's Weekly,* October 11, 1873. **70:** National Archives. **73:** Office of the Comptroller of the Currency. **74:** National Archives. **76:** National Archives. **77:** National Archives. **80:** Office of the Comptroller of the Currency. **84:** Office of the Comptroller of the Currency.

CHAPTER 5   **91:** Robert Friedberg, *Paper Money of the United States.* **94:** Board of Governors of the Federal Reserve System. **96:** Office of the Comptroller of the Currency. **103:** Board of Governors of the Federal Reserve System. **106:** Office of the Comptroller of the Currency. **109:** Robert Friedberg, *Paper Money of the United States.* **114:** Office of the Comptroller of the Currency.

CHAPTER 6   **119:** Courtesy of First National Bank of Bloomington, Indiana. **120:** United Press International. **121:** The Franklin D. Roosevelt Library, Hyde Park, New York. **125:** Library of Congress photo by Dorothea Lange. **127:** Office of the Comptroller of the Currency. **130:** Office of the Comptroller of the Currency. **135:** Office of the Comptroller of the Currency. **136:** Smithsonian Museum.

CHAPTER 7   **142:** American Bankers Association, *The Common Machine Language for Mechanized Check Handling.* **145:** American Bankers Association, *The Common Machine Language for Mechanized Check Handling.* **148:** Harris & Ewing, Washington, D.C. **153:** Courtesy of Indiana Bell Telephone Company. **158:** Office of the Comptroller of the Currency.

CHAPTER 8   **All illustrations:** Office of the Comptroller of the Currency.

The Comptroller and Bank Supervision has been prepared at the direction of the Office of the Comptroller of the Currency. It must not be reproduced in whole or in any substantial part unless prior written approval has been obtained from the Office of the Comptroller of the Currency, Washington, D. C. 20220.

Printed in the United States of America by the McCall Printing Company
First printing, April 1968

Library of Congress Catalog Card Number: 68-60034

Contents

Foreword

In recent years the Office of the Comptroller has received a growing number of inquiries from the academic and business communities about the history and functions of the Office. A variety of published materials, ranging from speeches and testimony of incumbent Comptrollers to official Annual Reports, has always been available. Yet no single work providing requested information in convenient form was ever prepared for classroom use or business reference.

Responding to an apparent public need, the Comptroller of the Currency two years ago commissioned this book by Professor Robertson, a leading student of the financial history of the United States. In accordance with established procedures, this Office permitted unrestricted access to source materials and furnished research and other assistance without any stipulations regarding the scope of the published work or the conclusions reached. Like other scholarly publications of the Office, this book is published under the sponsorship of the Office of the Comptroller without official commitment to the views expressed.

During the period of preparation of *The Comptroller and Bank Supervision* the officials and staff of the Office have benefited from information and ideas developed in their historical setting. It is our hope that this examination of the role of one of the oldest of the regulatory agencies will prove equally beneficial to the reading public.

William B. Camp
Comptroller of the Currency

Washington, D.C.
January 1968

Preface

Economic historians have devoted a substantial amount of research time to the study of financial institutions, public and private. Yet for reasons to be indicated they have never taken a good, hard look at the Office of the Comptroller of the Currency. Because no one paid academic attention to the Office, its history and functions have remained obscure to the greater part of the academic and financial communities. This book, commissioned in 1965 by former Comptroller James J. Saxon, attempts in small compass to remove that obscurity.

I have tried to make the book attractive to a readership that will approach it at different levels of economic knowledge. It should be particularly useful to college undergraduates. At the same time I hope that my professional colleagues will find it informative and interesting and that members of the business community, especially commercial bankers, may find this an appealing subject.

Like every author, I am indebted to many people, not only for their help but for their kindness. Comptroller William B. Camp, the Deputy Comptrollers, and the executive staff went out of their way to assist me, patiently explaining technical points and even searching for elusive material. Former Comptroller Saxon gave generously of his time and knowledge, both during his tenure and after his retirement from the Office, and former Comptroller Ray M. Gidney responded thoughtfully and candidly to my queries.

To my immediate co-workers I am deeply indebted. I particularly wish to thank Miss Abby Gilbert and Miss Amy Millen. Miss Gilbert, my research assistant these past two years, helped greatly with the basic research work, reading enormous quantities of manuscript material and honing it down to manageable proportions. She assisted in the editorial process, compiled the bibliography, and meticulously checked facts and data for accuracy. Miss Millen was editorially responsible for the book's production. With taste and good humor she helped me to clarify parts of the manuscript that might otherwise have been incomprehensible to lay readers, and she saw the work through every pitfall from copy editing to the reading of final proofs. In the last stages of production, Miss Millen served spendidly as coordinator of all our forces. Allen Smeltz and Miss Catherine Berrett assisted me at crucial points, and Mrs. Lucille Leiher prepared the manuscript and gave me the benefit of her years of experience on many questions of usage. Mrs. Nancy MacClintock prepared the index. William Ingram of the McCall Printing Company served as liaison officer for production, and George Lohr contributed his artistry and long experience to the design of both pages and cover.

Officials of national banks and of the other two federal bank supervisory agencies, the Federal Reserve and the Federal Deposit Insurance Corporation, were uniformly cooperative and responsive. In particular, I wish to thank Merritt Sherman, Secretary of the Board of Governors of the Federal Reserve System, who made key historical records available to me. Dr. Hope Holdcamper, Albert Blair, and Donald King of the National Archives were patient and imaginative in servicing the Office archives, and various librarians in the Manuscript Division of the Library of Congress and The Historical Society of Pennsylvania served beyond the call of duty. Dr. Elfrieda Lang and her associates in the Lilly Library of Indiana University, and Miss Marion Wells, archivist of the First National Bank of Chicago, gave unselfishly of their time.

To fellow students of financial history I am indebted for unstinting aid in unraveling many historical perplexities. Professor Edwin L. Harper of Rutgers University, Professor Irwin Unger of New York University, Dean Ira O. Scott, Jr. of Long Island University and my colleagues at Indiana University, Professors Joseph A. Batchelor and David D. Martin, devoted many hours to helping me keep the historical record straight; and Gerald T. Dunne of the Federal Reserve Bank of St. Louis elucidated for me the legal and political environment in which many institutional changes occurred. Professor Gerald C. Fischer of Temple University made his notes and his then unpublished manuscripts freely available and in long conversations helped me more than he knew. And to Victor Abramson, formerly Director of the Banking and Economic Research Division of the Office of the Comptroller, I must express my gratitude for his perceptive suggestions for substantive changes and felicitous turns of phrase.

I can only add that my teaching colleagues at Indiana University bore with good grace the imposition of having on occasion to pinch hit for me during nearly two years of commuting to Washington, just as my family altered cherished plans to accommodate my work away from home. I hope that they will be pleased; I do thank them.

Ross M. Robertson

Bloomington, Indiana
January 1968

Bank Regulatory Agencies

Even the most casual visitor to Washington is likely to notice the buildings that house the three federal agencies charged with regulating the nation's commercial banks. The Federal Reserve is notable for its lovely marble structure, partly hidden in summer by the verdure of Constitution Avenue. On 17th Street rises the contemporary building of the Federal Deposit Insurance Corporation, its architecture testifying to the brusque, no-nonsense attitudes of the agency. And no one could miss the Treasury, the massive, classic building that encloses the Office of the Comptroller of the Currency from public view.

In a vague sort of way, the citizen who passes these buildings has a sense of what goes on inside. The Federal Reserve is responsible for managing the nation's money supply. The Federal Deposit Insurance Corporation administers the program whereby each depositor of a commercial bank is insured against failure of the bank up to $15,000. But the role of the Comptroller of the Currency is probably a mystery. To be sure, most people know that the *Treasury's* main job is to collect taxes, make disbursements, and manage the public debt. But what does the Comptroller of the Currency do?

The Office of the Comptroller of the Currency is a bureau within the Treasury that operates almost apart from that Department. The very name of the Office, descriptive when it was founded in 1863, no longer has meaning. For in modern times the relationship of the Comptroller to the currency is purely legalistic and ministerial, his main function now being to provide administrative regulation and supervision of the country's national banks. The Office considers applications for charters, approving or rejecting them after detailed and lengthy investigation. It grants permits for the formation of new branches of existing banks. It exercises broad administrative controls over bank mergers and consolidations. And it carries on, among other duties, supervision of the operations of national banks, conducting periodic examinations of their activities and continually issuing and reinterpreting rules and regulations under existing laws.

But the Office of the Comptroller of the Currency regulates only about 5,000 nationally chartered commercial banks. What of the approximately 9,000 commercial banks organized under the laws of the 50 states? Approximately 1,350 state-chartered banks have elected to join all national banks as members of the Federal Reserve System; these state member banks, as they are called, are subject to the administrative supervision of the Federal Reserve. Nearly all the rest of the state-chartered banks (7,385 at the end of 1966) are insured, nonmember banks. Because they are insured, and at the same time not members of the Federal Reserve System, they are subject to administrative regulation by the Federal Deposit Insurance Corporation; moreover, they are subject also to regulation by state authorities. Finally, a handful of state-chartered banks, 236 at last count, are noninsured and so fall entirely within the jurisdiction of state authorities.

To beginner and initiated alike, these interrelationships are puzzling. Table 1-1 helps to keep things straight, but the intellectually curious are likely to ask why the division of authority developed among the federal administrative triumvirate. For example, if three agencies have theoretical jurisdiction over national banks, how did the Comptroller of the Currency become in fact the administrator of national banks? Why did the Board of Governors of the Federal Reserve System assume the chief examining and supervisory authority over state member banks? Under what circumstances did the Federal Deposit Insurance Corporation acquire extensive regulatory functions when the other two agencies had been in business for many years at the time of the FDIC's inception?

TABLE 1-1

Supervisory Jurisdiction Under Existing Law

Types of Insured Bank	Federal Agency Having Jurisdiction
National banks [1]	Comptroller of the Currency Board of Governors of the Federal Reserve System Federal Deposit Insurance Corporation
State banks [2] that are members of the Federal Reserve System	Board of Governors of the Federal Reserve System Federal Deposit Insurance Corporation
State banks [2] that are not members of the Federal Reserve System	Federal Deposit Insurance Corporation

[1] National banks **must** be members of the Federal Reserve System; **all** member banks are insured by the FDIC.
[2] State banks are also subject to the jurisdiction of state supervisory agencies; the small number of noninsured banks are exclusively so.

Answers to these questions abundantly prove Justice Oliver Wendell Holmes' observation that a page of history tells us more than a book of logic. They begin far back in the story of American financial institutions. And they are very important answers, for the present fact is that a few agency heads, among the top public officials in America, influence materially the allocation of the financial resources of the country. In these agencies, to say nothing of the 50 lesser but important state bodies, is substantial authority to determine the number and location of commercial banks and their branches, the size of the individual institutions, the variety of services they provide, and the conditions under which they provide them. These authorities largely determine the structure and competitive environment of the commercial banking industry and so indirectly affect the use of financial services by business firms and households.

In banking, as in the rest of the business world, prices play their part in determining the amount and variety of the industry's output. The rate of interest—the price paid for the use of borrowed funds—is one of the most significant prices in the economy, for it largely determines in what proportions funds are channeled into different markets. Moreover, it drastically affects the competition of commercial banks with nonbank financial institutions like savings and loan associations, mutual savings banks, credit unions, and life insurance companies. Yet the price system is less useful as an allocator of resources in banking than it is in unregulated industries. For on the one hand, the total supply of commercial banks' stock in trade—money—is determined by the central bank. On the other hand, the amount and kinds of *investment* in banking are largely circumscribed by the regulatory authorities.

The Aim of the Book

This book will examine the emerging roles of these regulatory authorities. It will trace the evolution of the complex pattern of administrative and supervisory regulations and provide a brief analysis of the changing economic effects of these regulations on banks in particular and on the financial community in general. Books about money and banking crowd the shelves of libraries large and small, yet none of them attempts to sketch the history of commercial bank regulation in the United States. It is the purpose of this book to do just that.

Our topic is thus narrower than the reader might have supposed. For the most part, it leaves out of account the subject of stabilization policy, the strategy by which modern governments try to reduce the magnitude of swings in production, prices, and the level of unemployment. So it largely excludes the fascinating subject of regulation of the money supply and interest rates by the Federal Reserve, the American central bank. It omits

The United States Treasury Building, which lies just to the east of the White House, was completed in 1869 in substantially its present form.

the equally intriguing subject of management of the public debt, the intricate process by which the Treasury sells government securities in order to finance the government of the United States. Nor does it consider, except in passing, questions of deposit insurance, the financing of certain government agencies that cannot draw directly on Treasury funds, and the regulation of the securities markets.

The reader may at first be disappointed to learn that he will not be enlightened on questions of monetary and debt-management policy. For one thing, he may have the impression that the narrower subject of bank regulation, in the sense of supervision and administration, is mundane and without serious public-policy implications. Or he may feel that all the problems of intervention by the financial agencies are inextricably tied together, so that a narrower subject cannot be examined outside the context of the broader one. Until recently, the first objection had more than a little merit, and the second still has a certain validity.

Both historians and economists have largely avoided study of the supervisory functions of the several financial agencies. The people who administered the laws were often pedantic and dull—puritanical types who seemed bent on maintaining a *status quo* that slowed the growth of the institutions they were regulating. Students of money and banking were inclined to look on the regulatory function as being synonymous with bank examination, having to do only with figures and accounts and vouchers and auditors. In short, the regulators, if they made any social contribution at all, seemed to exercise a kind of negative authority, which protected the quality of bank assets by rooting out malfeasance or incompetence. Yet in the past five years this academic view of the supervisory role has been changing. The shift was triggered by the 1961 appointment to the Comptrollership of James J. Saxon, who viewed the role of bank regulators as positive and creative rather than negative and restrictive. But the tardy awakening of interest in the regulatory function should not mask the fact that for more than a century regulation has played a major role in the allocation of the financial resources of the country. What this role has been over the span of approximately 100 years is the subject of this book.

This central topic cannot be treated in a historic vacuum. In the next chapter we will introduce it by tracing the pre-Civil War evolution of commercial banking in this country. Throughout the course of our inquiry, we will take note of changing institutional arrangements in the private financial sector and among governmental agencies. Insofar as it is possible to do so, we shall keep a careful focus on the regulatory, as distinguished from the stabilization, aims of these agencies, but it will be necessary from time to time to treat their other activities. It is impossible, for example, to understand the tightening of supervisory rules that accompanied the Banking Act of 1933 without reference to the depression of 1930-1933 and the central bank's inability to cope with the deflation of that period. Similarly, it is hard to imagine contemporary public and managerial attitudes toward bank liquidity and consumer attitudes toward the safety of their funds without considering the phenomenon of the insurance of bank deposits.

But the economic historian is always confronted with the difficulty of separating the strands of historical change. He is compelled to abstract from the jumble of facts that is reality. It will be possible, at little cost except that of foregoing excursions down intellectual sidepaths, to stick largely to the subject of bank regulation and its effects on resource allocation in finance.

Why Banks Are Regulated

Some of the techniques of modern commercial banking were practiced by businessmen in ancient Persia and Greece. Even in the darkest of the Dark Ages the thin, tenuous lines of commercial exchange were kept alive by specialists who knew how to make payments across international boundaries without necessarily using gold or silver. But commercial banks in

Federal Reserve: Designed by the noted architect Paul P. Cret, the building that houses the Board of Governors of the Federal Reserve System was first occupied in 1937.

the modern sense did not emerge until venturers in 13th-century Genoa began the practice of extending credit to other venturers in trade and industry. From the time of the early Renaissance to the present, bankers, their customers, and the general public have considered banking a very special business, set apart from all others in many ways. Almost everyone realized, however dimly, that a banker must tread a narrow path between earning profits for his bank and keeping enough cash to meet customer withdrawals of funds. Because of their crucial role in financing the ventures of others, bankers have been viewed with awe frequently tinged with suspicion. But not until the early 18th century in England and the early 19th century in America was there a growing awareness that banks perform a social function even more important than that of financing other businesses. At first by issuing bank notes when making loans, and later by crediting the deposit accounts of borrowers when making loans, banks began to provide a portion of the money supply of an economy. As hard money (silver and gold coins) became less important in effecting transactions, the portion of the money supply provided by bank credit increased. Today, in the economically advanced countries of the modern world, commercial banks, operating under certain constraints imposed on them by governments through their central banks, for all practical purposes create the money supply. Clearly, then, the banking business is one in which households and business firms have a more than passing interest.

Pressures for regulation of banks grew as people realized that the failure of a bank could mean the loss of personal fortune or of a firm's working capital. Worse, the failure of a bank cast a pall over the entire community it served, as the means of financing already stricken businesses disappeared. Nor did the damage of failure necessarily stop with the foundering of a single institution. A run on one bank often generated uncertainty and panic among depositors of other banks in a community or region, and the spillover of failure could in turn be transmitted to more remote parts of the country. As harried banks all tried to increase their liquidity by selling securities, prices of securities fell dramatically. And if a bank chose to call loans or refuse to renew notes as they came due, the trouble was passed on to the customers of banks.

Thus, public concern about the condition of banks was especially acute in a day when no one seriously advocated governmental intervention to moderate the business cycle. For it was in times of economic downturn and accompanying financial panic that banks proved especially vulnerable. The only sure protection of the public seemed to be in an ever more complex set of rules and regulations aimed at keeping banks "sound." So we shall not be surprised to find that much of commercial-bank regulation in this country is aimed at weaknesses, real or fancied, that became apparent in depressions long since forgotten.

Indeed, we shall have more than one occasion to observe that American regulation of commercial banks looks backward rather than forward. Failing to realize that times change, supervisory authorities have tended to think more about past battles fought and lost than about strategic planning for a future that will be characterized by a high degree of economic stability. Until recently bank regulation was influenced far more by implicit theorizing about causes of the Great Depression than about mid-20th-century requirements for an imaginative and creative financial system in a growing economy.

It would be misleading, however, to suppose that impetus for bank regulation has come exclusively from customers of commercial banks. Many of the most restrictive banking laws have resulted from active lobbying by banks and by their trade associations. Although businessmen are inclined to praise free competition, the competitive environment they admire is usually one to be prescribed for an industry other than their own. For their own particular business they prefer less competition—the less the better. And so over the past century bankers and their trade associations have urged state and federal legislation to restrict chartering of new banks and licensing of new branches. To be sure, a handful of aggressive bankers, leaders in banks large and small, have consistently urged more competition among banks and between banks and other financial institutions. The American Bankers Association, ministering to a membership that spans a spectrum of bank sizes, is often publicly ambivalent toward regulatory problems, for, in general, smaller banks prefer more restraints on competition while larger ones prefer less. Indeed, the "dual" banking system, whereby charters are granted by both federal and state authorities, persists largely because state legislatures are more readily persuaded than Congress to pass laws favorable to small banks.

Finally, we should be reminded that government regulation in banking as in other fields of activity is often the result of bureaucratic initiative. It is an axiom of political science that regulators on administrative commissions and boards eventually identify the public interest with that of the firms they regulate. In the absence of any clear call from either the customers of banks or from banks themselves, supervisory authorities have asked for laws (and issued regulations under existing laws) that constrain banking activity. We do not impugn the motives or the integrity of public officials when we observe that over the past century many of them have been fearful of markets and suspicious of the allocative efficiency of the price system. Being fearful, they have often prevented the outcomes to which market processes were leading.

Youngest of the three federal bank regulatory agencies, the Federal Deposit Insurance Corporation dedicated its new building in 1963.

Few people would argue for complete absence of regulation in banking. The welfare of depositors is too delicately bound up with the welfare of banks to allow bank managers to seek, without constraints, maximum profits for their firms. Moreover, as providers of the country's money supply, commercial banks play a sensitive, crucial role in the maintenance of economic stability. The historic record suggests, however, that the government has intruded in financial marketplaces in such a way as to bring about a serious misallocation of resources. This misallocation, which led to a proliferation of small banks under a unit-banking system, helped turn the defeat of the Great Depression into ultimate rout. In an economy that will soon generate a trillion dollars worth of output each year, the problem will likely be one of too little finance rather than too much. Without forward-looking regulation we may find ourselves in the mid-1970s with insufficient banking resources in some areas and with units of less than optimum size in others.

Whether commercial bank supervision will in fact be forward- rather than backward-looking depends in part upon technical changes in the payments system, in part upon successfully achieving goals of economic stabilization, and in part upon legislative attitudes toward competition in banking. In recent years the tendency has been to discard restrictive rules of thumb and to make bank regulatory decisions on the basis of economic and legal analysis. Yet there remains continuing opposition to legislative and administrative attempts to permit increased investment in banking. The severity of business slumps, to which banks are so vulnerable, has been greatly reduced, but we have no assurance that depressions have been permanently eliminated. And while the increasing use of electronic devices in the payments mechanism makes old control systems more and more outdated, human beings will continue to make fundamental accounting judgments. We can only be sure that bank supervision will change slowly, probably in the direction of greater freedom for individual bank managers but plainly starting from the practices of the late 1960s.

It is therefore a useful exercise to inquire in some detail how the present structure of regulation developed. In the next chapter we survey the beginnings of bank regulation before 1863. Chapter 3 then describes the events that led to a major decision in banking regulation—the decision to grant national charters to commercial banks. Chapter 4, which brings us to the establishment of the Federal Reserve System, sketches the evolution of the dual banking system in this country. Chapter 5 considers the period 1914-1930, years that witnessed the proliferation of unit banks and the beginning of their wholesale destruction during the 1920s. Chapter 6 examines the regulation of American banks from the early 1930s to the mid-1950s, a period dominated by depression mentality in commercial banking unrelieved by attitudes in the state and federal regulatory agencies.

Chapter 7 discusses the forces that led to liberalization of old rules that were constricting the expansion and creative force of America's banks and summarizes the major administrative decisions made by the Comptroller of the Currency in the years 1961-1965. Chapter 8 closes the study with a description of current organization and functions of the Office of the Comptroller, and an epilogue contains a brief assessment of present relationships among the supervisory agencies.

The Antebellum Setting

Our history of commercial bank regulation could well begin with the passage of the National Currency Act of 1863. But the banking business a century and more ago was different from what it is today, and some of its institutional arrangements would scarcely be recognizable to modern Americans. Because banking practices of that day seem strange—even incomprehensible—to the present day reader, it will help to begin with a quick review of early financial history.

Like people in new lands everywhere, American colonials had serious problems with their money supply. During the first century or so of their economic development, they carried on a substantial portion of their trade through barter, and at one time or another almost every imaginable commodity, from furs to tobacco, was monetized. But with the growth of colonial trade, gold and silver trickled into the five main seaport cities, and by the end of the 17th century coins from all over the world were in general circulation. A continuing slightly favorable balance of trade provided our colonial forebears with a tolerably good specie supply by 1750.

Yet even before the end of the 1600s, the steady growth of trade required some resort to paper money. Promissory notes of well-known merchants might pass from hand to hand for several months, as did bills of exchange drawn on London. In anticipation of tax collections, enterprising treasurers of the several Colonies often issued promissory notes that passed, upon endorsement, as money.

At least three other kinds of paper were in circulation before the American Revolution. Several Colonies issued "bills of credit," promising to redeem them in specie at a future date. Or colonial governments might establish publicly owned "banks," unlike anything we should call a bank today, that issued "loan bills," paying them out to individuals in exchange for notes secured by land or personal property. Some colonial legislatures even allowed associations of landowners to form "land banks." Under these schemes, private venturers would contribute to the bank mortgages on real property, receiving in exchange paper bills that then passed as currency.

Although paper money was not promptly redeemed in some Colonies and so fell into disrepute, other Colonies experimented successfully with these ingenious additions to the money stock. Indeed, good experiences outweighed bad ones, and there was continuing agitation and popular support for more and more paper money. Only outright Parliamentary prohibition of such issues in 1751 and 1764 prevented the rapid growth of paper issues in late colonial days.

Paper money was not issued in serious excess until the Revolutionary War. To finance the Revolution, more than $400 million in Continental money, Quartermaster and Commissary Certificates of the central government, and paper money of the states were printed and put into circulation. The consequence was a runaway inflation, the only one ever experienced in the United States except in the Confederate South. But far from being frightened of paper money, people clamored for more after the break with England, and by 1786 no less than seven states were again issuing their own paper. Although the issuing states acted responsibly, the potential creation of money by 13 political units loosely knit under the Congress of the Confederation was a source of great concern to conservative, propertied leaders, furnishing one of the major arguments for a strong central government. In any case, a Constitution providing for a great common market and a central government potent enough to control the quantity of money was ratified in 1789. Not the least important provision of that Constitution was the clause that outlawed the emission of bills of credit by the states, reserving to the United States power over the money supply.

Although the Constitution ruled out money creation by the several states, it made no positive provision for a currency adequate to the needs of the new country. Coins circulated, of course, coins of all shapes and sizes from every civilized nation. Because of extensive trade with the West Indies and the Spanish colonies, the Spanish dollar and its fractions ("bits") predominated. This fact, plus the preference of Thomas Jefferson for a decimal system, led to the adoption of the dollar (rather than the pound) as the American monetary unit. After Congress passed the Coinage Act of 1792, American coins slowly made their way into circulation along with the foreign ones.

By the time the United States got its start as a nation, it was no longer possible for the economy to function properly on the basis of hard money alone.[1] Modern money forms—bank notes and deposits subject to check—

---

[1] There were nevertheless many hard-money advocates in the United States until the 19th century was nearly over. The idea that there was something immoral and dangerous about bank notes and bank deposits died hard.

were essential even then, and by the end of the 1700s the accepted note-issuing, deposit-creating institutions were commercial banks.

Early Commercial Banking

Commercial banks were not established in colonial America for two reasons. The opposition of British merchants, who made a good thing of financing their American counterparts, led to a tough Parliamentary position against colonial paper money in any form, as the Currency Acts of 1751 and 1764 testified. As important, perhaps, was colonial lack of experience with financial institutions, which were still embryonic in Europe. The first commercial banks began when merchants in major seaports found it more efficient to lend their spare funds through an intermediary—that is, a bank—than directly to each other.

The prevalence in colonial circulation of Spanish milled dollars, their edges designed to prevent chipping or shaving, led to the adoption of the dollar rather than the pound as the American monetary unit.

It was fitting that the first bank chartered in the United States should be located in Philadelphia, for several decades the financial center of the new country. The Bank of Pennsylvania, formed in 1781 under a resolution by the Continental Congress, was replaced in 1784 by a successor institution, the Bank of North America, which for a time held charters issued by both federal and state authorities. Two other banks were chartered in 1784—the Bank of New York and the Massachusetts Bank in Boston. Until 1790, these were the only commercial banks in the country. In that year the Bank of Maryland, in Baltimore, was added to a list that grew steadily until 1811, when there were 88 banks in the country. Banks established in these early years were "founded on specie." Their capitals were largely subscribed in specie—gold and silver—and it was fully intended in those days that both depositors and note holders would be able to obtain hard money on demand.

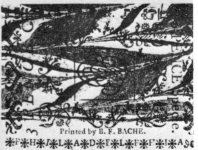

Notes in various denominations of the Bank of North America, first commercial bank in the United States.

These early American banks received deposits and made loans in the same way that commercial banks do today. Depositors could draw checks on their accounts, a practice followed by wealthy customers even in the earliest days. But more often both individuals and business firms made payments in cash. Thus, when a bank officer made a loan, he either credited the borrower's checking account with the amount or, more frequently, handed over the proceeds of the loan in bank notes, which the borrower would then use to pay his workers or remove his other obligations.

Bank notes were ordered by individual banks from private engravers, whose numerous designs could be modified according to the whims of a particular board of directors. Notes were ordinarily signed by the president and cashier of the bank and stored in the safe or vault until they were issued by a bank officer in the routine course of business. Not until the middle 1850s did the dollar volume of bank deposits exceed the dollar volume of bank notes outstanding. Some banks in large cities had by then withdrawn their "circulation," preferring to make all their loans by crediting the deposit accounts of borrowers.

During the first three decades of our national history commercial banks were scrupulously run, their managements so conservative that many a creditworthy borrower was doubtless turned away empty-handed. Some banks limited their discounts to 30 days, with no renewals, and most of the rest put a 60-day limit on their note maturities. Although some banks would make concessions to the requirements of farmers, sometimes extending them credit for as much as nine months, long-term paper was frowned upon. There were exceptions to any rule, of course, because the most inventive bankers were forever experimenting with new types of credit, finding new ways to earn profits for their stockholders while protecting the solvency of their institutions. Nevertheless, mortgage loans, whether on farm or city property, were for decades made only to favored customers; typically, they were unamortized and had maturities of from three to five years. Unlike their European colleagues, most early American bankers resisted the temptation to long-term involvements in the businesses they financed, though more aggressive big-city bankers gradually committed their institutions to the bonds of railroads and manufacturing companies as well as to those of states and municipalities. And gradually the sophisticated banks of the East began to engage in what was later called "investment banking," underwriting securities issues as well as buying the bonds of industry and government.

Banking practice tended to be less cautious, less conservative, as banks were formed at the cutting edge of the frontier. We should guard against the hasty inference that all Western and Southern banks were inferior to those of the East. Banking at its best was to be found in such states as

Ohio, Indiana, Iowa, and Louisiana before the Civil War. But it was in the new areas of the country that the demand for a circulating medium was insatiable, and it was in these areas that the malpractices so shocking to historians of another generation were most apparent.

Difficulties centered around the note issues of banks. Even in well-settled parts of the country, notes issued by different banks were accepted at widely varying rates. Notes of institutions long-established and known to redeem in specie were accepted at par over wide areas. Bills of other banks were received at discounts varying from one-half of 1 percent to 50 percent or more. As much as anything else, distance from the location of the issuing bank affected the acceptability of notes. For example, bills of Baltimore banks circulated at 1 to 2 percent discount in Washington, 40 miles away, while Washington paper was at 1 to 2 percent discount in Baltimore. Notes of Western banks located in states known for lax laws might circulate in the East at big discounts, even though they were issued by specie-paying banks with solid local reputations.

As the number of state banks increased to more than 500 in 1834 (see Table 2-1), heterogeneity of the currency implied other problems. The process of determining the value of genuine notes became more tedious and complex. To this difficulty was added the problem of how to detect the growing number of counterfeit bills. Finally, there was the requirement that notes of broken or liquidated banks, which remained in circulation for long periods, be detected.

Thus, the simplest transaction might require haggling over the amount of payment in the notes of a particular bank, and it is easy to perceive how burdensome it would be to make payments from one part of the United States to another. Indeed, many banks specialized in the pur-

TABLE 2-1

Number of State Banks, 1811 - 1862

Year	Number	Year	Number	Year	Number
1811	88	1841	784	1852	913
1815	208	1842	692	1853	750
1820	307	1843	691	1854	1,208
1830	329	1844	696	1855	1,307
1834	506	1845	707	1856	1,398
1835	704	1846	707	1857	1,416
1836	713	1847	715	1858	1,422
1837	788	1848	751	1859	1,476
1838	829	1849	782	1860	1,562
1839	840	1850	824	1861	1,601
1840	901	1851	879	1862	1,492

SOURCE: *Historical Statistics of the United States, Colonial Times to 1957*, pp. 623-624.

East side of the first Treasury Building: the building was occupied in 1800 and burned by the British in 1814.

chase and sale of domestic exchange in much the same way that modern money-market banks specialize in the purchase and sale of foreign exchange. Actually, in 1850 it was probably more difficult for a St. Louis merchant to remit to a New York supplier than it is for a modern Chicago business-man to remit to a manufacturer in Tokyo. Clearly, a growing industrial economy would have to find a better way.

The Start of Bank Regulation

Almost from the beginning of our national history, it was apparent that the money supply would not manage itself in a way satisfactory to the substantial citizens of the country. As the decades went on, a variety of regulatory devices were suggested and put into effect. A glimpse at our pre-Civil War financial history suggests the course that regulation was to take.

Federal Intervention

Throughout the years before 1863, Americans maintained a strange ambi-valence toward federal controls over banks and the banking system. From the first it was recognized that only federal regulation could provide a homogeneous, universally accepted currency. Moreover, there was a growing realization that only a bank with special privileges could affect the total money supply, keeping the note issues and deposits of the state banks within certain bounds. Yet there was great reluctance, most pro-nounced in the newly settled areas of the country, to allow so much author-ity to the federal government. To this reluctance was added the hostility of a large number of state-chartered banks, whose officers and stockholders were persuaded, rightfully, that banking was more profitable in the absence of federally chartered institutions. Nevertheless, two experiments with federal regulation left marks on 19th-century banking.

Soon after he became Secretary of the Treasury, Alexander Hamilton proposed the establishment of a Bank of the United States. In his famed *Report on a National Bank,* he argued that the young country required a major institution to provide a first-rate convertible paper currency, and to serve as lender to the Treasury and fiscal agent for the government. Over

This portrait of financier Alexander Hamilton, less flattering than the Trumbull rendering, hangs in the Treasury. It is this likeness that appears on every $10 bill currently issued.

the opposition of such major figures as Thomas Jefferson and Edmund Randolph, Congress in 1791 created the first Bank of the United States. With a capital of $10 million, one-fifth of it subscribed by the United States as a major stockholder, the Bank of the United States quickly became the most influential financial institution in the country. Following the clear intent of its charter, the Bank earned most of its income by carrying on a regular commercial banking business, though loans to the government were not unusual. As Hamilton had predicted, the Bank provided valuable services to the government, acting in many respects like a modern central bank. The Bank and its branches followed a conservative lending policy and on balance remained the creditor of the state banks, continually receiving a greater dollar volume of state-bank notes than the state banks received of the Bank's obligations.[2] Notes of the Bank of the United States and its branches ordinarily circulated throughout the country at par. The Bank gradually came to hold a substantial portion of the monetary gold and silver of the country, its vaults during the last three years of its existence containing about as much specie as the total holdings of the state banks. Moreover, the Bank gradually took on the responsibility of making specie loans to state banks, many of which came to rely on the federal institution for accommodation in times of stress.

By almost any criterion, the first Bank of the United States must be judged a success. In no comparable period of American history was there such a well-ordered expansion of credit, and after 20 years the monetary system had advanced remarkably from its inauspicious start. Yet a combination of fear and cupidity led to congressional opposition to the Bank's recharter in 1811. Ironically, Albert Gallatin's support of the bill to recharter did more harm than good with other members of Jefferson's party, and the bill failed by the narrowest of margins.

Grave problems of financing the War of 1812, and deterioration of the paper currency as state banks filled the void left by the first Bank, led to renewed support for a federal institution. After congressional wrangling over several bills, the second Bank of the United States was chartered in 1816. With a capital of $35 million, one-fifth of it again subscribed by the government, the second Bank was a major force in the economy. Despite a shaky start, the Bank prospered after 1823 under the leadership of Nicholas Biddle. By 1830 it had become a central bank, controlling the quantity of money in the economy and rendering services to the federal government as well as to commercial banks. At times it acted as a lender of last resort to commercial banks, and it undertook countercyclical action to offset swings in economic activity. Its notes and those of its branches

---

[2] Thus, the Bank was on balance in a position to present state-bank notes for redemption in specie, forcing the state banks to limit their circulation. Although not founded for this ostensible reason, the first Bank of the United States soon exercised a regulatory function.

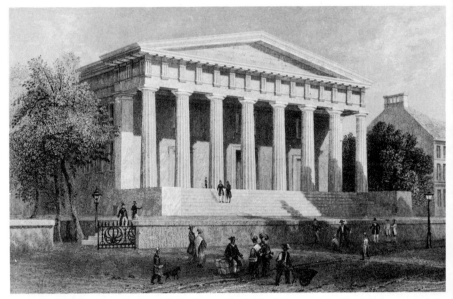

A steel engraving of the second Bank of the United States: the Bank was created by Congress in 1816 and located in Philadelphia.

were literally as good as gold, circulating without discount throughout the United States. Branches of the Bank provided banking facilities in backwoods areas, and greatly reduced the cost to the business community of transferring funds from one part of the country to another.

Once again, agrarian conviction that the Bank unduly restricted the money supply plus the jealousy of state bankers, especially in New York and Boston, furnished the basis of opposition to the Bank's recharter. Even so, the Bank might have survived if Biddle had not allowed Henry Clay, Presidential candidate of the Whigs, to make the question of recharter a campaign issue in the election of 1832. In the summer preceding the campaign, pro-Bank forces in Congress had passed a bill to recharter, which Jackson vehemently and swiftly vetoed. Jackson considered his victory in the autumn a confirmation of his action by the electorate; a year later, the government discontinued making deposits in the Bank, and for all practical purposes the United States again relinquished its central bank.[3]

During the second Jackson administration and the Van Buren administration that followed, continuing efforts were made to put the government on a hard-money basis. Toward the end of Van Buren's term, Western

---

[3] For two somewhat conflicting views of the forces at work to abolish an American central bank, see Bray Hammond, *Banks and Politics in America from the Revolution to the Civil War*, Princeton: Princeton University Press, 1957, and Jean Alexander Wilburn, *Biddle's Bank—The Crucial Years*, New York: Columbia University Press, 1967. In this, as in so many public issues, the decision turned ultimately on the demands, not of the majority of the electorate, but of political and business figures who wielded great power.

and Southern Democrats in Congress at last overpowered their Eastern colleagues and the Whigs, passing an Independent Treasury bill requiring the government to receive only gold and silver in payment of its obligations. But the Whigs repealed this legislation a year after winning the election of 1840. Twice Congress passed bills, drafted by Secretary of the Treasury Thomas Ewing, to charter a third Bank of the United States, only to have them vetoed by unyielding President Tyler. With the return of the Democrats to power in 1844, the battle was renewed to put the Treasury on a specie basis. In 1846, the Independent Treasury was reestablished; from that time on, government officials were "to keep safely, without loaning, using, depositing in banks, or exchanging for other funds than as allowed by this act, all the public money collected by them, or otherwise at any time placed in their possession and custody, till the same is ordered . . . to be transferred or paid out." The federal government was literally on a hard-cash basis. If the letter of the law were observed, the United States could have nothing to do with the money supply except to provide the coinage. Congress had not only killed the central bank but had insisted that the government have no dealings with state banks. Henceforth, all funds were to be kept in the vaults of the Treasury at Washington or in the subtreasuries in various cities, and neither notes of state banks nor checks drawn on state banks would be accepted in payment of obligations due the government.

Almost from the first, Treasury secretaries found themselves unable to adhere strictly to the Independent Treasury law. Even in the 1850s it would be necessary for the Secretary of the Treasury, by means that bordered on illegality, to get coin back into a banking system stripped of coin by tax payments. Nevertheless, the people had spoken. If there was to be regulation of banks and the banking system, it would have to be done by the states. Not until the 1830s, however, had anything like a modern regulatory pattern begun to form. By 1850 state laws adumbrated the complex of rules and regulations that would develop after the Civil War.

Charter and Entry

For the first half-century of our national history, banks were chartered by special act of a legislature, a common procedure for granting all corporate charters. By 1810 the corporate form was usual for banks, insurance companies, and turnpike companies, as it would one day be for railroads and large manufacturing companies. Banks, then, were not singled out for special treatment.

The requirement that charters be granted by a specific legislative act presumably had the advantage of insuring more than routine scrutiny of the incorporators. But there was an objection, loudly raised as the years passed, that the scrutiny was more often than not to see if the politics of the incorporators was that of the majority in the legislature. For those with political connections, obtaining a charter was fairly easy and inexpensive, and there was always the possibility of obtaining one with exceptionally liberal provisions. But those without political ties would often lobby unsuccessfully for a corporate charter, and as early as 1800 there was agitation by those who considered special charters undemocratic to secure "general" acts of incorporation. General laws enabled any group to obtain a charter provided the incorporators followed certain specified procedures and met certain statutory requirements. Gradually the proponents of general incorporation laws won out over those who insisted that their elected representatives should pass on *each* application.

As early as 1811 New York passed a law that permitted incorporation of small manufacturing concerns without special legislative act, and in 1837 Connecticut passed the first general statute that made incorporation the right of anyone. From that time on, acts to *permit,* if not *require,* general incorporation became more and more common.

So we should not be astonished to learn that the early 1800s saw a movement to make bank charters easier to obtain. There was a substantial opinion among the more radical Jackson supporters that banks should be abolished entirely; but by the middle 1830s such a turning back seemed impossible to most people, and only in a few states did no-bank legislation make headway. Moreover, when it became apparent that the second Bank of the United States would not be rechartered, the opportunities for profit were too great to be put aside on ideological grounds. There was a sharp increase in the number of state banks and in the dollar value of their capitalizations and note issues. New banks were chartered in great numbers in the developed East as well as in the

From 1836 to 1860, notes of state-chartered banks constituted the entire paper circulation, the issue of the great Suffolk Bank of Boston being literally as good as gold.

agrarian South and West, and state legislatures were literally flooded with requests for charters.

Thus, simple expediency, as well as belief in the democratic ideal of opportunity for everyone, led to much discussion of the idea of free banking. To the people of the time the adjective "free" meant that any individual or group of individuals, upon compliance with certain procedural steps prescribed in the statute, could start a bank. Michigan's Free-Bank Act of 1837 provided that ". . . any persons, resident of any of the counties of this State . . . desirous of forming an association . . ." could go into the business. A free-bank law with more historic significance was passed the next year by the Assembly of the State of New York. Drafted by Abijah Mann, a perennial architect of bank legislation, the New York statute freed up entry into the banking business, imposing at the same time certain restrictions on the incorporators. Most notable of these constraints was the requirement that the state Comptroller of the Currency was to issue bank notes to promoters of a bank only after they had deposited with the Comptroller an equal dollar amount of bonds of the United States, of the State of New York, or of certain other states approved by the Comptroller. Under certain conditions mortgages on New York land might be so pledged. In the event that a bank organized under this law failed to redeem a note on demand, the Comptroller could, upon notice, sell deposited securities to redeem the note. A final important section of the Act required banks organizing under it to keep a specie reserve in the vaults of at least 12½ percent of their outstanding notes.

The Free-Bank Law of New York was copied with varying success. For a variety of reasons, many states maintained effectual bars to entry up to and beyond the Civil War. Some states were still stockholders in their own successful bank systems, though there was a tendency for states to liquidate their banking interests, only Missouri, Ohio, and South Carolina maintaining theirs after 1850. During the 1840s and 1850s, by constitutional amendment or legislative prohibition, nine states made all banking illegal; and while such severe restrictions did not usually remain long, banks could not be organized in a handful of states at the time of the Civil War. But by then roughly half the states had free banking laws modeled on that of New York. The idea of readily available charters and bond-secured note issues was quickly becoming accepted throughout the country.

Supervision of Bank Operations

The first and second Banks of the United States were required by their charters to furnish statements of condition when called for by the Secretary of the Treasury, but not oftener than once a week. These reports were

The Treasury Building as it looked from 1840 to 1855, when the south wing was added.

to include the amount of the capital stock, obligations due the Bank, total deposits, and total notes on hand and in circulation. The Secretary did not make the reports public, nor did he make them available to Congress unless some member asked for specific information. The Secretary could, however, examine the general accounts of the books of the first and second Banks, and the books of the second Bank were open to a congressional committee for general examination. If the committee should find that the charter had been violated, the government could bring suit against the Bank to have it closed.

Almost from the start of commercial banking in the United States, there were sporadic, ineffective state efforts to prescribe rules for the business. One regulation limited note issue to some multiple of a bank's capital, the stipulation usually being that the "circulation" should not exceed two, three, or four times the capital account. Other rules, such as minimum denomination requirements for notes, were also common.

Condition reports, to either the governor or the legislature, and on either a regular or occasional basis might be required. When they were required, the request was usually made on the grounds that the state was a stockholder entitled to a statement of condition. These earlier reports were simple breakdowns of assets and liabilities by major categories, and contained no information the directors wished to keep secret. As late as 1829, banks in some jurisdictions refused to provide any information about their condition, contending that the running of the bank was a private affair and no one's business but the stockholders'.

Bank examination appears to have originated in those states where a stockholder relationship existed between the state and the banks. Before the 1830s examinations were not made on a regular basis and were ordinarily prompted by what appeared to be a false report of condition or rumored insolvency. Under these circumstances a governor or legislature appointed a prominent citizen or committee of citizens to make inquiry and submit a report. It was considered essential that a person designated to examine a bank be of impeccable reputation and considerable means, for disclosure of a bank's affairs was deemed a great risk to both bank and customers. In general, when examination was permitted before 1830, it was with the understanding that the examiner would only be allowed to verify a condition report previously submitted to the state, and that he would not have unrestricted access to individual accounts and detailed bank records. In 1837, banks in Louisiana refused to be examined, on the ground that the state was not one of their shareholders and was therefore without authority to look at private records.

Federal attempts to examine the condition of state banks developed purely by chance. On March 1, 1819, the House of Representatives, concerned over the administration of the second Bank, passed a resolution demanding an inquiry into its activities and those of state banks as well. All state banks and those in the District of Columbia were required to send the Secretary of the Treasury a statement showing the amounts of capital, notes issued and in circulation, public and private deposits, loans, and specie in vault.[4] On July 10, 1832, the House passed a resolution requiring the Secretary to compile annually a report to Congress on the condition of all state banks, the data to be obtained from records of the governors or legislatures of the several states. These reports were regularly submitted, though with huge gaps in the information, for 30 years. From 1836 to 1841 government depositories were required to submit weekly reports of condition, and the Secretary was authorized to inspect their general accounts and report annually to Congress.

Bank supervision in something like a modern sense came with the innovation of bank-obligation insurance systems. The first of these, the famed Safety-Fund System established by the New York legislature in 1829, was followed by five other schemes in Vermont, Indiana, Michigan, Ohio, and Iowa. With one exception, these five states followed the New York plan of requiring each bank in the insurance system to contribute annually into an insurance (safety) fund up to a certain maximum percentage of its capital. Indiana had no fund, the banks in that state merely signing a mutual-guaranty agreement protecting note holders and depositors against losses resulting from any bank's failure. Like Indiana, Vermont and Michigan protected both note holders and depositors against loss, as did New York from 1829 to 1842. From 1842 to 1866 the New

---

[4] These returns were presented as a composite figure in Secretary William Crawford's *Report on Currency* of February 12, 1820. See especially Statement C, *Reports of the Secretary of the Treasury of the United States, 1815-1828,* Volume II, Washington, D. C.: Blair and Rives, pp. 521-522.

York system protected only against losses to note holders, and the Ohio and Iowa plans similarly excluded protection to depositors.

Conceptually, insurance schemes and methodical supervision might have been introduced separately. But proponents of bank-obligation insurance systems felt that their acceptability would depend on assuring participating banks some control over risk so as to keep loss by failure to a tolerable minimum. Well-managed banks did not wish to be penalized by either the carelessness or malfeasance of bad bank managers. How strongly the profit motive worked to assure adequate supervision is suggested by the fact that in all but one early insurance system selection of the supervisory officials was to be by the participating banks.

In the states initiating these plans, two types of supervisory agencies were established. In New York, Vermont, and Michigan a board of appointed bank commissioners, apparently with no subordinate staff, performed the necessary duties. In Indiana, Ohio, and Iowa authority was given to banking boards, with actual supervisory functions performed by a committee of these boards or by specially appointed agents.[5] In general, salaries were sufficient to pay for full-time services of the supervisory officials, who were delegated ample authority for the performance of their duties. In New York, for example, inspections were made every four months, and examination of any bank could be requested by any three members of the insurance system. In Vermont and Michigan, as well as in New York, bank commissioners could obtain a court injunction against the continued operation of a bank in difficulties or operating illegally. In Indiana, Ohio, and Iowa supervisory officials had the power to close insolvent or badly managed banks, and banks could be closed for refusal to comply with examiners' orders. Supervisory officials could also prescribe lesser penalties. For example, they could order a change in the rate of dividend payments. In Indiana they could go so far as to establish, between certain statutory limits, the ratio of loans and discounts to capital for any bank.

The idea of scrutiny of the affairs of commercial banks attracted supporters even in the absence of insurance plans. One of the strongest commercial bank systems in the country emerged in Louisiana; without an insurance system, supervision there was tough and persistent in the years preceding the Civil War. On the other hand, both insurance and supervision were shortlived in Michigan. On the whole, the decade of the 1850s witnessed general acceptance of the notion that creditors of

---

5 For these and other details of the early insurance plans I have drawn on an unpublished work by Carter H. Golembe and Clark Warburton, *Insurance of Bank Obligations in Six States During the Period 1829-1866*, presently the property of the Federal Deposit Insurance Corporation. For published information on this subject, see the *Annual Report* of the FDIC, 1952, pp. 59-72. See also *Annual Report* of the FDIC, 1953, pp. 45-67; and Carter H. Golembe, "The Deposit Insurance Legislation of 1933," *Political Science Quarterly*, LXXV, June 1960, pp. 181-200.

banks could not rely exclusively on a market system for the protection of their rights.

Unit Versus Branch Banking

Over the past three-quarters of a century, the merits of unit versus branch banking have been volubly debated. Advocates of unit banks have insisted that, whether the units be small or large, banks without branches preserve a competitive environment and make banking services more readily accessible to small customers. Proponents of branch banking have taken the position that multi-office banks in the European tradition provide assurance of a safe, stable banking system, with little or no likelihood of failures and better service to customers because of greater mobility of funds. Branch-bank supporters have further insisted that because of this mobility of funds small communities are better served by branch systems than by unit banks.

As is usually the case in such arguments, both sides can cite historical precedent to suggest that their method of organization has been the "traditional" one. If the appeal to history is confined to the antebellum period, branch-bank advocates have an edge over their unit-bank antagonists. There is plenty of evidence to support the view that throughout the period branch banks were widely accepted as a legitimate form of organization, and that at the very end of the period branch systems showed great vitality and strength almost everywhere outside the New England and Middle Atlantic states.

During the latter part of the 18th century and the first decade of the 19th, the right of banks to have branches was not questioned. Typically, banks organized under the early charters had only one or two branches. But as years went on, banks in the Northeast tended to divest themselves of branches, not because of political opposition but because of a lack of economic impellent to keep them. In this early period branches were almost invariably intercity, there being no special advantage to maintaining intracity branches. In the long-settled regions of the United States, areas requiring a banking office were not without wealthy citizens who could provide the capital necessary to start a bank should there be a prospect of profitable operation. At the same time, no cost savings resulted from operating in two or more cities. The consequence was that in the late 1840s there were no branches of banks in any of the New England states, and only two for the State of New York.[6]

---

[6] In the 1850s a few small banks in Massachusetts, Connecticut, and Rhode Island began the practice of setting up part-time offices in nearby cities to increase their business. The banking commissioners of these states soon quenched such fiery entrepreneurial spirit, beginning a long history of interference with branching by administrative fiat.

Both the first and second Banks of the United States operated branches to the considerable advantage of both institutions. Despite Alexander Hamilton's objections (possibly because he feared competition with his own Bank of New York), the first Bank's charter made it lawful for the directors to establish offices anywhere for the purpose of discount and deposit. Branches were quickly opened in Baltimore, Boston, Charleston, and New York; Norfolk, Savannah, Washington, and New Orleans soon benefited from similar branches. The second Bank had a total of 27 offices and agencies; and while there was complaint in the early years of this Bank's operation about the insubordination of branch managers and the tendency of the branches to become disproportionately large, branch operation of the second Bank was on the whole successful. Branches of the Bank carried on an extremely profitable business, and their competition was felt by state banks everywhere, even in Indiana and Illinois, which did not actually have branches within their boundaries.

The two Banks of the United States set a pattern for the organization of branch systems that became typical in pre-1860 America. In a time of slow communication and transportation, it was impossible for a head office to exercise day-to-day supervision over a network of branches. In fact, each branch had its own board of directors; and though Nicholas Biddle gradually imposed a stronger discipline on his wide-reaching offices, local directorates never relinquished a certain autonomy.

This same principle of organization was carried over into the great branch systems of the West. The structure of one of the best of them, the State Bank of Indiana (begun in 1834), was imitated by the state banks of Ohio and Iowa. The board of directors of the bank was resident in Indianapolis, the capital city. Yet each of the 17 branches was locally organized, had its own capital subscribed by its own stockholders, and paid its own dividends, subject only to the Indianapolis board's approval. Each branch was in effect autonomous, with a supervisory board of control. The Indiana, Ohio, and Iowa systems were held in high esteem and by any touchstone must be judged successful. Several other states, notably Illinois, Kentucky, Tennessee, Delaware, and Vermont adopted the same type of system.

Branch systems of the kind in use today were not unknown, though with one exception they were confined to the South. The Bank of Missouri, a remarkable financial institution, was organized with a head office and five branches. This bank, so conservatively managed that its notes actually circulated at a premium over gold, was run by the head office, its branches having limited authority specifically delegated by the board of directors.

But it was in the South that this type of branch banking became a common form of organization. In Virginia, North Carolina, and South

Carolina, banks with several branches predominated. In Virginia, more than in any other state, a modern form of branch banking flourished. The Farmers Bank of Virginia was perhaps the largest branch organization in the country in pre-Civil War years. Its head office and 12 branches were managed as well as any of its contemporary financial institutions.

Branch banking took a different form in the South for purely economic reasons. Southern capital was largely committed to the plantation system and was not available for a unit bank in every community able to support one. Head offices of banks tended to be in urban centers; therefore, their branches, without local capital contributions in the areas they served, had to be directed from the top. It is foolish to attribute the special organizational characteristics of this kind of system to either European heritage or sociological environment in the South. As elsewhere, availability of resources and the prospect of profitable operations determined the varieties of financial institutions.

Banks and the Money Supply

Despite the banking troubles that beset certain areas, notably those without sufficient resources to support commercial banks, the various kinds of organization served well the communities in which they emerged. A mass of flamboyant prose to the contrary, American banking in antebellum days was of remarkably high quality, episodes of dishonest or bad banking being aberrations from a norm.

Some of these episodes have been recounted with gusto, particularly those describing the activities of wildcatters, who placed their banks far out in the woods to make redemption of notes difficult. Michigan's experience after the passage of the free-banking law of 1837 provided the classic example of wildcatting at its worst. On the frontier shaky banks frequently used operating methods that were scandalous to Boston bankers; and even in the State of New York, where banking was possibly the best in America, country banks would set up redemption offices in Albany and New York, "shaving" a discount of one-half of 1 percent or more in the process of redeeming their notes.

There is of course no blinking the fact that the chartering of banks by the several states resulted in difficulties that 20th-century Americans would find intolerable. By 1860 nearly all of the more than 1,500 state banks had outstanding, on an average, six denominations of notes, so that some 9,000 different kinds of paper bills were in circulation. Some were as good as gold; others, as we have seen, passed at varying discounts. Notes of failed and voluntarily liquidated banks stayed in circulation long after the doors of the issuing institutions had closed forever. And with such a variety of designs to choose from, counter-

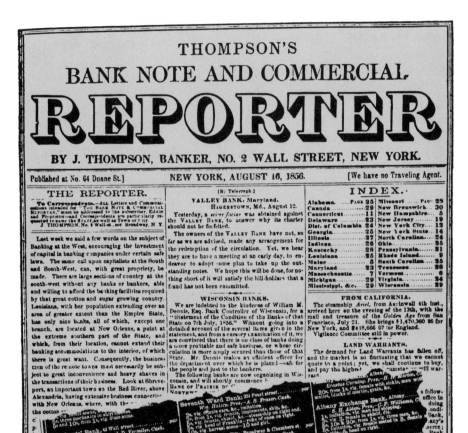

In antebellum days several firms provided an inexpensive "reporter" service to provide information to businessmen about the heterogeneous currency. Best known of the services was Thompson's Bank Note and Commercial Reporter, a weekly.

feiters practiced a profitable trade that bankers combatted with anti-counterfeiting associations, which in turn hired specialists called "snaggers" to ferret out makers of spurious bills.

The problem of judging the authenticity of a bill continued and was complicated by the difficulty of determining the discount at which valid notes should be accepted. The presumption was that well-worn notes or those perforated many times by the teller's staple were genuine. But businessmen needed more technical assistance, and they invariably relied on a "bank-note reporter" or "counterfeit detector." The best of these publications, like *Thompson's Bank Note and Commercial Reporter*, each week provided alphabetical listings, by states, of the notes of banks and the discounts at which they should pass, along with descriptions of known counterfeit bills. *Bicknall's Counterfeit Detector and Bank Note List* specialized in the identification of bogus bills, whereas *Hodge's Bank Note Safeguard* furnished 300 pages of facsimile reproductions of genuine notes. However helpful these lists and periodicals may have been, they suggest the plight of the businessman who many times a day had to take his reporter from the hook to see what a particular bill was worth—if, indeed, it was worth anything.

The pre-Civil War banking system had faults; but it worked, and it was anything but "chaotic," as many of the old historians alleged. A lack of any federal coordination of the banking system unquestionably meant increasing costs to businesses and households from fees and charges. There was, moreover, the unfortunate possibility of being stuck with a counterfeit note or the bill of a broken bank. But those who managed banks showed a remarkable sense of responsibility, ethical standards on the whole being at least as high as those of their contemporaries in the business world. Working with new and untried institutions, feeling their way along to generally accepted principles of operations, 19th-century bankers probably did not understand all the social implications of their business acts. They nonetheless understood some of them.

The settled fact remains that early banks encouraged a rapid development of the American economy that would have been impossible without them. Whatever the hardships and costs imposed upon firms and households, the net effect of early commercial bank activity was to reduce the cost of finance.[7] Moreover, the system assured the most aggressive entrepreneurs of a source of steady funds. No better way of guaranteeing creation of new money to finance new circuits of production could have been devised than this one, which allowed one group of enterprisers to set themselves up in business as dispensers of loans to another group of enterprisers who would take risks with the proceeds. Banks met the new

---

[7] Many of the alleged weaknesses of the banking system should not be attributed so much to banks as to an unstable economy with its pronounced cyclical swings.

country's demand for money by the simple process of exchanging the notes (and the deposit credits) of banks for the promissory notes of business firms—that is, by exchanging one kind of debt for another. The bank's instruments of indebtedness simply had more general acceptability, at least as a medium of exchange, than the debt instruments of commercial or industrial firms. The pre-1860 money supply was created by monetizing private debt. There is a good case to be made for the proposition that this monetization occurred at an optimum rate in the absence of interference by the federal government.

Restriction of the antebellum money supply to gold and silver coin would have been disastrous. By a substantial majority the electorate supported Jackson's stand against a central bank, which could have provided a homogeneous currency while placing various financial restraints on the economy. So for three decades after 1832 the money supply depended upon: (1) net additions to the quantity of specie resulting from importation of precious metals and from domestic mining, and (2) the paper money and bank deposits created by commercial banks operating under various state laws. In the next chapter we shall see how this arrangement was modified by the federal government.

Establishing
A National Banking System

By 1860 the United States was a major economic power. The preceding decade had been one of remarkable growth; at its close the United States was second only to Great Britain in manufacturing, and American agricultural products were steadily invading world markets. By modern standards the individual firm was still small, and the banks that served them were even smaller. But the use of the corporate form of business organization was spreading rapidly; and though few firms except railroad companies required an actual investment of as much as a million dollars, signs were clear that the concentration of industry would soon bring much larger business units.

A part of the reason for the country's growth lay in the fact that it constituted a great common market, which assured maximum participation in the benefits of specialization. By the early 1840s three great economic regions had emerged. Beginning after the War of 1812 the South provided through the cotton trade a major impellent to economic growth.[1] Cotton linked the United States to the Atlantic economy and the South to the Northeast, for it was the Northeast that provided the services necessary for transporting, financing, insuring, and marketing cotton. But the Northeast did more, for this section manufactured and exported goods to the West and to the South. The West in turn furnished the South a large portion of its food, at the same time exchanging its agricultural products for the manufactured goods of the Northeast. This tripartite regional specialization was at once the basis of strong economic bonds and weakening political divisions. For in the years before the Civil War a pronounced sectionalism directed political energies toward county seats and state capitals, and even by the standards of the time federal receipts and expenditures were incredibly small.

The wonder was not that ties of Union were severed in 1861 but that the Union had endured for nearly three-quarters of a century. The

---

[1] See Douglass C. North, *The Economic Growth of the United States, 1790-1860,* Englewood Cliffs, N. J.: Prentice-Hall, 1961, pp. 66-100.

...ict between North and South began before the American Revolution. The constitutional crisis that led to Civil War emerged in the divisions that separated American leaders during the Confederation and was forebodingly apparent in the Constitutional Convention of 1787. Southern and Western insistence on states rights and an ineffectual federal government did little to remove these divisions, and those who wished to preserve the Union were seriously hampered by a feeble and inadequately supported government in Washington. The sorry state of national affairs is suggested by two facts: when Salmon Portland Chase became Secretary of the Treasury in the dismal spring of 1861, there was less than $2 million in the Treasury, and the government had recently been required to pay as much as 12 percent for short-term funds.

Secretary Chase was a man of considerable gifts. An ex-Governor and ex-Senator from the state of Ohio, he had fought his way very nearly to the top of the Republican Party, standing in 1861 so close to the peak of power that he could command the second post in the Cabinet. A humorless man, authoritarian and domineering, he was nevertheless a person of integrity and steadfastness of purpose. Unfortunately for his country, Secretary Chase knew little about public finance, his experience having been limited to that of director and counsel for a commercial bank. But in those days political preferment rather than technical competence made a Secretary of the Treasury. Chase's ideas on public finance were simply the conventional wisdom of hard-money advocates, and he refused to consider imaginative plans suggested by some of his contemporaries for financing the War.

We need sketch only the barest outline of Secretary Chase's approach to the country's financial problems. In the first place, he was persuaded against vigorous and prompt taxation, taking ex-Secretary Gallatin's view that the government need only raise taxes sufficient to cover peacetime expenditures plus interest on the growing public debt. As a consequence, of the more than $3 billion spent by the Lincoln administration during four years of war, less than one-fifth was paid for by taxes. The remaining four-fifths was defrayed by issuing unredeemable paper currency and by borrowing.

As early as the summer of 1861, Secretary Chase began to use non-interest-bearing demand notes, authorized by Congress in small amounts, to pay government salaries.[2] With the passage of the Legal Tender Act

---

[2] These notes were not specifically made payable in coin. However, before the suspension of specie payments, the Secretary of the Treasury proclaimed them redeemable in coin in certain cities, and they were universally regarded as coin notes. For detailed discussion of the controversies and unending perplexities of Civil War financing, see Gerald T. Dunne, "President Grant and Chief Justice Chase: A Footnote to the Legal Tender Cases," *Saint Louis University Law Journal*, 5, Fall 1959, pp. 539-553, and Bray Hammond, "The North's Empty Purse, 1861-1862," *The American Historical Review*, LXVII, October 1961, pp. 1-18.

A demand note of 1861, the first noninterest-bearing note issued by Secretary Chase, shows Alexander Hamilton, and the statue of Columbia on top of the U. S. Capitol.

of February 25, 1862, the United States could issue $150 million of non-interest-bearing notes not redeemable in specie. Strictly speaking, this issue made legal tender for all private and public debts except payment of customs duties and interest on United States obligations, was the first paper money issued by the United States government. Printed by the newly established Bureau of Engraving and Printing, these United States notes, nicknamed *greenbacks* because of the vivid color on their reverse sides, became a permanent part of the American money supply. By the end of the War some $450 million of this paper had been authorized, an enormous amount for the time constituting almost half of the total amount of currency in circulation. As opponents of fiat-money financing had predicted, greenbacks almost immediately fell to a discount compared with gold and silver, so that two sets of prices were soon being quoted for goods and services and foreign exchange. In the darkest days of the War, greenbacks sold at a gold price as low as 35 cents on the dollar, though Northern victories brought them by the end of the War to slightly over

80 cents. During the War state-bank notes, redeemable only in greenbacks, depreciated similarly.

Depreciation of the paper currency was synonymous with rising prices. Only a little while after the issue of the first legal tender notes, it became clear that inflation would place a ceiling on the amount of paper money that could be issued. Since Secretary Chase remained adamant in his refusal to increase taxes, declining to use such authorization to tax as Congress granted him, the only recourse was to borrowing. Yet it was clear from the Treasury's successive efforts to finance its deficit that the market for government bonds would be continuously unfavorable. Chase and his advisers became obsessed with the notion that a plan of national-bank organization requiring banks to have bond-secured note issues would be of great help to wartime financing. At the same time Chase would be able to achieve a reform that he had publicly supported for years—the creation of a uniform paper currency. "I have never entertained a doubt," he wrote to Joseph Medill, "that it is the duty of the General Government to furnish a general currency. Its . . . duty . . . must now be performed, not merely as a duty but as a matter of policy." [3]

The Currency Act of 1863

The United States had experimented twice with a central bank, and for a time in the 1840s Congress had attempted to establish a third such institution. The ideal solution to many of the Treasury's problems would have been a central bank. Yet a serious proposal for another Bank of the United States would have raised an intolerable political storm. What other kind of scheme, in the Federalist-Whig tradition, might be devised?

For many years proposals were heard for a uniform currency that would have the advantage of federal coordination without the disadvantage of federal monopoly. As early as 1815, *Analectic Magazine* had run a sprightly review in which the author suggested a national, uniform currency that would be redeemable in either specie or government stock.[4] As might be expected, advice was also forthcoming from the academic community. In 1827 Professor John McVickar published "Hints on Banking," in which he was the first to suggest unifying the currency through a system of free banks, each bank to invest nine-tenths of its capital in government stocks pledged for the redemption of its notes. Twenty years later Millard Fillmore of New York urged the extension of free banking and suggested

---

[3] Salmon P. Chase to Joseph Medill, October 16, 1861, Chase Mss., Pennsylvania Historical Society.

[4] Until the Civil War and even a little later government debt instruments were commonly referred to as "stock."

the adoption of a national currency that would displace the individual issues of state banks, at the same time obviating the need for another central bank.

No less than three specific plans for a uniform national currency based on Treasury bonds were presented directly to Secretary Chase during the last half of 1861. The first of these came in an August letter from blueblood Orlando Bronson Potter of New York. Potter recommended that banks duly authorized by loyal states could secure their circulation by depositing with an appropriate Treasury official United States stocks, "thus making the stocks of the United States a basis of banking on which alone a national circulation can be secured." Such bills, appropriately stamped and signed by a Treasury official, would in effect be guaranteed by the United States. With a common design and a government guaranty, such an issue would achieve the goal of uniformity while leaving the state banking systems intact, for Potter had a simple faith that banks without a national circulation could not compete with banks that adopted one.

In November, New York tycoon Eleazar Lord sent a pamphlet to Chase outlining another plan for bond-secured notes. "Let the Treasury Department (or a bureau under the responsibility of the Secretary) be authorized to propose to the existing banks throughout the country, and to new banking companies, to invest their capital at once, or gradually, in part or wholly, in national stock . . . to deposit the said stock with his department as security for circulating notes to a like amount."[5] But Lord proposed a currency convertible into United States bonds that would in turn be redeemable in specie 20 years later.

In the winter of 1861, a third suggestion was made to Secretary Chase by Silas M. Stilwell, a former New York Assemblyman. Stilwell wrote a draft bill that Secretary Chase gave to Edward Jordan, Solicitor of the Treasury, for revision. Chase was so pleased with the result that he had the public printer prepare 30,000 copies for distribution by Stilwell.[6] Stilwell's pamphlet developed the idea that the use of government bonds as security for the national currency would stimulate the demand for them and so enable the Treasury to pursue its policy of heavy deficit financing. Another advantage was added to the list of arguments for national banks when Stilwell alleged that considerable benefits would result from the use of national banks as government depositories.

Thus, Secretary Chase was at once predisposed to a plan of national banks by his own theory of war finance and guided to a plan by several

[5] Eleazar Lord, *A Letter on National Currency Addressed to the Secretary of the Treasury*, New York: A.D.F. Randolf, 1861, p. 6. Toner Collection, Rare Book Division, Library of Congress. (See Frontispiece.)

[6] Silas M. Stilwell, *Private History of the Origin and Purpose of The National Banking Law and System of Organized Credits for The United States*, New York: Trow's Printing and Bookbinding Co., 1879, pp. 4, 10.

Thomas Sully's portrait of Salmon Portland Chase, Secretary of the Treasury under Lincoln and later Chief Justice of the Supreme Court.

concrete proposals. By the time he issued his *Report on the State of the Finances* on December 9, 1861, the main outlines of the forthcoming banking system had emerged.

> The [plan] contemplates the preparation and delivery, to institutions and associations, of notes prepared for circulation under national direction, and to be secured . . . by the pledge of United States bonds and other needful regulations.
>
> In this plan the people . . . would find the advantages of uniformity in currency; . . . effectual safeguard . . . against depreciation; . . . a large demand for govern-

ment securities, of increased facilities for obtaining the loans required by the war, . . . A further and important advantage [was] increased security of the Union. . . .

To public officials and bankers alike, Chase's proposal seemed revolutionary; for though the ideas were neither original nor novel, they had not had widespread public discussion, and they flew in the face of public sentiment.

To be sure, the beleaguered Secretary was cheered by some favorable comment, delivered in person or through the press. Powerful Congressman Samuel Hooper of Massachusetts expressed cordial approval, as did Economist Amasa Walker and Alfonso Taft, father of the 27th President. Joseph Medill, influential editor of the *Chicago Tribune,* vigorously enlisted support for the plan, and Robert Walker, a former Secretary of the Treasury, came out foursquare for Mr. Chase's "free banking system."

Yet it was clear from the outset that a powerful opposition would burgeon. Some of it was of the "yes-but" variety. New York securities broker James M. Brown, for example, wrote Chase to commend him on

United States notes were, strictly speaking, the first paper money issued by the federal government. One of a series of early designs, this note depicts an American buffalo between famed explorers Lewis and Clark.

his "highly interesting and very able *Report*" and then proceeded to say why it should not be adopted. An improvement in the market for government bonds would be offset, he believed, by a deterioration in the market for securities that would be sold by state banks to buy Treasury issues. Moreover, Brown worried, the scheme amounted to a forced loan from the banks that would "provide a substitute for the ordinary mode of borrowing by tempting existing Banks to increase their circulation and inducing the formation of New Banks and Associations by the profit derivable from an issue of paper to be provided for them by the Currency Bureau. . . ." [7]

More to the point, James W. Taylor, a leader of the banking fraternity, warned Chase about the reaction of the commercial banks, and John J. Knox (later to be the fourth Comptroller of the Currency) questioned the strength of the inducement offered state banks to join the system, implying that only a differential tax on state-bank notes would provide such inducement. George R. Messersmith, President of the Chambersburg (Pennsylvania) Bank, asked his friend Jay Cooke to persuade the Secretary not to "swallow up the banks." Simeon Nash wrote Chase that it was too late to deny the power of states to create banks, that the interest of state banks lay against the plan, and that in any case the time for moving to a national system was not propitious, requiring as it did a change in the entire investment of the country's banking capital then fully loaned to commerce and industry. George S. Coe, President of New York's dominant Bank of Commerce echoed, "We want something more immediately effective. . . ." [8]

Members of both the Senate and the House were bombarded with correspondence. Senator William Fessenden of Maine, Chairman of the Finance Committee, later to succeed Chase as head of the Treasury, received a letter from James Gallatin, son of the distinguished former Secretary of the Treasury, arguing that "to establish a system of currency on the basis of the government debt, similar to the system prevailing in this State, is very much less objectionable, than the issue of a government paper by the government." [9] But much of Fessenden's mail opposed the Secretary's plan as did that of Senator John Sherman, able member of the Senate Finance Committee who would one day be its chairman.

No amount of opposition, however formidable, would deter Secretary Chase. His *Report* was referred to the House Subcommittee of Ways and Means, then composed of three powerful and financially knowledgeable

---

[7] James M. Brown to Salmon P. Chase, December 11, 1861, Volume 53; January 1, 1862, Volume 54, Chase Mss., Library of Congress.
[8] George S. Coe to Salmon P. Chase, December 12, 1861, Chase Mss., Library of Congress, Series 2, Volume 110.
[9] James Gallatin to William P. Fessenden, December 14, 1861, Fessenden Mss., Library of Congress, Volume 2.

businessmen—E. G. Spaulding of New York, Samuel Hooper of Massachusetts, and Erastus Corning of New York. During the Christmas holidays of 1861 Spaulding prepared his first draft of a national bank bill and had 200 copies printed for the Committee of Ways and Means. Spaulding almost certainly was aided by Edward Jordan, Solicitor of the Treasury, and Silas M. Stilwell. He also used a copy of the New York banking laws sent from Albany by Congressman Corning. Finally, Congressman Hooper incorporated certain passages from the Massachusetts statutes.

John Thompson, founder and editor of Thompson's Bank Note and Commercial Reporter, *was one of many prominent figures who forwarded a uniform-currency plan to Secretary Chase.*

By the time Congress reconvened after the Christmas recess, the banks had suspended specie payments. Suspension diluted the enthusiasm of some Congressmen hitherto favorably disposed toward a bill to create more banks. Thaddeus Stevens, Chairman of the Committee of Ways and Means and the most influential figure in the House, led a ferocious opposition. Though Spaulding reported the bill to the whole Committee, it was clear that it would not pass. In any case the Treasury needed relief more immediately and directly than ultimate support of the bond market. So Spaulding made the legal tender section of the bank bill into a separate measure, and in February of 1862 the Legal Tender Act became law. Within a month, Chase's plan for a national banking system was dead, and greenbacks began to pour out of the engraver's plant.

Congress had refused to meet the desperate financial problems of early 1862 with a bill that would not be effective for months or even years. But if Secretary Chase was discouraged, pessimism was not evident in his papers or diary. He obstinately kept pressing for his legislation. On July 11, 1862, the very day on which Congress authorized another issue of greenbacks, Congressman Hooper introduced a bill to provide for a "National currency secured by a pledge of United States stocks." Again, Thaddeus Stevens was in noisy and fearsome opposition. Alarmed, Chase successfully appealed to Senator Sherman to champion the bill in the Senate. Yet Congress took no action during the summer and autumn, and even Chase began to show his discouragement. On December 4, in his second *Report,* he again urged the adoption of his plan for a uniform and stable currency, outlining in more detail than a year previously procedures for the establishment of banking associations and mentioning for the first time their prospective usefulness as public depositories. His final argument, one not without merit, was that temporary redemption of the proposed bank notes with United States legal tender notes would hasten specie redemption.

Public reaction to the second message, this time relatively mild on both sides, simply recast the old arguments. Once again, it was not theory that prevailed so much as vested interests, for clearly the majority of commercial banks saw nothing but trouble for themselves should the legislation pass. James M. Brown was frank to say that "though Bankers may be as generous and patriotic as other people, yet as a *rule* business advantages and considerations will be the *test* they will apply to it, and not their feelings as citizens and Patriots." [10] Less candid opponents merely argued that, although the bill had merits, immediate action was necessary, and the bank scheme would fare better when conditions were more settled. A parade of leading bankers came to Washington to express their disapproval, not the least of them being Hugh McCulloch, president of the prestigious Bank of Indiana, who flatly stated that banks would not submit to examinations and other novel restrictions provided in the bill. And A. B. Clark of Clark and Company, New York City, was more prophetic than he knew when he wrote Chase that to attract banks in his state the federal provisions would have to be as liberal as those of the banking law of New York State. Mr. Sherman's bill, he added, was certainly not as liberal and he predicted that "if passed but a very few if any Banks will be organized under it, and the object which you wish to accomplish will entirely fail." [11] But the forces that were to secure passage of the revolutionary measure were too great to be resisted.

There was first of all the support of President Lincoln, who in his Annual Message of December 1, 1862, specifically urged passage of the National Currency Act. The public credit would be greatly improved, he said, and "negotiation of new loans greatly facilitated by the steady market demand for Government bonds which the adoption of the proposed system would create." [12] Again in a special financial message in mid-January Lincoln pressed Congress for early passage of the bank bill. Secretary Chase meanwhile was exerting every pressure he could, leaving the impression with Congress that he could not continue the financial management of the country without passage of the bill.

---

[10] Brown to Chase, *op. cit.,* February 24, 1863, Volume 72.

[11] A. B. Clark to Salmon P. Chase, February 12, 1863, National Archives, Record Group 56, Treasury Department.

[12] *Congressional Globe,* 37th Congress, 3rd Session, 1863, 62, Appendix p. 2. As a young Whig politician in Illinois, Lincoln had argued for national regulation of the currency.

Senator John Sherman, a foremost 19th-century political figure who never quite achieved the Presidency, was largely responsible for Senate passage of the Currency Act of 1863.

As matters turned out, congressional approval of the bank bill was secured with the support of three of Chase's Ohio cronies, Senator John Sherman and the Cooke brothers, Jay and Henry. It was Sherman's bill, introduced into the Senate on January 26, 1863, after a similar House bill had foundered, that became law. It was Sherman who compromised at crucial points, who debated the issue masterfully, and who at last squeezed it through the Senate by a margin of two votes. But it was the Cooke brothers who in both House and Senate managed to glean the finally conclusive support.

The father of Henry and Jay Cooke, Eleutheros Cooke, had campaigned with Chase in Ohio. While Governor of Ohio, Chase became well-acquainted with Henry Cooke, then editor of the *Ohio State Journal* and a leading Republican in the state. Henry Cooke supported Chase in his campaign for the Senate and later, after Chase went to the Treasury, backed his successor, John Sherman. Although Jay, fast gaining prominence as a financier in Philadelphia, had never met Chase, it was inevitable that he should make his acquaintance after the national election of 1860.[13] The two met in the summer of 1861, and the following autumn Chase went to Philadelphia to seek Jay Cooke's advice on his pressing problems of government finance.

From that time on Jay and Henry Cooke were extremely close to the Administration. But not even Jay Cooke's success in the sale of bonds for the Treasury meant as much to Chase as the brothers' help in getting the bank bill through Congress. Henry was the manager on Capitol Hill, daily informing Jay of his progress in gaining the support of both House and Senate members. But the Cookes' success lay in an intensive newspaper campaign that covered most of the loyal states. As sole Treasury agent for the sale of government bonds, Jay Cooke had spent large sums in newspaper advertising. He felt that he had a right to claim space in news columns, which carried on a drumbeat of comment about the merits of the national banking system. He similarly commandeered editorial space, often supplying material in his own hand, and clippings of the ensuing articles from hometown newspapers were then placed on each legislator's desk. Editorial opinion plus a flood of ·constituents' letters generated by employees of the Cooke organization had a magical effect. On February 6 Henry could write his brother that the "medicine" was doing its work and that Congressman Spaulding had remarked, "What a wonderful change in popular sentiment. Everybody seems to be going in for the Bank bill." [14]

Henry was more sanguine than he had a right to be. Even after the bill passed the Senate on a vote of 23 to 21, the House threatened not to take it up. But on February 20, eight days after Senate passage, a reluctant House of Representatives passed the bill. On February 25 the President signed it.

The issue of who actually wrote the National Currency Act has often been discussed and never finally resolved. The fairest judgment seems to be that it was a composite bill: the original details were outlined by Potter; the Stilwell-Jordan draft was used by Spaulding in drawing up a bill for the Congress; and Spaulding's effort was revised by Hooper and finally amended by Sherman. No other claims to authorship, including those championing the Cookes, are valid. Most of the early schemes stressed the utilization of a bond-secured note issue to provide a national

---

[13] Neither Jay nor Henry, nor their father for that matter, made any bones about the importance for their personal finances of an old Ohio friendship with the new Secretary of the Treasury.

[14] Henry D. Cooke to Jay Cooke, February 6, 1863, Cooke Mss., Pennsylvania Historical Society.

currency, but it was Salmon P. Chase who originally suggested the idea of independent national banks, combining the concepts of free banking and federal control.

After more than 30 years of remaining aloof from American banking, the federal government once again established a relationship with banks and bankers. The Currency Act of 1863 was loosely drawn, full of ambiguities and uncertainties, and destined to be replaced by a more orderly statute little more than a year later. Yet Congress had made a major move, one that would not be undone. There had been no widespread sentiment for passage, and only accusations of "disloyalty" in time of war, administrative pressure, and modern lobbying techniques secured a favorable vote. Secretary Chase had gotten what he wanted, a uniform currency bill that would presumably strengthen the market for Treasury securities. But more than two years would pass before the system would fasten itself securely on the American economy.

It was clear nonetheless that the national banking system was permanently lodged. Henceforth five or more people could form an "association" to carry on the business of banking, provided they could raise a capital stock of $50,000 in cities of 10,000 or less and $100,000 in cities of over 10,000. Upon compliance with the technical provisions of the Act, each association would be required before beginning business to deliver to the Treasurer of the United States interest-bearing government bonds in an amount equal to one-third of the association's paid-in capital. Moreover, each association might deposit bonds to the full amount of its paid-in capital as security against its note issue, which could not exceed 90 percent of the current market value of the United States bonds deposited. The administrator of the Act, designated the Comptroller of the Currency, would issue uniformly engraved notes to the requesting associations, a stipulation being that the total amount of such issues should not exceed $300 million. The total note issue was to be apportioned among the states in accordance with a formula that gave equal weight to population on the one hand and "existing banking capital, resources, and business" on the other.

Experience and Revision

The arrangements made for administration of the National Currency Act indicated congressional sensitivity to the importance of the legislation. The law established within the Treasury a separate bureau, designated the Currency Bureau.[15] Its chief officer, the Comptroller of the Cur-

---

[15] References to the "Currency Bureau" are common until the close of the 19th century, when the name fell into disuse.

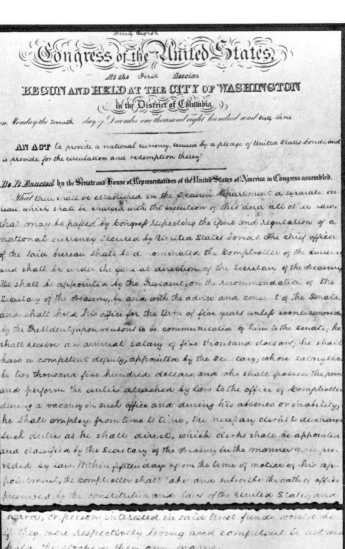

Beginning and closing passages of the National Bank Act of 1864 showing Abraham Lincoln's signature.

rency, was to function under the general direction of the Secretary of the Treasury. Appointment to a five-year term would be by the President with the advice and consent of the Senate; and a unique clause in the statute provided that early removal by the President would likewise be with the advice and consent of the Senate. Moreover, the Comptroller was required to report annually to Congress at the beginning of its session, the report to come directly and not through the Secretary of the Treasury.

Congress obviously considered the Comptrollership a major job. As the repeated use of the word "currency" suggests, the Office was conceived to be the administrative apparatus by which the issue of national-bank notes would be controlled. The obvious person for such a position would be a seasoned banker.

Perhaps as many as a dozen names were suggested to Secretary Chase as potential nominees. The first man to be offered the position was Thomas W. Olcott, President of the Mechanics and Farmers Bank of Albany, New York, who forthwith turned down the job. The second candidate to receive an invitation was Joseph Patterson, friend of Jay Cooke and President of the Western Bank of Philadelphia. Upon Patterson's refusal, Secretary Chase was free to negotiate with Hugh McCulloch, a man unknown to Chase personally but a banker widely admired because of his superb management of the Bank of Indiana. A leading lobbyist against the national banking system in 1862, McCulloch had gradually come to the conclusion that a uniform circulation was essential. He decided to resign the lucrative presidency of the Bank of Indiana and go to Washington "to organize the National Currency Bureau, with the understanding, however, that I should remain in Washington no longer than might be necessary to give the new banking system a successful start." [16]

Months were spent attending to the details of organizing the Bureau. Not until June 20 was the first organization certificate issued to the First National Bank of Philadelphia, and the first of the new national-bank notes were not in circulation until December. As of the date of the first *Report* of the Comptroller (November 28, 1863) only 134 banks had been organized under the Act, 94 of them in the four States of New York, Pennsylvania, Indiana, and Ohio. The response was, to say the least, disappointing, for the banks chartered were on the whole small and there was only one conversion from a state-bank charter. Indeed, throughout the period spanned by the Currency Act of 1863—from February 25, 1863 to June 3, 1864—only 456 charters were issued, and less than 20 of these were conversions.

Clearly there was no rush to move from state to national charters. In

---

[16] Hugh McCulloch, *Men and Measures of Half a Century*, New York: Charles Scribner's Sons, 1889, p. 165.

This portrait of Hugh McCulloch, first Comptroller of the Currency and later Secretary of the Treasury, hangs in the office of the present Comptroller.

his memoirs, Comptroller McCulloch indicated four reasons for the unwillingness of state banks to become national banks.

First: The apprehension that the national system might prove to be a repetition of the free-bank system of the West, which had been a disreputable failure.

Second: The opinion that in becoming national banks, and issuing notes secured by Government bonds, their interests would be so identified with the interests of the Government, their credit so dependent upon, so interwoven with, the public credit, that they would be ruined if the integrity of the Union should not be preserved.

Third: The danger of hostile legislation by Congress, or the annoyances to which they might be exposed by Congressional interference with their business for partisan purposes.

Fourth: The requirement, that in order to become national banks, they must relinquish the names to which they had become attached, and be known by numerals.[17]

Of these four objections McCulloch felt that he could successfully refute the first three. The fourth continued for some time to give him organizing troubles, for Secretary Chase was obstinate on the question of the titles of national banks, insisting that such corporate identities as the Fifth National Bank of Chicago or Tenth National Bank of New York be exchanged for old and valued names.[18]

McCulloch knew, of course, that the basic statute would have to be tightened and strengthened. In the archives of the Treasury Department is a notebook containing a paste-up of the sections of the Currency Act of 1863, with lengthy emendations in Comptroller McCulloch's own hand. In his *Annual Report* of 1863, McCulloch suggested so many revisions that their incorporation amounted to a complete rewriting of the law. Again, a minority of reluctant legislators resisted for a time the passage of another statute. But the decision had been made, once and for all, in the winter of 1863; on June 3, 1864, the National Bank Act was passed, this time by substantial majorities. It left a permanent imprint on the nation's economic system, providing the legal framework for national-bank charters that persists into the present day. For convenience, the provisions of the Act can be summarized under three headings.

Organization. Five or more persons could form an "association" for the purpose of carrying on a banking business.[19] Incorporators were to draw up articles of association and file them with the Comptroller of the Currency. Associations in towns of less than 50,000 were required to have a minimum capital of $100,000 and those in cities of 50,000 or more a capital of at least $200,000. With the approval of the Secretary of the Treasury, associations in towns of less than 6,000 inhabitants might be organized with a minimum capital of $50,000. Strict rules required total capital to be paid in after only a few months of operation.

---

[17] Ibid., p. 168.

[18] Secretary Chase's attitude toward the question of names of national banks is suggested by his response to Comptroller McCulloch's request that the Bank of the Ohio Valley be allowed to enter the system under that corporate title:

The Associations have an undeniable right to select their name—but I deeply regret any determination to depart from the style thus far adopted. It will be unjust to the Banks which have already taken the National disposition to give any sanction to such a departure and will occasion work for which the acceptance of the Bank of the Ohio Valley to the System will be no compensation—though that acceptance is certainly much to be desired.

See Chase's handwritten note on W. W. Scarborough's letter to Hugh McCulloch, November 16, 1863, National Archives, Record Group 101, Comptroller of the Currency.

[19] The word "associations" was used in this and much state banking legislation to avoid the use of the word "corporation." No one was deluded by the euphemism.

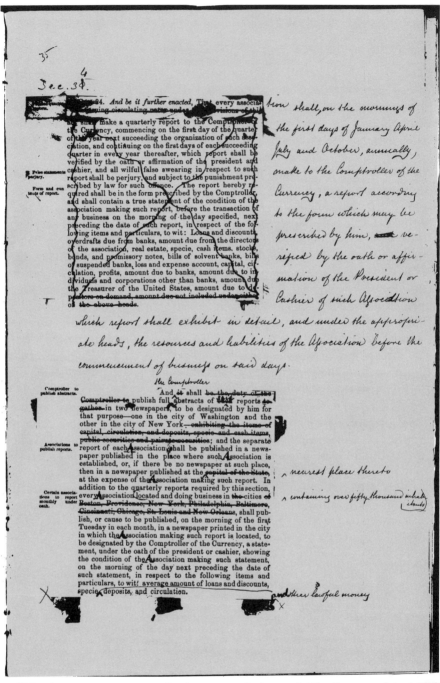

A page from an old notebook showing proposed changes in the Currency Act of 1863, made in his own hand by Comptroller McCulloch. These changes were incorporated in the National Bank Act of 1864.

Note Issue. To secure its note issue each national bank was required to buy bonds of the United States equal to one-third (later one-fourth) of the dollar amount of its paid-in capital stock. Having deposited its government bonds with the Treasurer of the United States, each bank would receive notes, engraved in a standard design but with the name of the issuing bank on the obverse side, in the amount of 90 percent of the par or market value (whichever was lower) of bonds deposited. A national bank could have any amount of government bonds in its portfolio, but the amount of its notes outstanding could not exceed its capital in dollar amount.

Reserves. By 1860 several state laws required banks to keep cash reserves against deposit and note liabilities. In strict practice banks based on specie kept reserves of gold and silver in their own vaults. But as time went on, the custom emerged of keeping deposits, known as correspondent accounts, with banks in other cities.[20] The National Bank Act recognized prevailing practice by permitting new associations to keep their reserves in two forms—as cash in vault or as deposits with a national bank in one of 17 "redemption" cities. Banks located in New York City (later called a "central reserve" city) were exceptions in that they were required to keep their entire reserve as cash in vault.[21] Banks in the 16 other redemption cities (later redesignated "reserve" cities) were required to keep half their reserves as cash in vault but might keep the other half as deposits with national banks in New York. Banks in all other cities and towns (country banks) had to keep two-fifths of their reserves as cash in vault but might deposit the remaining three-fifths in a national bank in a redemption city. Reserves, in whatever form they were maintained, were set at 25 percent for banks in redemption cities and at 15 percent for country banks.

Originally reserves were to be calculated as a percentage of notes outstanding plus deposits. Beginning in 1874, national banks were no longer required to keep reserves against notes but were to keep on deposit with the Treasury a 5 percent redemption fund that could also be counted as part of reserves against deposits. From that time on national banks calculated their minimum legal reserves only as a percentage of deposits.

The National Bank Act of 1864 met the greater part of McCulloch's objections to the earlier legislation. Many ambiguities were removed, and minor concessions were made to bankers in the direction of milder con-

---

[20] If a bank manager in Indianapolis, Indiana, knew that a substantial portion of checks drawn by depositors would be payable to Chicago firms, he found it convenient to keep funds in a Chicago bank to meet this flow of obligations. In case of local emergency these deposits would serve him almost as well as cash in his own vaults, for he could either use them to meet obligations of his bank in Chicago or have the funds transferred back to Indianapolis.
[21] The 1864 law provided that cash be "lawful money." At that time "lawful money" meant gold, silver, and greenbacks.

One of the very early national-bank notes, duly signed by the President and the Cashier of the Third National Bank of Pittsburgh, Pennsylvania. The reverse shows Sir Walter Raleigh in England exhibiting corn and smoking tobacco imported from America.

straints. The objective of a uniform national currency was admirable, and a national charter might bring increased prestige and perhaps greater customer confidence. Yet it soon became apparent that there were few inducements to persuade state banks to take out national charters. State bankers could see little reason for giving up comfortable (and sometimes nonexistent) supervision under state charter for the uncertainties of national regulation. Under a national charter regular bank examinations would be mandatory, and each institution would be required to submit a statement of condition upon the request of the Comptroller of the Currency. Reserve requirements were for the most part higher than under the state rules. Real estate loans by national banks were restricted to such an extent that they could scarcely be made, and loans could not be made on the security of a bank's own stock. The range of permissible investment was narrower than for state banks. The prospect of profits under national supervision seemed much slimmer than under state supervision.

Thus, to the disappointment of Chase and McCulloch, growth of the system continued slow through 1864. Especially vexing was the refusal of large, well-established banks of the East, holding a substantial proportion of the banking resources of the country, to leave the havens of state charters. Both Chase and McCulloch worked incessantly but to little avail to persuade established banks to convert. With the help of Jay Cooke and some subtle financial pressure, a few large state banks were persuaded to go national, and Cooke was instrumental in founding a $5 million bank (The Fourth National Bank of New York), a substantial institution for the time. But by early 1865 it was clear that if a national system were to emerge existing institutions would for the most part have to be coerced into participation.

Since the beginning of the controversy over a uniform currency law there had been considerable jockeying among members of Congress to place first national and then state banks at a tax disadvantage. After passage and repeal of various statutes, this wrangling resulted in a tax for revenue purposes only that did not discriminate between national and state institutions. In the opinion of Secretary Chase and Comptroller McCulloch it had become necessary to create a tax differential so severe that state banks would have to transfer to national status. On March 3, 1865, Congress imposed a tax of 10 percent upon state-bank notes. Banks put their notes into circulation by lending them to borrowers. If the interest on a loan were 7 percent per annum and a bank were required to pay a tax of 10 percent per annum on the amount of its notes outstanding, there would obviously be a loss on the transaction.

As Table 3-1 indicates, the tax was indeed effective. A majority of state banks immediately changed to federal jurisdiction, and in 1866 less than 300 state banks remained. These were for the most part institutions

TABLE 3-1

Number and Resources of National Banks and State Commercial Banks and Loan and Trust Companies, 1863-1870

	Number of Banks		Resources (millions of dollars)	
Year*	National	State	National	State†
1863	66	1,466	$ 16.8	$1,185.4
1864	467	1,089	252.2	725.9
1865	1,294	349	1,126.5	165.8
1866	1,634	297	1,476.3	154.8
1867	1,636	272	1,494.5	151.9
1868	1,640	247	1,572.1	154.6
1869	1,619	259	1,564.1	156.0
1870	1,612	325	1,565.7	201.5

* As of various call dates, approximately June 30 for years indicated.
† State-bank resources are estimated.
SOURCE: Comptroller of the Currency, Annual Report, 1931, pp. 3 and 5.

that had long since dropped the practice of issuing notes when they made loans. After the Civil War deposits were far more important than notes in cities; within a decade after Appomattox banks in all but backwoods areas could make their loans simply by crediting the account of the borrower, so that after 1875 the tax on state-bank notes would no longer be an economic deterrent to operation under state charters.

But the tax on state-bank circulation achieved its aim. The national banking system was given the needed boost and new banks with large capitals began to seek charters. Though a great many bankers sensed that they would be able to hang onto state charters and so to maintain dual—that is, federal and state—control over the banking system of the country, Treasury officials no longer had to beseech the financial community to cooperate. National banks were here to stay.

The First Half Century Of
Federal Bank Regulation

The differential tax on state banks and the ensuing swing to national charters came as the country confronted the formidable business of reestablishing the ties of Union. The states of the Confederacy would have faced an uncertain future under the most enlightened public economic policy. Such policy as could be detected was for the most part anything but enlightened. The emancipation, which provided no land for the former slaves and no compensation to former slave owners for the loss of their capital, began a desperate period of struggle to restore the economic system of the South. A vengeful and cruel attempt at Reconstruction made the woeful prospect all but hopeless. Moreover, the South, traditionally short of finance, would be handicapped for almost a century by a continuing scarcity of imaginative financial leadership.

The North had problems of its own, of course. In the minds of conservative, solid citizens not the least of these was the problem of getting back to specie payments. On August 31, 1865, $100 in gold exchanged for $144.25 in greenbacks or checks drawn on bank deposits.[1] Businessmen wanting to return to a gold basis as quickly as possible agitated to have the greenback retired. The resumption of specie payments became the most controversial economic question of the day, one that was debated for years.

To secure the resumption of specie payments the premium on gold would have to drop to zero. Two alternative monetary policies were proposed. It appeared to some that the best course would be to reduce the general price level by contracting the supply of paper money. The price of gold would presumably decline with the general fall in prices, and when the mint price was reached resumption could take place. The second course would be to allow the economy to "grow into" resumption.

---

[1] Put the other way around, the gold price of $100 in greenbacks on this date was $69.32. For the variation in gold prices in terms of other money between 1865 and 1879, see Comptroller of the Currency, *Annual Report,* 1879, pp. xiv-xv.

Counting cash in the vaults of the New York Subtreasury, one of the key offices in the Independent Treasury system.

Such a course would hold the money supply constant while allowing the growth of the economy to bring about a gradual decline in prices. Again, the market price of gold would fall, ultimately reaching the mint price by a slower and less painful route.

Actually, Hugh McCulloch, Secretary of the Treasury in the Johnson Administration, initiated a severe policy of monetary contraction that was approved by Congress in the Contraction Act of April 1866.[2] But the deflationary medicine was bitter, and in February of 1868 Congress ended contraction. From 1868 to 1874 the Republican Administration paid lip service to gold resumption yet took the sensible course of not contracting the money supply. But when the Democrats won the congressional election of 1874, lame-duck Republicans, afraid of the antipathy of Western and Southern legislators toward resumption, hurried to pass legislation providing for a return to gold payments in four years. The Gold Resumption Act of 1875 was a major piece of legislation. After January 1, 1879, the United States was to maintain strict convertibility between green-

---

[2] This law authorized redemption of greenbacks at a rate of $10 million a month for six months and $4 million a month thereafter. See Act of April 12, 1866, 14 Stat. 32.

backs and gold.[3] For all practical purposes the United States would from that time on be on the gold standard.

The national banking system was thus forged in a setting of continuing controversy over the amount and kind of currency to be used. Moreover, Westerners and Southerners complained endlessly about the special lack of circulating medium in *their* sections of the country. Thus, to the problem of determining the amount of money in circulation was added the perplexing one of its proper apportionment among the states. An issue that may seem academic to modern Americans was real and vital to the people of that time, and many who knew little about most facts of economic life took strong sides in the public argument.

Bank Chartering and Entry

Constraints on Entry

Through the power to tax, Congress had forced the conversion of the great majority of state banks to the national system, but continuing concern and suspicion kept institutions holding roughly 10 percent of the country's banking resources from converting. For more than a decade after the establishment of the national banking system, another major restriction, which had nothing to do with the merits of a particular charter application, inhibited entry. Under the Currency Act of 1863, the total circulation of nationally chartered banks was limited to $300 million. Moreover, the original statute provided for the apportionment of this circulation among the states and territories, one-half on the basis of population and the other half on the basis of wealth, resources, and existing banking facilities. This distribution formula was omitted from the 1864 Act, but it was restored by the Act of March 3, 1865, when it became apparent that without such a formula the national banking system would be largely confined to the Middle Atlantic and New England states. On the same day, as a provision of the law levying the 10 percent tax on state-bank note issue, the Comptroller was required until July 1, 1865, to give preference in granting charters to state banks (with capitals of $75,000 or more) over new associations.

Caught between seemingly contradictory statutes, Comptroller McCulloch had to decide which of the two laws took preference. The conversion of state banks in preference to granting new charters meant that a disproportionate amount of Eastern banks would enter the system, violating the "distribution rule." But since there could be no truly national banking system without conversion of the state banks, McCulloch and his

---

[3] In 1878 Congress ordered that no further greenbacks be destroyed or retired and authorized a greenback circulation of $347 million, the amount that remains outstanding today. See Act of May 31, 1878, 20 Stat. 87.

R.N.P

Files Nov 2 1866

Treasury of the United States.
Division of National Banks.
Washington **Nov. 2° 1866**

Sir—

I am in receipt of yours of this date, requesting that I will decline to receive any further amounts of bonds designed for deposit to secure circulating notes under the National Currency Act, "as the amount already received, and of which we have advices, will be sufficient to secure the entire $300,000,000 of National Currency authorized by law."

In reply, I have to say that your request will be complied with, and that no further deposits of bonds for the purpose stated will be received except with your consent.

Very Respectfully,

H. R. Hulburd Esq
Depy & Actg Comptroller of the Currency

As this letter to Acting Comptroller H. R. Hulburd testifies, notes issued by national banks had by 1866 reached the authorized limit of $300,000,000.

immediate successors chose the alternative of preferring conversion, despite the violation of the apportionment law.[4]

[4] Professor George L. Anderson has pointed out that Comptroller McCulloch could have taken a different tack, reconciling the two laws by "confining the preference law to operation within states and with respect to the quota of circulation assigned to each state by the apportionment law. Thus a state bank in Ohio would have the preference over a new bank in Ohio in competing for the quota of national circulation assigned to Ohio by the apportionment act. Instead of following this rule the officials of the Treasury

58   **The Comptroller**

For more than a decade the upper limit on circulation harried the national chartering authority and was a source of continuing annoyance to the Southern and Western states. The unequal distribution of national-bank circulation was an issue in the presidential campaign of 1868, and Governor Horatio Seymour, the Democratic candidate, time and again roused Midwesterners with his demand for more national banks. The South, even worse off, made similar demands for a fair share of the circulation, but the section's political potency was insufficient to stir much congressional sentiment. An attempt in the summer of 1868 to authorize an increase of $20 million of circulation in the South had failed of passage, and redistribution of existing circulation, though often suggested, was not adopted as a remedy until an Act of July 12, 1870. This statute provided for an increase in the national-bank circulation of $54 million but retired an equal amount of 3 percent certificates eligible for reserve purposes. This law also provided that $25 million of the circulation of Eastern states should be redistributed after the $54 million of new circulation was "taken up." Once again, the Southern and Western states failed to get their due. A decision of the Comptroller held that the new circulation had to be assigned to banks with completed organizations. For the sole purpose of forestalling the exhaustion of the $54 million, many banks filed applications for circulation and then did not complete the formal process of issuance, with the consequence that the $25 million never was redistributed. At last, in June of 1874, Congress passed a law providing for the immediate redistribution of $55 million, but by this time circulation was being voluntarily *retired*. Finally, in a section of the Specie Resumption Act of 1875, Congress removed all restrictions on the national-bank circulation.

Despite the requirement that he sell his wares to an unfriendly clientele, Comptroller McCulloch did not consider himself bound to automatic approval of charter applications. Although he never articulated a philosophy of bank chartering, his views can be inferred from an 1864 *Manual of Instructions* sent to prospective organizers of national banks and from cryptic notes in his own hand on letters requesting forms for charter applications. Even in these beginning years, when every effort was made to strengthen the system through numbers, national-bank charters were not handed out indiscriminately. Before mailing forms for meeting procedural requirements for a national-bank charter, McCulloch insisted on having three kinds of information. First, he wanted a summary of the economic potential of the community in which the proposed bank would

---

Department ignored the apportionment law completely and permitted state banks, largely in New England, to enter the national system and absorb over $50,000,000 of circulation set aside for the South and over $30,000,000 assigned to states of the West." See George L. Anderson, *The National Banking System, 1865-1875: A Sectional Institution*, abstract of a doctoral thesis, University of Illinois, 1933.

INSTRUCTIONS AND SUGGESTIONS

OF THE

COMPTROLLER OF THE CURRENCY

IN

REGARD TO THE ORGANIZATION AND MANAGEMENT OF
NATIONAL BANKS.

TREASURY DEPARTMENT,
Office of the Comptroller of the Currency, 1864.

For the instruction and guidance of persons who may
desire to organize National Banks, under the national
currency act, the following suggestions and forms have
been prepared:

1. In proceeding to organize an Association, the first
thing to be done is to obtain the necessary subscriptions
of stock. This may be accomplished through commissioners to be appointed for that purpose, or in any other
manner that may be found to be the most convenient.
No form is required by the Act, and it is not thought
necessary that any should be furnished by this bureau.
It is only necessary that the subscriptions should be
made in such manner as will create a legal liability on
the part of the subscribers to take and pay for the stock
subscribed for by them respectively according to the
requirements of the Act.

2. After the stock is taken, the associates should enter
into Articles of Association, according to the requirements
of the 5th section of the Act; and the following is submitted as a general form for such articles, to be modified
in such proper manner as will meet the views of the
persons forming Associations:

The first page of the first edition of a Manual of Instructions, *published in
1864. This manual, originated by Comptroller McCulloch, was revised and
issued at irregular intervals by succeeding Comptrollers over a period of more
than 50 years.*

be located—its population, the kinds and amount of business done there, and its prospects for growth. Second, he required information from responsible people about the character and business ability of those proposing to organize a bank. Finally, he investigated the extent of banking facilities in the city of the proposed bank and in nearby communities to ascertain the extent of potential competition. Many a letter of inquiry contains such remarks as "Send law but express opinion bank not needed" or "Delay" or "Discourage, near Athol Depot." Procedures were less formal than those that ultimately emerged, but the first Comptroller made an investigation of the same kind that would be required a century later.

Freeman Clarke, who succeeded to the Comptrollership upon McCulloch's appointment as Secretary of the Treasury, also took the view that the Comptroller could exercise some discretion in the granting of a bank charter. Like McCulloch, he operated within the constraints of provisions restricting the circulation, as did the third incumbent Hiland R. Hulburd. John J. Knox, Hulburd's successor, had to contend with a maximum-circulation constraint for only a short while. After the limitation was repealed, Comptroller Knox could comment enthusiastically in his *Annual Report* for 1875:

> The national banking system was intended to be a free system, and from the beginning the organization of banks was open to all; but the amount of circulation originally authorized having subsequently become exhausted, the establishment of banks with circulation was, of necessity, for a time suspended. The act of January 14, 1875, however, removed all restrictions in this respect; and since that date every application which has conformed to the requirements of the law has been granted.[5]

During Knox's tenure of just over 12 years, the conviction gradually emerged that the Comptroller could play only a passive role in the granting of charters. Wrote Knox in the 1881 *Annual Report*:

> . . . the Comptroller has no discretionary power in the matter, but must necessarily sanction the organization, or reorganization, of such associations as shall have conformed in all respects to the legal requirements.[6]

Thus, by the 1880s the spirit of free banking pervaded the Office. Almost imperceptibly there began what many have called a "charter race" between the Comptroller of the Currency and state banking authorities. Until about 1880 the note-issue privilege of national banks gave federal charters a competitive edge. Another advantage of a national charter was its familiarity to nonresident investors, who were more likely to commit their capital to such a charter in undeveloped sections of the country. But after 1880 the competitive advantage swung steadily in favor of state charters with the consequence that the dual banking system achieved a viability no one could have predicted two decades previously.

---

[5] Comptroller of the Currency, *Annual Report,* 1875, p. xv.
[6] Comptroller of the Currency, *Annual Report,* 1881, p. 11.

A national-bank note of the series of 1902 containing a portrait of John J. Knox, fourth Comptroller, whose tenure of 12 years is second longest in the history of the Office.

The Decline in Profitability of Note Issue

The one undeniable advantage possessed by national banks after 1865 was the privilege of issuing notes. On the face of it, the issuance of notes returned a handsome profit as long as the bonds on which they were based sold at or close to par, as they did between 1864 and 1880. For example, in January 1879 the 4 percent bonds due in 1907 (see Table 4–1) and eligible as collateral for national-bank notes sold for $99.75, yielding approximately 4 percent to maturity. Costs of issuing $90 worth of notes approximated 96 cents a year. Phillip Cagan has calculated the net return to one of these bonds, paid for by using $90 of allowable note issue plus $9.75 of the bank's own capital, at 31 percent per annum.[7] But the Treasury soon began to run a surplus, and as it retired callable bonds and

[7] See Phillip Cagan, "The First Fifty Years of the National Banking System—An Historical Appraisal," *Banking and Monetary Studies,* Deane Carson (ed.), Homewood, Illinois: Richard D. Irwin, Inc., 1963, p. 22. The calculation is as follows:

$$\frac{.04\ (99.75)\ - 0.96}{99.75\ - 90}$$

TABLE 4–1

Security for National Bank Notes
(November 1, 1878)

Class of Bonds	Authorizing Act	Interest Rate (percent)	Amount
Loan of February 1861 (81s)	Feburary 8, 1861	6	$ 2,276,000
Loan of July and August 1861 (81s)	July 17 and August 5, 1861	6	34,416,550
Loan of 1863 (81s)	March 3, 1863	6	19,790,900
Consols of 1865	March 3, 1865	6	825,700
Consols of 1867	March 3, 1865	6	8,172,100
Consols of 1868	March 3, 1865	6	1,764,500
Ten-forties of 1864	March 3, 1864	5	70,688,850
Funded Loan of 1881	July 14, 1870 and January 20, 1871	5	125,926,750
Funded Loan of 1891	July 14, 1870 and January 20, 1871	4½	49,397,250
Funded Loan of 1907	July 14, 1870 and January 20, 1871	4	30,566,300
Pacific Railway Bonds	July 1, 1862 and July 2, 1864	6	5,584,000
Total			$349,408,900

SOURCE: Comptroller of the Currency, *Annual Report*, 1878, p. 42.

purchased others in the open market, the price of government securities eligible to back notes began to rise. In January 1882 the 4 percent bonds due in 1907 sold for $117.94 to yield about 3 percent, and the return on them fell to about 9 percent per annum.[8] In the next few years the return on eligible bonds drifted downward so that other assets brought a far better return.

Thus, issuance of national-bank notes was profitable or not according as interest rates rose and fell (that is, as bond prices fell and rose). The volume of national-bank notes outstanding decreased from the early 1880s to the early 1890s, and Horace White, late 19th-century authority on money matters, predicted in 1894 that a bond-secured note issue would ultimately disappear.

In any case, the national-bank note circulation had shrunk from a figure of more than $337 million in 1880 to less than half that amount in 1890. The circulation of national-bank notes rose to a spectacular high of more than $700 million in 1914. In large part the revival of national-bank notes

---

[8] *Ibid.*, p. 23. The calculation was then as follows:

$$\frac{.03 \ (117.94) \ - \ 0.96}{117.94 \ - \ 90}$$

the result of statutory changes that made them more profitable. For example, after a decade of urging by the Comptroller, Congress in 1900 authorized the issue of currency up to 100 percent of the par value of the bonds held as security. The semi-annual tax on national-bank currency was lowered from one-half to one-quarter of 1 percent. Finally, the classes of bonds eligible as security for national-bank circulation were extended to include 2 percent consols payable 30 years after their issue in 1900. In the generally good times of the early 1900s, interest rates rose steadily, as they did so, the price of the consols fell so much that a good profit was once again made on the circulation.

Nevertheless, the issue of notes by a commercial bank was an anachronism by the early 1880s, and only the special provisions of the National Bank Act, along with the fancied advertising value of having a bank's name on nationally circulated bills, kept the notes outstanding in volume. For the function of note issue, usually (though not necessarily) a major part of the business of commercial banks in the 1850s, was obsolescent 30 years later. Business practices were changing rapidly. Customers of banks withdrew the proceeds of loans in the form of paper bills with less and less frequency, preferring instead to leave their borrowed funds on deposit subject to the convenience of withdrawal by check. Gradually bank managers thought less in terms of the mechanics of note issue and more about maintaining appropriate (or required) reserves against deposits. Decade after decade the business of note issue became less significant; by 1890 it was obvious to bankers everywhere, even in the most remote parts of the country, that bank notes were entirely dispensable.

Resurgence of State Chartering

Indeed, by the early 1870s it had become clear that a national charter was not essential to a profitable banking business. Moreover, for bank organizers with no aspirations toward operations on a national or substantial regional scale, state charters had positive advantages.[9]

1. Lower capitals were required in most state jurisdictions and under nearly all circumstances. Until 1900 the minimum capital required for a national bank was $50,000. In the West and South state minimum capital requirements of $10,000 were not infrequent, and some states prescribed no capital minimums at all.

2. Reserves required against deposits were lower under most state banking laws than under the National Bank Act. Furthermore, national banks had to observe substantially stricter rules regarding the amount of cash

---

[9] For a full discussion of the growing importance of state-bank charters in the late 19th century, see George E. Barnett, *State Banks and Trust Companies Since the Passage of the National-Bank Act*, Washington, D. C.: National Monetary Commission, 1911.

Portrait of William Barret Ridgely, eleventh Comptroller of the Currency, who served from 1901 to 1908.

held as reserve, and the Comptroller of the Currency was in general more severe in dealing with reserve deficiencies than were his state counterparts. Finally, several state laws distinguished between time and demand deposits, permitting lower reserves against the former, while the national law made no distinction between time and demand deposits and required the same reserves against both.[10]

3. In general, national banks operated under much stricter rules of both lending and investment policy than did their state-chartered competitors.[11] Before 1913 the National Bank Act for all practical purposes pro-

---

[10] Comptroller of the Currency, *Annual Report*, 1912, p. 11.

[11] We should not be so naive as to conclude that the prohibition of certain practices assured compliance on the part of national banks. A long-time official of the Office testified in his memoirs, perhaps with some exaggeration, that at the turn of the century "probably seventy-five per cent of the examiners' reports, and about the same percentage of reports of condition made by the banks, disclosed violations of law of one kind or another, making it necessary to write letters to that number of banks." See Thomas P. Kane, *The Romance and Tragedy of Banking*, New York: The Bankers Publishing Company, 1930, p. 366. See, also, pages 365-386 for a discussion of the most common types of violation.

hibited loans on real estate, which in some areas constituted a major portion of competing banks' business. Until 1906 a national bank could not lend to a single borrower more than 10 percent of its paid-up capital, a limitation that became increasingly harmful in the competition with other institutions. And whereas state banks and trust companies frequently had wide latitude in purchasing the stocks of banks and other corporations, national banks were barred from such activity.

4. Standards of bank supervision and examination were much higher in the national jurisdiction.

In a word, rules governing the entry and operations of banks chartered by the states were far less onerous than those prescribed for national banks. From 1864 to 1914 (and, for that matter, to the present day) a dual banking system developed because one set of rules was easier than the other. It was as simple as that, and the data testify to the truth of the proposition.

As Table 4–2 shows, the revival of state banking began in the 1870s; by the early 1880s the relative growth of the state-bank system was unmistakable. Between 1880 and 1900 the number of national banks increased from 2,076 to 3,731; in the same 20-year period, the number of state banks jumped from 650 to just over 5,000. In 1900 resources of national banks were not far short of double those of state banks. A few years later, in 1907, state banks outnumbered national banks by nearly two to one, and resources of state banks were about the same as those of national banks.

State banks were apparently forging steadily ahead in the competition. National banks continued to enjoy a certain prestige, perhaps, but a large proportion of the state institutions gained growing public confidence and custom. More significant than prestige to some banks was the attraction of the word "national" in a corporate title to correspondent banks and big companies. For the rules governing national banks were uniform throughout the country, and anyone hesitant about making a commitment to a bank in another city could ordinarily reduce his risks by choosing a federally chartered institution. But these advantages, though real, were many times offset by the greater flexibility of state banks and trust companies, which often enabled them to take business that national banks could not touch.

Chartering Philosophy

The period from 1880 to the Panic of 1907 comes as close to being one of free banking as the country has ever experienced. With few exceptions state supervisory authorities had little discretion in granting bank charters. At the national level variation in the attitudes of successive Comptrollers was slight; for the most part they approved new charters, provided the letter of the law was observed. To be sure, the 1884 edition of *Instructions in Regard to the Organization, Extension, and Management of National Banks* required that a new application be endorsed by a member of Congress or be accompanied by letters from prominent citizens "vouching for the character and responsibility of the parties, and the necessities of the community where the bank is to be located." In the 1891, 1893, 1897 and 1900 editions of this manual the "necessities" criterion was omitted.

Under Comptrollers Knox, Cannon, and Trenholm charters were granted routinely. Data on new-bank formation between 1891 and 1900 suggests at first inspection that Comptrollers Lacey and Eckels may have been more strict in their approval policy. Yet the decade of 1890s was one of bad times; there were perhaps 1,000 bank failures during those 10 years, and

TABLE 4–2

Commercial Banks in the United States, 1870-1914

Year *	State † Banks	National Banks	Year *	State † Banks	National Banks
			1892	3,773	3,759
1870	325	1,612	1893	4,188	3,807
1871	452	1,723	1894	4,188	3,770
1872	566	1,853	1895	4,369	3,715
1873	277	1,968	1896	4,279	3,689
1874	368	1,983	1897	4,420	3,610
1875	586	2,076	1898	4,486	3,581
1876	671	2,091	1899	4,738	3,582
1877	631	2,078	1900	5,007	3,731
1878	510	2,056	1901	5,651	4,163
1879	648	2,048	1902	6,171	4,532
1880	650	2,076	1903	6,890	4,935
1881	683	2,115	1904	7,970	5,327
1882	704	2,239	1905	9,018	5,664
1883	788	2,417	1906	10,220	6,046
1884	852	2,625	1907	11,469	6,422
1885	1,015	2,689	1908	12,803	6,817
1886	891	2,809	1909	13,421	6,886
1887	1,471	3,014	1910	14,348	7,138
1888	1,523	3,120	1911	15,322	7,270
1889	1,791	3,239	1912	16,037	7,366
1890	2,250	3,484	1913	16,841	7,467
1891	2,743	3,652	1914	17,498	7,518

* All figures as of June 30, or nearest available date.
† Excludes unincorporated banks and mutual savings banks.
SOURCE: Board of Governors of the Federal Reserve System, Members of the Staff, *Banking Studies*, Baltimore: Waverly Press, 1941, pp. 418-419.

A cartoonist for Harper's Weekly *portrayed three hypothetical figures who played key roles in the Panic of 1873.*

investors were probably deterred by the accumulated bank investment of the 1880s. In any case, Comptroller Eckels in 1896 urged Congress to amend the National Bank Act, to reduce minimum capital requirements in small towns to permit branches of national banks in communities of less than 1,000, and to lower the proportion of a small bank's capital mandatorily invested in government bonds. Comptroller Charles G. Dawes supported the capital-reduction proposal, and it became law in the Gold Standard Act of 1900. Henceforth, national banks in places of 3,000 inhabitants or less might be chartered with a capital of $25,000, and within a few years more than 2,500 of these applications were approved. From 1900 through 1907 there is little evidence of restrictions on chartering by the Comptroller.

A marked change in attitudes occurred with the appointment of Comptroller Lawrence O. Murray in April of 1908. The severe, if short-lived, depression of 1907-1908 and its accompanying money panic doubtless colored his thinking, but his decisions marked a more fundamental turn in the charter philosophy of the Office. The 1911 edition of the *Instructions Relative to the Organization and Management of National Banks* required three prominent public officials of a community to state their "belief that the conditions locally are such as to insure success if the bank is organized and properly managed." In successive reports, Comptroller Murray remarked the increasing care taken by the Office to scrutinize charter applications, observing that particular attention would be paid to applications from small communities.[12] He noted, not without some wishful thinking,

---

[12] That the Comptroller should use discretion in chartering banks was shocking to an old-line official of the Currency Bureau. With questionable accuracy, Deputy Comptroller Kane wrote: "No Comptroller of the Currency before Mr. Murray ever assumed the right to determine the question of the business needs for a new bank, or an additional association, in any city, town or place. . . . Nowhere in the national banking laws could authority be found, expressed or implied, vesting the Comptroller with such discretionary power, and in the absence of any provision of this nature, Comptrollers from McCulloch to Ridgely held that they had no discretion in the matter." See Kane, *op. cit.*, pp. 393-394.

that state authorities were cooperating in refusing bank charters where prospective business did not warrant them. But the brakes applied by Comptroller Murray, though slowing perceptibly the rate of increase of national banks during his tenure, were eased by his successor John S. Williams, and state authorities continued to charter new banks at an incredible rate.

Bank Supervision in a Dual System

State Supervision in Embyro

We observed in Chapter 2 that two types of state-bank supervision emerged before 1860. In several of the New England and Middle Atlantic states, banking departments or boards of bank commissioners acquired these responsibilities. Although departments or boards had varying degrees of authority, they gradually developed workable supervisory techniques. Even more effective, perhaps, was the type of bank supervision that evolved in the Midwest, notably in Indiana, Missouri, Ohio, and Iowa. Here central boards of directors supervised the branches, or semi-independent banking offices, that constituted units in the state systems. But these state systems were all liquidated soon after the passage of the Currency Act of 1863, many of the branches becoming independent national banks.

As late as 1863 a large number of states had made no provision for bank supervision. Since it was assumed that state banks would go out of existence with the national legislation, for a time little effort was made to extend the scope of state-bank supervision. But beginning with the resurgence of state-bank chartering in the 1880s, the states once again began to create supervisory authorities. Slowly at first, then gradually picking up speed, states provided for (a) regular examination of banks and (b) permanent authorities charged with the supervisory function.

In 1885, 10 states had authorized regular examination of banks and nine had provided for a supervisory official or board. Between 1886 and 1900, 21 additional states made regular bank examination mandatory, and 10 additional states created supervisory authorities. By 1914 all the states required regular examinations, though not until 1931 would all the states create official supervisory authorities.

The quality of state-bank supervision in these early years varied tremendously. With rare exceptions, supervisory officials and their staffs, including bank examiners, were strictly political appointees, often with no experience in commercial banking or even more broadly in finance. Up to 1914 few supervisory boards had much control over charter applications, either because they had no discretionary power in granting them or were subject to increasing political pressures. Salaries, especially for

A letter from Secretary Chase to cashiers of all national banks setting forth requirements for becoming a government depository and financial agent of the United States.

examiners, were incredibly low, and in many jurisdictions rapid turnover of personnel made even annual examinations impossible. Indeed, it was universally agreed that, with a few exceptions that simply proved the rule, state banking standards and supervision were distinctly inferior to those of the national system. As of 1914 the quality of bank supervision in a substantial majority of states could only improve.

Evolving Federal Supervision

The National Bank Act explicitly provided for supervision, including continued scrutiny of bank records. The implied powers of the Comptroller of the Currency were such that, despite some problems of enforcement, national banks were subject to more than routine authority.[13]

Examination. In the beginning, under the assumption that the National Bank Act was essentially a currency measure, the aim of examination was to make sure that the condition of banks would enable them to redeem their notes when they were presented. But after a decade or so of experience it became clear that, under the American system of unit banking, supervision would have to become more exacting. In general, the scope and quality of national-bank supervision improved more or less continuously to 1914. Yet after 50 years examination procedures were far from perfected.

The subject of examination was discussed by succeeding Comptrollers in almost every *Annual Report* starting with the first one. Hugh McCulloch found no fault with the original Section 51 in his detailed emendation of the Currency Act of 1863. The following year McCulloch wrote that he was "instituting a system of examinations which will do much to expose and check improper practices on the part of the bankers, and violations of the wholesome provisions of the law." [14] He also observed that in the primary investigation of applications he was "requiring the most satisfactory references or credentials in regard to the standing and responsibility of the persons proposing to organize national banks. . . ." [15] On September 15, 1864, he sent to every examiner the first of what would become a series of detailed instructions to the examining force. These instructions were necessary, he thought, though no ". . . cast-iron rules, covering minute details, can be issued to examiners. . . ."[16]

Succeeding Comptrollers elucidated at some length their philosophy of

---

[13] For three-quarters of a century, the remedial powers of the Comptroller were not clear. For any continuing infraction he could revoke the charter of a national bank, a disciplinary action so drastic that it would be invoked only for the most serious violations. Strictly speaking, the Comptroller had to rely on cooperation from officers and directors of banks in order to correct lesser violations. Nevertheless, the growing prestige of the Office and the weight of authority that grew with it, plus the latent threat of charter revocation, soon gave the Comptroller of the Currency adequate coercive power.

[14] Secretary of the Treasury, *Report on the Finances*, 1864, p. 49.

[15] *Ibid.*

[16] Comptroller of the Currency, *Annual Report*, 1891, p. 26.

bank examination. H. R. Hulburd, for example, wrote in his *Report* in 1869: "Perhaps no one thing has done more to promote the safety and sound management of national banks than their liability to examination without previous notice. . . ." John J. Knox expressed similar sentiments: "The excellent system now in operation is in strong contrast with the generally lax systems of bank reports and supervision which prevailed previous to the passage of the national-bank act." [17] He held that it was "the duty of the examiner to ascertain whether the officers of the bank and its directors are complying with the requirements of the law and whether they are in any way violating any of its provisions, to the end that in such case they may be enforced by the proper authority." [18] In Knox's view the role of the government was to stir directors and officers to full and active responsibility, while at the same time supervisory officials could in no way accept responsibility for the management of a bank's funds. Knox went on to note that though the detection of embezzlement might occur as an incident of an examination it was certainly not the principal object of examination. "It is scarcely to be expected," he wrote, "if a robber or a forger is placed in control of all of its assets, that a national bank can be saved from disaster by the occasional visits of an examiner." [19]

Knox's successor, Henry W. Cannon, generalized further the functions of an examiner. Examination, in his opinion, went beyond a mere inspection of ledgers to a close scrutiny of the *business* of the bank—that is, the responsibility and prudence of its management and the total quality of its loans and its investment portfolio. Examiners, he believed, should consult with officers and directors concerning broad principles of bank management and should be especially solicitous to see that banks were maintaining their prescribed lawful money reserves and that banks were not themselves borrowing from other banks. Although Comptrollers as early as Freeman Clarke wrote letters to banks commenting upon the results of examination reports and requesting correction of weakness, Comptroller Cannon made critical analysis from Washington an integral part of examination. Cannon established the tradition that it was the function of supervision to correct basic managerial difficulties when they were incipient and not simply to perform what amounted to routine audits. He insisted that malfeasance could best be prevented through examination of the bank by a committee of directors, that it was not the function of examination to attend to minute details:

> . . . there are many ways of evading [the] law, and it is a physical impossibility for the Government to maintain . . . constant espionage over the affairs of the national banks. . . . Any attempt to direct the making of loans and to

---

[17] Comptroller of the Currency, *Annual Report,* 1869, p. x; Comptroller of the Currency, *Annual Report,* 1878, p. 17.
[18] Comptroller of the Currency, *Annual Report,* 1881, pp. 35-36.
[19] *Ibid.,* p. 38.

Portrait of Henry W. Cannon, fifth Comptroller of the Currency, who served from May 1884 to March 1886.

dictate to the directors and managers . . . would . . . be impracticable. . . . it is not the intention of the bank act to interfere with the business of [an] association . . . .[20]

Comptrollers Trenholm, Lacey, and Eckels successively dwelt on the importance of supervision of a bank's affairs by its board of directors, and by 1900 the idea of the fundamental responsibility of boards of directors for detecting embezzlement and other dishonesty was accepted.

With experience, the Office of the Comptroller of the Currency made other suggestions for improvement of the supervisory system. In both his *Annual Reports* Trenholm recommended the appointment of supervisory examiners to be paid by the Treasury rather than by bank assessment. Trenholm enumerated four advantages to be secured from this change in supervisory procedures:

[20] Comptroller of the Currency, *Annual Report,* 1884, pp. xlix-l.

1. Banks could be specially examined at any time between the dates of ordinary examinations without exciting alarm in a community or reflecting upon the management of a bank.
2. Protection against arbitrary or improper conduct upon the part of a local examiner would be afforded banks, especially those in remote localities.
3. Supervising examiners would carry throughout the country a knowledge of correct and uniform methods of business and could instruct both local examiners and bank officers.

A plea for reimbursement from a bank examiner who received his compensation under the fee system.

Sandusky, O, Aug. 31. 1865.

Dear Sir,

Enclosed please find list of National Banks of Ohio examined by me during the month of August with account $475. for my commissions, for which, if found correct please remit.

Very Respectfully,

J. D. Whitney
Bank Examiner,

H. R. Hulburd Esq.
Deputy Comptroller
Washington, D. C,

4. Since their circuits would begin and end in Washington, the special examiners would supply the Comptroller with comprehensive information, enabling the Office to understand needs and circumstances that must vary according to the peculiarities of different sections of the country.[21]

Trenholm's successor, Edward Lacey, continued to insist upon the appointment of supervisory examiners to be paid from public funds. Comptroller Eckels likewise asked for two general examiners. At last, in 1899 Comptroller Charles G. Dawes (one day to be Vice President of the United States) persuaded Congress to provide funds for special examiners.

Comptroller Lawrence O. Murray, who came to the Office in April of 1908, took the questionnaire approach toward improving supervision. In September he wrote to the presidents of all national banks asking their opinion of the examination procedure and their suggestions as to how it might be improved. Of the more than 3,600 replies, slightly over half viewed the current system as entirely satisfactory. But a large number of bank presidents were not loath to offer opinions as to how the service might be improved. Among a host of recommendations, the most important were that examiners should be paid salaries instead of fees, that more time should be devoted to examination, and that the number of supervisory examiners be increased. A surprisingly large number of respondents suggested that bank examiners should indeed make careful audits in order to assist bankers in detecting skullduggery. Not surprisingly, bankers in large cities favored establishing agencies whereby there could be some collusion in collecting credit information and in enabling bankers to determine the advisability of extending credit to large borrowers.

Comptroller Murray worked harder, perhaps, than anyone in the history of the bureau to improve bank supervision. Like his predecessors, he urged the appointment of directors' committees to supplement the work of national bank examiners, in the summer of 1912 going so far as to ask that committee reports of examination be forwarded to Washington. Through these reports, Murray felt, dishonest employees could be detected, forged paper discovered, and losses that had escaped official examination turned up. But to his disappointment, Murray found that a large portion of such examinations were altogether ineffective and that a large percentage of bank directors did not have the slightest notion of what constituted an effective inspection. So the Comptroller replied with a circular to all banks outlining proper procedures.

Murray's main contribution to supervisory procedures seems to have been his insistence that the examination of charter applications be done in person rather than by correspondence. Despite Murray's efforts, on September 9, 1913, in reporting the bill creating the Federal Reserve System

---

[21] Comptroller of the Currency, *Annual Report,* 1886, p. viii; Comptroller of the Currency, *Annual Report,* 1887, p. 10.

to the House of Representatives, Carter Glass could remark with truth: "For some years the national banking act has been found to be seriously defective in its provisions for examinations. In attempting the organization of a more closely woven system of banking the committee therefore feels impelled to urge the necessity of stiffening existing examination requirements. . . ." [22]

The Fee System. If examination of national banks was not entirely satisfactory after half a century of experience, the difficulty could be largely attributed to the method of paying the examining staff. Pay was hardly munificent, but it was the method by which examiners were reimbursed that was most at fault.

Both the 1863 and 1864 laws provided that:

> . . . every person appointed to make such examination shall receive for his services at the rate of five dollars for each day by him employed in such examination, and two dollars for every twenty-five miles he shall necessarily travel in the performance of his duty, which shall be paid by the association by him examined.

This brief examiner's form and the first known report, written in longhand on the letterhead of the examined bank, show why examinations could be conducted in a single forenoon or afternoon.

---

[22] Comptroller of the Currency, *Annual Report*, 1914, p. 116.

Correspondence between the field examiner and the Bureau sheds light on the tribulations of early members of the field force. W. Coombs, who covered the State of Pennsylvania, wrote McCulloch on September 30, 1864, that his expenses had been larger than ever before "owing to having considerable carriage fare, and Philadelphia expenses" and requested $350. A year later, a New England examiner, Noah Woods, complained that "to date" he had received no pay for examining 61 banks and requested the Comptroller to tell him how much he was entitled to. Complaints to the home office became so frequent that in 1869 Comptroller Hulburd asked Congress to change the law, providing for an increase in compensation of examiners and an assessment of the banks in proportion to the time and labor spent on their examination. No appropriation of money would be necessary, he assured the legislators, since all expenses would be defrayed by the banks. But not until February 19, 1875, did Congress approve an amendment providing that all bank examiners assigned to nonreserve cities and states other than Oregon, Nevada, and California receive compensation based upon the capital of the examined bank. The scale estab-

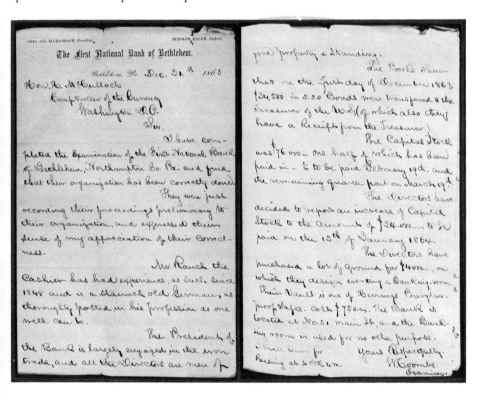

lished is shown in Table 4–3. Examiners in reserve cities, the three designated states, and the territories were to have their compensation fixed by the Secretary of the Treasury upon the recommendation of the Comptroller.

TABLE 4–3

Scale of Examination Fees Established in 1875

Bank Capital	Fee
Less than $100,000	$20
$100,000 - $299,999	$25
$300,000 - $399,999	$35
$400,000 - $499,999	$40
$500,000 - $599,999	$50
$600,000 and over	$75

The banks continued to bear the cost of examination, paying their fees in accordance with the statutory scale. Examiners received no other compensation; moreover, from their gross receipts they had to pay the wages of assistants and all expenses incident to their travel. Although as a rule of thumb it was assumed that an examiner's net income would average about two-thirds of his gross, his true compensation must have varied considerably. Obviously, it was to any particular examiner's advantage to hurry his work and get on to a new job, the fee being the same whether he took one day or three days. Moreover, to minimize travel expense examiners ordinarily followed predictable routes, going the shortest possible distances from one bank to another. Needless to say, banks could make fairly accurate guesses as to the approximate date of forthcoming examination and could make their preparations accordingly.

Beginning with Comptroller Cannon in 1884 successive Comptrollers pleaded for both higher pay and a different method of paying the examination force. Cannon, for example, believed that fees based on the capital of a bank were unfair, that a formula including both capital and average deposits should be used. In his *Report* of 1887 Comptroller Trenholm recommended that Congress drastically change the system of compensation, suggesting that certain examinations be paid out of congressionally appropriated funds and hinting that it might be well to abolish the fee system entirely. In 1893 Comptroller Eckels went further to recommend to Congress that the Comptroller be allowed to fix the compensation of all examiners without regard to fees earned. Four years later he asked that the fee system be abolished and that examiners be paid a fixed salary with an allowance for travel and other necessary expenses. "With a fixed salary," he wrote, "instead of an already-determined fee, examiners would be in [a] position to apportion their time, in making examinations, in accordance with the needs of the banks examined. Only in this way can be had that complete scrutiny of a bank's affairs which is due to the officers and shareholders and to its patrons and the general public." [23] Three years later, Eckels' successor, Comptroller Dawes, echoed his sentiments, as did Comptrollers Ridgely and Murray. Yet not until the passage of the Federal Reserve Act did Congress finally abolish the fee system.

Removal of inequities of reimbursement did not, of course, solve all the problems of bank examination. The geographic assignments of bank examiners were such that they were rarely in touch with each other, so that there was lack of uniformity in procedures and principles. The fact that examiners hired their own assistants, who were in no way responsible to the Comptroller, made for wide variations in quality of the staff. Moreover, as late as 1913 banks could engage in the most outrageous practices aimed at avoiding the examiner's wrath. It was not uncommon to transfer bad assets to other banks or corporations during the period of examination, borrowing more acceptable securities in the meantime. The affiliates of commercial banks might be in a condition so bad as to jeopardize a bank's solvency, yet affiliates were beyond the authority of national supervision.

Despite the difficulties, a loyal corps of civil servants, working long hours and suffering the pains of pre-World War I travel, assured a quality of national-bank supervision not ordinarily reached by state banks. But for all their labors, forces were at work to undermine the good achieved by the most effective oversight of financial institutions.

Reports of Condition. The problem of call reports occupied the early Comptrollers. In his first *Annual Report,* McCulloch noted that the portion of the law dealing with quarterly reports needed strengthening. In 1867 Comptroller Hulburd criticized both the quarterly reports (a detailed statement of the bank's affairs) and the monthly statement (showing the bank's average circulation, deposits, lawful money, and balance available for redemption of their circulating notes.) About the former he observed, tongue in cheek:

> It is known, understood, and anticipated, by all who have dealings with the banks, that they are in the habit of preparing systematically for making creditable exhibits on quarter day. It is certainly a point gained to know that the banks can make a good showing at least once every quarter; but it would be more satisfactory to know that they do so at all times.[24]

---

23 Comptroller of the Currency, *Annual Report,* 1897, p. lxxv.
24 Comptroller of the Currency, *Annual Report,* 1867, p. vii.

Charles G. Dawes, who later gained fame as an international figure and as Vice President of the United States, was Comptroller from 1898 to 1901, while he was still in his thirties.

He attacked the monthly report as being too vague to give any useful information at all.

Hulburd recommended that, in addition to a more detailed monthly report, a full statement of condition be submitted five times a year as of a past date announced without warning by the Comptroller. Hulburd's suggestions, for such a detailed monthly report plus the five "call" reports to replace those then in use, were ignored for two years. On March 3, 1869,

Congress approved an act encompassing Hulburd's recommendations, and the third Comptroller thus initiated the practice of the surprise call date. The ability of the Comptroller to choose random call dates would prevent the practice, known as "windowdressing," of doctoring the records to show a condition not warranted by the fact. The success of this new supervisory tool pleased Hulburd, for he wrote that it enabled the banks to set forth "the actual working condition . . . without manipulation or preparation. . . ."[25]

The 1869 law also empowered the Comptroller to call for special reports. Any association that failed to report was subject to a penalty of $100 for each day of delay. Furthermore, every national banking association had to report to the Comptroller, under oath, the amount of dividends declared and its net earnings in excess of dividends within 10 days after declaration. Failure to comply also brought a penalty of $100 per day.

The usefulness of these reports of condition became so great that in 1889 Edward Lacey remarked that associations in reserve cities had long expressed a desire to receive more frequent information on the condition of their correspondents and other banks. That year the American Bankers Association passed a resolution requesting the Comptroller to publish a detailed report of condition during the first half of the year. Lacey asked Congress to provide the necessary funds for this semi-annual publication. Nothing came of the request, and the following year he repeated it, stating that "Twelve months seems a long time to wait, in this progressive age, for information so important."[26]

Multi-Office and Multi-Unit Banking

Branches of National Banks

When the national banking system was established, there was little or no controversy over branch banks. As we have observed, there were at that time two types of branch systems in the United States, the great state systems of the Midwest and the Southern systems dominated by a head office. Examination of the legislative history of the Currency Act of 1863 and the National Banking Act of 1864 (statutorily redesignated the "National Bank Act" in 1874) reveals no special concern about branches, and not until passage of the 1865 law levying the 10 percent tax on state-bank notes was there statutory mention of the matter. This legislation allowed state banks converting to national charters to keep their branches provided that definite capitals were assigned to the "mother bank and

---

[25] Comptroller of the Currency, *Annual Report,* 1869, p. viii.
[26] Comptroller of the Currency, *Annual Report,* 1890, p. 57.

branches." There was no apparent controversy over this section of the Act and no suggestion that branch systems would not be allowed to develop.

Moreover, there is no evidence that the framers of the 1863 and 1864 legislation meant to preclude branch banking. Nevertheless, two clauses in the National Bank Act were so interpreted by McCulloch and other early Comptrollers. Section 6 of the Act required persons forming an association to specify "the place" where business would be carried on, and Section 8 required that usual business be transacted at "an office or banking house" located in the city specified in the organizer's certificate. As Professor Gerald C. Fischer has pointed out, this use of singular nouns was common in state free-banking statutes, which were usually modeled on the New York Free-Bank Law of 1838. Actually, the phraseology of the New York law can in turn be found in the special charters under which earlier banks in the state received their authority to do business, such a use of singular nouns being found in the charters of banks with branches as well as those without branches. For example, in Ohio, which had both a state bank with many branches and unit banks organized under a free-banking statute, the phrase "the place of business" is used in the law that applied to branches of the state bank as well as to unit banks.[27] The intention of the framers of the original New York statute, as well as those who uniformly followed the original wording, was to outlaw the location of many offices in inaccessible places for the purpose of hindering note redemption. In other words, early legislators wanted to make sure that a single place of business was designated for official purposes, and there is no evidence at all that they were thereby precluding the establishment of other offices as deemed necessary by individual bank managements.

To date, an intensive search of the correspondence of Hugh McCulloch has yielded no formal decision or explicit statement of principle regarding the legality of branches of national banks. We do know that he required the so-called branches of the State Bank of Indiana to enter the national system as units, an understandable procedure in view of the near autonomy of these separate branches under the peculiarities of that state's arrangements. McCulloch's successor, Freeman Clarke, did make an explicit ruling. As a condition of granting a national charter to the Washington County Bank in Williamsport, Maryland, Comptroller Clarke required the bank to divest itself of its branch office in Hagerstown. He wrote: "The 6th Section [of the law] requires that [the organizers] shall specify in their organization certificate the particular place (not places) at which their operations of discount and deposit shall be carried out."[28] Whatever Con-

---

[27] Federal Reserve Board, "Branch Banking in the United States," Report of the Committee on Branch, Group and Chain Banking, 1932, pp. 52-70.

[28] Clarke's handwritten note appears on the back of a letter to him from a bank official. D. Weisel to Freeman Clarke, August 18, 1865, National Archives, Record Group 101, Comptroller of the Currency.

gress had intended, this decision was followed by Comptrollers for years. For several decades the opinion made little difference, one way or another. In the North and East branch banking had nearly disappeared. In the South, where in antebellum years multi-office banking of the 20th-century type was concentrated, many branch banks were destroyed by the War, were dissolved by state authorities, or entered the national system with each former branch as a unit. And the free-banking spirit that pervaded the West made it possible to form one or more new banks in the towns and cities where organizers felt business could support them.

As a result, the branch-bank question did not become an issue until near the end of the 19th century. In 1887 and again in 1888, the Comptroller of the Currency recommended that national banks be allowed to establish additional offices in the head-office city, but nothing came of the suggestion.[29] During the 1890s, however, there was a growing demand for increased banking facilities in small towns, and leaders in government and business suggested with increasing frequency that branches of established banks would solve the problem. Thus, the first strong advocates of branch banking based their case largely on rural need, Comptroller Eckels' 1896 proposal for branches, in places of less than 1,000 population that had no national bank, being a typical public-policy prescription. Consequently, the force of branch-banking arguments was greatly weakened with passage of a 1900 statute reducing to $25,000 the capital requirements for a national bank in a place of 3,000 inhabitants or less.[30] With the ensuing rapid creation of small banks by the hundreds, the chief argument for branch banking was undermined. By the same legislative stroke, the ultimate potential of the anti-branching lobby in state legislatures was bolstered by thousands of new country-bank offices.

For two or three years there was a continuing discussion of the issue, as Congress took up branch banking bills that had been drawn up. In a classic profession of faith in branch banking, Comptroller William B. Ridgely in 1902 placed the Office squarely on the side of branch-bank proponents:

> I believe in branch banking. Theoretically it is the best system, as it is more economical, more efficient, will serve its customers better and the organization can be such as to secure in most respects better management. Owing to co-operation between its branches, it can be made safer than any system of independent banks. If I were outlining a new system for a country in which

---

[29] Comptroller of the Currency, *Annual Report,* 1887, pp. 4, 7, 26; and *Annual Report,* 1888, p. 4.
[30] Act of March 14, 1900, 31 Stat. 48. It is a curious and interesting detail of history that this legislation should be found in the Gold Standard Act of 1900, which dealt with what seemed at the time a more monumental subject, namely the establishment *de jure* of United States adherence to the gold standard.

James H. Eckels, ninth Comptroller of the Currency, served from April 1893 to December 1897.

there was none, I would adopt this system; and I regret that it was not adopted or permitted in the beginning of the National banking system. I believe the National banks would be stronger and better to-day if branches had been permitted and the system had been developed with the branch feature an essential part of it. [31]

But the first economic pressure for branch banking had disappeared, to be gradually renewed as the continuing growth of cities moved their peripheries farther and farther away from the business centers. Moreover, as Professor Fischer has remarked, much support for branch banking had come from advocates of currency reform, who felt that extensive branch banking would aid their cause. When it appeared that political opponents of branch banking were becoming increasingly hostile, these supporters turned to new plans not likely to incur so much opposition.

In 1900, banks with branches accounted for only 2 percent of the resources of American commercial banks. Thus, the branch-banking movement lost momentum before it was even well under way, but even the

---

[31] "Proceedings of the American Bankers Association 28th Annual Convention," *The Commercial and Financial Chronicle* Supplement, 75, November 22, 1902, p. 59.

next 15 years would see a slow, steady increase in branching as economic forces began to exert inexorable pressure for change.

Chains and Groups

Although the simplest way to organize a multi-office bank is to utilize the device of branching, other means may achieve the same end. In general, wherever branch banking is prohibited or restricted, two other forms of multi-office banking will thrive—groups and chains. A "group" of banks consists of two or more banks under the control of a holding company that may or may not be a bank. In contrast to a branch system, a group of banks may operate across state lines, though some groups are intrastate and are obvious substitutes for branch systems in states that prohibit branch banking. A chain of banks is similar to a group but is characterized by the control of several independently incorporated banks by an individual or a group of individuals or through interlocking directorates. Although chains tend to center around a nucleus bank, ordinarily the largest in the chain, they may be simply a "string" of banks organized for the sole purpose of achieving several office outlets.

Origins of groups and chains are obscure. Historically, chains appear to have emerged first at almost the same time in the South and Midwest, probably in the 1880s. By 1902 at least two chains were operating in North Dakota, and by 1911 the Witham chain had 125 banks located mainly in Georgia and Florida with a few units in New York and New Jersey. By the turn of the century several chains had been organized in the Pacific Northwest, though there is no record of the number of banks or the total resources involved. In New York, the Morse-Heinz chain of six banks called public attention to chain organization with a spectacular failure that sparked the Panic of 1907.

By 1900 aggressive entrepreneurs were starting to form banking groups.[32] When it became apparent that the linkage of banks through common ownership was profitable, companies were formed for the purpose of holding stock in several banks. In the early days, groups, like chains, tended to take advantage of one or two names familiar to the financial community and already associated with the ownership of more than one institution. For example, in 1900 Adam Hannah, well-known for his interest in several country banks, became the first head of the Minneapolis holding company that took control of a number of banks. On the other hand, some groups maintained the anonymity of a single corporate name. Thus, the Union Investment Company, organized in 1903 in Minnesota, gained control of 31 banks within five years.

---

[32] The term "group banking" was not in common use until the mid-1920s. Gerald C. Fischer, *Bank Holding Companies*, New York: Columbia University Press, 1961, p. 18.

Groups and chains, like branch-banking systems, were only beginning to make their influence felt by 1914. In the financial exuberance of the 1920s these novel forms of business organization would make rapid headway as alternate forms of multi-office banking.

1914 To The Great Depression

During the first half century of its history the national banking system did all it was engineered to do, and more. Yet as the 19th century drew to a close there was spreading concern that the monetary system was seriously defective. A few sophisticated and unusually perceptive businessmen and political figures, along with a handful of university professors, saw that only a central bank would provide an adequate remedy. Actually, some rudimentary central bank functions were performed in the latter half of the century by harried Secretaries of the Treasury, who violated the independent Treasury law to protect the money market from destabilizing swings in monetary reserves. The correspondent banking system, after a century of development, performed the so-called service functions of a central bank—providing cash, collecting checks, effecting long distance remittances, and the like.

The great difficulty with the system was that it had a propensity to break down in times of economic stress. During recurring monetary panics, banks suspended cash payments, and the currency supply all but disappeared. Fundamentally, the problem was one of structure. New York banks, which held a large part of the country's monetary reserves, were a focal point for interbank deposits because of the city's financial pre-eminence; moreover, they attracted correspondent accounts by paying interest on deposits and collecting checks drawn on Eastern banks. Since the funds so attracted involved a cost, they had to be put to some profitable use. In an embryonic money market there were relatively few short-term securities for banks to hold, so they tended to lend their excess funds "at call" to dealers in securities.

Country banks and reserve city banks in the interior withdrew deposits from the New York banks whenever they needed cash. Even when business was "normal," there would be seasonal movements of funds that were sometimes disturbing. But bank managers in New York ordinarily could predict routine flows of funds to the interior and could prepare for them in advance. Every few years, however, as economic activity slid into the first stages of a major economic downturn, the demand for cash remittances to the interior would become greater than New York banks could meet, even by letting their own reserves fall seriously below the legal minimum.

At such times each bank had to think of its own solvency. A point was quickly reached at which cash could no longer be paid out. Most analysts, including the most highly respected academicians, tended to think, as their fathers and grandfathers had before them, that something was seriously wrong with the "currency." Indeed, a distinguished National Monetary Commission sponsored voluminous studies, published in 1912, that described for the public the weaknesses of the monetary system. The major defect, according to the Commission, was an "inelastic" currency—that is, a supply of coin and paper money that did not expand and contract in accordance with the "needs" of the business community. The quantity of currency, it was argued, should increase and decrease with the rise and fall of business activity. Moreover, since the chief manifestation of seasonal panics was a disappearance of cash, it was believed that bank reserves should be "pooled" to make them readily available in times of stress.

Modern economics would not be so concerned with the "elasticity" of the currency. What was really needed was a central institution that could *create* reserves and inject liquidity at appropriate times. Writers of that period, who thought the problem could be solved by putting cash reserves in a central place, forgot that reserves *were* pooled in New York in banks that could not create more cash.

Advent of a Central Bank

The basic plan of the National Monetary Commission, introduced as the Aldrich Bill,[1] provided for the establishment of a weak central bank, to be known as the National Reserve Association, with its head office in Washington and 15 branches located in various parts of the country. The Association would carry a portion of the member banks' reserves, determine discount rates, and, most important, issue currency based upon gold and commercial paper that would be a liability of the Reserve Association and not of the federal government. The Association would be managed by a board composed of government officials and private members and would be controlled by a board of 46 directors, 42 to be chosen by banks and four by the government. Bankers, favoring private control of banking, supported the bill; agrarian radicals criticized it as being exclusively a bankers' bill. To William Jennings Bryan and his followers passage of the Aldrich Bill meant the continuation of the "Money Trust" and Wall Street's control of

---

[1] The bill was named after the Chairman of the Commission, Senator Nelson Aldrich of Rhode Island.

the nation's credit resources. Their objections were given increased weight by the shocking findings of the Pujo Committee in 1912.

President-elect Woodrow Wilson was obliged to formulate an alternative to the Aldrich Bill. Silent during the campaign on the issue of monetary reform, Wilson in his own thinking had not gone beyond general objectives and was unfamiliar with the details of alternative proposals. Bankers, who supported the Aldrich Plan, asked James B. Forgan, president of the First National Bank of Chicago and member of the American Bankers Association's Currency Commission, to intercede with the President. An agitated colleague sent Forgan the views of the banking community:

> . . . It is understood here that the President-elect is studying the whole currency question with an open mind, but that he has certain tempermental [sic] peculiarities which incline him, once he has made up his mind that he understands a thing, so that he obstinately will refuse to open his mind to any arguments to the contrary. It is known of course that he has been taking advice chiefly from the radical element of the Democratic party represented by Bryan. . . . It is said to be highly important that while the President is seeking light that he should get the real truth from some such competent authority as yourself. . . . I think you can present certain fundamentals that must be embraced in any plan and can make it so clear to him that his mind will become fixed when he grasps the real rudiments. . . . In other words, the plan is, while he is making up his mind, to seize the opportunity to make it up for him in the right way rather than let the radicals convince him wrongly to the detriment of any possibility of sound legislation.[2]

Meanwhile, the House Banking and Currency Committee, chaired by Virginia's Representative Carter Glass, decided that it must obtain the President's views on the matter. During the spring and autumn of 1912 the Committee had worked on a proposed banking bill drafted by its economic adviser, H. Parker Willis. Glass and Willis wished to discuss this bill with Wilson and met with the President-elect at his home in Princeton. Willis' draft called for a reserve system privately and locally controlled, with 20 or more independent reserve banks. In order to bring the national banks into the system, Willis further proposed to broaden their lending powers and to allow them to distinguish between demand and time deposits for reserve purposes. Both Glass and Willis stressed the importance of decentralizing the system and breaking the concentration of power in Wall Street. Wilson tentatively agreed to the plan but questioned a provision giving the Comptroller of the Currency general supervision over the reserve system on the grounds that it did not provide sufficient coordination and control. Wilson realized that a central bank in the traditional European mold would be politically impossible, even if economically desirable, but he wanted a "capstone to be placed upon the structure"—a central board to control, coordinate, and perform the functions of a central bank. It was

---

[2] Joseph T. Talbert to James B. Forgan, February 26, 1913, James B. Forgan Papers, The First National Bank of Chicago.

Wilson, then, who perceived a way of reconciling the radicals' demands for decentralization with the practical necessity for centralized control—the idea of the Federal Reserve Board.

At the end of January 1913, Willis and Glass presented their revised plan to Wilson. The reserve system was to include 15 or more regional banks, owned and controlled by the member banks, which would hold a portion of member-bank reserves, issue currency against gold and commercial assets, and be controlled by a Federal Reserve Board of six public members and three bankers chosen by the directors of the regional banks. Wilson was delighted; but the Democratic Party was almost split in the ensuing storm of protest, for Glass and Willis had merely drafted a somewhat decentralized Aldrich Plan, with control once again in the hands of bankers. In response, the left wing of the Party demanded public control of the Board and complete government responsibility for the issue of currency.

Both Secretary of State Bryan and Robert L. Owen, Chairman of the Senate Committee on Banking and Currency, were adamant on these two points, and Owen made it known that he had drafted a bill of his own. Secretary of the Treasury William McAdoo, fearing that the scheme would die in intra-Party squabbling, resolved to find a solution. With the help of John Skelton Williams, soon to be Comptroller, and Senator Owen he prepared the outline of a new bill, which called for a National Reserve Bank in the Treasury Department, to have 15 branches and be administered by a National Reserve Board of political appointees. A National Currency Commission functioning in the Treasury would issue the currency. Glass was dismayed upon reading the bill, for he was convinced that Williams and Owen were the real authors. When he asked McAdoo if he were serious about the proposal, the Secretary bluntly replied: "Hell, yes!" Glass now felt that hope for currency reform was dim, for to Party opposition on the left was added the hostility of the nation's leading bankers on the right.[3] Backed by James B. Forgan and A. Barton Hepburn, former Comptroller of the Currency and president of the ABA's Currency Commission, Glass had a showdown with the President. Wilson agreed to support the Glass bill and to insist upon two provisions calculated to mollify the Democratic radicals—governmental control of the Federal Reserve Board and a currency issue that would consist of obligations of the United States.

The Glass-Owen bill still had to confront the hostility of the banking community. At a last-minute conference held on June 25, attended by McAdoo, Glass, Owen, and five members of the Currency Commission, the President agreed to several changes demanded by the bankers.[4] Among

---

[3] See Gerald T. Dunne, "A Christmas Present for the President," *Business Horizons*, 6, Winter 1963, especially pp. 47-54.

[4] Members of the ABA Currency Commission in attendance were James B. Forgan, George M. Reynolds, Festus J. Wade, Sol Wexler, and John Perrin.

Federal Reserve Bank notes were provided originally as a replacement for national-bank currency. Three-times issued (for various reasons) and three-times withdrawn, Federal Reserve Bank notes (as distinguished from Federal Reserve notes) are no longer in circulation.

them was a change in the provision to end the bond-secured note circulation of national banks. In order to protect the banks' large investment in the 2 percent bonds that supported the national currency, it was agreed that national-bank notes would be gradually retired, the 2 percent bonds redeemed, and new notes issued to replace them. More important was the President's concession to establish a Federal Advisory Council, composed of representatives of the banks in each region, in lieu of banker representation on the Federal Reserve Board.

Banker opposition nevertheless remained almost unanimous. Many wrote Hepburn and Forgan protesting the disposition of the national-bank notes and the principle of coercion embodied in the bill. Bank executives did not understand the reason for retiring the national-bank notes, which as late as 1913 seemed to be part of a bank's public image. The issue of coercion was emotionally charged. One banker wrote: "I am unwilling to be forced into taking stock in a bank or anything else that I have no active voice in managing." The growing disposition on the part of the Administration to force national banks into system membership also disturbed the Currency Commission. On December 9, two weeks after the bill had been brought to the Senate floor, John Perrin wrote Senator Owen:

> Two alternatives must be faced: Either the possibility must be considered of the Government promoting the establishment of an entirely new banking system with a view to driving out of existence in considerable measure the existing banks, or, on the other hand, present banks generally must be influenced either by compulsion or inducement into participation.[5]

A compromise proposal would have extended the transition period by six years to 1920. But two days later the Glass-Owen bill was amended so that refusal to accept the terms of the Act within 60 days would bring punitive action. Perrin again tried to change the attitude of the bill from threatened punishment to promised rewards, arguing that special advantages should be offered to those banks subscribing early. Forgan continued to insist that there should be no compulsion requiring the national banks to comply or be dissolved.[6] Despite the unremitting efforts of banking's leadership, coercion remained a feature of the Act. It would be mandatory for all national banks to become members of the new Federal Reserve System.

National-bank officers, alarmed over these and other provisions, began talk of withdrawing from the national banking system. "After a careful reading of the Bill," wrote one irate president, "will have to say, most emphatically, I do not see a single thing to recommend it from the standpoint of our little Bank." Another small-town banker wrote from Texas that a large majority of the country banks would surrender their national charters. John Hamilton warned, "This measure would certainly drive 60 per cent of the national banking institutions out of business and cause them to re-organize under state charters." In July a Boston banker wrote: "I am considering the policy of endeavoring to get the banks here to join in a statement to the powers at Washington that they *might* withdraw from the national system if the bill went through in its present form." Even Forgan threatened to withdraw his powerful and financially important First National Bank of Chicago. Removing himself from the emotional impact of the law upon the national bankers, he assessed the effect of the new legislation:

> The fact that a large number of national banks are likely to withdraw from the system, or to put it in another way, the fact that the bill will not be sufficiently attractive to induce the national banks generally to go into it and will certainly have no attractions for State banks appears to me to be the most alarming thing in connection with the bill, and it is most desirable that the attention of the powers at Washington should be drawn to it. If the bill is not sufficiently attractive to draw the national banks generally into the system and

---

5 James B. Forgan Papers, The First National Bank of Chicago.
6 *Ibid.*

to attract the larger State banks through the country the result will be a complete fiasco . . . as it would mean the complete destruction of our present national banking system because all the national banks refusing to go into it must either continue under State charters or be dissolved. . . .[7]

Forgan was in a sense correct, for events would soon prove that membership in the new system had few attractions for banks having an option. Nevertheless, confronted with the choice of giving up their national charters or staying in the new organization, most national bankers decided to remain, realizing as they did that their remonstrance had helped to forge a statute that would be tolerable.

On December 23, 1913, President Wilson signed the bill establishing the Federal Reserve System. Some 80 years after they let the previous central bank die, Americans reluctantly accepted once again the idea of a central bank. In an illusory attempt to decentralize authority, a Federal Reserve Bank was organized in each of 12 districts, each district enclosing an area of similar economic activity and containing enough banking resources to support a strong Reserve Bank. The system was to be headed by a Federal Reserve Board of seven members, including *ex officio* the Secretary of the Treasury and the Comptroller of the Currency and five others to be appointed by the President. Membership in the System would be compulsory for national banks; state banks, upon compliance with certain requirements, might become members. Upon joining the System, a commercial bank was required to purchase shares of the capital stock of the Federal Reserve Bank of its district up to the amount of 3 percent of its combined capital and surplus (another 3 percent might be required). Thus, member banks nominally owned the Federal Reserve Banks, with a limitation on the annual return to their stock of a 6 percent cumulative dividend. But three of the nine directors of each Bank were to be appointed by the Board in Washington, one of them to be designated Chairman of the District Bank and Federal Reserve Agent.[8] The Act originally provided that member banks might retain a part of their reserves as cash in vault, but in 1917 the rule was changed to require *all* the legal reserves of member banks to be in the form of deposits with the Federal Reserve Bank of its district.[9]

The framers of the Federal Reserve Act did not intend that the new central bank should execute a monetary policy directed toward stabilizing the economy. In fact, the Federal Reserve did not seriously undertake such responsibility for nearly four decades after its founding. Nevertheless, the

[7] James B. Forgan to Thomas P. Beal, July 29, 1913, James B. Forgan Papers, The First National Bank of Chicago.

[8] There is little question that the framers of the Federal Reserve Act intended Federal Reserve Agents to be the chief executive officers of the several Banks. But the district boards, six of their members elected by the member banks of the district, designated a "Governor" as chief operating officer, and the Agent gradually assumed only an advisory and ministerial role.

[9] Beginning November 24, 1960, all currency and coin held by a member bank could once again be counted as reserves.

WOODROW WILSON
FOUNDER
OF THE FEDERAL RESERVE SYSTEM

WE SHALL DEAL WITH OUR ECONOMIC SYSTEM
AS IT IS AND AS IT MAY BE MODIFIED
NOT AS IT MIGHT BE
IF WE HAD A CLEAN SHEET OF PAPER
TO WRITE UPON
AND STEP BY STEP WE SHALL MAKE IT
WHAT IT SHOULD BE

FIRST INAUGURAL ADDRESS
WOODROW WILSON

Just inside the entrance to the Federal Reserve Building is this modest statement of the hopes of a great President for financial stability.

basic idea of the new central banking scheme was to correct deficiencies in the monetary system. There is little in the legislative history of the Act, or in the statements of those most closely involved in its passage, to suggest that the Federal Reserve would have more than minimal supervisory responsibility. Yet, as we shall see presently, the very notion of a central bank implied a linkage with other supervisory authorities.

Retrogression of the National Banking System

Between 1900 and 1914, the year in which the Federal Reserve began operations, the number of commercial banks in the United States increased from about 9,000 to just over 25,000; as of June 30, 1914, there were 17,498 state-chartered banks and 7,518 national banks. During World War I state-chartered banks increased much more rapidly than national banks.

In 1921 the number of commercial banks in this country stood at the incredible level of more than 29,000, approximately 21,000 of them state banks and about 8,000 of them national banks.[10] The year 1921 marked the high point of commercial bank numbers, though in the early 1920s two successive Comptrollers of the Currency followed reasonably liberal chartering policies because of their anxiety to maintain the number of national banks and so the strength of the Federal Reserve System. "It is desirable, indeed necessary," wrote Comptroller Daniel R. Crissinger, "to bring into the Federal reserve system the largest possible proportion of the banking power of the country. National banks are required to be members of the Federal reserve system, and they must inevitably constitute the real foundation of that structure." [11] Even so, Crissinger observed in his 1921 *Annual Report* that "95 applications, with capital of $4,530,000, were rejected" and that the principal causes of rejection were "lack of demand for additional banking facilities in the various communities or the reported unsatisfactory financial standing or character of the applicants." From 1924 on, chartering policy became progressively more restrictive, the rejection rate for the years 1926-1930 approximating one-half of the applications received. In his 1927 *Annual Report,* Comptroller Joseph McIntosh wrote:

> This bureau is subject at all times to the demand for charters for new national banking associations. One of its most difficult problems is to avoid conflict between the interests of the applicants and the needs of the community for additional banking facilities. . . . An analysis of the applications which this office has received for the establishment of new banks shows that there is too often a desire to organize banks in localities where the communities are amply served and which would not support new institutions with a likelihood of any fair measure of success.

---

[10] Some series show slightly more than 30,000, doubtless because the enumerators included certain private banks that are not represented in the smaller figure.
[11] Comptroller of the Currency, *Annual Report*, 1922, p. 2.

*Comptroller
Joseph W. McIntosh,
in whose tenure
during the 1920s
the rate of chartering
of national banks
dropped sharply.*

Extreme care should be exercised in granting charters, both for National and State banks. This has been my policy with respect to national bank charters. During the current year only 44 per cent of the number of applications received for the establishment of new national banks was approved, as compared with 52 per cent the previous like period and an average of 72.8 per cent over the eight prior years, with a high of 82.7 per cent just subsequent to the World War. In other words, despite the fact that the number of applications received remains about the same, the number approved by this office is constantly becoming fewer and in the current year a less number of applications was approved than has been approved any year during the past 10-year period.[12]

In 1928, Comptroller John W. Pole reported that the Office was exercising a "policy of extreme care in granting charters for national banks" and that less than 40 percent of applications received were approved.

---

[12] Comptroller of the Currency, *Annual Report,* 1927, pp. 13-14.

But both McIntosh and Pole continued to voice the concern of their immediate predecessors, Crissinger and Henry M. Dawes, over the failure of the national banking system to maintain its relative strength. In 1927, McIntosh noted that in the preceding three years 253 national banks had converted to state charters, taking with them aggregate resources of more than $1 billion. Moreover, he observed, total resources of national banks had dropped from about 75 percent of the total of commercial-bank resources in 1884 to about 46 percent in 1926. And in 1930 Comptroller Pole expressed the gloomy view that the "national banking system has within recent years declined in size, importance, and influence and has become thereby relatively less effective as an instrumentality of the Federal Government. Through the diversion of commercial banking from the national to the various State banking systems, Congress has lost control over the major portion of commercial banking resources in the United States." [13] As indeed it had, for in 1930, according to the Comptroller's calculations, the national

[13] Comptroller of the Currency, *Annual Report,* 1930, p. 5.

TABLE 5–1

Aggregate Loans and Investments of Large Banks Lost to the National and State Banking Systems by Consolidation and Conversion, by Years, 1921-1931*

Year	National charters given up		State charters given up	
	Number	Loans and investments (in millions of dollars)	Number	Loans and investments (in millions of dollars)
1921	11	$ 565,423	3	$ 57,642
1922	3	70,724	7	84,035
1923	12	238,752	4	104,073
1924	6	128,500	7	108,850
1925	4	98,272	6	91,001
1926	14	359,533	5	169,228
Total 1921-1926	50	$1,461,204	32	$ 614,829
1927	9	$ 117,177	15	$ 982,070
1928	16	309,778	18	356,248
1929	27	1,844,416	17	637,359
1930	15	158,951	8	913,666
1931	6	129,829	7	498,543
Total 1927-1931	73	$2,560,151	65	$3,387,886

* Banks with loans and investments of $5,000,000 or more at time of conversion or consolidation.
SOURCE: Committee on Branch, Group, and Chain Banking, appointed February 26, 1930, by the Federal Reserve Board.

Number of Banks in the United States, Exclusive of
Mutual Savings Banks and Private Banks,* 1914-1930

Date (June)	Member banks			Nonmember state banks (exclusive of mutual savings and private banks)	All state banks	All state and national banks
	State	National	Total			
1914	—	7,518	7,518	17,498	17,498	25,016
1915	17	7,597	7,614	17,731	17,748	25,345
1916	34	7,571	7,605	18,219	18,253	25,824
1917	53	7,599	7,652	18,657	18,710	26,309
1918	513	7,699	8,212	18,891	19,404	27,103
1919	1,042	7,779	8,821	18,604	19,646	27,425
1920	1,374	8,024	9,398	19,261	20,635	28,659
1921	1,595	8,150	9,745	19,672	21,267	29,417
1922	1,648	8,244	9,892	19,141	20,789	29,033
1923	1,620	8,236	9,856	19,034	20,654	28,890
1924	1,570	8,080	9,650	18,458	20,028	28,108
1925	1,472	8,066	9,538	18,101	19,573	27,639
1926	1,403	7,972	9,375	17,591	18,994	26,966
1927	1,309	7,790	9,099	16,810	18,119	25,909
1928	1,244	7,685	8,929	16,196	17,440	25,125
1929	1,177	7,530	8,707	15,551	16,728	24,258
1930	1,068	7,247	8,315	14,730	15,798	23,045

* Banks in continental United States only. "All State banks," "national banks," and "all State and national banks" were taken from the Comptrollers' abstracts and annual reports, except that for December 1931 the state-bank figures were compiled by the Division of Bank Operations of the Federal Reserve Board from state-bank abstracts. State-bank members were compiled from Federal Reserve Board abstracts and call reports, and nonmember banks were derived by deducting member banks from the total of national and state banks.
SOURCE: Committee on Branch, Group, and Chain Banking, Federal Reserve Board.

banking system's proportion of total banking resources had shrunk to less than 40 percent.

Actually, measured in loans and investments, in the years 1920-1926 losses of the national system through surrender of charters were just about offset by net gains in the years 1927-1928. This turnabout doubtless resulted from passage of the McFadden Act, which, in addition to the liberalization of national-bank branching, gave national banks a number of additional powers and made their charters perpetual instead of for only 99 years.[14] The retrogression of the national banking system was obviously not the consequence of serious net losses on account of conversions. Instead, state banks that were members of the Federal Reserve System were simply growing faster than national banks. In the 11 years 1920-1930 loans and invest-

---

[14] The limitation of national-bank charters to 20 and then 99 years had unquestionably hurt national banks in their competition for trust business.

ments of state member banks increased nearly 74 percent, while those of national banks increased 24 percent and those of state nonmember banks grew only 17 percent.

Comptroller Pole was acutely aware of the problem of bank failures. In his 1930 *Annual Report,* he observed that in the fiscal year ending June 30, 1930, there had been 640 failures, 82 of them national banks and 558 state banks. He noted that bank failure was obviously most pronounced in the agricultural states, with the failure rate being negligible in the East and on the West Coast, where business was more diversified. He added that the failure in the past 10 years of 5,600 banks, with $2 billion of deposits, "constitutes one of the main factors responsible for the crystallization of a strong sentiment in favor of some change in our banking structure which will bring to our rural districts, where more than four-fifths of these failures have occurred, the benefits and protection of the strong well-managed banks now operating in our commercial centers."[15]

Comptroller Pole was prepared to argue that the salvation of commercial

---

[15] Comptroller of the Currency, *Annual Report,* 1930, p. 2.

TABLE 5–3

Loans and Investments of Banks in the United States Exclusive of Mutual Savings Banks and Private Banks, 1914-1930

(in millions of dollars)

Date (June)	Member banks			Nonmember state banks (exclusive of mutual savings and private banks)	All state banks	All state and national banks
	State	National	Total			
1914	—	8,313	8,313	8,410	8,410	16,723
1915	76	8,688	8,764	8,582	8,658	17,346
1916	229	10,086	10,315	9,972	10,201	20,287
1917	556	11,897	12,453	11,248	11,804	23,701
1918	4,594	13,913	18,507	8,727	13,321	27,234
1919	6,530	15,712	22,242	9,404	15,934	31,646
1920	8,012	17,547	25,559	10,712	18,724	36,271
1921	8,226	15,895	24,121	10,090	18,316	34,211
1922	8,477	15,705	24,182	9,677	18,154	33,859
1923	9,702	16,805	26,507	10,590	20,292	37,097
1924	10,109	17,058	27,167	10,938	21,047	38,105
1925	11,225	18,293	29,518	11,694	22,919	41,212
1926	12,025	19,159	31,184	12,263	24,288	43,447
1927	12,519	20,237	32,756	12,331	24,850	45,087
1928	12,999	22,062	35,061	12,874	25,873	47,935
1929	14,254	21,457	35,711	13,132	27,386	48,843
1930	13,907	21,749	35,656	12,638	26,545	48,294

SOURCE: Committee on Branch, Group, and Chain Banking, Federal Reserve Board.

banking lay in the extension of branch systems. The controversy that had been building steadily for more than a decade was now coming to a point of settlement.

The Rise of Branch Banking

As we have observed, branch banking began a slow but substantial growth just after the turn of the century. By 1915, 397 banks maintained branches; of this group, 12 were national banks and 385 were state banks.[16] The 397 institutions operated 785 branches; 832 offices were in the head-office city, and 350 were outside the head-office city.

Six years later, of more than 29,000 commercial banks, 530 maintained a total of more than 1,281 branches. Because of the rapid increase in the number of unit banks during the previous two decades, the number of branch offices constituted only 6 percent of the total number of banking offices.[17] Nevertheless, banks with branches accounted for nearly 15 percent of the total commercial banking resources of the country, suggesting that relatively large banks were expanding by acquiring branches. From 1920 on, branch banking increased in relative importance as the number of unit banks was steadily reduced by suspension and failure and as the number of branch offices steadily increased. By 1930, 751 commercial banks, 166 national banks and 585 state banks, maintained 3,522 branches. Of the total of branch-bank offices, 3,140 were in the head-office city and 1,133 were outside the head-office city. Banks with branches were by this time almost equal in total resources to the much larger number of banks that had no branches.

Branch banking would have shown even more dramatic gains in the absence of legislation, federal and state, passed with the primary intention of protecting unit banks from competition. In some states this legislation completely stopped an increase in multi-office banking, leaving the large banks of those states to squeeze themselves into increasingly inefficient banking houses. In other states, anti-branching legislation led to the expansion of two forms of multi-unit banking, groups and chains, which flourished where the more straightforward branch-bank organizations were illegal.

During the first quarter of the 20th century, the economic forces compelling the growth of branch banking tended to promote intracity branching rather than intercity branching. As cities pushed outward and increasing traffic congested the streets, banks found it progressively more difficult to

---

[16] It will be recalled that state banks converting to national charters could keep their branches, provided definite capitals were assigned to each of the branches. For data sources, see *Historical Statistics of the United States, Colonial Times to 1957,* p. 635, and *Federal Reserve Bulletin,* October 1938, p. 880.

[17] The expression "branch-bank offices" is used in this book to denote *all* offices of branch banks, including home offices. Whenever the word "branches" is used alone, home offices are excluded.

reach households. Yet it was almost precisely at this time that the American middle class was becoming affluent enough to make household and small personal accounts profitable. In a society of spatially separated communities, where villages and hamlets flourished only a few miles apart, uncertain communication and bad roads slowed the establishment of branch offices outside the home city. Even before 1920, however, intercity branches were increasing in a dozen states, notably in California. By the mid-1920s intercity branching was on its way to becoming the more important type, as banks moved to place offices in the burgeoning suburbs.

Underlying these changes, their character in part determined by the urbanization and then the suburbanization of a peripatetic population, were the increasing returns to scale in banking. The market advantages of larger units were reinforced by technical advances in handling checks, making bookkeeping entries, and processing data, as well as by the proportionately greater use that big banks could make of free Federal Reserve services. More fundamental was the advantage to large units of first-class managerial talents; for in an increasingly complex world financial institutions, possibly more than any other business firms, benefited from the improving quality of management that, within certain limits, came with size.

Yet the specific course of branch banking in the United States was unquestionably diverted and shifted by statutory and regulatory resistance to basic economic forces. This resistance, though by no means universal, persisted in wide geographic areas. Even so, at both federal and state levels the trend after 1915 was toward liberalization of late 19th-century judgments about branch banking.

For nearly 50 years, the predecessors of Comptroller Lawrence O. Murray had ruled that national banks could not have branches. In 1911 Murray asked Attorney General Wickersham for an opinion on the question, and Wickersham replied that the power to branch was not implied in the National Bank Act. In 1915 the Federal Reserve Board, apparently concerned over the statutory discrimination in favor of its state member banks, recommended national-bank branching within the main-office city or county. A controversy that had smouldered for years erupted at the 1916 convention of the American Bankers Association, which adopted resolutions opposing branch banking in any form. So vehement was the opposition to the Federal Reserve proposal that it was dropped forthwith.

Only the devious path of the National Bank Consolidation Act of 1918 opened the way to multi-office structures for existing national banks. This statute permitted a national bank that had converted from state to national charter, keeping its branches, to consolidate with another national bank, retaining the branches involved in the consolidation. Thus, in states permitting branching, a national bank could acquire branches by organizing a state bank with branch offices, converting the state bank to a national charter, and then merging with it. An awkward procedure, the method nevertheless enabled more than 100 national banks to acquire branches in less than a decade.

By the early 1920s the problem of providing banking facilities convenient to residential areas of a city was shifting to the problem of creating outlets for the suburbs, to which higher income families were emigrating from their old homes in the central city. For years the Office of the Comptroller had considered the possibility of allowing metropolitan banks to open "offices," thus equalizing competition with metropolitan state banks that were permitted to branch. In 1921 Comptroller Crissinger reported that a bill had been introduced to permit limited branching of national banks in those states authorizing the operation of branches by state banks, but there was no congressional response. Crissinger then held that national banks might open intracity offices or tellers' windows wherever state branching was permitted. These offices could receive deposits and cash checks but could not make loans or carry on other business requiring policy decisions. In his *Annual Report* for 1922, Crissinger again asked that national banks be granted branching authority, at least to the extent enjoyed by state banks. He wrote:

> At this point a situation is presented which must be looked squarely in the face and dealt with in complete frankness. National banks are compelled to compete with State institutions, and if the laws of the States are more liberal than are the national banking laws they will constitute an inducement to banks to operate under the laws of the States rather than of the Nation. The very fact that the Federal reserve system establishes a measure of financial assurance, a concentration of reserves, and an elasticity of the currency, which operate to the advantage of all kinds of banks, whether State or national, makes it easier for State banks to carry on under the more liberal charters which many States issue. So long as all banks enjoy the general advantages accruing from the workings of the Federal reserve system, there is obvious temptation to the particular institution to supplement these benefits by taking advantage of the wider liberality of State charters. But it is apparent that if all banks should yield to this temptation the maintenance of the Federal reserve system would at length be impossible; and just in proportion as an increasing number of banks prefer the State to the national charter, the aggregate power, security, and responsibility of the Federal reserve system must be diminished.
>
> In short, if the Federal reserve system is to be perpetuated and maintained in the strength and authority which are desirable, there must be national banks in sufficient number and strength. And if national banks are to be assured in such numbers, they must be given charters liberal enough to constitute inducement to remain in the system.
>
> All this seems so plain that the statement of it may appear unnecessary. But we have reached the time in the competition between the State banks and the National banks when it is obvious that in many States there is a decided tendency away from the national and toward the State forms of charter.[18]

18 Comptroller of the Currency, *Annual Report,* 1922, p. 2.

Again, Congress showed no disposition to act.

Crissinger's immediate successor, Comptroller Henry M. Dawes, was a vigorous opponent of branch banking. "Branch banking," he once said, "is concentration carried to the nth degree. . . . It seems to me that there is no room for compromise on this subject and that a determination should be reached as to whether the United States wishes to embrace a national system of branch banks or to preserve its coordinated independent units. It can not do both." [19] Yet in his 1923 *Annual Report,* Comptroller Dawes had been willing to admit that:

> . . . a fair and reasonable solution of the question of branch banking in the United States can be made by Congress through the enactment into law of the substance of the resolutions recently adopted by the Federal Reserve Board, at the same time granting to national banks the power, with the approval and under the general supervision of the comptroller, to establish and operate branch banks or branch offices under similar territorial restrictions. . . . [20]

D. R. Crissinger, Ohio friend of President Harding, was a liberal Comptroller who resigned to become Governor of the Federal Reserve Board.

---

[19] Henry M. Dawes, "Would Extension of the Branch Banking System Be Beneficial?," *Congressional Digest,* 10, December 1931, pp. 309, 313.

[20] Comptroller of the Currency, *Annual Report,* 1923, p. 16.

The plain fact was that national banks were operating under increasingly serious disadvantages and their inability to branch was beginning to place a severe strain on the national banking system. Dawes requested an opinion from Attorney General Daugherty about the legality of additional offices of the kind that his immediate predecessor had authorized. This time the Attorney General responded favorably, holding that national banks could operate limited-service offices within their city of location. In the five-year period 1922-1926, more than 200 of these offices were established, relieving somewhat the considerable pressures that were building.

In 1922, the First National Bank in St. Louis forced a test case of the power of a national bank to branch. Acting under advice of its counsel, the bank established a branch office in a separate building distinctly removed from the main banking house. The branch carried on a full banking business, and the directorate of the bank announced its intention to form other branches. This action flew in the face of a Missouri statute providing that "no bank shall maintain in this State a branch bank or receive deposits or pay checks except in its own banking house." The attorney general of the State of Missouri thereupon filed suit in the Missouri Supreme Court to determine the authority of the bank to have a branch bank in St. Louis. It was contended that the laws of Missouri prohibited the establishment of branch banks and that the prohibition applied to the First National Bank in St. Louis, because national banking laws did not permit a national bank to establish branches. Counsel for the bank replied that the State of Missouri was without authority to proceed against a national bank and that the First National Bank was within its charter powers in establishing a branch. The Supreme Court of Missouri held that the Missouri statute applied to national banks, whereupon the case was brought to the Supreme Court of the United States. Argued in May of 1923, it was reargued in November of that year. The Solicitor General contended that the State of Missouri was without jurisdiction in attempting by a *quo warranto* proceeding to inquire into the powers of a corporation chartered by the United States government. He further contended that upholding the State of Missouri would infringe upon the sovereignty of the United States. The opinion of the Court, rendered in 1924, upheld the Supreme Court of Missouri, three justices dissenting.[21] The Supreme Court held that a national bank has no charter power to establish a branch bank and that the First National Bank in St. Louis was in violation of the Missouri statute. The Court added that the enforcement of the statute against the national bank did not conflict with federal law because the prohibition was against acts not permitted by federal law.

By the time of this decision the Comptroller of the Currency had prepared recommendations for a federal statute governing national-bank

---

[21] *First National Bank in St. Louis v. State of Missouri,* 263 U.S., pp. 640-668.

branching, and in 1924 bills containing his suggestions were introduced in both the House and Senate. After three years of noisy debate, the McFadden Act was passed in 1927. For the first time the law permitted national banks to open *de novo* branches unlimited with respect to function. Nevertheless, many considered the McFadden Act to be an anti-branching bill, for it allowed members of the Federal Reserve System to establish new branches only within the limits of "the city, town, or village in which said association is situated if such establishment and operation are at the time permitted to State banks by the law of the State in question."

Almost at once agitation began for liberalizing this restrictive law, which effectively precluded further branching outside their home cities of banks subject to federal regulation. In his *Annual Report* for 1929, Comptroller Pole expressed a twofold concern, (1) that the "country-bank" system was being undermined by the continuing high rate of failures of small institutions, and (2) that holding companies were being formed in large numbers for the purpose of bringing together a number of banks in a single operating group. The latter development, he said, was a substitute for branch banking, "whereby each operating unit leans for support upon the . . . holding company, and receives the benefits of its moral and financial support; its prestige and good will; its extension of the wider type of banking service; and the benefits of its highly trained management." Although he did not have complete statistics, Pole believed that group operations were attempting to do what could be much more simply accomplished by extending ". . . adequately capitalized large city banks to the outlying communities within the economic zone of operations of such banks. . . ." In a word, Pole proposed that national banks be allowed to branch over their trade area.[22] In the same year President Hoover, likewise noting the growth of group and chain banking, suggested to Congress that it consider permitting national banks to branch in limited areas. The battle over branching was far from settled and would soon rage again.

Bank Supervision in Early Federal Reserve Years

The Federal Reserve Act made specific provision for supervision of member banks. Since national banks were required by law to enter the System, whereas state-chartered banks could elect membership, a period of testing different kinds of arrangements was bound to follow.

---

[22] Comptroller of the Currency, *Annual Report*, 1929, pp. 4-5.

Only five years previously, Comptroller Henry M. Dawes had remarked that the terms "economic spheres, financial zones, etc., are mere balderdash, given a different interpretation by every individual who uses them. The city is the natural unit for community endeavor. It is a clearly understandable and definite thing and the confines of a city are not now and never will be so large that personal contact between the banker and his clients can not be established either instantaneously by telephone or in a few moments by conveyance." See Comptroller of the Currency, *Annual Report*, 1924, p. 5.

John W. Pole, Comptroller from 1928 to 1932, was aware of the economic forces at work to change the structure of American commercial banking.

The law establishing the Federal Reserve provided that the Comptroller of the Currency was to examine each member bank at least twice a year. But it also authorized the Federal Reserve Board to examine member banks at its discretion, and another provision gave further authority to the 12 Federal Reserve Banks to make special examinations of member banks within their districts. Thus, the Comptroller of the Currency, the Board in Washington, and the Federal Reserve Banks of the several districts could each look into the affairs of member banks; in addition, state authorities maintained their old supervision of banks within their jurisdictions. Obviously, arrangements had to be made that would reduce multiplicity of bank examinations and a burdensome, repetitious series of call reports. It was particularly important that supervision be made reasonably palatable to state banks so that they would not be deterred from joining the System.

Although the Federal Reserve Act made no other major revisions in the national banking laws, it did make substantial changes in supervisory procedures. The statute changed the method of paying examiners from a fee to a salary system, with salaries to be fixed by the Federal Reserve Board upon the recommendation of the Comptroller of the Currency. Power of appointment of examiners was vested in the Comptroller subject to the approval of the Secretary of the Treasury. Costs of examination were to be assessed against the banks in proportion to the resources of the banks examined.

Friction Between the Comptroller and the Board

Almost from the first, relations between the Office of the Comptroller and the Federal Reserve Board were strained.[23] Conflict arose at once over the contents of examination reports and the Board's powers to demand certain information. Only a little while after the Federal Reserve System began operating, Comptroller John Skelton Williams, not celebrated for his tact, sent a circular to all member banks instructing them to send the Federal Reserve Agents of their districts a duplicate of the next report of condition, omitting certain schedules such as interest rates charged, number of depositors, bills rediscounted, and liabilities of directors as payers or endorsers. The Agent in San Francisco wrote plaintively to Board member Adolf Miller: "It has been my conviction that the Federal Reserve banks should have a gradually increasing, rather than a decreasing, amount of information regarding their member banks. . . ."[24] Within a few weeks letters were pouring in from other Agents, protesting Comptroller Williams' circular and arguing that the deleted information should not be kept from the Reserve Banks. There were, moreover, continuing complaints from Reserve Banks about the difficulties of obtaining copies of examination reports of national banks. The Governor of the Federal Reserve Bank of Chicago wrote the Board: "While it is true we are at the present time receiving some information through the local National Bank Examiner, it

---

[23] In these early days the Board and its staff were housed in the Treasury Building, as was the Comptroller of the Currency. Both the Secretary of the Treasury and the Comptroller of the Currency were members of the Board, *ex officio*. But physical and official proximity could not prevent extended controversy induced by a statute that created so much overlapping authority.

[24] Federal Reserve Board, Record File 241.2: Examination of Member Banks: 1914-1924, April 30, 1915.

is also true that his information does not fully serve the purpose and I trust an arrangement may be made whereby we will again be accorded the privilege of having access to the Examiners' reports. . . ." [25] Acting Comptroller Thomas P. Kane told the Board somewhat testily that in response to the complaints of Reserve Banks a blank form was being drafted for use in furnishing them information.

In general, it was the position of the Comptroller's staff, in both Washington and the field, that Federal Reserve officials were not empowered to scrutinize highly confidential portions of examination reports. The only information really necessary for Reserve Bank use, they held, was that required in the extension of credit via the discount window. Reported one committee:

> In requesting access to the complete reports of examination, the Federal Reserve banks appear to be operating upon the assumption that the credit extended by them is an extra hazardous risk and of an abnormal character justifying them in demanding information not exacted by other banking institutions and in no way relating to the solvency of the bank. This point of view is not warranted by past banking experience and if the extending of accommodations is to be restrictive and surrounded with burdensome exactions, the success of the system is in jeopardy. [26]

In response to this comment, Vice Governor Frederick A. Delano wrote the Comptroller that the committee report "fails utterly to comprehend the new order of things." The Comptroller's Office, he implied, was comparing Federal Reserve Banks, which were wholly owned by the member banks, with large national banks that had previously been correspondents of other banks. In Delano's view, the Comptroller's Office misunderstood the nature of the central bank and the kind of control it should exercise.

National bank examiners apparently continued to send Federal Reserve Agents only abstracts of examination reports. In the fall of 1915, the Board once again discussed the possibility of obtaining the entire report, which would be held in the joint custody of the Governor of each Reserve Bank and the Governor of the Board. The power of the Federal Reserve Board over the reports was crucial in determining its right to demand them from the Comptroller. On October 18, 1915, the Board's Chief Counsel held that the examination reports of national banks formed part of the records of the Comptroller of the Currency and were under his supervision and control. Thus, the Federal Reserve Board could not, as a matter of right, or by

---

[25] Federal Reserve Board, Record File 241.3: Examination of National Banks: 1915-1920, August 27, 1915.

[26] Federal Reserve Board, Record File 011.2: Comptroller of the Currency: 1908-1916, July 16, 1915. Members of the committee were Charles Starek (Deputy Reserve Agent of the Federal Reserve Bank of New York), Sherrill Smith (Chief District Examiner at Chicago), and James D. Brennan (Chief District Examiner at Boston).

A Federal Reserve note, series of 1918: Federal Reserve notes (as distinguished from Federal Reserve Bank notes) would one day become, for all practical purposes, the paper currency of the country.

reason of any supervision over the Bureau, require full reports made by examiners to the Comptroller. At a Board meeting the following February, Governor Harding pointed out that "the Comptroller has the authority to furnish these reports but he also has the right under the law to refuse to deliver them for the use of the Federal Reserve Board."

Negotiations with the Comptroller's Office were soon concluded. On March 10, 1916, Comptroller Williams wrote Governor Charles Hamlin that new forms were being prepared, so drawn that the main portion could be sent to Federal Reserve Agents and the supplementary portion, containing confidential information, to the Comptroller.[27] Meantime, Federal Reserve Banks would be given access to the full examination report. Even the Board seemed to feel that the confidential nature of these reports created grave problems. At an ensuing Board meeting it was emphasized that duplicates of examination reports of member banks supplied to Federal Reserve

---

[27] As another break with tradition, the Comptroller announced that after June 1 examined banks would also receive copies of the reports.

Banks were to be used only by the Agent and the Governor of each Bank and were not for the scrutiny of the Bank's directors or junior officers. At the same time, the Board took the position that if a copy of the full report were not furnished for the use of the Agent and the Governor of each Bank, it would be necessary for the Bank to exercise its right to make its own examination.[28]

Hoping to correct weaknesses before they appeared in examinations, Comptroller Williams enlarged and amplified the reports of condition (which he demanded on a bi-monthly basis) to include information about a bank's condition not previously requested. In December of 1915 the Board's Committee on Audit and Examination recommended that the form of the report of condition be altered to increase its usefulness in providing statistical data for the Board, at the same time making the form less objectionable to member banks. Bureaucratic tempers continued to rise, for at a Board meeting early the next February Governor Harding asked that a statement be included in the Annual Report:

> The Board is given no power whatever in the matter of reports of condition which are made to the Comptroller of the Currency by member banks, which contain, besides the essential facts relating to the financial status or solvency of the individual member banks, much statistical information. The Board has no voice whatever as to the dates or frequency of these reports, and has no control over the matter that is included in them.[29]

Five months later the agencies were still squabbling, and the San Francisco Agent reported tartly that an Idaho national bank had failed to forward copies of a call report made to the Comptroller. The Board referred the letter to Comptroller Williams.

The two-year discussion of the Federal Reserve Board's right to examination reports of national banks, not to mention the hassle over call reports, had not improved relations between the agencies. Indeed, before agreement was reached on the form of reports, Vice Governor Delano recommended that Section 21 of the Federal Reserve Act be amended to give the Board almost complete powers over the Comptroller's Office and provide that "all administrative orders, rulings and circulars issued from the office of the Comptroller of the Currency . . . be approved by the Federal Reserve Board." [30] But Secretary of the Treasury William McAdoo strongly advised "effective cooperation between the Board and the Comptroller's office," and other Board members urged a conciliatory attitude.

Settling the Issue

Meanwhile, at both Board and Bank levels, the Federal Reserve wrestled with the problem of System participation in examinations and, more gener-

---

28 Federal Reserve Board, *Minutes: 1916,* July 7, 1916, pp. 753-754.
29 *Ibid.,* February 5, 1916, p. 156.
30 *Ibid.,* p. 158.

ally, in the total supervision of member banks. At the outset state member banks resisted examination by the Comptroller's examiners, even though the Board reserved the right to designate the ones to be selected for this work.[31] A circular of October 17, 1914, expressly directed the several Federal Reserve Banks to adopt a uniform plan of examination and look to the recruitment and training of a force of examiners. To prevent a multiplicity of examinations the circular also provided that special examinations, to be conducted by Federal Reserve Banks, might be made in connection with the regular examinations by national or state examiners. On February 24, 1915, the Board agreed that, in those states where supervision by state authorities was not of a standard acceptable to the Board, the initial examination of an applying institution was to be made either by a Board-designated examiner or by a national bank examiner assigned by the Comptroller at the request of the Board. On June 7, 1915, the Board issued Regulation M, whereby every state bank or trust company while a member of the System was subjected to examination by the Board. But to avoid duplication the Board could at its discretion accept examinations by state authorities "found to be of the same standard of thoroughness as national bank examinations." [32]

State member banks continued their complaints about examinations by the Comptroller of the Currency. Ostensibly, they objected to the expense, contending that they had to pay for the examination of the state authorities that chartered them. But the real reason for their hostility and continuing resistance was an unwillingness to subject themselves to the more rigorous examination procedures of the federal authority. Federal Reserve Agents argued that federal examination was deterring state-chartered banks from joining the System, and in June 1917 the Federal Reserve Act was amended to exempt them from this requirement.[33]

Although the 1917 amendment removed state member banks from the supervision of the Comptroller, substituting that of the Board or the Federal Reserve Banks, the statute expressly provided that expenses were to be assessed against the banks examined. But to make membership more attractive by reducing member-bank costs, Federal Reserve Banks adopted the practice of absorbing the expenses of examination. An open violation of the law, this absorption was manifestly unfair to national banks. Nevertheless, the practice continued. On April 7, 1923, the Federal Reserve Board

---

[31] Federal Reserve Board, *Minutes: 1914,* August 20, 1914, p. 49.
[32] Federal Reserve Board, Record File 125: Regulations and Circulars of Organization Committee Minutes, Circular No. 14, June 7, 1915, p. 5.
[33] By 1917 it was apparent that liberal terms of admission to the System would have to be statutory, for only 53 state-chartered banks had joined up to that time. The examination amendment was one of several aimed at enticing the state banks. Henceforth, state member banks could withdraw from the System on six months' written notice to the Federal Reserve Board, could retain their full charter and statutory rights subject to the restrictions of the Federal Reserve Act, and were relieved of the limitations on national banks regarding loans to a single borrower.

ruled that Reserve Banks should assess state member banks to defray costs of examination. The ruling met with loud protests; state banks maintained that they had joined the System on the assurance that they would not be so assessed, and many threatened to withdraw. Since a major source of annoyance was the requirement of paying both a state and federal authority, a Federal Reserve committee recommended that state banks secure from their legislatures a statute permitting or requiring state supervisors to accept federal examinations in lieu of their own.[34] Many voices in Federal Reserve councils argued that Reserve Banks should bear the cost of examining all members banks, national as well as state. But it was feared that earnings of Reserve Banks would not ordinarily be sufficient to absorb the entire expense, and the committee felt that the Banks should do so only when they had excess earnings, charging all member banks in proportion to their resources just as the Comptroller assessed national banks. The 1923 committee implied that if this latter solution were not accepted, Federal Reserve Banks would have to reduce examination to a minimum, for continuing efforts to charge state member banks for examination seemed certain to lead to serious attrition in System membership. Alternatively, the committee contended, state examinations would be accepted in lieu of those by Federal Reserve Banks, even though the former were "entirely inadequate and unreliable, as they always are in most of the States." [35]

Actually, the issue would not be settled for many years. During the rest of the 1920s, different Reserve Banks began to vary their practice, so that by 1930 some Banks were not charging at all and others were assessing a substantial part of the costs.

Meantime, the Comptroller of the Currency continued to standardize the process of examination. In 1930 Comptroller Pole could write that the name "Comptroller of the Currency" was then something of a misnomer since "his primary function is that of a bank supervisor" and that the most important work done by the Office was that "involved in the regular examinations of national banks." Not without some pride he added:

> There are now in the Bureau of the Comptroller of the Currency, in addition to the Comptroller, three Deputy Comptrollers and a Chief National Bank Examiner with the necessary number of assistants and clerical personnel to perform the work of the Washington office. In addition there is a field force of one hundred and forty-eight national bank examiners operating under twelve District Chief National Bank Examiners with headquarters in the respective Federal Reserve cities.[36]

---

[34] Federal Reserve Board, Record File 241.2: Examination of Member Banks: 1914-1924, December 18, 1923, pp. 4-5.
[35] Ibid., p. 3.
[36] J. W. Pole, "Extent of Federal Supervision of Banking Today," Congressional Digest, 10, December 1931, p. 293.

Office of the Comptroller in Jeopardy

With the advent of the Federal Reserve System the continued existence of the Office of the Comptroller was in serious doubt. In large part congressional animosity was prompted by Federal Reserve officials, who deeply resented the intransigence of the old-line agency on jurisdictional questions. But a part of the problem developed out of the character and personality of the 13th Comptroller, John Skelton Williams, who held office from February 2, 1914, to March 2, 1921. During his term of office he created innumerable personal enemies, exacerbated difficulties with the Federal Reserve Board, and at one time or another incurred the wrath of commercial banks, large and small. Members of Congress reacted by introducing five bills to abolish the Office of the Comptroller of the Currency, three resolutions to investigate the conduct of the Comptroller, and two bills to provide for "proper" cooperation between the Comptroller and the Federal Reserve Board.

Before he was in office two full years, Comptroller Williams was forced to defend his policies against an attack in the press. He refuted the intimation that his alleged harsh attitude toward the national banks was forcing them into the state system and defended the examination fees he was charging. Three years later, in June of 1919, he again defended his examination policies, criticized as inadequate in a resolution of the California legislature, by coldly informing the legislators that examinations can serve as warnings but cannot prevent impending failures. In harsh correspondence and public speeches, Williams criticized the policies of the Federal Reserve Board. Although his attempts to protect the banks of the South and West were praised in Congress by his supporters, Williams was strongly opposed for confirmation in 1914. Upon the expiration in 1919 of the statutory period of his appointment, he served for more than two years under a law that permitted the continuance in office of Treasury Department officials pending the appointment of their successors.

Bills were introduced in three successive Congresses (the 65th, 66th, and 67th) to abolish the Office of the Comptroller of the Currency. The bills of Senator John M. Weeks of Massachusetts and Representative William M. Calder of New York proposed to transfer the functions of the Bureau to the Federal Reserve Board. Congressman Louis T. McFadden of Pennsylvania, who in 1924 would introduce banking legislation drawn to the order of Comptroller Dawes, wrote three bills that began: *"Be it enacted, . . . That the Bureau of the Comptroller of the Currency in the Treasury Department, and the office of Comptroller of the Currency be, and they are hereby abolished. . . ."* He further recommended that the Federal Reserve Board perform the Comptroller's duties.

Neither the Senate nor the House Banking and Currency Committees held hearings on any of these bills, and they died in committee. However, one of the McFadden measures was debated in the House at the time of its introduction. During the debate in February 1919, Williams' supporters questioned McFadden's reasons for introducing such a bill. He was pointedly asked whether the Federal Reserve Banks had brought pressure to bear upon Williams to carry out what McFadden maintained was a deliberate policy of transferring funds from state banks and trust companies to national banks.[37] McFadden had to admit that he did not know if the purpose of such a transfer was to strengthen the Federal Reserve System but added: "I need only point to the fact that during the term of office of

John Skelton Williams, stormy and controversial Comptroller during the period of adjustment to the Federal Reserve Act, 1914-1921.

[37] As Comptroller of the Currency, John Skelton Williams had no authority to switch substantial deposits from one bank to another. But he also served as Director of Finance and Purchases of the Railroad Administration and was a member of the War Finance Board and the Farm Loan Board.

the present Comptroller of the Currency many controversies have taken place between him and the banks and bankers all over the country." [38] He remarked further that he had been trying to abolish the Office since 1914; if the extremely autocratic powers of the Comptroller were necessary, he said, bankers would prefer them to be vested in a board rather than in one man.

During the first session of the 67th Congress, hearings were held on H.R. 4906, to amend Section 10 of the Federal Reserve Act, introduced by Representative McFadden on April 22, 1921. One of the main points of this bill was a proposal to abolish the Office of Comptroller of the Currency. On Wednesday, June 21, Governor Harding of the Federal Reserve Board was called to testify before the House Committee on Banking and Currency. Harding was asked if, in his judgment, the Office of the Comptroller of the Currency was a necessary function under the Federal Reserve Plan. Harding replied: "I do not think it is." It was then suggested to Harding that the reason for trying to abolish the Office was psychological; that perhaps the former Comptroller, Williams, was not temperamentally adapted to dealing with the bankers and the Board, and that the bill was more of a personal criticism of Williams than of the Bureau. Harding responded that for two years the Board had considered attempting to abolish an office that the Federal Reserve Act made redundant. Moreover, the Federal Reserve Advisory Council had made a similar recommendation, and many banks approved the proposition, which would remove the Comptroller's supervisory authority. Furthermore, the Federal Reserve System had created a duplication of powers, especially in the field of examination, and costs could be reduced by simplifying the structure of authority. Harding went on to say that if the Office were abolished, the Board, which was not seeking any additional power, would find ways and means to discharge the extra duties. The examination of the national banks, conducted by the Comptroller according to a rigid schedule, would be performed by the Federal Reserve Banks on a schedule that would vary according to the condition of a bank.[39]

This bill, like its predecessors, died in committee. None of the proposals to abolish the Office of the Comptroller of the Currency were successful. But if John Skelton Williams could not be curbed by abolishing the Comptroller's Office, Congressman McFadden and others were determined to subject him to congressional investigation. McFadden introduced two resolutions, the first on February 15, 1919, and the second during the following session on July 14, 1919, demanding that the Speaker of the House appoint a committee of seven members to inquire into Williams' conduct as Comptroller. These resolutions were referred to the Committee on Rules but died in subcommittee.

[38] *Congressional Record,* 65 Congress, 3rd Session, 1919, 57, p. 3452.
[39] U.S. Congress, House, Committee on Banking and Currency, *Hearings, Amendment to Abolish the Office of the Comptroller of the Currency,* 67th Congress, 1st Session, June 21, 1921, pp. 39, 40, 46, 47.

Despite these attempts to investigate the Comptroller's conduct, the controversy between him and the Federal Reserve Board did not abate, and Congress felt that it had to act. During the first session of the 67th Congress, Representative William F. Stevenson of South Carolina introduced two bills that would provide ". . . for proper cooperation between the Comptroller of the Currency and the Federal Reserve Board." No hearings were held on either bill, the first introduced on May 18, 1921, and the second on May 24, 1921, and they died in the House Banking and Currency Committee. On July 22, 1921, Senator George P. McLean of Connecticut introduced a resolution authorizing the Committee on Banking and Currency to investigate the administration of the Office of the Comptroller of the Currency and to report its findings and recommendations. During the debates McLean was asked why he had introduced the resolution. He replied: "That was done at the suggestion of the Federal Reserve Board." It was then asked why the Board wanted the Comptroller investigated. McLean answered testily that he had not been aware of any objections to his resolution and that the investigation would prove to be a wise move. At the following session the resolution was reported from the Committee to Audit and Control the Contingent Expenses of the Senate and agreed to by the Senate. But there is no evidence that the investigation was held, nor was there a public report of findings.

Although nothing came of these bills and resolutions, they testified to congressional annoyance with relations between the Comptroller's Office and the Federal Reserve Board. By 1923 matters had not improved, and in his *Annual Report* Henry M. Dawes wrote at length about the controversy. "The agitation . . . continues to be a source of annoyance and a disorganizing factor in the operation both of the Federal reserve system and of the comptroller's office." Dawes asserted that there was no duplication in the examination function, a strong argument used by those wishing to abolish the Office. Moreover, with his present independent status the Comptroller had a responsibility to the national banks, but if they were to fall under the direction of the Board, the latter would be obliged to direct their operations in the interest of their greatest creditors, the Federal Reserve Banks. "The whole principle," he said, "is wrong . . . unfair and . . . vicious. . . ." [40]

By this time, former Comptroller Crissinger had become Governor of the Federal Reserve Board, a change calculated to mend relationships. Henry M. Dawes, brother of former Comptroller Charles G. Dawes, was a strong figure, not inclined to be bullied or browbeaten. Finally, Comptrollers McIntosh and Pole worked cooperatively to make the System a viable institution. By 1930 both agencies had plenty of troubles without creating more internecine strife.

---

[40] Comptroller of the Currency, *Annual Report,* 1923, pp. 18-19.

Quarter Century Of Readjustment: 1930-1955

The decade of the 1920s saw the coming to full flower of the great American economic system. In the short space of 10 years, the productivity of American manufacturing plants jumped by 50 percent. Just as important, the benefits of increasing output were being shared among an ever greater proportion of the population. These benefits often took the form of an increasing variety of household equipment, remarkably improved in quality. Appliances of all kinds relieved the burden of household work, and the player piano, the phonograph, and the radio added a new gaiety to family life. These blessings gave a sense of economic euphoria that was felt in all economic strata. Only in the agricultural sector was there some grumbling, for many American farmers were saddled with debts incurred during World War I. But even the farm sector seemed on the whole healthy, and there was a widespread view that the secret of unending prosperity had been found.

Disillusionment came with savage swiftness. The depression that began with the autumn of 1929 was the more disastrous because most people had been assured that the bitter hardships of economic slumps could be avoided. Indeed, American political leadership could not bring itself to the realization that catastrophe was in the offing, so the decline in economic activity was allowed to run its course with scarcely any remedial measures taken to correct the fundamental disequilibrium. As late as September 1931 there was still a chance to prevent disaster, but no one, in or out of government, had the good sense to take measures aimed at correcting the financial debacle. So defeat was turned into rout, largely because the financial system simply disintegrated, and the economy slowly ground to a halt.

It is hard for modern Americans to imagine the extent of the depression. The gross national product in current prices declined almost one-half, from $104.4 billion to $56 billion; in constant prices the decline was nearly one-third. Industrial production fell by more than one-half, as wholesale prices dropped one-third and consumer prices one-fourth. But the heartrending statistics were those of unemployment and sliding household incomes. Civilian employment fell by about 20 percent, and unemployment rose from 1½ million to more than 13 million. The data show that one quarter of the civilian work force was unemployed, but under-utilization of skills, as when trained engineers made a few dollars by washing windows, meant that the real unemployment rate was much higher than the simple figures show. By the most conservative estimate nearly half the nation's bread-winners were out of work or drastically reduced in circumstances.

The trauma of the Great Depression affected the entire business community. But more than any other business, commercial banking was especially hard hit. The continuing slide of 1929-1933 was attributed, not without reason, to the failure of the banking system to hold up under stress. A large part of the electorate, not realizing that it was the duty of the central bank to provide liquidity for the commercial banks, laid the entire blame on commercial bankers. In the whole history of our country, no single group had been so bitterly castigated. Bankers were not entirely without fault, of course, but the disintegration of the financial system, which became very nearly complete in the days just preceding the inauguration of Franklin D. Roosevelt, was the result of causes far more serious than risky banking practices and an occasional dishonest banker.

The real heroes of the banking crisis were the personnel of the Office of the Comptroller of the Currency and their counterparts in the state banking departments. Unstinting work, far beyond the call of duty, brought the financial system back to something like normal working order by 1935. The economy recovered, though with agonizing slowness, only to receive a sharp setback in the "recession" of 1937-1938, brought on by central bank authorities who, in an incredible miscalculation, took steps to prevent inflation when the economy was still performing far below capacity.

Meantime, commercial banks drifted along, their managements too shocked and fearful to finance American business more aggressively. Even in the later 1930s, the prospects of commercial banks were by no means exciting. Hard as it is for modern Americans to realize, the economy was still floundering a decade after the beginning of the depression, with one-sixth of the work force still unemployed or seriously underemployed. But the outbreak of war in Europe early in September 1939 stimulated military buying; and purchases of foreign governments, particularly Great Britain, began to revive the flagging economy, which showed signs during 1940 of achieving full recovery. Employment and payrolls rose, industrial production increased rapidly, and there were indications of a return to genuine prosperity. But not until 1941, when the Treasury began to run massive deficits, did the economy get back to operation at something like its vast potential.

Commercial banks, again more highly liquid, did not participate at once in returning good times. Interest rates would remain abnormally low for many years, and both the depression and World War II biased the asset structure of commercial banks from high-yield loans to low-yield securities.[1] Furthermore, most bank managers looked complacently on increasing competition from the nonbank financial intermediaries, annoyed, perhaps, with the savings and loan associations and the special tax advantages accorded them, but not really concerned at the inroads they were making in finance. Indeed, from the onset of the Great Depression, when opportunities for high-yield loans began to decline, bank managers were increasingly unenthusiastic about time deposits, and only the most progressive could foresee the drastic change in this view that would come in the mid-1950s. But for that matter, scarcely anyone could have predicted the great change in commercial-bank competition that would begin then.

Shown is a specimen national-bank note issued not long before the withdrawal from circulation in 1935 of this form of Treasury currency. In that year the Treasury retired the bonds eligible to "back" national-bank notes. Except for an occasional bill that emerges from a safety-deposit box or other hiding place, schoolboys no longer experience the thrill of finding a note with the name of a familiar town on its face.

---

[1] *Vide infra*, pp. 143-144.

Thursday, October 24, 1929, remains Black Thursday in the minds of those who witnessed this panic scene on Wall Street that day. The precipitate decline in the market adumbrated the catastrophe to come.

Rescue Operations

The Banking Crisis

The stock market crash of late 1929 sent tremors throughout the financial community, accelerating briefly the rate of failure of bank and nonbank institutions. In early 1930 it appeared that the economy was headed for only a modest slump, and public officials assured the electorate that "prosperity was just around the corner." The money stock held very nearly constant, and until late in the year the problem of bank failures appeared no worse than it had been during the 1920s. Unfortunately, at the end of 1930 and the beginning of 1931, when many observers could point to faint signs of an upturn, the first of three successive waves of bank failures struck the economy. President Hoover's response to increasing trouble was a recommendation to form a National Credit Corporation, a private corporation to be owned by banks and formed for mutual self-aid. But the stronger banks of the system were unwilling to bail out the weaker ones, and by January 27, 1932, the Corporation had lent only $155 million to 575 institutions.[2] Meantime, during the last half of 1931 a second wave of bank

---

[2] *New York Times,* January 20, 1932.

failures was precipitated by a Federal Reserve increase in the discount rate that was calculated to staunch the gold outflow. In the last three months of the year more than 1,000 banks failed, a clear indication of a terrifying increase in the rate of bank failure. During the latter half of 1931 more than $1 billion of deposits disappeared as a result of bank suspensions; but this contraction of the money supply was only a fairly small portion of the total decline in deposits of nearly $6 billion that occurred during the latter half of 1931, as banks contracted their loans and sold securities to maintain some semblance of liquidity.

To arrest the deflation and the further disintegration of the banking system, the Reconstruction Finance Corporation was established early in 1932. The RFC was authorized to make loans to a wide variety of business firms, among them commercial banks, savings banks, trust companies, and other financial institutions. Beginning in February 1932, the Corporation lent to banks in danger of failure and later to those in process of liquidation. The RFC was also authorized to invest in the common stock of commercial banks; it ultimately made loans of nearly $2 billion and purchased almost $1 billion of bank stock, a major effort that unquestionably saved a great many institutions, particularly large ones. For a time, depositor confidence was bolstered, and from March 1932 to the end of the year it appeared once again that the banking system might remain intact.

A frightening manifestation of the financial disaster that accompanied the Great Depression was a "run" on a bank. Lines of anxious depositors often stretched for blocks.

y late 1932, however, rising unemployment and falling incomes were ing their reciprocal effect on business sales and income. Once more the banks were confronted with a drain of currency and gold, as less affluent householders put cash in hiding places and the richer and more knowledgeable put gold in safety deposit boxes or sent it abroad. Early in 1933 a third wave of bank failures began, threatening this time to inundate the entire economic system. The problem became so grave that only the suspension of all banking activity would serve as a first step in its resolution.

As early as 1930, the State of Oregon had passed legislation allowing banks to suspend payments for a period of 60 days, while they arranged with their depositors for orderly withdrawals. A handful of other states passed similar legislation, and in 1932 mayors of cities and towns began the custom of ordering bank holidays for a period of days. But not until October 31, 1932, when the Governor of Nevada authorized the closing of banks for a period of 12 days, was there a statewide moratorium.[3]

Beginning early in 1933 other states adopted the same tactic, and by March 4 all the banks in 30 states had closed their doors, while withdrawal restrictions were authorized in most of the others. On March 6, as one of the first acts of his administration, Franklin D. Roosevelt ordered the suspension of all banking transactions for a period of four days. During this time banks could make change, cash government checks, switch checks to drawers' accounts when no cash payment was required, and perform similar routine functions absolutely essential to carrying on daily business. But the sobering fact was that the financial system had broken down. Many banks closed for the "holiday" would never open their doors again.

Opening the Banks

The problems confronting officials of the Treasury, the Federal Reserve, and the Office of the Comptroller were formidable. If, as President Roosevelt had said in his inaugural address two days before, "the only thing we have to fear is fear itself," allaying apprehension was perhaps the first order of business. But "nameless, unreasoning, unjustified terror" would return quickly if concrete steps were not taken to put the nation's financial affairs in order.

On March 9, 1933, Congress passed the Emergency Bank Act which approved and confirmed the Proclamation of March 6. The Act vested in the President power to close the banks and gave to the Secretary of the Treasury authority to regulate the business of the banks during such emergency

---

[3] This holiday was ordered after the suspension of the Wingate chain of 12 banks which accounted for nearly half of the state's 26 banks and about one-half of their resources. It was necessary to extend the holiday for an additional three weeks, although not all Nevada banks took advantage of it. See Cyril B. Upham and Edwin Lamke *Closed and Distressed Banks*, Washington, D.C.: The Brookings Institution, 1934, pp. 9-12.

period as the President might designate. A major provision, one that did much to stabilize the banking community, gave authority to the Comptroller of the Currency to appoint conservators, who would conserve the assets of a national bank on behalf of depositors and creditors and would bring about the reorganization of those banks that appeared salvageable. Other provisions authorized national banks to issue preferred stock and gave the Reconstruction Finance Corporation authority to purchase preferred stock whenever the Secretary of the Treasury, with the approval of the President, deemed new funds necessary for the reorganization of banks. To tide certain banks over the immediate emergency, the Comptroller of the Currency was authorized to permit banks under conservators to receive new deposits, which were to be segregated and made subject to withdrawal without restriction.[4]

The President immediately issued his Proclamation of March 9, which extended until further notice the terms of the Proclamation of March 6. The next day the President by Executive Order authorized the Secretary of the Treasury and the appropriate supervisory authority in each state to permit the opening of banks on the condition that state nonmember banks obtain a license from a state authority and member banks obtain a license from the Secretary of the Treasury. Procedurally, applications for a license from the Treasury were filed with Federal Reserve Banks, and upon approval by the Secretary issued by Federal Reserve Banks.[5]

On March 11 President Roosevelt announced a definite schedule for the reopening of the country's commercial banks. Licensed member banks located in the 12 Federal Reserve Bank cities could open on March 13. Licensed member banks, located in the 250 cities of the country with recognized clearinghouse associations, could open on March 14. Finally, all other licensed member banks might open on March 15. The schedule for opening nonmember state banks was left to the decision of the several state authorities. By April 12, 1933, the licensing program was completed. At that time 4,789 national banks, 636 state member banks, and 7,392 nonmember banks, or a total of 12,817, were open for business.[6]

Although the reopening of the banks had so far proceeded smoothly, supervisory agencies were left with an almost overwhelming task of reconstruction. As of March 16, 1,070 banks under the jurisdiction of the Comp-

---

[4] Other provisions of the Act enlarged the powers of the Federal Reserve; of particular importance was the provision liberalizing the definition of collateral for rediscount at Federal Reserve Banks.

[5] The Secretary approved licenses for state member banks upon the recommendation of the Federal Reserve Bank of the district in which they were located; licenses for national banks were approved upon recommendation of the Comptroller of the Currency.

[6] These banks had deposits as follows: national banks, $16.5 billion; state member banks, $9.5 billion; nonmember banks, $5 billion.

The licensing of banks was accomplished with incredible speed. Yet of the nearly 13,000 banks licensed, only 15 member banks and 206 nonmember banks suspended business between the end of the bank holiday and the end of 1937.

troller, with deposits of nearly $890 million, were in receivership. Almost two years later, at the end of 1934, depositors of these banks had received about one-half of the amount due them, but 946 banks were still going through the painful process of winding up their affairs.

The most constructive work performed by the Comptroller's Office was the resuscitation of national banks remaining unlicensed on March 16. There were 1,417 unlicensed banks, with deposits of almost $2 billion, under the jurisdiction of the Comptroller. For most of these banks the Comptroller appointed conservators, who during the period of conservatorship were to husband the assets of their banks, following strict rules regarding the paying out of funds.[7] During the remainder of 1933 and all of 1934, the job of revitalizing these banks continued. On the whole, results were remarkably favorable. Of the 1,417 banks, 1,093 were reorganized under old or new charters, absorbed by other national banks, or had approved plans for reorganization; 30 went into voluntary liquidation, paying their depositors in full; and 294 banks were placed in receivership. At the end of 1934 the remaining depositor liability of the 1,417 banks amounted to only 5 percent of the amount of deposits frozen at the end of the banking holiday.

The success of conservatorships seems all the more striking when we reflect that most of the conservators appointed were officers of the banks that had gotten into difficulty under their leadership. But the Comptroller was faced with a problem of moving rapidly. Experienced bank receivers were simply not available to assume positions as conservators, for the number of old staff members had been quickly exhausted, and new personnel were already in receivership jobs. Despite some objection to the procedure, the Comptroller continued to place former officers of banks in charge of their conservatorship. Operating under rigid rules prescribed by the Comptroller, these officers probably performed more successfully than would less competent conservators brought in from outside the banking field.

By executive order of March 18, 1933, the President in effect authorized the appointment by appropriate state authorities of conservators for state member banks. State-bank supervisors followed different plans for the non-member banks under their jurisdiction. Some state authorities followed the procedure of either licensing a bank for reopening or placing it in receivership immediately. Other banking commissions were authorized to appoint conservators who acted much like their counterparts under the Comptroller's supervision. Other states put all unlicensed banks under the dicta-

---

[7] During the existence of a conservatorship, the Comptroller could require a conservator to "set aside and make available for withdrawal by depositors and payments to other creditors, on a ratable basis, such amounts as in the opinion of the Comptroller may safely be used for this purpose." The Comptroller could also authorize the receipt of "trust deposits," to be kept in cash or government bonds or as a deposit with a Federal Reserve Bank. See Upham and Lamke, *op. cit,* pp. 50-51.

This "Hooverville," located in Central Park, New York, poignantly evokes the memory of a time when half the nation's households either had no income or were seriously reduced in circumstances.

torship of a single official. But whatever method was followed, a substantial majority of the 148 state member banks and the nearly 3000 nonmember banks remaining unlicensed on April 12, 1933, were removed from restrictions by the end of 1934.

The collapse of the banking system had very nearly destroyed the edifice of American capitalism. But a strong and confident President took precisely the steps necessary to halt the complete disintegration of the financial system. Courageous and unflagging efforts of the supervisory authorities restored order long before anyone viewing the chaos of March 1933 would have anticipated.

The Reaction: Bank Chartering, 1931-1955

During the decade of the 1920s almost half the nation's commercial banks disappeared. Over the nine-year span, 1921-1929, 5,411 banks failed. From 1930 to 1933, 8,812 banks suspended operations, nearly half of them going under in 1933 alone. Of the 14,000 banks that suspended business between 1921 and 1933, 11,300 were state banks and 2,700 were national banks. Most of the failed banks were small; more than 90 percent of them were in communities with less than 25,000 inhabitants, and 85 percent had total assets of less than $1 million.

Preoccupied as they were with rescue operations during the period 1933-1935, neither the Comptroller of the Currency nor state authorities could give much thought to future chartering policy. Although nearly 800 new national charters were approved in those three years, more than 700 of them were worked out with the cooperation of the Comptroller of the Currency to save banks in difficulty.

Of the many post-depression changes in public-policy attitudes toward banking, none was more drastic than the new view of bank chartering. The ruin of the banks had been the consequence of a more deep-rooted cause than "overbanking." Urbanization of the American population began in earnest in the 1920s, inexorably taking people from the agricultural communities and their purchasing power away from small-town businesses. Moreover, mortgages made on the basis of high World War I land values went steadily into default. With the deterioration of assets that occurred when loans to farmers and to businesses dependent upon farmers went bad, thousands of institutions found themselves in severe straits. At the onset of the depression, frightened depositors rushed to demand their money, with the consequence that even good assets had to be liquidated in falling markets. At last, as business declined disastrously, the very best credit risks could not meet their obligations.

Yet the excesses of chartering of the period 1880-1925 had clearly been a large part of the problem, for the failures that began a decade before the economic disintegration of the early 1930s were a response to the previous high rate of bank investment, particularly in rural areas. For 40 years, banks had been springing up in hamlets and villages of 200 and 300 inhabitants; in a South Dakota community of 300 served by a state bank, the competition became ruinous when the Comptroller of the Currency granted a national charter to another group in the same place. County-seat towns of less than 1,500 people often boasted three or four banks, and a Midwestern county with a population of 10,000 was blessed with 18. Nearly everyone agreed that free banking should stop if it meant continuing competition between state and federal authorities. A corollary of this proposition was that some kind of federal control had to be exercised over bank formation under state charter.

As it turned out, the Federal Deposit Insurance Corporation became the agency to exert this control. By the end of 1935, a few months after the permanent plan of federal deposit insurance was introduced pursuant to the Banking Act of 1935, more than 90 percent of United States commercial banks were "admitted to insurance." Since federal authorities could now withhold deposit insurance, considerable power would henceforth be exerted over state chartering.

Actually, the matter would not be finally settled until 1939. The Banking Acts of both 1933 and 1935 had specified that insured banks should ultimately become members of the Federal Reserve System, and membership implied that the Federal Reserve would have supervisory responsibility. But the inexorable legislative pressures of nonmember banks led finally to the removal in 1939 of the membership requirement. Indeed, the ultimate decision in this controversy was suggested in 1938, when the Office of the Comptroller of the Currency, the Federal Reserve, and the Federal Deposit Insurance Corporation agreed to a formal division of responsibility of the examination function.

Comptroller "Jefty" O'Connor, California politician and vibrant personality, participated in the tremendous job of restoring the nation's banking system to something like normal performance.

The period of free, or nearly free, banking that began around 1880 had clearly come to an end well before the onset of the Great Depression. Marked selectivity in chartering started in the mid-1920s, at both state and federal levels, and even in the absence of economic catastrophe increasing care would have been exercised in creating new banks. But the cautious attitudes after 1935 were in large part the result of fears engendered by the depression, and it would be 25 years before the timidity of bankers would disappear. Those responsible for the supervision of banks were just as cautious as commercial bankers. Like the bankers they regulated, supervisors of state banking departments, as well as Comptrollers J. F. T. O'Connor and Preston Delano, considered their main responsibility to be the preservation of banks. Their attitudes were understandably defensive, and after the repair work of 1931-1935 was completed, it was clear that there would no longer be business as usual.

Indeed, as early as 1934 Comptroller O'Connor observed that "great caution should be exercised in the future in the establishment of either State or national banks, or branches of either, in order to prevent a repetition of the failures of a few years ago." [8] And for the first time a Comptroller could make an unequivocal statement about his legal authority to regulate bank chartering:

> The Comptroller's Office, under existing law, is in a position to require national banks to maintain adequate, sound capital, and also to prevent the organization of a new national bank unless it has adequate, sound capital, and unless there is need for additional banking facilities in the location chosen, and a reasonable prospect that the bank will operate successfully. [9]

The Banking Act of 1935 clearly gave to federal authorities permanent discretionary authority over bank charters. Moreover, the statute specifically required the agencies to consider certain criteria in their administration of the law. Among them were: adequacy of a prospective bank's capital structure; its future earnings prospects; the character of its management; and the convenience and needs of the community it would serve. Thus, standards that had been intermittently used by the Office of the Comptroller, and increasingly by state authorities, were finally written into the law.

The year 1936 began a 20-year period of drastic reduction in the rate of formation of new banks. On the average, 70 new institutions were started annually from 1936 to 1955. This rate was not constant over the entire period, for it began to pick up in the early 1950s as profits of commercial banks improved in the postwar years. Actually, in the decade 1936-1945, 480 new state banks were chartered; the figure for the decade 1946-1955 was 705. The corresponding figures for national banks were 55 and 156. From

---

8 Comptroller of the Currency, *Annual Report*, 1934, p. 14.
9 *Ibid.*

1936 to the end of 1955, applications for national-bank charters averaged about 43 each year, or one-seventh the annual average from 1911 through 1935. Over the two decades from 1936 to 1955, national-bank charters accounted for less than one-sixth of the nearly 1,400 banks organized.

There were several reasons why only 211 national banks were chartered in this 20-year post-depression span. Relatively low returns to capital invested in commercial banking were partly responsible, while discouraging preliminary discussions and a rejection rate on applications exceeding 40 percent in some years must have deterred prospective bank organizers. But the most obvious reason for the low number of bank charters was the attitude of post-depression Comptrollers. Although there was comparatively little discussion of chartering policy in successive annual reports, it was apparent that the Office of the Comptroller was for 25 years extremely reluctant to admit new banks to the competition. In a drastic swing of the pendulum of authority, "convenience and needs" were severely scrutinized, and decisions to charter new banks went from the extreme of free banking to the extreme of unduly restricted approval.

Early in his tenure, Comptroller Delano, in his *Annual Report* for 1938, could point with some pride to the fact that "there were no primary charters issued for national banks during the year ended October 31, 1938." [10] During the next few years, only a few national charters were issued annually. In his 1945 *Report,* Comptroller Delano noted "the increased flow of applications for bank charters" and pointed to "the likelihood of an even greater number of such applications in the near future. . . ." [11] Although he felt it appropriate to discuss some of the "problems and principles" of chartering policy, Delano confined his analysis to a repetition of firmly established dogma—that study must be made of "such intangibles as the experience and skill of the existing or proposed managements, the future earnings prospects of the banks, the convenience and economic needs of the communities to be served, and the adequacy of the capital structures in view of the geographical location." The Comptroller, Delano felt, was "not charged with and does not undertake the enforcement of the antitrust laws," but was "obligated to exercise his discretionary power in the light of the purposes which the statutes in this field were designed to achieve." [12] But if it was the role of the Comptroller to lessen the possibility of monopoly in banking, as Delano's statements suggested, there is little evidence that he wished to take the route of providing new banks to lessen the possibility of monopoly power. While giving lip service to the "undesirability of either hampering entrance into, or mobility within, the banking field," Comptroller Delano seemed more concerned to prevent the dangers

---

[10] Comptroller of the Currency, *Annual Report,* 1938, p. 1.
[11] Comptroller of the Currency, *Annual Report,* 1945, p. 4.
[12] *Ibid.*

Comptroller Preston Delano, a gentle bureaucrat, whose tenure in office of nearly 15 years is unsurpassed by any other Comptroller.

of excess banking capacity in any particular community. In 1948 he could remark that "the National Banking System apparently has stabilized numerically, for the time being at least, the number of banks in the System having remained in the neighborhood of five thousand for some five years." [13]

In 1951, Comptroller Delano again reflected on the question of achieving an optimum investment in the commercial banking industry. In his *Annual Report* for that year he wrote:

> We recognize the desirability of competition wherever possible, since we believe that sound and healthy competition between banks redounds to the public welfare through increased adequacy of credit facilities, fair rates of interest, and the prevention of undue concentration of monetary and economic power. Hence, in considering applications for new banking offices in communities having only one bank, we give considerable weight to this factor. In communities where competition already exists, the factor is given somewhat less weight, for excessive competition can result in such a weakening of existing banking institutions as to bring consequences so injurious to the welfare of the community as to outweigh any benefits to be anticipated from increasing the intensity of competition in such cases.[14]

[13] Comptroller of the Currency, *Annual Report*, 1948, p. 1.
[14] Comptroller of the Currency, *Annual Report*, 1951, p. 3.

130   **The Comptroller**

These words, while suggesting a judicious attempt to provide an appropriate number of new commercial banks, find little support in the statistics. Only seven national banks were chartered in 1950, and only nine in 1951.

At the same time, state authorities showed little more disposition to charter new banks. A survey made by the Joint Economic Committee of Congress, published in 1952, suggested that state authorities looked primarily to the prospect of profitable operations and improvement of the competitive environment as the chief reasons for granting new charters. Like the Comptroller, they gave lip service to the ideal of avoiding too much competition and at the same time of providing bank resources where none existed. Yet it is clear from their questionnaire responses, repeated over and over again, that they were anxious to avoid the "overbanking" of the 1920s. Without any question, this concern dominated chartering philosophy among state as well as federal supervisors.

Continued Growth of Multi-Office and Multi-Unit Banking

In the turmoil of the early 1930s the course of branch banking was unclear. In the five years 1931-1935 the number of branch banks increased from 751 to 822, while the number of branches dropped from 3,522 to 3,156. In these years, however, there was a marked change from intracity to intercity branching, the number of branches in head-office cities declining by about 750 and the number of "outside" branches rising by 375. Between 1935 and 1950 branch banking made steady, if unspectacular, gains. In this 15-year period, the number of banks maintaining branches increased from 822 to 1,241, and the number of branches grew from 3,156 to 4,721. The proportion of branches located outside the head-office city increased steadily during the early part of the period and then remained approximately constant during the first postwar decade.

Beginning in the early 1950s, branch banking accelerated its rate of increase. By the end of 1955, there were 1,659 branch banks in the country maintaining 6,710 branches. Branch-bank offices constituted a little more than 40 percent of the total number of banking offices, and branch banks accounted for approximately 55 percent of the banking resources of the country.

Although the rate of branch-bank expansion over the quarter century from 1930 to 1955 seems impressive, it was slower than it would have been under more liberal federal law. Legislation removing restrictions on branching was very nearly passed by Congress in the early 1930s, as the electorate's disenchantment with the banking system turned to vindictive anger. Indeed, almost any bill aimed at strengthening the financial system could have passed the Congress. Once again, however, the supporters of small unit banks won the day by securing the passage of legislation that undermined the chief argument of branch-banking proponents.

As the banking system encountered increasing turbulence in the early thirties, opinion seemed to swing in favor of permitting strong branch systems in every state. In the press, in speeches, and in hearings before congressional committees, Comptroller John W. Pole continued to advocate branching over trade areas. The Comptroller wished to avoid establishing lines along political boundaries, preferring instead to place branches strategically in economic areas large enough to support branches of substantial size. Senator Carter Glass, a major voice in policy matters affecting the banking system, actually introduced a bill to permit statewide branching, and even branching across state lines, to a distance of 50 miles from the parent bank. Even the American Bankers Association began to soften its opposition to branching, indicating that "community wide" branching in cities and "county wide" branching in rural areas might be economically justifiable.

But such proposals for change often led to bitter, if minority, opposition in Congress. This minority pressed for insurance of bank deposits as the only needed protection for the unit banking system. The arguments of the deposit-insurance advocates unquestionably played a part in stopping the movement toward a liberal branch-banking law, though the astonishingly influential small-bank lobby might have defeated the branching proposals anyway. The law providing today's basic rule for national-bank branching became a part of the Banking Act of 1933. In effect, this provision allowed national banks to branch in any state within the geographical limits specifically authorized by the laws of that state. The statute read in part as follows: [15]

> A national banking association may, with the approval of the Comptroller of the Currency, establish and operate new branches: (1) Within the limits of the city, town or village in which said association is situated, if such establishment and operation are at the time expressly authorized to State banks by the law of the State in question; and (2) at any point within the State in which said association is situated, if such establishment and operation are at the time authorized to State banks by the statute law of the State in question by language specifically granting such authority affirmatively and not merely by implication or recognition, and subject to the restrictions as to location imposed by the law of the State on State banks.

To the basic geographic limitations on branching of national banks were added certain discriminatory capital requirements for member banks branching outside their head-office cities. These requirements, often much higher than those for nonmember banks, were a serious deterrent to many banks that might otherwise have extended their geographic influence. In 1952 the law was changed to permit member banks wishing to add

---

[15] Act of June 16, 1933, 48 Stat. 189.

branches to meet the capital requirements of state law for branch banks. In his 1952 *Annual Report,* Comptroller Ray M. Gidney remarked that "provisions of the new law are proving to be eminently satisfactory." [16]

National banks might be "on a parity, for all practical purposes, with State chartered banks," as Comptroller Gidney further remarked. But 17 states then limited branching, and 11 states prohibited branching entirely. Again, largely as a result of remaining branch limitations, chain and group banking were by the mid-1940s clearly in the ascendancy.

Both types of multi-unit banking were struck a serious blow by the depression. Chain banking, which had developed much less rapidly than group banking after 1925, was particularly hard hit. Between 1931 and 1939, the number of chain systems and the number of banks in chains declined by about one-half. But with the advent of war-induced prosperity, chain systems began a resurgence. In 1939 there were 96 chain systems consisting of 424 banks with under a billion dollars of deposits. By 1945 there were 115 chains consisting of 522 banks with deposits of $4.6 billion. Although accurate data for the 1950s are not available, the evidence suggests that in the first postwar decade assets of chain systems grew at about the same rate as those of all commercial banks.

The Federal Reserve Board reported 97 groups, consisting of 978 banks, in operation in 1931. By 1936 these figures had dwindled to 52 and 479, respectively. Between the middle 1930s and 1948, the relative importance of groups in the commercial banking system changed little, with groups over this span of time controlling approximately 7 percent of commercial banking offices and 11 percent of commercial bank deposits. Beginning in 1949 the largest bank holding companies entered a period of remarkable expansion. One authority estimates that deposits of 15 leading groups rose between 1949 and 1956 at approximately twice the rate achieved by all commercial banks.[17] In 1957, 44 bank holding companies with a total of 1,368 banking offices held deposits of more than $15 billion.

Like commercial banks in general, chains and groups flourished as the economy emerged from the sub-par performance of the 1930s. Yet at least one of the variables influencing the growth of chains and groups was the statutory change affecting branch banking in the state jurisdictions. The number of states permitting statewide branches doubled from nine in 1929 to 18 in 1939; in the same years, the number of states allowing *some* form of branch banking rose from 19 to 36. These relaxations of restrictions

[16] A floor on capital requirements of national banks and their branches is established by federal law. Specifically, "the aggregate capital of every national banking association and its branches shall at no time be less than the aggregate minimum capital required by law for the establishment of an equal number of national banking associations situated in the various places where such association and its branches are situated." Regardless of the number of branches a national bank may have in one place, the capital requirements for all of them are only what they would be for *one* bank.

[17] See the forthcoming book of Gerald C. Fischer, *American Banking Structure: Its Evolution and Regulation,* New York: Columbia University Press, 1968.

unquestionably played a part in retarding the growth of multi-unit systems during the 1930s. Similarly, as a hard core of states held to their severe limitations on branching, multi-unit banking became an alternative form of achieving the advantages that branch systems would otherwise have provided.

Bank Examination: Cooperation Among Federal Agencies

Having resolved the critical problems associated with banking operations, federal supervisory agencies could attend to the more mundane, day-to-day questions of examination and control of the commercial banks. Even if the economy had emerged rapidly from economic doldrums, problems of coordination and cooperation would have arisen. In an environment of seriously deficient output and high levels of unemployment, a solution to these problems seemed almost impossible.

The unfortunate fact was that, so long as recovery remained only a dim hope of the future, loans could not be accurately assessed as to probability of repayment, and many investments were seriously depressed in value. The application of rigorous standards to the valuation of financial assets would have meant serious impairment of the capitals of most commercial banks and continued pressures on the banks to remain as liquid as possible. But what the country needed, of course, was an assertive, aggressive attempt on the part of commercial banks to meet legitimate demands for funds, which were at best well below that required to assure a healthy, profitable banking system.

Added to these difficulties was the inability of the two established agencies, the Federal Reserve and the Office of the Comptroller, and the new agency, the Federal Deposit Insurance Corporation, to agree on principles and procedures. To be sure, most of the tension between the Federal Reserve and the Comptroller's Office was allayed as they joined in rescuing the banks. But friction developed between the Office of the Comptroller and the FDIC, and to a lesser extent between FDIC and Federal Reserve, as the new agency took on the job of supervising insured nonmember banks. For the role of the new Corporation in the supervisory process was by no means clear at the outset, and continuing personal antagonisms between Comptroller J. F. T. O'Connor and Chairman Leo T. Crowley of the FDIC did not help to clarify it.[18]

---

[18] Friction doubtless originated over the question of examination of insured nonmember banks. In 1933, Comptroller O'Connor had generously made available to the FDIC the services of a substantial number of experienced national bank examiners in order to facilitate examination of banks before their admittance to insurance. Yet O'Connor doubtless felt that either the Comptroller's Office or the Federal Reserve would perform the regular examination function, for in his *Annual Report* for 1934 he wrote that the "Federal Deposit Insurance Corporation does not examine banks in the sense that the Comptroller of the Currency and the Federal Reserve Board examine them, since the Corporation has no supervisory functions." (Page 5.)

The upshot of years of discussion of examination procedural problems was intervention by the President. In his message to Congress of April 14, 1938, announcing the desterilization of Treasury gold, Franklin Delano Roosevelt expressed the hope that federal banking supervision might be better coordinated in order to stimulate the flow of credit to business and agriculture. The Secretary of the Treasury thereupon initiated a series of conferences attended by representatives of the Office of the Comptroller, the Board of Governors of the Federal Reserve System, and the Federal Deposit Insurance Corporation. The purpose of these discussions was to seek agreement on general policies and on specific regulations involving bank supervision. The outcome of the conferences was a revision and standardization of classifications of both loans and securities in the administration of bank examinations.[19]

Perhaps the most important change was the new loan classification to be used on examination reports. Instead of placing them in the old categories of "good," "slow," "doubtful," and "estimated loss," loans would be assigned the designations I, II, III, and IV. Loans would be designated Class I if repayment appeared to be assured, and Class I loans would not be listed in the examination reports. Class II would include loans or portions of loans involving a substantial and unreasonable degree of risk with the possibility of actual loss. Class III would include loans or portions of loans of doubtful ultimate collection and with probable substantial, though not definitely ascertainable, losses. In Class IV would be listed loans or portions of loans estimated as losses. Fifty percent of the total of Class III loans and all of Class IV loans were to be deducted in computing the "net sound capital" of a bank.

The agreement among the agencies similarly revised examination procedures with respect to bank investments. Basically, the new procedures di-

---

[19] Board of Governors of the Federal Reserve System, *Federal Reserve Bulletin*, July 1938, pp. 563-564.

These gold coins were among the last to be struck at the mint, for gold was finally withdrawn from the American circulation in 1933-1934. Only two of the 1933 double eagles are in existence.

vided securities between those of investment character and those considered speculative. The former were to be in Group I, the latter in Group II. Defaulted bonds would be listed in Group III and all stocks in Group IV. The agency conferees estimated that about 90 percent of the total securities held by banks would fall in Group I, while Group II securities were estimated at not more than 5 percent of commercial bank holdings. Fifty percent of the net depreciation of Group II investments and all of the net depreciation of Group III and IV securities were to be deducted in determining the "net sound capital."

It is noteworthy that Group I securities were to be valued "by investment and not by fluctuating market standards." Examiners were not to take daily quotations into account when making their reports, but instead would show Group I securities at their book value. "By severing appraisal of bank investments from current market quotations," the official Federal Reserve statement said, "it is believed that the banks will be encouraged to purchase securities of sound business and industrial concerns, whether large or small, for their true worth and not for speculative gains." [20] Group II securities were to be shown in examination reports at their average market price for the 18 months preceding the date of examination.

This official pronouncement of the agencies suggested a novel attitude toward bank examination.[21] In a word, examiners were not to adhere to rigid, traditional standards, but instead were to take into consideration the economic climate in which they were making examinations. The philosophy of lenient and uniform supervision was officially summarized in four succinct paragraphs:

---

[20] *Ibid.*

[21] During the financial crisis of 1932-1933 the supervisory agencies had ". . . eased the burden on the banks by mitigating the rigors of examination," especially by waiving rules for the valuation of portfolios. See Upham and Lamke, *op. cit.*, p. 11. But there was no coordinated action between the Federal Reserve and the Office of the Comptroller, nor do official documents of either agency indicate that examination standards changed during the crisis.

Under the new designations, the principle is clearly recognized that in making loans, whether for working capital or fixed capital purposes, the banks should be encouraged to place the emphasis upon intrinsic value rather than upon liquidity or quick maturity.

Similarly, the revised examination procedure recognizes the principle that bank investments should be considered in the light of inherent soundness rather than on a basis of day to day market fluctuations. It is based on the view that the soundness of the banking system depends in the last analysis upon the soundness of the country's business and industrial enterprises, and should not be measured by the precarious yardstick of current market quotations which often reflect speculative and not true appraisals of intrinsic worth.

A primary purpose of the program is to encourage the private banking system of the country to adapt its lending and investment functions to present-day requirements of commerce, industry, and agriculture. It is designed to afford the banks a broader opportunity for service to the community and for profitable outlet for some of their abundant, idle funds. As the banks avail themselves of the opportunity, the necessity will be diminished for creation of government agencies to furnish credit facilities which the banks should provide.

The program is based upon sound banking principles. The banks will be required to continue the present practice of charging off losses and of establishing and maintaining adequate reserves against doubtful and speculative loans and securities.[22]

The use of an "intrinsic soundness" test instead of a "current market value" test in valuing bank investments was indeed a departure from orthodoxy. In the view of many observers this change marked a genuine advance in examination philosophy, for it implied an awareness by bank supervisors of an obligation to vary examination criteria with changes in business activity. By relieving examination pressure to liquidate "intrinsically sound" assets during deflationary periods, supervisors would presumably reinforce an "easy" monetary policy. On the contrary, tougher attitudes toward intrinsic values in times of inflationary pressure, along with a closer scrutiny of the "soundness" of bank loans, would presumably aid the monetary authority in times of "tight" monetary policy. Whether such a view of the examination process could in fact be translated into action by examiners in the field remained to be seen.

Yet a little reflection would have convinced most knowledgeable officials that cyclically varying standards for the worth of assets could not be effectively imposed by a large corps of examiners in the field. No forseeable degree of cooperation among the three federal agencies, nor among the state authorities, would result in a consensus permitting uniform prescriptions for economic stabilization. Only chaos would be the consequence of allowing each examiner to make his *own* estimate of asset values relative to a particular phase of the business cycle. And though in the late 1930s

---

[22] *Ibid.*

theoretical tools were being developed to help policymakers control the amplitude of economic fluctuations, only a small minority of government officials had more than the haziest notion of how to affect, through fiscal or monetary policy, swings in output, employment, and prices. With ignorance of economics as great as it was a generation ago, any hope that bank supervision could somehow add to economic stability seemed doomed to failure.

7
Bank Supervision In
A Stabilized Economy

As World War II came to a victorious close, Americans were apprehensive about the postwar depression that seemed sure to come. Each of the great wars, from the Revolution on, had been followed by a severe economic slump, and there was no reason to think that the experience at mid-20th century would be any different. The United States had certainly not entered World War II in good economic health; for 11 long years, from 1929 to 1940, the American economy had performed far below its vast potential, and only the advent of world conflict had restored equilibrium at high levels of employment and income. Many of the country's respected economists hypothesized that mature capitalist economies were prone to stagnate for the reason that the high level of savings generated each year could not be profitably invested in business plant and equipment and business inventories. It was only natural that people should be fearful about the performance of an economy no longer stimulated by massive wartime deficits and required to absorb more than 10 million returning servicemen into the civilian work force.

Nevertheless, the economic euphoria of World War II years persuaded a majority of the electorate that permanent prosperity could be engineered by appropriate fiscal policies aimed at preventing unemployment. As early as 1945, Congress considered a bill that would place at the disposal of the Secretary of Commerce a $40 billion "annual investment fund" to be spent, if necessary, to assure full employment. After lengthy debate on this proposal, a revised version of the original "full employment" bill was passed as the "Employment Act of 1946." It would henceforth be the federal government's responsibility to ". . . promote maximum employment, production, and purchasing power." Although the word "maximum" was intentionally ambiguous, knowledgeable people assumed that the government would in the future act quickly to stimulate a flagging economy.

Moreover, it was assumed that the newly created Council of Economic Advisers, to be a part of the Executive Office of the President, would provide both the President and Congress with timely notice of impending economic downturns. The statute further provided that the House and Senate form a Joint Committee on the Economic Report, which would examine the reports of the President and the Council that were to be submitted at least annually, and, after hearings, report to Congress.

For more than two years after the war the economy expanded rapidly as households took advantage of their highly liquid positions to make purchases of durable goods, long postponed because of wartime shortages. After the removal of controls in the summer of 1946, prices rose rapidly, and by the late summer of 1948 the postwar inflation was twice that of the wartime years. Late 1948 saw a downturn big enough to cause uneasiness; but the gross national product fell by only 4 percent, and unemployment rose to little more than 5 percent of the work force when the upturn began. The onset of the Korean War brought the output of the economy quickly back to something like its tremendous potential.

Just as many observers were beginning to comment that the decade of the 1950s would be one of continuing boom, the recession of 1953-1954 began. The drop was about the same as that of 1948-1949; industrial production fell 10 percent, and the gross product less than 4 percent. The decline was not serious. Nevertheless, it caused great concern, if only because many were aware that output could not even stand still—let alone fall off—if net annual additions to the work force of ¾ of a million people were to be absorbed.

The reassuring outcome of the 1953-1954 recession was that it did not deteriorate into a progressive, cumulative downward spiral. For the second time in only a few years it appeared that there were strong sustaining forces in the economy. A continuing rapid increase in population and a substantial rate of household formation bolstered the demand for consumer goods. Indeed, the most important resistance to this recession was consumption expenditure, as personal income remained insulated from the general decline in spending and income. The distribution of population among age groups was favorable, for young people ate more food and wore more clothing. To these natural supports were added the automatic stabilizers: unemployment insurance payments, a reduction in the total tax bill as the incomes of corporations and individuals declined, support of falling agricultural prices, and some increase in social security payments. With a short time lag, the stabilizers counteracted the downward movement in business activity.

By the mid-1950s optimistic pronouncements were heard from government, business, and the academic community that "modern" stabilization policy had licked the old-fashioned depression. There was still a good bit of worry over inflation, for prices had risen about 8½ percent from mid-1955 to mid-1957. And there was growing concern over a retardation in the rate of growth of the economy, which was indicated by an increasing gap between output and productive capacity of more than $40 billion and by an unemployment rate that reached 7½ percent toward the end of the recession of 1957-1958. When another recession came on in 1960, though ever so briefly, there was agitation for steps to assure a substantial boost in the rate of economic growth. For the time had now come when the economy had to grow enough each year to absorb more than a million new entrants into the work force; and as the postwar baby crop came to adulthood in the middle and late sixties, the problem of maintaining full employment would become increasingly severe.

Fortunately, there were by this time at least 15 years of experience under the Employment Act of 1946. Besides the Council of Economic Advisers, three other agencies were closely tied to the problems of stabilization policy—the Federal Reserve, the Treasury, and the Bureau of the Budget. Each agency had its own bias about what public policy ought to be; yet there was substantial agreement among them on goals, and there was a consensus among the advising economists that income taxes were then so high as to contribute a serious barrier to economic progress.

President Kennedy came to office in early 1961, just as the economic indicators were showing some signs of improvement after their adverse turn the year previously. He was persuaded that the problem of a slowing rate of economic growth was in large part the consequence of an unduly restrictive monetary policy. In the 10 years following the Treasury-Federal Reserve "Accord" of 1951, the money supply had increased at an annual rate of 2.1 percent, less than many economists and bankers thought necessary to support a real growth of the economy on the order of 4 percent a year.

At a meeting of the agencies charged with stabilization policy, held very early in his Administration, President Kennedy expressed the view that a tight money policy could not be allowed to induce another recession. A marked change in monetary policy ensued, as the Federal Reserve began its "Operation Twist," an attempt to raise short-term rates of interest, so as to make foreign short-term investment in dollar securities profitable enough to staunch the gold drain while keeping long rates low enough to encourage domestic investment in plant and equipment. From 1961 to the summer of 1967, a period of sustained high performance of the economy, the money supply increased at a rate of about 3.3 percent per annum, well above the average rate of increase in the fifties.

Although the money managers undoubtedly contributed to the buoyancy of the economy, the key to the successful stabilization policy of 1961-1967 unquestionably lay in a clever, and to some extent lucky, handling of fiscal

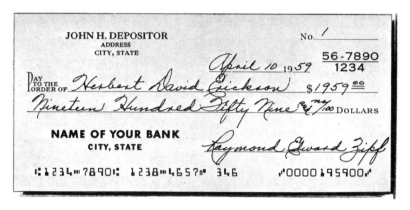

In April 1959 the Bank Management Commission of the American Bankers Association published this illustration of "The Check of the Future." Magnetic imprintation of checks had even then begun to revolutionize bank operating procedures.

matters. For months before his death in 1963, President Kennedy had worked persuasively for a substantial reduction in corporate and personal income taxes. The grave economic problem of the day, as the Presidential advisers saw it, arose from the fact that as the economy approached full-employment levels of income, high tax rates drained the purchasing power of households and business firms so drastically that full-employment national income could not be reached. A tax-reduction bill was not the easiest kind to get through Congress, for organized labor was at first opposed to it on the grounds that many welfare programs would have to be reduced because of a smaller tax take. Conservative Senators and Representatives contended that a reduction in tax rates would mean an increase in the Treasury deficit and so would lead to renewed inflationary pressures. But at last the bill making a substantial reduction in tax rates in 1964, to be followed by a smaller reduction in 1965, became law.

The results were encouraging beyond the best hopes of those who argued for changing tax rates as the basis of stabilization policy. Instead of dropping in calendar 1964, Treasury receipts actually rose, as they continued to do in succeeding years. The tax cuts stimulated consumer buying and business investment in fixed plant and inventories, with the consequence that cash receipts of the Treasury jumped $2.5 billion in calendar 1964, $8.5 billion in calendar 1965, and $18 billion in calendar 1966. Despite rising defense expenditures, the deficits in the administrative budgets for 1964 and 1965 were of a magnitude of only $3 billion, and on a basis of reckoning that counts both receipts and expenditures on an accrual rather than a cash basis (the so-called national-income-accounts budget), there was an actual surplus in 1965 and 1966. But what is far more important, the economy continued the longest uninterrupted upward surge in history.

No responsible economist or public official maintained that the
to eternal prosperity had been found. But it was apparent by the mi
1960s that an intelligent stabilization policy could do much to secure a
steady rate of economic growth, with little possibility of a return to the
horrors of serious depression and unemployment. The problem of bank
supervision has assumed new dimensions in this environment, for the concern of the last quarter of the 20th century may well be over too few
financial resources rather than too many.

The Changing Character of Commercial Banking

It was in the 19th- and early 20th-century tradition of American commercial banking that banks should be primarily committed to short-term,
"self-liquidating" paper. During World War I and through the decade of
the 1920s bankers considered themselves almost exclusively lenders to business. By present standards loan-to-deposit ratios were extremely high, and
cash assets and low-yield securities were considered necessary evils, buffers
against the vagaries of an economic climate not yet modified by governmental intervention. As the Great Depression ran its course, banks reduced
their volume of loans greatly, increasing somewhat their holdings of government securities. By 1934 the total amount of investments exceeded the
amount of loans, though it was not until 1943 that the income from the
former exceeded the income from the latter.

In 1945 it looked as though banks had changed from holders of private
debt to holders of public debt. Many observers commented that the banking system had ceased to perform its primary function of furnishing short-
term credit to commerce and industry, that banks had in fact become investment trusts specializing in Treasury issues. Bankers retorted that the
demand for loans had fallen off seriously during the 1930s and that the
government, by building its own facilities and lending directly to business
during World War II, had unnecessarily usurped the banking function.

During the postwar years there was a rapid growth of loans as banks,
seeking higher profits, shifted out of Treasury issues, which they could sell
at or above par until the Treasury-Federal Reserve Accord of 1951. By 1955,
for both national banks and state member banks, loans surpassed investments in dollar volume.[1] Even with the return toward a historically normal
distribution of assets, many thought that the economic functions of banks
had been permanently modified, and that the banking system would keep
its role as a residual lender to government.

At the time of World War I time deposits of commercial banks began
a slow but steady increase in relative importance, during the 1920s grad-

---

[1] For state nonmember banks, loans did not surpass investments in dollar volume until
the end of 1959.

ually approaching demand deposits in total dollar volume. By 1930 they were practically equal in amount, one series indicating that time deposits actually surpassed demand deposits in dollar volume for a few months of that year. But with the deepening depression and declining opportunities for high-yield loans, bank managers made only token efforts to attract and hold time deposits, and agnostic attitudes toward active attraction of these deposits became a part of commercial-banking mentality for perhaps a quarter of a century. Not until the latter part of the decade of the 1950s were bankers under any particular compulsion to attract funds in order to increase their lending volume.

Everything considered, it seemed to most observers of the contemporary scene that the banking community of the mid-1950s, while admittedly inclined toward more aggressive competition than had been witnessed for a generation, still operated in the traditional mold. But young managers, many of them recruited from the colleges and universities into organized bank training programs, were beginning to take over policy-making functions. Unlike their fathers and grandfathers, they understood that in an economy committed to stabilization of employment and incomes old rules of thumb about loan to deposit ratios and capital to risk-asset ratios were no longer reliable guides to action. Furthermore, they were willing to introduce new systems for handling the swelling tide of paper flowing through the banks, and so succeeded in substantially reducing costs. The result of these changes was a widespread recognition of the prospect of steadily increasing profits, which by the late 1950s impelled imaginative managers to seek an escape from the antiquated regulatory apparatus of federal and state authorities.

In the meantime, commercial banks were collectively under the pressure of competition from a group of financial institutions known as nonbank intermediaries. These institutions—notably savings and loan associations, life insurance companies, mutual savings banks, credit unions, and uninsured pension funds—were making inroads on commercial-bank business before World War II, but it was not until after the war that they seemed to pose a serious threat. In particular, savings and loan associations waged vigorous campaigns to capture both the savings and the customer loyalty of American households, and the banking community became concerned that the S & Ls would soon be given wider lending and investment privileges.[2]

Although the nonbank intermediaries, like commercial banks, grew and

---

[2] Savings and loan associations, like the other nonbank intermediaries, are the *customers* as well as the *competitors* of commercial banks, for they, like all other business firms, must keep funds on deposit in a bank. Reluctant to offend good customers, some individual bankers made no public statements denigrating the thrift institutions, leaving the hatchet work up to their trade associations. Other bankers were vehement in their denunciation of the "unfair" competition of the other intermediaries.

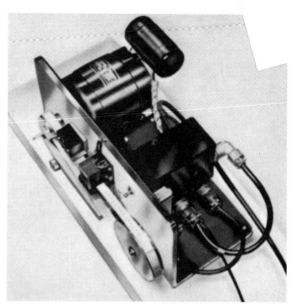

New systems meant all kinds of new equipment. Shown is a magnetic printing tester to be used in evaluating the signal level of individual printed characters on checks.

prospered because they were profitable, their managers were successful in leaving the impression that they were altruistically motivated. It was an easy impression to give because of the historic consumer orientation of the nonbank intermediaries. With a few obvious exceptions, they render some kind of service to the household unit. They insure a life, invest in securities to provide for retirement income, lend money on residential real estate, make personal loans, and so on. On the other hand, they all take in savings. They serve as a go-between, linking the household unit to the demander of funds, which may be another household unit or a business firm. A nonbank intermediary *must* make some kind of appeal to the household unit (consumer) if it is to obtain funds. A commercial bank *may* make such an appeal, and in recent years many of them have made heroic efforts to do so. But historically the important relationships of banks were with other *businesses* rather than with household units.

An interesting question is what might have been the outcome of our financial system if commercial banks had from the beginning furnished services long since taken over by nonbank intermediaries. The historical fact is that they did not, in part because they failed to seize profit opportunities when they appeared, but more importantly because the several regulatory agencies would not let them. Another historical fact is that after World War II the nonbank intermediaries made relative gains that appeared phenomenal. In 1946, commercial banks held 70 percent of the assets of the four major intermediaries—commercial banks, life insurance companies, savings and loan associations, and mutual savings banks; in 1955 the figure stood at 57 percent. Claims against commercial banks (that is, total deposits) amounted to 64 percent of the major liabilities of the same intermediaries in 1945; a decade later they were 54 percent. Banks were obviously losing out in the competition.

The nonbank intermediaries enjoyed a remarkable postwar growth for several reasons. In general, they were favored by beneficial tax laws, and an especially brilliant group of entrepreneurs innovated effective advertising and public relations programs. Their long-time relationships with families, particularly as lenders for cherished goals and in time of need, gave them an advantage over commercial banks. But more important was their ability to maintain a massive savings flow, largely because of restrictions placed on commercial banks by Federal Reserve Regulation Q, which placed a ceiling on the rates banks were permitted to pay on time and savings deposits. Since January 1, 1936, banks were allowed to pay a maximum interest rate of $2\frac{1}{2}$ percent on time deposits. On January 1, 1957, 21 years later, the Federal Reserve raised the maximum rate to 3 percent.[3] This may not seem like much of a boost, but the effect of the change on commercial-bank competition with the nonbank intermediaries was considerable. Between 1948 and 1956 increases in time deposits had been moderate, growing at an average yearly rate of $4\frac{1}{2}$ percent. But between 1957 and 1963, the annual rate of growth of time deposits was 12 percent.[4] A simple change in the rules of the game, arbitrarily ordered by the monetary authorities, made it possible for commercial banks to pay rates for time deposits close to those of the savings and loan associations, with the consequence that in many important markets commercial banks made a substantial breakthrough. There began a drumbeat of appeals to households to do *all* their financing at a "full-service" bank.

By 1960 the commercial-banking industry had metamorphosed. The changing *esprit* of the managerial corps was translated into lending and investment policies aimed at higher profits; and if new business could be developed with a swelling tide of time deposits, so much the better. Managements tied to the past—plodding and unimaginative, with a pronounced tendency to be hereditary—were giving way to new groups that associated venturing with profits. For it was clear by the late 1950s that high-profit

---

[3] See Board of Governors of the Federal Reserve, *Federal Reserve Bulletin*, April 1967, p. 602.

[4] Later changes in the permissible rate payable under Regulation Q were made on November 24, 1964, and December 6, 1965. The first of these changes permitted banks to pay up to $4\frac{1}{2}$ percent on time deposits of 90 days or more; the second allowed a maximum rate of $5\frac{1}{2}$ percent on all time deposits and made possible the expansion of negotiable certificates of deposit as significant money-market instruments. The argument of the text is simply that the modest changes of 1957, 1962, and 1963 were sufficient to enable commercial banks to compete for savings.

banks differed from low-profit banks by having smaller percentages of their assets in U. S. government securities and cash assets, and higher percentages in installment loans, residential mortgages, municipal bonds, and business loans. Since 1948 loan-to-deposit ratios had risen, interrupted only in periods of sagging economic activity, as had the ratio of risk assets to total assets. Over the same time period the liquidity ratio had fallen, though not without interruptions, and the capital-risk asset ratio had steadily drifted downward.[5]

These changes, though frequently noted, were not generally viewed with concern, except in an occasional Federal Reserve speech that sounded a somber note. There was a growing realization in the banking community, however, that supervisory restrictions would inhibit the rate of growth of the industry unless some modifications were quickly made. Indeed, as early as the mid-1950s the American Bankers Association pressed for passage of the Financial Institutions Act of 1957, which would have simplified and codified the banking law that had not had a systematic overhaul since enactment of the Currency Act of 1863. But after Senate passage, the House of Representatives failed to enact the bill. Simplification and codification of the banking law were thereby postponed, for these objectives could be reached only through congressional action. But many of the other provisions of the Act, which aimed at improving the competitive position of commercial banks and at increasing the allocation of resources to banking, could be achieved by administrative action. Yet the Federal Reserve was not then disposed to rapid innovation, and the FDIC had no real authority over the country's largest banks. The thoughts of those desiring change turned to the Office of the Comptroller of the Currency.

The Comptroller's Office as a Power Center

On April 16, 1953, Comptroller Ray M. Gidney was appointed to succeed Preston Delano. An agreeable, soft-spoken man, Comptroller Gidney ran the Office in a quiet, competent fashion. As the figures demonstrate, his policies with regard to chartering and branching were more liberal than those of his predecessor. The very fact of his reappointment in 1958 suggests that his service was eminently satisfactory.

Once again, however, economic change was beginning to require forthright and vigorous, even radical, leadership in the Comptroller's Office. After the inauguration of President Kennedy, Secretary of the Treasury C. Douglas Dillon and the then Undersecretary of the Treasury Henry H. Fowler considered at length the appointment of a new Comptroller of the Currency. The selection of James J. Saxon, a former Treasury official with

---

[5] The liquidity ratio is defined as cash minus required reserves plus government securities due within five years as a percentage of total deposits. Risk assets consist of assets other than cash and government securities.

*Ray M. Gidney, 20th Comptroller of the Currency who
served from 1953 to 1961, maintained a conservative
chartering policy but encouraged the certification of
de novo branches.*

years of experience in commercial banking, was announced on November 15, 1961, his appointment to be effective the next day.

The consequences of this appointment were immediate and extensive. A cordial, vigorous extrovert, Saxon brought to the Office of the Comptroller a strong sense of purpose and an inclination to rely on the advice of intellectuals. One of his first moves was to appoint an economist to his immediate staff.[6] Comptroller Saxon was equally prompt to expand the legal staff, which was soon to have its workload increased many-fold. He simultaneously began a gradual program of decentralizing those functions of the Office essentially performed by the field staff, giving much greater autonomy to the regional offices and providing those offices with a professional advisory staff.

Decisions, Rulings, and Regulations

Within a few months Saxon was ready to move toward substantial change in the role of the Comptroller's Office. In public addresses and in con-

---

[6] Later a full fledged Department of Banking and Economic Research was established, and there was inaugurated *The National Banking Review,* a scholarly journal distinguished among government publications because it published articles often in dissent from the views of the publishing agency.

versation with leaders of the banking community, the new Comptroller let it be known that the Office would be more receptive than it had been in the recent past to applications for new charters and new branches. He also informed the financial world at large of his intention to seek major legislation that would relieve the national banking system of the restraints imposed upon it as a consequence of a previous generation's struggle with the problem of bank failures in an unstable economy. Finally, the new Comptroller announced that the Office would resume leadership in matters of bank supervision that it had held until the 1930s.

With drastic changes in mind, Saxon was well aware of the necessity of support from the national banks. On February 1, 1962, he asked each of them for ". . . its judgment concerning needed changes in the laws, policies, and regulations affecting its operations." At the same time he appointed an Advisory Committee of 24 bankers and lawyers, including two state bankers, to review the national bank responses and report the conclusions and recommendations of the Committee. The Committee, under the leadership of Frank E. McKinney of Indianapolis, published its findings in September 1962 in a 189-page volume, *National Banks and the Future*. Although the Committee was divided almost equally on certain issues, and although the Comptroller was in disagreement with some recommendations, the Report of the Advisory Committee charted much of the course that would be followed. In general, the Committee recommended many technical changes that would broaden the lending and investing powers of national banks and that would enable many of them to expand the scope of their activities.[7]

At the outset Comptroller Saxon also knew that he would run into opposition from state and federal agencies as well as from state banks certain to feel threatened by expansion of the national system. Exacerbating the difficulties of cooperation with the Federal Reserve and the FDIC were squabbles over the design of examination forms and reports of condition, and tensions reminiscent of the days of John Skelton Williams rose between the Federal Reserve and the Office of the Comptroller.[8] To the congressional hostilities and pressures generated by the state and federal agencies were added those of the smaller commercial banks, largely through their trade association and lobbyist, the Independent Bankers Association.

The data, to which we turn presently, provide a substantial measure of the changes brought about during the tenure of Comptroller Saxon, but they fall far short of indicating the nature and extent of his administrative innovations. On a few occasions Comptroller Saxon was able to secure the

---

[7] Comptroller of the Currency, *National Banks and the Future*, Report of the Advisory Committee on Banking, Washington, D.C.: U. S. Government Printing Office, 1962.

[8] Early in his tenure Saxon made several attempts to enlist the cooperation of the Board of Governors of the Federal Reserve System, but differences between the two agencies over substantive matters were too serious to be negotiated.

passage of recommended legislation, as, for example, when he succeeded in obtaining transfer of authority over the trust powers of national banks from the Federal Reserve to the Office of the Comptroller.[9] But in general legislation aimed at removing old statutory prohibitions was opposed by the Board of Governors of the Federal Reserve System. Moreover, the Office encountered the persistent opposition of several influential members of the House Committee on Banking and Currency, who were especially resistant to laws calculated to extend the influence of the larger banks. As a consequence, the Comptroller was forced to achieve most of his goals through changes in administrative rules and regulations. His course was made easier by the statutes granting permissive powers to the Comptroller of the Currency, which are perhaps the broadest drawn of all the regulatory laws.

Decisions made pursuant to these statutes covered a vast range. A summary of the principal changes is contained in the Comptroller's *Annual Report* for 1963, one of the most candid documents ever published by a regulatory agency.[10] Comptroller Saxon repeatedly affirmed that his fundamental test of a new regulation or procedure was the requirement that it be essential to the "solvency and liquidity" of the banking system. "Wherever," he wrote, "a restrictive control did not meet this test, we have endeavored to broaden the discretionary powers of the national banks, insofar as this appeared desirable and was permissible under existing law.[11]

Restrictive controls were eased by making substantial changes long requested by a majority of national banks and set forth, for the most part, in the Report of the Advisory Committee. A number of modifications were made in the direction of liberalizing lending limits of national banks and in making national banks more competitive with other institutions in many categories of real-estate loans. Successful efforts were made to enable the trust departments of banks to offer a full range of fiduciary services. The Comptroller broadened the investment powers of national banks by including in the "general obligations" of a state or political subdivision of a state certain securities hitherto ruled unavailable for customary trading by national banks, and he specifically authorized them to underwrite revenue bonds. National banks were authorized to bring their corporate practices into closer congruence with other types of contemporary firms by reforming procedures and policies for declaring stock dividends, for raising

---

[9] This statute was enacted on September 28, 1962. For details, see Comptroller of the Currency, *Annual Report*, 1963, p. 13.

[10] The theme section of this report, "Years of Reform: A Prelude to Progress," is contained on pages 1-32. Published in late 1964, this material provides the substance of Saxon's philosophy of regulation and a major part of his achievements. Additional insights may be obtained from the appendices, which contain addresses, selected congressional testimony, and important correspondence of Comptroller Saxon. The *Annual Report* for 1964 and the *Annual Report* for 1965-1966 provide further detailed material illuminating the philosophy of the 21st Comptroller.

[11] Comptroller of the Currency, *Annual Report*, 1963, p. 2.

capital through the issuance of senior securities, and for adopting employee incentive stock-option or stock-purchase plans. Among a large number of other rulings aimed at freeing the competitive environment of national banks were authorizations to engage in direct-lease financing of personal property, to act as agents for the issuance of insurance incident to banking transactions (retaining the commissions received therefrom), to receive savings deposits from profit-making corporations, and to acquire directly (as distinguished from indirectly through a subsidiary Edge Act or agreement corporation) the stock of foreign banks.

To all except the initiated, rulings such as these have a hopelessly technical, and even trivial, ring. What difference does it make if a bank's lending limits are raised? Or why should a bank be concerned about the official definition of "improved" property? Or who cares whether banks have the privilege of underwriting revenue bonds? The answers to such questions as these suggest why officers of national banks demanded a change in the Office of the Comptroller and why, generally speaking, they supported Saxon. If state-chartered banks can lend to a single borrower an amount equal to 15 or 20 percent of their capital and surplus, whereas a competing national bank can lend only 10 percent, the state-chartered bank has a competitive advantage. Or if a small bank must enlist the participation of a large bank because it cannot lend sufficient amounts to its best customers, the large bank may ultimately take over much of the small bank's best business. Or if a national bank cannot make loans on "unimproved" property—so defined because there are no buildings on it—state-chartered banks or savings and loan associations will finance housing developments from their initial stages. Or if the largest commercial banks cannot underwrite revenue bonds, competition in the bidding is artificially restricted and costs to taxpayers may thereby be increased.

Consider a somewhat more elaborate example. Banks, more than any other type of business, have always made a practice of trading on their equities, usually in a range of 8 to 15 percent of their total liabilities. Nevertheless, from the earliest days of commercial banking in the United States there has been an aversion to bank borrowing. It is one thing, apparently, to have depositors for creditors and another to have nondepositors for creditors.[12] However this may be, national banks have in recent years made growing use of unsecured promissory notes and capital notes and debentures. At the end of 1965, $364 million of the former and $1,134 million of the latter had been issued by national banks.

Both instruments became popular following favorable decisions by Comp-

---

[12] Those who insist that raising bank capital by borrowing is a questionable practice argue that the very nature of banking, which implies a heavy indebtedness to depositors, requires that a bank's capital be entirely contributed by the shareholders and that not even undivided profits should be included in unimpaired capital and surplus.

troller Saxon regarding their use. Early in his tenure he ruled that unsecured promissory notes (commercial paper) ". . . may be issued at face amount or at a discount, in negotiable or nonnegotiable form, and in any maturity," and that "the proceeds may be used for any normal banking purpose." [13] Unlike capital notes and debentures, these securities are not subordinated to the rights of depositors, and the amounts that may be borrowed in this way are restricted by the borrowing limitations in 12 U.S.C. 82. Because these notes are subject to borrowing limitations, Saxon ruled, they cannot be considered deposits and so are not subject to interest ceilings and reserve requirements. Ruling further that capital notes and debentures are subordinate in right of payment to all deposit liabilities of the issuing bank, the Comptroller held that the proceeds of such securities might be included as part of the aggregate amount of unimpaired capital and surplus of a bank to determine the bank's lending limits.

Although the dollar amount of funds subsequently raised in this manner was small in comparison with total liabilities of commercial banks, borrowing to augment capital has become an important means of increasing lending limits. The chief operating officer of one of the great money-market banks in New York remarked in the late summer of 1966, "I do not know what we would have done without our issue of debentures a year ago." For, he went on, prestigious customers and not a few banks had been reluctant to take advantage of other rulings of the Comptroller that liberalized limits on loans to a single borrower. The inclusion of borrowed money in the capital accounts substantially and unequivocally raised these limits and so made it possible for institutions to accommodate favored customers without sharing their business with participating banks.[14]

A liberalization of lending rules of particular significance to national banks in their competition with the nonbank intermediaries was in the category of real-estate loans. Comptroller Saxon's changes restated legal definitions of real-estate loans and allied terms, and extended changes made in 1955 in the direction of increasing loan-to-value limits and maturities of amortized loans on residential real estate and of total bank lending limits on such real estate. Since these innovations there has been almost no net change for national banks in the ratio of total real-estate loans to gross loans and discounts. However, for national banks there has recently been a decided upward trend in the ratio of conventional urban residential mortgage loans to total loans and discounts. Although it is still too soon to tell, the data suggest that national banks and possibly state member banks are becoming strong competitors in the market for urban residential

---

[13] Comptroller of the Currency, *Annual Report*, 1963, p. 22.
[14] The Office of the Comptroller has been inclined to limit indebtedness in the capital accounts to 25 or 30 percent of the total. However, banks of some size presently have borrowings of more than 35 percent of their capital accounts, and some commercial bankers say that they foresee a time when half the capital of a bank may be borrowed.

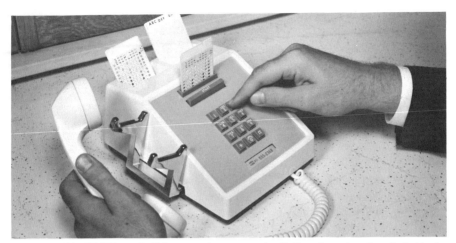

The TOUCH TONE card dialer permits automatic dialing by using punched plastic cards, with subsequent data inputs by pushbuttons or by card. This or a similar data-input device may ultimately be used for electronic monetary transfer.

mortgages, reversing the postwar drift toward a decreasing share of this market.

Direct Allocation of Banking Resources

Decisions of the Comptroller, like those of the other regulatory agencies, indirectly influence the allocation of resources in banking and, for that matter, in finance. Yet the effects of such administrative rulings are often masked, and we sometimes follow a will-o'-the-wisp of change consequent upon such rulings without ever being able to reckon the ultimate effects. But certain administrative determinations have demonstrably plain effects in the marketplace. Chief among these are approval of new charters, certification of *de novo* branches, and action on mergers.

Approval of Charters. The drastic reduction in the rate of formation of new banks that began in 1935 continued through Comptroller Gidney's tenure, though in the late 1950s there was some easing of the clamp on charters. In the five-year period 1956-1960, 168 national banks were chartered; in the same quinquennium, 435 state banks were started.

Beginning in 1962 the Comptroller's Office publicized its willingness to receive more applications for new charters. In 1961, Comptroller Gidney's last year in office, 97 applications were received. In 1962, 176 applications for new charters came in, the number soaring to 490 in 1963, and 468 in 1964. This three-year total of 1,134 charter applications was more than had been submitted in the previous 20 years. In the four-year period 1962-1965, the Office granted 513 new charters, while state authorities, unquestionably stimulated to greater liberality by the Comptroller's actions, granted 502.

The banking community and, to some extent, the public at large understood that the closed-industry image had changed and that, at least for a time, a decision had been taken to increase the banking resources of the country in trade areas where they were deficient. Comptroller Saxon took the view that, despite the considerable regulation to which they are subject, commercial banks are not public utilities and are not entitled to complete protection from competition. Nevertheless, the Office was concerned to prevent overinvestment in banking by trade areas, and the economists on the staff were continually on the alert for signs of such overinvestment. As early as 1964, in the *Annual Report* for that year, it was noted that new charters would have to be rejected for particular areas once a certain level of investment was reached. The rate of rejection of charter requests climbed steadily in 1963-1964, reaching 70 percent in 1965.

Certification of Branches. A substantial proportion of the new charters granted during Comptroller Saxon's tenure was for banks organized in states with severe limitations on branching. In states permitting county-wide, contiguous-county, and statewide branching there was an acceleration in the 1961-1965 rate of new-branch certifications, although the step-up was not as marked as it was in the case of new charters.

In 1955, there were 12,057 unit banks in operation and 1,659 banks with branches. In 1960, the comparable figures were 11,143 and 2,329, the number of branches having increased from 6,710 to 10,216.[15] Comptroller Saxon took the view that *de novo* branches should be certified where state law was permissive and where the economics staff could project community circumstances that indicated profitable support of a new branch. From the end of 1960 to the end of 1965, the number of national banks maintaining branches rose from 905 to 1,331, an increase of 48 percent. Meantime, the number of branches operated by national banks increased from 5,298 to 8,754, a jump of 64 percent. (Branches of state banks rose in this interim from 4,918 to 6,732, an increase of 37 percent.) At the end of 1965, offices of national banks operating branches totaled 10,085, compared with the state-bank figure of 8,541.

At the end of 1966 there were more than 30,400 banking offices in the United States. The number of unit banks was falling, and the number of branch-bank offices was steadily rising. With branch-bank offices accounting for about 65 percent of total banking offices and branch banks controlling almost 70 percent of the country's banking resources, the United States was no longer committed to the principle of unit banking.

Action on Mergers. For half a century after passage of the Sherman Act, banks were not threatened with antitrust litigation, nor did the more spe-

---

[15] Data on the number of banking offices in the United States are published annually in the April issue of the *Federal Reserve Bulletin*. See, especially 1956, pp. 398-399; 1961, pp. 486-487; 1966, pp. 600-601; and 1967, pp. 658-659.

cific prohibitions of Sections 7 and 8 of the Clayton Act seem a cause for apprehension. Mergers were considered a means of rescuing foundering institutions, or improving operations, rather than a way to monopolistic restraints. Moreover, many observers felt that since banking was regulated by specific federal and state statutes the antitrust laws did not generally apply.

The first faint rumblings of commercial bank exposure to Sherman Act prosecution came in the 1940s. In 1945, the Justice Department filed suit against a New York trade association, composed of mutual savings banks and trust companies but including one commercial bank, alleging a Section 1 Sherman Act violation. Three years later, a similar suit was brought against the Chicago Mortgage Bankers Association, which included several commercial banks, the defendants being charged with fixing minimum fees and rates in connection with their lending activities. After more than a decade of inattention to such activity, the Justice Department, in 1961, brought a price-fixing charge against certain New Jersey banks alleging collusion in setting service and other charges. Similar action was shortly taken against banks in Dallas, Texas, and in certain Minnesota cities. In each case, groups of commercial banks were charged with conspiring to fix various rates and terms, whether of interest to be paid or charges for services. In each instance, proceedings were terminated by consent decree or other agreement, and some defendants were fined after pleading no contest. Early in 1962, the Comptroller's Office instructed all national banks to determine service charges and banking hours without collusion, whether through clearinghouse agreements or otherwise. Individual boards of directors were made responsible for determination of such practices, and national bank examiners were instructed to insure compliance. Comptroller Saxon considered these activities within the sphere of his authority and maintained a close surveillance on national banks regarding them.[16]

Section 8 of the 1914 Clayton Act aimed at the prohibition of interlocking corporate managements. After much congressional deliberation, directors and other officers of banks above a certain size were specifically prohibited from sitting on more than one board, though exceptions in this and subsequent amending legislation, notably the Banking Act of 1935, made the law fuzzy and uncertain of enforcement. The Board of Governors of the Federal Reserve System has held hearings on alleged Section 8 violations, but these cases have not found their way into the courts on appeal. Data on exemptions granted by the Federal Reserve as authorized by the statutes are not available.

In 1962, the Comptroller's Advisory Committee on Banking recommended ". . . that the law and its application by the supervisory authorities should restrict interlocking directorates, and not only between competing

---

[16] See Comptroller of the Currency, *Annual Report*, 1963, p. 29.

commercial banks (as is now the case) but also between commercial banks and certain other types of competing financial institutions. . . .[17] Comptroller Saxon consistently took the view that conflicts of interest in the financial structure should be removed and that laws regarding interlocking directorates should be clarified and strengthened.

Like clearinghouse association agreements, acquisition of commercial banks through purchase by nonbanking corporations of stock or assets came under administrative and legislative scrutiny in the 1940s. After years of discussion among the federal supervisory agencies and the Department of Justice, the Board of Governors of the Federal Reserve System in 1948 initiated a proceeding under Sections 7 and 11 of the Clayton Act against the Transamerica Corporation, a West Coast holding company, alleging a violation of Section 7 because of systematic acquisition of the voting stock of independent banks in five states. The Board's 1952 order to Transamerica to divest itself of 47 majority-owned banks was set aside by a Circuit Court of Appeals in 1953, and the Supreme Court refused to review the lower court's decision.

Meanwhile, some congressional sentiment was developing for legislation that would bring bank acquisitions under the control of federal bank regulatory agencies. For example, a 1945 bill sponsored by Senator Estes Kefauver would have exempted bank acquisitions from Section 7 of the Clayton Act, requiring that bank mergers be approved by the Comptroller of the Currency, the Federal Reserve Board, or the Federal Deposit Insurance Corporation. Neither this nor subsequent attempts to include federal agency control of bank acquisitions secured congressional approval. When the 1950 Celler-Kefauver Amendment to the Clayton Act was passed, merger by asset acquisition as well as stock acquisition was brought within the Section 7 provision of the Clayton Act. Bank mergers were not included in this legislation, probably because the bill would not have passed if they had been included.

Despite repeated attempts to bring bank mergers and consolidations under the proscriptions of Section 7, notably by Congressman Emanuel Celler and Senator John Sparkman in 1955, a succession of bills for this purpose failed to gain congressional approval. After a decade of consideration, the Bank Merger Act of 1960 provided for administrative control of bank mergers by the federal agencies, and made explicit the consideration of banking as well as competitive criteria in determining the merits of a particular merger. In addition to the effects of a merger on competition, regulatory agencies were to consider at least five banking criteria, including "the convenience and needs of the community to be served."

Careful review of the legislative history of the 1950 and 1960 legisla-

---

[17] Comptroller of the Currency, *National Banks and the Future,* Report of the Advisory Committee on Banking, 1962, p. 94.

TABLE 7-1

Mergers of State and National Banks, 1946–1966*

Year	Number of national banks merged into state banks	Number of state banks merged into national banks	Number of national banks merged into other national banks	Totals of merged national banks
1946	17	8	22	30
1947	8	10	20	30
1948	6	3	23	26
1949	11	3	21	24
1950	8	12	16	28
1951	21	10	9	19
1952	13	11	26	37
1953	21	24	42	66
1954	42	66	60	126
1955	47	52	74	126
1956	26	55	50	105
1957	26	55	28	83
1958	13	39	42	81
1959	27	38	47	85
1960	11	44	43	87
1961	16	44	26	70
1962	23	48	62	110
1963	15	58	41	99
1964	16	44	52	96
1965	19	39	40	79
1966	14	36	39	75

* Includes mergers, consolidations, and purchase and sale transactions.
SOURCE: *Annual Reports* of the Comptroller of the Currency, 1946-1966.

A Stabilized Economy   157

James J. Saxon was Comptroller of the Currency for exactly five years, from November 16, 1961 to November 15, 1966. In this short period of time, bank regulation changed in many ways to fit the needs of the 20th century.

tion left no doubt in the minds of most economists and lawyers about the intent of Congress to exclude commercial bank mergers from Clayton Act prosecution. But the 1960 statute did not explicitly state such exclusion, and in the *Philadelphia National Bank* decision of 1963, the Supreme Court, though wondering aloud why the Celler-Kefauver Amendment made no explicit mention of mergers not subject to Federal Trade Commission jurisdiction, could perceive "the basic Congressional design" and could infer that bank mergers were subject to the Clayton Act.

This opinion, when coupled with the decision in the *Lexington* case, subjected commercial banks to more stringent antitrust regulation than applied to firms in unregulated industry. The Bank Merger Act of 1966 imposed a single set of standards upon the banking agencies, the Department of Justice, and the courts by which to assess the legality of a merger. The Comptroller's Office then had to make an antitrust judgment and, finding a substantial lessening of competition, could approve a merger only if banking advantages outweighed the competitive disadvantages. The Department of Justice could then postpone a bank merger by merely commencing an action against it instead of seeking an injunction in the courts.

Comptroller Saxon held the view that, in the expansion of banking, mergers may often be preferable to new charters or *de novo* branching.[18] He felt strongly that the Comptroller of the Currency, along with the other federal regulatory agencies, had been unnecessarily hindered by the Justice Department and the courts in the determination of optimum allocation of commercial-bank resources. It was his contention to the end of his tenure on November 15, 1966, that decisions made by the bank-regulatory authorities would be based on a surer perception of the nature of competition in banking than that of the Justice Department. The consequence of Justice Department interference, he felt, would be less competition in national markets as medium-sized banks could not, through merger, achieve optimum size. On the other hand, the structure of banking in local markets being that of a few firms competing among themselves and against the nonbank intermediaries, precluding mergers would have no demonstrable local-market effects except, perhaps, to place commercial banks at a disadvantage with other financial institutions.

The Saxon Position

Comptroller Saxon was without question a stormy and controversial figure. As he has been frank to say, some of the turbulence of his term developed unnecessarily over procedural matters and as a consequence of

---

[18] Comptroller of the Currency, "The Banking Structure in Evolution," *Annual Report*, 1964, p. 5.

unintentional slights to government colleagues. A frequently mentioned example of diplomatic failures during his tenure was his refusal, after a few months in office, to attend meetings of the FDIC Board of Directors. A precedent had been set by his predecessor, Comptroller Delano, who made a practice of sending a proxy to FDIC Board meetings. Saxon felt that his own time could be put to more productive use than attending meetings largely devoted to details of minor administrative problems. Moreover, he was often called on to vote on matters affecting the competitive position of national banks, and to avoid possible conflict of interest he thought it best to abstain from discussion and voting. Nevertheless, his practice of sending major staff officers to meetings, bolstered by the appointment of a liaison officer for FDIC affairs, failed to mollify critics, who felt that the Comptroller himself should vote on administrative questions ranging from establishing the salaries of chauffeurs to approval of insurance applications of new state banks.

Yet the debate over Saxon's policies turned on substantive matters. In general, national-bank officers approved his regime. Executives of larger banks were almost unanimously in favor of his rulings, and a large majority of officers of smaller national banks gave staunch support to his policies. In their judgment his decisions were well within a tradition that gives wide latitude to the Comptroller of the Currency. They represented an infusion of new ideas required by a growing and increasingly complex economy, and they meant increased profits to institutions, big and little, that really wished to compete. On the other hand, officers of small state banks and a few national banks feared and distrusted Saxon, for they were persuaded that an extension of his branching philosophy meant an end to small unit banks in America. Their alarm was first expressed in a public forum during the so-called Saxon hearings, which Representative Patman conducted to investigate the Comptroller's alleged nefarious activities in disregarding state laws on branching and in refusing to cooperate with state authorities in dividing up choice new branching sites between state and national banks.[19] But Saxon's powerfully reasoned, articulate defense was more than adequate to win the respect of the press and, as nearly as such opinion can be judged, of the public at large.

The 21st Comptroller's most potent adversary was the Federal Reserve, which continually laid its immense prestige and power on the line to forestall permanent acceptance of decisions that flew in the face of traditional central-bank attitudes. In the midst of the controversy, Vice President Robert N. Hilkert of the Federal Reserve Bank of Philadelphia underscored the polarization of the conflict in a speech delivered in a series of meetings of bankers and businessmen. He described the technical nature of

---

[19] See *Conflict of Federal and State Banking Laws,* Hearings before the Committee on Banking and Currency, House of Representatives, 88th Congress, 1st Session, 1963.

the dispute—over such questions as whether debentures are capital or surplus, whether national banks should be allowed to hold savings deposits of corporations, and so on. Then he got to his major point: "The Federal Reserve's basic disagreement with the Comptroller seems to boil down to whether bank supervision should be substantially relaxed at this time. Mr. Saxon seems to be saying it should, and the System is saying that it shouldn't."[20] Stressing the basic philosophic difference between the two agencies, Mr. Hilkert remarked that relaxation of bank supervision would be all right if serious depressions could be ruled out. But in his view they could not: "The late Norbert Wiener, an M.I.T. professor, said that fast-accelerating automation will bring a depression that will make the 1930's seem like a joke. I don't agree with him but I can't completely ignore the thought. At the very least the coming years will be an unsettled period for the Nation as a whole." [21]

The issue would not be settled, either during Comptroller Saxon's tenure or for a long time after. But it was nevertheless clearly joined. Is modern stabilization policy effective enough to allow the freer allocation of resources in banking? Or is it not? For those who respond affirmatively, Comptroller Saxon moved in the direction of essential historic change. For those who respond negatively, the Federal Reserve's conservative ties to the past suggested the only prudent course. In general, a younger generation of economists and political scientists tended to side with Saxon's position, while those whose outlooks reflected memories of the depression years were inclined to the Federal Reserve view.

James J. Saxon argued, during his term in office and afterward, that the controversy between the Comptroller of the Currency and the Board of Governors was the inevitable consequence of Federal Reserve insistence upon a position as undisputed arbiter of the banking system. He saw the tension between the two agencies during his tenure as evidence of a continuing struggle for power that began with the framing of the Federal Reserve Act. It erupted during the term of John Skelton Williams, came temporarily to a halt with the 1935 removal of the Comptroller from his ex-officio position on the Board, and resumed a quarter of a century later when Saxon's rulings posed a threat to the long-held dominance of the central bank.

Thus, in Saxon's judgment the problems of bank supervision were deeper and more broadly based than the simple issue of maintaining the "soundness" of commercial banks. He saw in the portfolio diversification of nonbank intermediaries and in the extension of services they offered a threat to the competitive position of commercial banks, so he moved to increase the banks' competitive strength by expanding their powers. Impressed with

---

[20] Robert N. Hilkert, "The Muddle in Bank Supervision," *Business Review*, Federal Reserve Bank of Philadelphia, June 1964, p. 4.
[21] *Ibid.*, p. 5.

environmental changes that left regions of rapid growth with a shortage of finance, Saxon encouraged investment in banking where it appeared that resources so committed would earn a competitive return. And with the reduction in lending risks that has accompanied the increasing stability of the economy, Saxon could act to remove hindrances to competition among banks and between banks and nonbank intermediaries. He was convinced that the social risk of banks unduly constrained by legislation would be greater in the last third of the 20th century than the social risk of bank failure. And, it might be added, Comptroller Saxon was persuaded that a little competition among the bank regulatory agencies themselves would in the long run serve the public weal.

Contemporary Banking Supervision

After a century and a half of experimentation and practice, responsibility for bank supervision in the United States remains divided. Diffused among three federal and 50 state agencies, jurisdictional authority is often fuzzy and overlapping. Nevertheless, the day-to-day machinery of bank examinations, the scrutiny of reports, the occasional liquidation of a failed bank, and the communication of advice and counsel runs smoothly and, on the whole, efficiently. In the upper echelons of the agencies, where policy is made, there is recurring conflict over the content of particular rules and regulations, although conference and compromise may often lead to workable resolutions of problems. In the abrasive give and take of expressing divergent views and opinions, bank supervisors in the several agencies shape policy courses preferable in many ways to those that would be charted by a single authority.

A persuasive case can be made for codifying and simplifying federal banking law, as was proposed in the Financial Institutions Act of 1957. Equally impressive arguments can be advanced for putting all supervisory functions of the federal banking agencies in the hands of a single new agency. In 1965 two bills were introduced to create a single supervisory authority. One (H.R. 6885) would have placed all examining and supervisory functions of the three existing federal agencies under the Secretary of the Treasury; the other (H.R. 107) would have created a Federal Banking Commission of five members, transferring all functions to it. Both bills would have abolished the Office of the Comptroller of the Currency and would have placed the management of the Federal Deposit Insurance Corporation under the Secretary or the Commission, eliminating the FDIC Board of Directors. Present supervisory functions of the Federal Reserve would have been transferred to the Secretary or the Commission, leaving the Board of Governors only with the duty of executing monetary policy.

But legislation aimed at abolishing the Comptroller's Office has mustered little support in Congress, and successive Comptrollers have pressed to make their responsibility over the national banking system complete.

The Federal Reserve, while insisting that it wishes to be relieved of supervisory functions, makes no serious move to relinquish this relationship with state member banks. And FDIC officials are convinced that the insurance function cannot be properly administered without some continuing influence on the heterogeneous rules and regulations prescribed by state banking authorities. No one can say, of course, what Congress will do, but the best guess for the near term is that the present federal and state agencies will continue to make supervisory policy.

The Conceptual Role of Supervision

Over the years the statutes, federal and state, have ordinarily provided only the most general instructions for achieving the objectives of supervisory policy, which have themselves never been clear. Bank supervisors have been enjoined to promote "safe" banking or a "sound" banking system. They have been explicitly directed to prevent "unsound" or "speculative" loans and investments, and more broadly to limit the risks to which banks may expose themselves. In a general way, supervisory authorities are asked to give a certain nebulously defined protection to the public and

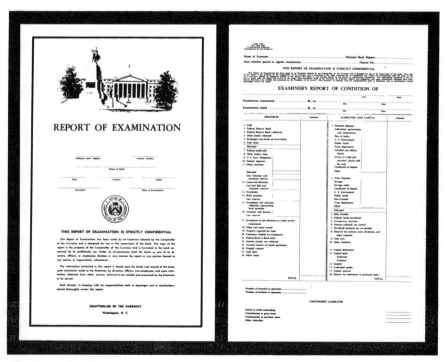

Bank examination remains the most time-consuming function of the Office. Shown is the front of a current Report of Examination.

to customers and shareholders of banks, and in the event of failure or liquidation of a bank, specifically to its depositors.

Bank Examination

In assessing the role of bank examination, in some respects the key function of supervision, it is possible to defend two distinct and almost opposite views. On the one hand, it can be argued that bank examination is crucially important in the sense that it guarantees the quality of bank assets and so validates the money supply, which is created by commercial banks. At the other extreme, it is possible to argue that bank examination is an unnecessary function, one that involves interference with bank management and a waste of social resources. Those who would defend the latter position point to the fact that in Great Britain bank examination is unknown. Indeed, the banking system of the United Kingdom is under a minimum of supervision, such supervision as there is being the responsibility of the central bank.

There is, of course, an in-between position, one that argues for bank examination only as a protection against dishonesty. Those who take this view contend that routine bank examination really cannot determine the "quality" of a particular piece of paper, especially if the piece of paper is a promissory note. About all that can be determined from inspection is whether the note is current and whether the credit seems excessive in relation to the financial resources of the borrower. But even these criteria ordinarily do not attest to the basic soundness of the asset. Experience has shown that loans to borrowers with impeccable credit ratings may go desperately sour with a general downturn in economic activity; similarly, loans to marginal or even bad credit risks may turn out quite well as long as the performance of the economy is at or near its potential. But even though middle-of-the-roaders would deny that examination helps to improve asset quality, they would admit that under a predominantly unit-banking system examination protects against the malfeasance and misfeasance of bank employees, particularly of senior officers in small- to medium-size institutions.

Actually, the role of examination is conditioned largely by the banking structure of a country. In the United States, where the great majority of banks are small units, some check other than that of internal audits is necessary. In countries like England and Canada, where the banking system consists of a few large banks with many branches, there is relatively less opportunity for minor employees to tap tills or alter records, the reason being that they are always reporting to someone higher in the chain of authority. Moreover, branches are subject to the constant surveillance of departments in the home office, and the falsifying of assets is far more diffi-

The detail of an examiner's report of condition has increased considerably since the turn of the century. Modern examination is so thorough that concealment of questionable banking practices is next to impossible.

cult under such scrutiny than it is in the case of a small bank, where senior officers have unlimited access to the records and are subject to no check except that of internal audits.

In American practice three concepts of bank examination have been formulated.[1] Examination can be viewed as a more or less mechanical process of checking on the legality of a bank's transactions, as a verification, if you will, of the honesty of a bank's management. More broadly, a bank examiner may be presumed to have the right to counsel and advise the officers of banks, going so far on occasion as to suggest changes in managerial practice and remonstrating against policies that appear to incur undue banking risk. In addition to investigation, then, examination may imply some continuing, if unobtrusive, supervision of bank management. Finally, bank examination may be considered an aid to general monetary policy, the implication being that standards of examination will vary with economic fluctuations. Under such a concept, examiners would be expected to encourage lending in times of economic slump by taking a more lenient attitude toward marginal loans; on the contrary, they would reinforce

---

[1] See G. L. Bach, *Federal Reserve Policy-Making*, New York: Alfred A. Knopf, 1950, pp. 104-107.

restrictive credit policy in times of inflationary pressure by discouraging loans that might otherwise pass without question.

On at least one occasion in recent banking history, at the time of the agreement of 1938, the federal agencies went so far as to make explicit their commitment to vary examination standards in order to facilitate the task of achieving economic recovery.[2] At least until the late 1940s Federal Reserve officials entertained the idea of making supervision an adjunct of stabilization policy, but serious advocacy of such a course has gradually disappeared. In the continuing depression of the 1930s, it was possible to use for a time the "intrinsic soundness" rather than the "fair market" criterion of valuing assets. But as the American economy regained its fundamental vitality, attempts to have examiners in the several agencies vary their judgments to suit top-level policy decisions were bound to end in frustration. The examination staff of the Office of the Comptroller has consistently tried to maintain a more or less unvarying standard of judgment regarding bank assets, and the Federal Deposit Insurance Corporation has been inclined to follow the same rule. Federal Reserve supervision is thoroughly decentralized, examiners in the field reporting to the 12 Reserve Bank chief examiners. And though the Board's Division of Examinations performs a review function, and staff conferences achieve some standardization and coordination of procedures, the fact remains that field examiners are considerably removed, physically and in supervisory attitudes, from policy-making offices in Washington.

In a word, examiners assigned to the duties of work in the field take a rather narrow view of the function of examination. No amount of directives and conferences are likely to achieve a workable variation of examination criteria to meet swings in economic activity. The consequence is that the second of the concepts of examination, which combines investigation of a bank's affairs with exhortations to remedy practices increasing banking risk, is the one most likely to have the long-term approval of the supervisory agencies.

Supervision and the Allocation of Banking Resources

The apparatus of call reports, bank examination, and consultation between examiners and bank executives constitutes the central activity of bank supervision and consumes the time of the greater part of the personnel. In the minds of many people this function constitutes the *raison d'etre* of the supervisory agencies. As our historical inquiry has made clear, supervisors also significantly influence the allocation of banking resources and, more broadly, of financial resources.

---

[2] *Vide supra,* pp. 135-137.

Rulings and Regulations. Banking law, though voluminous, is silent on a great many matters with which bank supervisors must deal. Consequently, rulings on particular points at issue and regulations issued to provide continuing guides on recurring procedural matters constitute the principal forms of bank regulation. Examples from the foregoing chapters come readily to mind. For more than half a century, national banks did not ordinarily have branches merely because a Comptroller of the Currency and his successors, despite the silence of the banking laws, ruled that they could not have them. In the early 1920s national banks began to branch in earnest, as another Comptroller ruled that "offices" were permissible within the city of a bank's location. In the 1930s a Comptroller decided that conservators of national banks could be former officers of those banks and need not be impartial "outsiders." Comptrollers of the Currency, as well as the Board of Governors of the Federal Reserve System, have ruled that member-bank purchases and sales of "federal funds" are not in fact "purchases and sales" but "loans and borrowings," yet another Comptroller maintained that they are not loans and borrowings and therefore are not subject to statutory restrictions. Comptrollers of the Currency had long ruled that national banks could not act as agents in the sale of insurance incidental to bank transactions (without regard to community population), yet another Comptroller ruled that they could.

The list of rulings and regulations pursuant to statutory authority is literally endless. Administrative determinations by agencies at both federal and state levels have as real an influence on banking operations, and more generally on financial institutions, as do requirements spelled out in the statutes. The implied powers of the agencies are so great that a liberal construction of the laws of the several jurisdictions gives almost unlimited power to single individuals, boards, and commissions. To be sure, as a consequence of a particular ruling or of the issuance of a specific regulation there may be loud complaints from the business community, sharp reaction from legislators, and even an ultimate attack in the courts. The fact remains that over long periods of time a Comptroller of the Currency or a board in Washington or a state capital may by a simple pronouncement greatly affect the transfer of resources into and out of the banking business. In this respect the regulation of banks is akin to that of public utilities, and many of the prerogatives of management in nonregulated businesses are thus not available to bank managements.

Approval of Charters, de novo Branches, and Mergers. Supervisory officials affect the allocation of resources in banking in an even more direct way. No bank may be formed without a charter, which must be approved by them.[3] No bank may expand, either through the acquisition of new

---

[3] The Federal Deposit Insurance Corporation does not approve charters. It can, however, refuse insurance to a newly organized state bank, so that in practice the FDIC does affect entry, particularly of small, state-chartered institutions.

capital or by the formation of new branches, even where the latter are permitted by the statutes, without explicit permission of a regulatory authority. Nor may a bank expand through the acquisition of another bank without the approval of a bank supervisory agency, and even then mergers are subject to attack by the Justice Department provided that litigation commences within 30 days of final agency approval.

Clearly, then, investment in banking does not necessarily follow the prospect of profits. Almost from the beginning of commercial banking in the United States, there was recognition of the fact that banks are special institutions, that the banking industry plays a role so central to the well-being of the economic system as to require special scrutiny and continuing oversight. Within the past generation the reasons for supervision of commercial banking have become less compelling because of (a) the innovation of deposit insurance, (b) improved techniques for stabilizing output (and so income) of the economy, and (c) the increasing relative importance of branch banking. But the tradition of bank supervision is so well established in this country that it is hard to imagine any serious turning away from the basic controls over entry.

Nonetheless, there are strong indications that modern supervisory agencies are more responsive to economic requirements and less amenable to personal and political pressures than they used to be.[4] For example, before the Comptroller of the Currency issues a charter, his staff conducts an elaborate and exhaustive investigation that reveals the background and resources of the organizers, the present banking facilities available to the area to be served by the proposed bank, and the likely effect of a new firm on competition in that area. A national bank examiner makes an on-the-scene investigation of the proposed bank's prospects. Before a charter is granted or rejected, a number of expert judgments, from economists and lawyers as well as from experienced examination personnel, are considered. A simpler procedure is followed before a permit to open a *de novo* branch is issued. However, the economic and legal investigation preceding a merger decision is even more complicated and exhaustive than that required before approval of a charter, and a major case may require months of work by a score or more of staff members with the highest professional qualifications.

In a word, the work of supervisory agencies is less tied to tradition, to rules of thumb, than it was even a decade ago. The concept of supervision has changed to a reliance on an intellectual basis for decisions rather than on the prejudgments, the "sense" of what is appropriate, that used to guide one man or a board. Those who wish to know what bank supervision is are best informed by observing what bank supervisors do. A brief exami-

---

[4] We should not be so naive as to suppose that such pressures have disappeared or that they ever will. No businessman welcomes competition, and new charters are almost invariably opposed by the bankers whose business will be affected by new competition. The opposition is simply less effective than it used to be.

William B. Camp, 22nd Comptroller of the Currency: like his predecessors, Comptroller Camp will maintain a continuity of supervisory procedures while making administrative changes required by a rapidly growing economy.

nation of the organization of the Comptroller's Office may further comprehension of the activities of the oldest supervisory agency.

The Office of the Comptroller Today

For more than 100 years, the Comptroller of the Currency has maintained about the same status in the administration of the federal government. He is still appointed by the President with the advice and consent of the Senate, and his term of office remains five years unless he is removed sooner by the President for reasons communicated by the President to the Senate.[5] Although the law provides that the Comptroller of the Currency "shall perform his duties under the general directions of the Secretary of the Treasury," the Comptroller operates with a degree of autonomy not enjoyed by any other bureau within an Executive Department. To be sure, the Secretary of the Treasury recommends an appointment in the first place, and in modern times it is scarcely to be imagined that the Comptroller and the Secretary could work to opposite purpose. Moreover, urgent political requirements of the President have on occasion been transmitted to the Comptroller through the Secretary of the Treasury.[6] The fact remains that for months and even years a Comptroller of the Currency can run his bureau as though he were physically located outside the Treasury, with no official ties to it.

The Comptroller reports directly to Congress through an annual report explicitly ordered by the statute. Yet he and his Office are, in the absence of further legislation, outside congressional purview for the simple reason that funds for maintaining the Office are obtained from assessments on national banks and not from congressional appropriations. Despite the quasi-autonomy of the Office, the staff are considered civil servants, though not until 1942 were examiners subject to competitive procedures of the Civil Service Commission as a condition of employment.[7]

Although the Comptroller of the Currency can draw on a wide variety of talent and obtain technical assistance in minute detail, he must make the final decision on all major questions of national-bank regulation. Because he is not required to compromise his views with other members of a board or commission, the personality and abilities of the man in the office give that Office its tone and largely determine the creativity of a particular administration. This fact accounts for the great swings in influence of the

---

[5] This stipulation about removal is not provided for any other Presidential appointee.

[6] For example, it appears that in the fall of 1947 considerable pressure was brought to bear on the Comptroller by Secretary John Snyder to permit branching of banks owned by Transamerica Corporation. See Marriner S. Eccles, *Beckoning Frontiers*, New York: Alfred A. Knopf, 1951, pp. 448-449.

[7] Since 1946 the Comptroller's Office has had an excepted status under Civil Service, first under Schedule A authority and since 1955 under Schedule B authority. The effect of the Schedule B exception is that the Comptroller may conduct his own noncompetitive examinations. This excepted status could be withdrawn at any time.

OFFICE OF THE COMPTROLLER OF THE CURRENCY

Chart of Organization

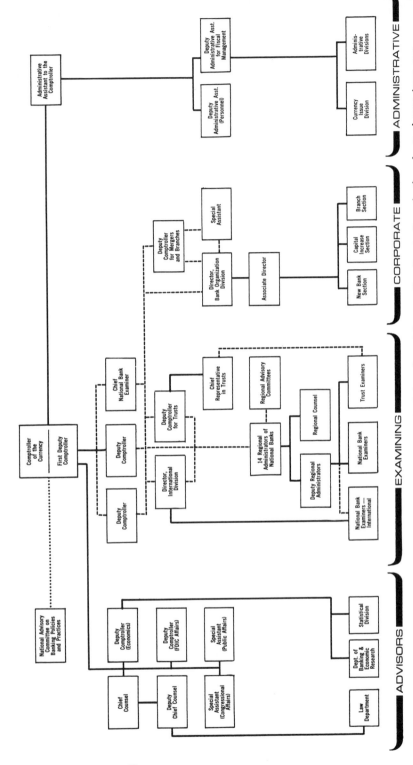

The organization of the Office of the Comptroller under the administration of Comptroller Camp. Organization charts change from one Comptroller to another to suit the style and personality of the incumbent.

Office of the Comptroller, as some incumbents have preferred to remain anonymous and withdraw from wider administration councils while others have vigorously and forthrightly advocated policy moves calculated to result in controversy. Thus, strong Comptrollers like Charles G. Dawes, Williams, Crissinger, Pole, O'Connor, and Saxon have tended to bring the Office into the arena of public discussion and public policy-making, whereas men like Knox, McIntosh, Delano, and Gidney have silently kept away from involvement in public debate. It goes without saying that major changes have been advocated and on occasion adopted during the tenures of the more aggressive incumbents.

The Staff of the Comptroller

The Currency Act of 1863 provided for the appointment of a Deputy Comptroller.[8] Since the passage of the original Act, three other deputies have been added, in 1908, 1923, and 1959. In the latter year Congress amended the National Bank Act to limit to four the number of deputies that the Secretary of the Treasury can appoint. These four deputies are known as statutory deputies, because their positions are defined in the law. With the expansion of the national banking system in the 1960s, Comptroller Saxon was required to increase his immediate staff, and he created a group of "nonstatutory" deputies. They are appointed by the Comptroller rather than by the Secretary, and their terms of office depend upon his wishes and those of his successors. These functional deputies are in effect administrators who head departments organized to provide information and expert opinion.

The deputy Comptrollers of the Currency have invariably been career men, more often than not examiners who have come up through the ranks. Each deputy is assigned a particular set of responsibilities, his work being in large part determined by the principle of staff organization selected by the Comptroller. With a single exception, Comptrollers of the Currency have preferred geographical rather than functional organization of the staff. Until 1962 the four statutory deputies were placed in charge of certain districts, each coterminous with the Federal Reserve districts, and assignment was made on a basis of the deputy's preference or special knowledge of a particular geographical area. Although Comptroller Saxon grouped the responsibilities of his deputies along functional lines, Comptroller Camp has returned to a geographical basis of allocating responsibility.

---

[8] Until the 1920s, the Deputy Comptrollers were considered more or less permanent fixtures of the Office, continuing from administration to administration as a basis of continuity of policy. Thus, Thomas P. Kane, who worked in the Office continuously for more than 36 years, was Deputy Comptroller from 1899 to 1922.

APPLICATION TO ORGANIZE
A NATIONAL BANK AND
REPRESENTATIONS OF APPLICANTS

dated

_____ , 19 _____

THE COMPTROLLER OF THE CURRENCY
Washington, District of Columbia

APPLICATION

WE, THE UNDERSIGNED, intending to organize and operate a national bank in accordance with the provisions of the National Bank Act, as amended, do hereby make application to the Comptroller of the Currency for permission to organize said national bank, and propose as follows:

1. That the main office of said national bank be located at _____

_____ , in the _____ of _____ , County

of _____ , State of _____

2. That, in order of preference, said national bank have one of the following titles:

_____

_____

_____

_____

The form of applying for a national-bank charter is simple enough, but organizers are subject to close personal and financial scrutiny.

In the absence of the Comptroller, the First Deputy becomes by law the acting Comptroller of the Currency. In that position, he is empowered to sign charter and branch certificates, approve or reject applications for charters and permits for branches, and authorize bank mergers. He is technically responsible for the administration and supervision of the Office, but the actual workload of administrative detail has been assumed by the Administrative Assistant to the Comptroller, a position created in recent years. In current practice the First Deputy, in addition to his responsibility for certain national bank regions, is primarily responsible for changes in examination policies and procedures, and his administrative work is confined exclusively to bank problems.

In 1962 the field organization of the Office was drastically revised with the establishment of 14 regions that bore only superficial resemblance to the previous 12 districts coterminous with Federal Reserve districts. The First Deputy is presently concerned with National Bank Regions 1 (Boston), 13 (Portland), and 14 (San Francisco); another deputy has been assigned Regions 3 (Philadelphia), 5 (Richmond), 7 (Chicago), and 9 (Minneapolis); and a third deputy is responsible for Regions 2

(New York), 6 (Atlanta), 8 (Memphis), and 11 (Dallas). Following a practice used in the past, Comptroller Camp has assigned the Chief National Bank Examiner three regions: 4 (Cleveland), 10 (Kansas City), and 12 (Denver).

The fourth statutory deputy, the Deputy Comptroller for Economics, is responsible for a staff function rather than for administration of several regions. Retaining in part the arrangements made by Comptroller Saxon, Mr. Camp has kept three functional deputies—the Deputy Comptroller for Mergers and Branches, the Deputy Comptroller for Trusts, and the Deputy Comptroller for FDIC affairs.

The flow of information to deputies, whether statutory or nonstatutory, comes largely from interchange of ideas with the banking community, from discussions with colleagues in day-to-day associations, and from field administrators and examiners. Although any staff member is free to go directly to the Comptroller, much substantive information and many staff problems are initially discussed with the First Deputy. All of the deputies have unrestricted access to the Comptroller, and since the Washington office is small relative to most bureaus, "bureaucratic" attitudes are minimal. The deputies have a close and informal relationship with each other and with other staff members.

In general all trust and international problems go first to the appropriate functional deputy or department head for analysis before consideration by a statutory deputy, who may seek further advice from the Chief Counsel or from the Director of Economic Research. Charter, branch, and merger matters are ordinarily considered by the appropriate statutory deputy and one or more functional deputies. Although no rigid distinctions can be made, the three statutory deputies and the Chief National Bank Examiner, each with primary responsibilities, make "line" decisions, whereas the fourth statutory deputy and the nonstautory deputies presently preside over "staff" organizations.

Besides the Comptroller of the Currency, the Deputy Comptrollers, and the Chief National Bank Examiner, there are a number of major administrative offices in the bureau, some statutory and some nonstatutory. In addition to his administrative responsibility for three regions, the Chief National Bank Examiner oversees the examination functions of the Office.[9] He is responsible for reviewing all reports of examination as they come from the field, having them checked for accuracy by assistants, and rating the condition of national banks according to standards established by the Office. He also aids in recruiting and training national bank examiners, deals with regional personnel on examination problems, and refines exami-

---

[9] In 1918 the Secretary of the Treasury first asked Congress to create the post of Chief National Bank Examiner, and in 1923 the National Bank Act was amended to establish the position. Comptroller Henry M. Dawes made the first appointment in 1923.

PRIMARY ORGANIZATION

EXAMINER'S REPORT OF AN INVESTIGATION OF AN APPLICATION FILED TO ORGANIZE

(Proposed bank title)   (City, Town, or Village)   (County)   (State)

Other acceptable titles:

(a) _____ (b) _____

Date application filed with Comptroller _____

Date investigation made by National Bank Examiner _____

*Date briefed _____

SUMMARIZATION AND RECOMMENDATIONS

1. Proposed initial capital structure as shown on application:

Capital $ _____ (_____ shares, $ _____ P. V. $ _____ Sale Price)
Surplus
Undivided profits
Total

Proposed initial capital structure suggested by Examiner:

Capital $ _____ (_____ shares, $ _____ P. V. $ _____ Sale Price)
Surplus
Undivided profits
Total

Regional Comptroller's comments regarding capital structure:

Are the organizers agreeable to the capital structure proposed by the Examiner?
If not, what are the objections?

2. Population of city, town, or village in which   Last decennial census _____
   proposed bank is to be located: Present estimate _____

3. Estimated population of the area which
   proposed bank is expected to serve: Radius of area _____ Mile(s).

4. Banking facilities: Number of existing banks and branches operating within radius of the area noted above _____

5. Rental cost or investment in banking house—furniture and fixtures:

6. Distances and geographical directions between the proposed bank and the location of existing banks and branches in that area.
   (If banks are uninsured or nonpar, so indicate).

Name of Bank or Branch and Address	Distance and Direction from Proposed Bank	Capital Structure	Total Loans	Total Deposits

(Use insert sheet)

On-the-scene examination of a new bank's chances for success was begun more than 50 years ago during the tenure of Comptroller Lawrence O. Murray.

nation policies and procedures through continuing discussion with the First Deputy and the Comptroller. By means of regular staff meetings with key figures in the regional offices, the Chief National Bank Examiner becomes aware of new banking techniques and practices and in turn suggests new supervisory policies.

In 1960 each deputy and the Chief National Bank Examiner were assigned an Assistant Chief National Bank Examiner to aid with the work of reviewing examination reports and applications for charters and *de novo* branches. After analysis of reports and applications, these assistants then made recommendations to the appropriate deputy concerning their disposition. They were also assigned responsibility for liaison with the regional offices and for the voluminous correspondence with national banks. Their duties extended to *ad hoc* conferences with staff representatives of the Federal Reserve and the Federal Deposit Insurance Corporation. One Assistant Chief National Bank Examiner was made head of the field educational programs. Having completed a tour of duty in Washington, the assistants were then assigned a position of major responsibility in the field, often as District Chief National Bank Examiner. Assistant Chief National Bank Examiners were in turn aided by a number of administrative assistants, who were themselves considered to be in training for senior positions in the field.

In 1961 Comptroller Saxon sent the Assistant Chief National Bank Examiners and their administrative assistants to regional offices upon completion of their training and abolished their positions in Washington. Comptroller Camp, however, has reinstated the positions in Washington, his immediate purpose being to reduce the workload of the deputies. Once again, this group first receives examination reports from the field, giving them a second screening after a preliminary review by regional administrators in the field. The appropriate deputies and the Chief National Bank Examiner ordinarily make final decisions, occasionally conferring with the Comptroller on critical or peculiarly complex problems.

The expansion of the national banking system has meant a considerable increase in strictly bank supervisory work. To relieve the First Deputy of much of the routine office responsibility, Comptroller Saxon in 1961 created the post of Administrative Assistant to the Comptroller, who took over the housekeeping duties of the bureau. The creation of this position enables an incoming Comptroller to have his own personal assistant among an executive corps composed of career people. The Administrative Assistant is concerned with efficient operation of the Office in addition to taking primary charge of management studies and management-executive development programs. A Deputy Administrative Assistant for Personnel handles the voluminous paperwork involved in recruiting, maintaining liaison with the Civil Service Commission, and processing promotions and separations from the service.

The Office of the Comptroller continues to receive its income from the assessment of national banks. A Deputy Administrative Assistant for Fiscal Management, responsible to the Administrative Assistant, has been recently appointed to oversee the internal financial structure of the Office. Under his jurisdiction, receipts and disbursements are carefully accounted for and are made a matter of public record. His office maintains the accounting system, receives checks in payment of examination fees, deposits funds to the Comptroller's Treasury account, and makes authorized disbursements. The Auditor for the Comptroller of the Currency, responsible only to the Comptroller, audits the accounts of the Disbursing Office, preparing and submitting periodic reports to the Comptroller, tabulating information, and making special statistical analyses. The office of the Auditor is a particularly sensitive one, because the funds of the Office are not audited by the General Accounting Office (GAO) and cannot be as long as they do not come from congressional appropriations. However, since 1938, at the request of the Comptroller, an outside audit has been conducted by the staff of the Bureau of Accounts of the Treasury Department. The 1967 audit was performed by an independent firm of certified public accountants.

In addition to the Administrative Assistant, Comptroller Saxon appointed a number of special assistants who have performed the same work for Comptroller Camp. Created to deal with special problems, these positions may, of course, be abolished at the pleasure of the Comptroller. The three special assistants are currently responsible for congressional relations, public and press relations, and branch matters.

The Staff Divisions

Staff divisions or departments have existed almost since the beginning of the Office.[10] Over the years, successive Comptrollers have enlarged some and abolished others. With the increasing variety of banking services and the growing importance of branches and mergers, staff functions are more important today than they have ever been.

Legal Division. This division is headed by a Chief Counsel, who is assisted by a Deputy Chief Counsel and by Associate Chief Counsels. The department is divided into several sections including bank operations, litigation, corporate practices, and special assignments. The division serves as counsel to the Comptroller, advising him on legal questions of corporate structure, bank organization and operations, and on those arising out of charter, branch, and merger applications. The attorneys prepare opinions and rulings and, on occasion, review and draft legislative proposals. In the past several years the volume of legal correspondence with national banks as well as litigation in branch and merger cases has increased significantly. The Legal Division prepares briefs and argues nonmerger cases in federal courts in cooperation with the Justice Department. The Bank Merger Act of 1966 authorized the Comptroller's Office to intervene in merger litigation in its own right and to defend its decisions against suits instituted by the Justice Department.

Banking and Economic Research Division. This department, created in 1962 by Comptroller Saxon, conducts banking studies that are utilized internally and were often published in *The National Banking Review,* a scholarly journal formerly sponsored by the Office. The Research Department provides economic analysis and opinions on charter, branch, and merger applications. It assists in developing arguments necessary in litigation and provides the Comptroller with information for use in speeches or in congressional testimony. Most of the flow of information from the De-

---

[10] In the early 1930s there were five permanent divisions: Examining, Insolvent Banks, Legal, Organization, and Statistical. To these were added two emergency divisions, the Division of Conservatorship and the Reorganization Division.

A charter certificate signed by the Comptroller of the Currency is a valuable business franchise.

partment to the Comptroller is through the Director of Economic Research, but senior economists are regarded as personal advisors and have easy access to the Comptroller.

The Statistics and Data Processing Division operates under the Department of Banking and Economic Research. From examination reports, call reports of condition, and income and dividend reports, the statisticians compile information for day-to-day use in analysis and interpretation and for publication in economics monographs and the *Annual Report* of the Comptroller.

Organization Division. The Organization Division supervises all matters pertaining to the organization of national banks and banks in the District of Columbia. It is divided into sections that specialize in the technical procedures necessary to proper applications for national-bank charters, new branches, and mergers. The capital-increase section, working with the Legal Division, oversees the technical, administrative, and legal problems associated with the purchase and sale of banks, authorization to increase capital stock, the sale of new bank stock, issuance of capital notes and debentures, stock dividends, and preparation of articles of association. Although the basic work of this division is clerical, the Director of the Division ordinarily gives an opinion on the advisability of the several kinds of application.

Examination Division. This division receives and analyzes all reports of examination. Since policy decisions have previously been made either in the field or by senior officers in Washington, its work is largely clerical. Its major effort is devoted to maintaining surveillance over banks having unsatisfactory reports of condition.

Currency Issue Division. The work of this department is ministerial and removed entirely from monetary and supervisory policy. Members of the department issue Federal Reserve notes upon proper authorization from Federal Reserve Banks. Historically, this division was in charge of issue and redemption of national-bank notes. But in 1935 the circulation of national banks was retired; and though for a time the division participated in destroying worn and unsightly paper money, even this negative role was relinquished in 1966.

Insolvent National Bank Division. Fortunately, the work of this division is minimal, because the Federal Deposit Insurance Corporation is now in charge of all liquidation of insured banks. The division is small, and its personnel devote the greater part of their time to disposing of problems that remain from the 1930s.

The Field Staff. The "districts" or "regions" of the Office were for 45 years coterminous with the Federal Reserve districts, and the field offices were located in or near Federal Reserve Banks. The district offices were for a long time headed by a District Chief National Bank Examiner, who recruited and trained examiners, assigned them to duty, and reviewed their reports before sending them to Washington. In 1962 Comptroller Saxon changed the regions to follow state lines and created two new ones in the Northwest. The chief administrative officer of each of the 14 regions was then designated a Regional Comptroller of the Currency. In 1966 the title of Regional Comptroller was changed to Regional Administrator of National Banks.

With the abolition of the positions of Assistant Chief National Bank Examiner and their administrative assistants in the Washington office, and with the implementation of a plan for decentralizing many of the Office functions, regional offices gained authority and autonomy. The Regional Administrator of National Banks was now more than a Chief National Bank Examiner; he had become primarily an administrator, acting for the Comptroller and dealing directly with the banks on a wider variety of matters. He still hired examiners, supervised their training, and was completely responsible for personnel in the regional office. Problems originating in the field were first considered by the Regional Administrator, who would in some cases pass them on to Washington with his opinion. In keeping with the expanded role of the office, Regional Administrators are not always chosen from the list of national bank examiners, but may come from other divisions in the Washington office. A Deputy Regional

Administrator in each region, himself a national bank examiner, has been assigned responsibility for administration of the examination functions and for reviewing reports of examination.

Comptroller Saxon believed that national banks should have a closer and more immediate relationship with the Office. For this reason, he appointed attorneys to the positions of regional counsel in order that banks might receive legal opinions immediately or within a few days. (Formerly questions were relayed to Washington, and answers were sometimes not received for weeks.) Later, regional economic advisors were added to the field staff so that the Comptroller could have an opinion on economic and banking conditions from an on-the-spot observer.

Comptroller Camp has maintained the basic structure of field organization established by Comptroller Saxon. However, there has been a tendency to return some authority to Washington, and certain functions have been restored to the Washington office to achieve uniformity of action.

Personnel of the field staff now comprise about three-fourths of the employees of the Comptroller's Office. Nearly all of them are national bank examiners, and positions are subject to an examination either in the Treasury Department or in a field office. A specialized staff of National Bank Examiners-International examine branches of national banks in Europe, South America, Africa and Asia. Their duties correspond to those of the domestic force, although particular attention is paid to foreign exchange transactions, especially Eurodollar trading. Most of today's recruits have a bachelor's degree with a background in finance, accounting, or general business. The examiners still have the century-old responsibility of investigating charter, new branch, and merger proposals; and they examine national banks and branches three times every two years and affiliates whenever an examination is deemed necessary. Examination reports are sent from the field to the regional office, where a chief clerk verifies them and corrects statistical errors and omissions. Final drafts of reports are then typed for review by the Regional Administrator and his Deputy, and copies are sent to Washington and to the examined bank. The Washington office in turn sends a copy to the Board of Governors of the Federal Reserve, and, upon request, to the Federal Deposit Insurance Corporation.

Epilogue

AT the beginning of our historical inquiry, we asked how the three federal bank agencies came to their present division of labor and why 50 state supervisory authorities have retained a potent influence on bank supervision. The careful reader can now see, despite the theoretical jurisdiction over national banks of three federal agencies, why the Comptroller of the Currency is in fact the Administrator of those banks. He has perceived how the Federal Reserve came to assume the chief examining and supervisory authority over state member banks. And he will recall the circumstances of FDIC acquisition of extensive regulatory functions over nonmember banks, the long previous experience of the other two agencies in the business of supervision notwithstanding. A word of summary may add meaning to episodes that, taken separately, seem fortuitous.

It is a curious and interesting fact that in an economic world dominated by the idea of *laissez-faire,* Americans chose first to regulate banking. In 1791, only two years after our beginnings under the Constitution, the federal government established the first Bank of the United States and so intervened to secure an allocation of financial resources different from what private markets would have ordered. From that day to this, legislators in both federal and state jurisdictions have continued their intervention in the private market place, with the consequence that the American banking system today is surely different from the one that would have emerged in the annealing fires of unregulated competition.

At the time of the Civil War, Congress unquestionably intended that all commercial banks should be chartered by the federal government and that state jurisdiction over banks should disappear. The national banking legislation of 1863 and 1864 was passed over the almost unanimous opposition of those who directed the fortunes of state-chartered banks, and such was the tenacity with which some of them held on to their state charters that a prohibitive tax did not do all of the state banks in. As the issue of bank notes became increasingly less necessary to profitable commercial banking, state banking systems made a phenomenal recovery, and by the end of World War I state banks were relatively more important than national banks in both numbers and total resources.

Meantime, the federal government once again intervened in the private financial sector by establishing a central bank. Again, a public policy move was undertaken in spite of the ferocious opposition of the banking community, and after more than three years of System experience, only 53 state-chartered banks had joined the Federal Reserve. Since a major objection to system membership was extensive supervision by the Comptroller of the Currency, the Federal Reserve agreed to take state-chartered member banks under the protective wings of the several Reserve Banks with results that were gratifying in terms of the ensuing increase in the number of state member banks.

The Federal Deposit Insurance Corporation was in one sense the outcome of more than a century of discussion about the advisability of insuring bank obligations. The proximate cause of its founding was the disaster of the Great Depression, which persuaded a majority of Congress that losses of small depositors should henceforth be socialized. Once again there was widespread banker resistance to federal intervention, yet to most bankers a scheme of deposit insurance seemed preferable to statewide and possibly interstate branch banking, which was the only feasible alternative if a stable banking system were to be achieved. Although the original statutes had required insured banks to become members of the Federal Reserve System and so to be subject to Federal Reserve supervisory authority, nonmember banks ultimately secured the removal of this obnoxious requirement. And so a third federal agency emerged to share regulatory authority with the other two.

Just as the establishment of the Federal Reserve had created tensions with the Office of the Comptroller, then the old-line supervisory agency, so the founding of the FDIC created strains with the other two federal agencies engaged in bank supervision. But by 1938 the three agencies had agreed upon a division of labor and had even reached accord on principles of valuation, for examination purposes, of different classes of securities. By this time, too, the Federal Reserve had resolved the problem that had long perplexed its officials of how to charge for bank examination. The final decision was to absorb those charges, the consequence being that state member banks would not have to pay for their own federal supervision.[1] National banks continued to pay for supervision from assessments levied by the Comptroller on each national bank. Costs of FDIC supervision of state nonmember banks were to be met out of the gross assessment income of the FDIC, derived from an annual assessment on each insured bank in the amount of 1/12 of 1 percent of its deposit liabilities.[2] Finally,

---

[1] Actually, these supervisory costs are a charge against Federal Reserve earnings, which in turn come primarily from interest on United States government securities acquired in the course of open-market operations. Since most of these earnings are turned back to the Treasury, the incidence of the cost of Federal Reserve supervision is ultimately on the Treasury.

[2] In current practice, all operating expenses of the FDIC, plus any insurance losses, are paid from assessment income. After these payments, one-third of the remainder, or "net assessment income," is paid as an addition to the FDIC's insurance fund and two-thirds as a refund to the insured banks. Since most of the operating expenses of the FDIC are incurred in connection with its examining and supervisory functions, national banks and state member banks contribute substantially to what is essentially the supervision of state nonmember banks.

state supervisory authorities continued to levy a charge on state-chartered banks, either as a payment for each examination performed or as a supervisory fee collected on an annual basis.

The lackluster, conservative nature of bank supervision from the middle 1930s to the early 1960s was the almost inevitable result of depression-induced banker psychology. To be sure, supervisory authorities had always been cautious about innovation. There is no question, for example, that Comptrollers of the Currency, strictly interpreting the statutes, made decisions that inhibited the growth of national banks relative to state banks during the period 1880-1920. By the same token, during these years more liberal state supervisory authorities tended to expand the powers of banks, allowing them to resist the growing encroachment on their business of the nonbank intermediaries. Yet in the free-wheeling capitalist era of the late 19th and early 20th centuries plenty of resources were devoted to commercial banking in the traditional American concept of the business. Moreover, political (legislative) insistence on local control of banks led to a faulty banking structure that buckled and nearly disintegrated in an era preceding serious attempts at economic stabilization by the federal government.

Historians enjoy the often unrewarding contemplation of historical might-have-beens. Students of financial history cannot resist the temptation to inquire what might have been the outcome of the American financial system if, from 1860 on, commercial banks had extended their business so that it became coincidental with that of financial institutions in general. Nor can they resist the further temptation to guess at what might have been the outcome if banks with such wide powers had been permitted to branch across state lines. The resulting agglomerations of financial power would surely have been awesome.

The historical facts are clear. Through a combination of statutory and administrative prohibitions, powers of banks were sufficiently restricted to permit the emergence of healthy, nonbank intermediaries. Similarly, as a consequence of the strenuous resistance of small banks, especially in the agricultural midlands, branching was severely inhibited. For a generation after the depths of the Great Depression, the commercial banking system retrogressed in the face of increasing competition from tax-favored nonbank intermediaries, which made a strong appeal to households while commercial banks were still thinking of business firms as their chief source of income. Yet rapidly rising personal incomes, the growth and urbanization of the population, and the increase in the size of nonfinancial institutions created pressures that brought an end to that retrogression.

In some jurisdictions, banks could, of course, escape the trammels of anti-branching legislation by forming groups or chains. In other jurisdictions, mergers, which were significantly high beginning in the early 1950s, provided a means to achieve size sufficient to provide competitive advantages. Yet it was the emergence in the mid-1950s of a new managerial corps, armed with new ideas and techniques and willing to compete vigorously in all financial markets, that turned the competitive tide toward commercial banks and away from nonbank intermediaries. Interest rates rose slowly but inexorably in the two postwar decades. As short rates rose relative to long rates, nonbank intermediaries that made a business of borrowing short and lending long were at a further disadvantage. To achieve a substantial victory, commercial banks had only to escape from the overburden of constraints that supervisory authorities had laid upon them.

As it turned out, Comptroller James J. Saxon was largely instrumental in removing these constraints.[3] Most of them had been imposed by administrative regulation. They were the composite result of decisions made by men long dead, in the context of another time and another set of economic circumstances. Although there was much discussion of the "legality" of Comptroller Saxon's decisions, the Office of the Comptroller suffered only a few serious rebuffs in the courts. Moreover, the lifting of restrictions at the federal level was followed by a similar easing of the rules in the important state jurisdictions, with the consequence that the total environment of financial institutions was remarkably changed in the decade of the 1960s. In this new environment, commercial banks made a vigorous comeback in their competitive struggle with the nonbank intermediaries, and within the commercial banking industry those firms inclined to expand the variety of services offered most strongly supported Comptroller Saxon's changes.

Since Comptroller Saxon's retirement from office, the question is frequently asked whether his policies are in fact reversible. In one sense the answer is clear. Although there have been and will continue to be changes in particular rulings, the great body of his decisions, which, taken together, constitute a whole new attitude toward bank supervision, will remain intact.

The only major setback to Comptroller Saxon's basic policies has been in the field of antitrust. The Bank Merger Act of 1966, while preserving the right of the Department of Justice to attack a merger transaction within a 30-day period following final approval by one of the three federal supervisory agencies, nevertheless seemed to give the agencies fundamental control over merger approvals. In four cases filed after the 1966 Act the lower courts ruled in favor of the approving agency, holding that

---

[3] It is ironic that deft manipulations of a monetary policy instrument, changes in permissible rates payable by commercial banks under Regulation Q, should have eased the path of change for Comptroller Saxon by making banks strongly competitive for time and savings deposits. But this intrusive regulation, for which there is no excuse in a tolerably free economy, is a two-edged sword; it can cut both for and against all financial institutions and its use is destabilizing.

the 1966 Act was the paramount statute, that the government had the burden of proving an anticompetitive effect, and that such an effect was not outweighed by "convenience and needs." The Department of Justice persistently refused to plead under the Bank Merger Act of 1966, charging a Section 7 Clayton Act violation in each instance. Against a substantial unanimity of opinion of lower court justices, the Supreme Court of the United States, by unanimous opinion in the *Houston* case, reversed in one sweep all the lower courts that had considered the issue. Whatever the intent of Congress, the bank regulatory agencies were for the time being substantially reduced in their abilities to approve bank mergers and make the approvals stick.

Yet our historical sketch has taught us that administrative decisions, themselves liable to continuing modifications, are forever made subject to the vagaries of a changing legislative and judicial climate. Within that climate the Office of the Comptroller will exercise its authority and judgment, largely under the direction of an officer whom we may appraise as follows:

1. The Comptroller of the Currency has vast administrative powers that have been exercised under a statute so broadly drawn as to permit wide latitude in judgment. As a federal administrator, the Comptroller affects resource allocation in banking, and more broadly in finance, his decisions determining in large part the number and size of the institutions, the banking structure, and the nature of competition in the market.

2. With the exception of the Presidency itself, no office in government reflects more keenly the personality and style, the intellectual equipment and philosophy, of its incumbent. The performances of the 21 Comptrollers who preceded Comptroller Camp have ranged in quality from routine administration of a meddlesome, intrusive bureaucracy to imaginative and creative reshaping of the competitive environment of financial institutions. The inhibiting influence of the permanent staff of subordinates, while certainly not absent, has probably been less constricting than that of any other commission, bureau, or department of the federal government.

3. The Comptroller of the Currency has nevertheless been historically subject to great pressures from the banking industry, directly from the managers themselves or organized banking groups, and indirectly through officials of the several state and federal agencies. These pressures spring from two basic motivations. The first is purely selfish, as when the chief operating officer of a bank (or his representative in Congress) protests a charter or the approval of a new branch on the grounds that "dangerous" competition would ensure. The other, more subtle, pressure is often ostensibly in the public interest and may be well-intentioned. It comes from an official in some other agency of government who believes that the conservative, prudent decision in the regulation of banking is to take no

action at all. The consequence has been great time lags in the approval of changes required by a growing economy.

Victor Hugo has remarked the impossibility of containing an idea whose time has come. It is similarly impossible to resist, through regulation, the inexorable outcome of economic forces, provided that the economy is not in the vise of totalitarian control. Ancient rulings may for a time distort and delay the allocation of resources dictated by the market system, but the restraints so exercised begin ultimately to retard the rate of economic growth demanded by contemporary society. At last, continuing adherence to the rules of another generation becomes more dangerous than the adoption of new rules, however they may seem to break with old notions of "sound" banking. In the modern setting of a stabilization policy guaranteed to prevent wide swings in economic activity, venturing in the public interest, like venturing in the private interest, becomes progressively less risky.

Appendix A

Comptrollers of the Currency, 1863 to the present

	Name	Dates of Tenure	State
1	McCulloch, Hugh	May 9, 1863—Mar. 8, 1865	Indiana
2	Clarke, Freeman	Mar. 21, 1865—July 24, 1866	New York
3	Hulburd, Hiland R.	Feb. 1, 1867—Apr. 3, 1872	Ohio
4	Knox, John Jay	Apr. 25, 1872—Apr. 30, 1884	Minnesota
5	Cannon, Henry W.	May 12, 1884—Mar. 1, 1886	Minnesota
6	Trenholm, William L.	Apr. 20, 1886—Apr. 30, 1889	South Carolina
7	Lacey, Edward S.	May 1, 1889—June 30, 1892	Michigan
8	Hepburn, A. Barton	Aug. 2, 1892—Apr. 25, 1893	New York
9	Eckels, James H.	Apr. 26, 1895—Dec. 31, 1897	Illinois
10	Dawes, Charles G.	Jan. 1, 1898—Sept. 30, 1901	Illinois
11	Ridgely, William Barret	Oct. 1, 1901—Mar. 28, 1908	Illinois
12	Murray, Lawrence O.	Apr. 27, 1908—Apr. 27, 1913	New York
13	Williams, John Skelton	Feb. 2, 1914—Mar. 2, 1921	Virginia
14	Crissinger, D. R.	Mar. 17, 1921—Apr. 30, 1923	Ohio
15	Dawes, Henry M.	May 1, 1923—Dec. 17, 1924	Illinois
16	McIntosh, Joseph W.	Dec. 20, 1924—Nov. 20, 1928	Illinois
17	Pole, John W.	Nov. 21, 1928—Sept. 20, 1932	Ohio
18	O'Connor, J. F. T.	May 11, 1933—Apr. 16, 1938	California
19	Delano, Preston	Oct. 24, 1938—Feb. 15, 1953	Massachusetts
20	Gidney, Ray M.	Apr. 16, 1953—Nov. 15, 1961	Ohio
21	Saxon, James J.	Nov. 16, 1961—Nov. 15, 1966	Illinois
22	Camp, William B.	Nov. 16, 1966—	Texas

Deputy Comptrollers of the Currency

	Name	Dates of Tenure	State
1	Howard, Samuel T.	May 9, 1863—Aug. 1, 1865	New York
2	Hulburd, Hiland R.	Aug. 1, 1865—Jan. 31, 1867	Ohio
3	Knox, John Jay	Mar. 12, 1867—Apr. 24, 1872	Minnesota
4	Langworthy, John S.	Aug. 8, 1872—Jan. 3, 1886	New York
5	Snyder, V. P.	Jan. 5, 1886—Jan. 3, 1887	New York
6	Abrahams, J. D.	Jan. 27, 1887—May 25, 1890	Virginia
7	Nixon, R. M.	Aug. 11, 1890—Mar. 16, 1893	Indiana
8	Tucker, Oliver P.	Apr. 7, 1893—Mar. 11, 1896	Kentucky
9	Coffin, George M.	Mar. 12, 1896—Aug. 31, 1898	South Carolina
10	Murray, Lawrence O.	Sept. 1, 1898—June 27, 1899	New York
11	Kane, Thomas P.	June 29, 1899—Mar. 2, 1923	Dist. of Columbia
12	Fowler, Willis J.	July 1, 1908—Feb. 14, 1927	Indiana
13	McIntosh, Joseph W.	May 21, 1923—Dec. 19, 1924	Illinois
14	Collins, Charles W.	July 1, 1923—June 30, 1927	Illinois
15	Stearns, E. W.	Jan. 6, 1925—Nov. 30, 1928	Virginia
16	Awalt, F. G.	July 1, 1927—Feb. 15, 1936	Maryland
17	Gough, E. H.	July 6, 1927—Oct. 16, 1941	Indiana
18	Proctor, John L.	Dec. 1, 1928—Jan. 23, 1933	Washington
19	Lyons, Gibbs	Jan. 24, 1933—Jan. 15, 1938	Georgia
20	Prentiss, William, Jr.	Feb. 24, 1936—Jan. 15, 1938	California
21	Diggs, Marshall R.	Jan. 16, 1938—Sept. 30, 1938	Texas
22	Oppegard, G. J.	Jan. 16, 1938—Sept. 30, 1938	California
23	Upham, C. B.	Oct. 1, 1938—Dec. 31, 1948	Iowa
24	Mulroney, A. J.	May 1, 1939—Aug. 31, 1941	Iowa
25	McCandless, R. B.	July 7, 1941—Mar. 1, 1951	Iowa
26	Sedlacek, L. H.	Sept. 1, 1941—Sept. 30, 1944	Nebraska
27	Robertson, J. L.	Oct. 1, 1944—Feb. 17, 1952	Nebraska
28	Hudspeth, J. W.	Jan. 1, 1949—Aug. 31, 1950	Texas
29	Jennings, L. A.	Sept. 1, 1950—May 16, 1960	New York
30	Taylor, W. M.	Mar. 1, 1951—Apr. 1, 1962	Virginia

31	Garwood, G. W.	Feb. 18, 1952—Dec. 31, 1962	Colorado
32	Fleming, Chapman C.	Sept. 15, 1959—Aug. 31, 1962	Ohio
33	Haggard, Hollis S.	May 16, 1960—Aug. 3, 1962	Missouri
34	Camp, William B.	Apr. 2, 1962—Nov. 15, 1966	Texas
35	Redman, Clarence B.	Aug. 4, 1962—Oct. 26, 1963	Connecticut
36	Watson, Justin T.	Sept. 3, 1962—..............	Ohio
37	Miller, Dean E.	Dec. 23, 1962—..............	Iowa
38	DeShazo, Thomas G.	Jan. 1, 1963—..............	Virginia
39	Egertson, R. Coleman	July 13, 1964—June 30, 1966	Iowa
40	Blanchard, Richard J.	Sept. 1, 1964—..............	Massachusetts
41	Park, Radcliffe	Sept. 1, 1964—June 1, 1967	Wisconsin
42	Faulstich, Albert J.	July 19, 1965—..............	Louisiana
43	Motter, David C.	July 1, 1966—..............	Ohio
44	Gwin, John	Feb. 21, 1967—..............	Mississippi

Administrative Assistants to the Comptroller

1	Larsen, Arnold E.	Dec. 24, 1961—July 1, 1962	Nebraska
2	Faulstich, Albert J.	July 2, 1962—July 18, 1965	Louisiana
3	Chase, Anthony G.	July 21, 1965—Feb. 25, 1967	Washington
4	Wickman, Wayne G.	Feb. 27, 1967—	Texas

Appendix B

Banks Remaining of the First 50 National Charters

Charter Number	Present Name of Bank	Location	Date of Founding
2	First New Haven National Bank	New Haven, Conn.	1792
4	State National Bank of Connecticut	Bridgeport, Conn.	1863
8	First National Bank of Chicago	Chicago, Illinois	1863
10	Third National Bank and Trust Co. of Dayton	Dayton, Ohio	1863
12	First National Bank of Erie	Erie, Pennsylvania	1852
17	First National Bank of Richmond	Richmond, Indiana	1863
19	First National Bank of Portsmouth	Portsmouth, N. H.	1824
20	Fifth Third Union Trust Company	Cincinnati, Ohio	1858
23	Purdue National Bank	Lafayette, Ind.	1853
24	First National Bank of Cincinnati	Cincinnati, Ohio	1863
25	First National Bank of Marietta	Marietta, Pa.	1863
28	National City Bank of Evansville	Evansville, Ind.	1850
29	First National City Bank of New York	New York, N. Y.	1812
30	First National Bank of Wilkes-Barre	Wilkes-Barre, Pa.	1863
31	Penn Central National Bank	Huntingdon, Pa.	1863
35	Fishkill National Bank	Beacon, New York	1863
36	First National Bank of Findlay	Findlay, Ohio	1863
39	First National Bank of Towanda	Towanda, Pa.	1863
42	First National Bank of Strasburg	Strasburg, Pa.	1863
43	First National Bank of Salem	Salem, Ohio	1863
45	First National Bank and Trust Co. of Ellenville	Ellenville, N. Y.	1863
46	First National Bank of McConnelsville	McConnelsville, Ohio	1863
47	Terre Haute First National Bank	Terre Haute, Ind.	1863

Appendix C

Historic Banking Legislation

The National Currency Act of 1863 (excerpts)

An Act to provide a National Currency, secured by a Pledge of United States Stocks, and to provide for the Circulation and Redemption thereof.

Feb. 25, 1863.

Be it enacted by the Senate and House of Representatives of the United States of America in Congress assembled, That there shall be established in the Treasury Department a separate bureau, which shall be charged with the execution of this and all other laws that may be passed by Congress respecting the issue and regulation of a national currency secured by United States bonds. The chief officer of the said bureau shall be denominated the comptroller of the currency, and shall be under the general direction of the Secretary of the Treasury. He shall be appointed by the President, on the nomination of the Secretary of the Treasury, by and with the advice and consent of the Senate, and shall hold his office for the term of five years unless sooner removed by the President, by and with the advice and consent of the Senate; he shall receive an annual salary of five thousand dollars; he shall have a competent deputy, appointed by the Secretary, whose salary shall be two thousand five hundred dollars, and who shall possess the power and perform the duties attached by law to the office of comptroller during a vacancy in such office, and during his absence or inability; he shall employ, from time to time, the necessary clerks to discharge such duties as he shall direct, which clerks shall be appointed and classified by the Secretary of the Treasury in the manner now provided by law. Within fifteen days from the time of notice of his appointment, the comptroller shall take and subscribe the oath of office prescribed by the Constitution and laws of the United States; and he shall give to the United States a bond in the penalty of one hundred thousand dollars, with not less than two responsible freeholders as sureties, to be approved by the Secretary of the Treasury, conditioned for the faithful discharge of the duties of his office. The deputy comptroller so appointed shall also take the oath of office prescribed by the Constitution and laws of the United States, and shall give a like bond in the penalty of fifty thousand dollars. The comptroller and deputy comptroller shall not, either directly or indirectly, be interested in any association issuing national currency under the provisions of this act.

Sec. 3. And be it further enacted, That there shall be assigned to the comptroller of the currency by the Secretary of the Treasury suitable rooms in the treasury building for conducting the business of the currency bureau, in which shall be safe and secure fire-proof vaults, in which it shall be the duty of the comptroller to deposit and safely keep all the plates and other valuable things belonging to his department; and the comptroller shall from time to time furnish the necessary furniture, stationery, fuel, lights, and other proper conveniences for the transaction of the said business.

Sec. 5. And be it further enacted, That associations for carrying on the business of banking may be formed by any number of persons, not less in any case than five.

Sec. 6. And be it further enacted, That persons uniting to form such an association shall, under their hands and seals, make a certificate which shall specify—

First. The name assumed by such association.

Second. The place where its operations of discount and deposite [sic] are to be carried on; designating the State, Territory, or district, and also the particular city, town, or village.

Third. The amount of its capital stock, and the number of shares into which the same shall be divided; which capital stock shall not be less than fifty thousand dollars; and in cities whose population is over ten

> Bureau of currency.
>
> Comptroller of currency; appointment; term; salary.
>
> Deputy comptroller; salary; duties.
>
> Clerks.
>
> Oath and bond of Comptroller and deputy.
>
> Rooms in Treasury building for bureau.
>
> Fire-proof vaults.
>
> Banking associations, how formed.
>
> Certificate to specify what.

thousand persons, the capital stock shall not be less than one hundred thousand dollars.

Fourth. The names and places of residence of the shareholders, and the number of shares held by each of them.

Fifth. The time when such association shall commence.

Sixth. A declaration that said certificate is made to enable such persons to avail themselves of the advantages of this act.

Certificate to be acknowledged, certified, and preserved in office of comptroller.

Authenticated copies.

The said certificate shall be acknowledged before a judge of some court of record or a notary public, and the acknowledgment thereof certified under the seal of such court or notary, and shall be transmitted, together with a copy of the articles of association which shall have been adopted, to the comptroller of the currency, who shall record and carefully preserve the same in his office. Copies of such certificate, duly certified by the comptroller, and authenticated by his seal of office, shall be legal and sufficient evidence in all courts and places within the United States, or the jurisdiction of the Government thereof, of the existence of such association, and of every other matter or thing which could be proved by the production of the original certificate.

Capital stock, how paid in.

Sec. 7. And be it further enacted, That at least thirty per centum of the capital stock of such association shall be paid in at the time of the commencement of its banking business, and the remainder of the capital stock of such association shall be paid in instalments of at least ten per centum each on the whole amount to which the association shall be limited, as frequently as one instalment at the end of each succeeding two months from the time of the commencement of its banking operations, until the whole of the capital stock shall be paid in.

Comptroller to examine and see if requisitions of this act are complied with.

Sec. 9. And be it further enacted, That whenever a certificate shall have been transmitted to the comptroller of the currency, as provided in this act, and the association transmitting the same shall notify the comptroller that at least thirty per centum of its capital stock has been paid as aforesaid, and that such association has complied with all the provisions of this act required to be complied with before such association shall be authorized to commence the business of banking, and that such association is desirous of commencing such business, the comptroller shall immediately proceed, in such manner as he shall by general rules prescribe, to examine the condition of such association; to ascertain especially the amount of money paid in on account of its capital stock; the name and place of residence of each of the directors of such association, and the amount of the capital stock of which each is the bona fide owner, and generally whether such association has complied with all the requirements of this act to entitle it to engage in the business of banking; and shall cause to be made, and attested by the oaths of a majority of the directors and by the president or cashier of such association, a statement of all the facts necessary to enable the comptroller to determine whether such association is lawfully entitled to commence the business of banking under this act.

If lawfully entitled to begin banking, comptroller to give certificate to that effect.

Sec. 10. And be it further enacted, That if, upon a careful examination of the facts so reported, and of any other facts which may come to the knowledge of the comptroller, whether by means of a special commission appointed by him for the purpose of inquiring into the condition of such association, or otherwise, it shall appear that such association is lawfully entitled to commence the business of banking, the comptroller shall give to such association a certificate under his hand and official seal, showing that such association has complied with all the provisions of this act required to be complied with before being entitled to commence the business of banking under it, and that such association is authorized to commence said business accordingly; and it shall be the duty of such association to

Certificate to be published.

cause said certificate to be published in some newspaper, published in the city or county where such association is located, for at least sixty days next after the issuing thereof: *Provided,* That if no newspaper is published in such city or county, such certificate shall be published as the comptroller of the currency shall direct.

Sec. 11. And be it further enacted, That every association formed pursuant to the provisions of this act may make and use a common seal, and shall have succession by the name designated in its articles of association and for the period limited therein, not, however, exceeding twenty years from the passage of this act; by such name may make contracts, sue and be sued, complain and defend in any court of law or equity as fully as natural persons, and may make by-laws, approved by the comptroller of the currency, not inconsistent with the laws of the United States or the provisions of this act, for the election of directors, the management of its property, the regulation of its affairs, and for the transfer of its stock; and shall have power to carry on the business of banking by obtaining and issuing circulating notes in accordance with the provisions of this act; by discounting bills, notes, and other evidences of debt; by receiving deposits; by buying and selling gold and silver bullion, foreign coins, and bills of exchange; by loaning money on real and personal security, in the manner specified in their articles of association, for the purposes authorized by this act, and by exercising such incidental powers as shall be necessary to carry on such business; to choose one of their number as president of such association, and to appoint a cashier and such other officers and agents as their business may require; and to remove such president, cashier, officers, and agents at pleasure, and appoint others in their place; and their usual business shall be transacted in banking offices located at the places specified respectively in its certificate of association, and not elsewhere.

Association may have common seal, name, and continue not over twenty years. Powers of association.

Business, where to be transacted.

Sec. 12. And be it further enacted, That the shares of associations formed under this act shall be deemed personal property, and shall be transferable on the books of the association in such manner as may be prescribed in the by-laws or articles of association; and every person becoming a shareholder by such transfer shall, in proportion to his shares, succeed to all the rights and liabilities of the prior holder of such shares; and no change shall be made in the articles of association by which the rights, remedies, or security of the existing creditors of the association shall be impaired. For all debts, contracted by such association for circulation, deposits, or otherwise, each shareholder shall be liable to the amount, at their par value, of the shares held by him in addition to the amount invested in such shares.

Shares to be personal property.

How transferable.

Shareholder personally liable to twice the amount of his shares.

Sec. 13. And be it further enacted, That it shall be lawful for any association formed under this act, by its articles of association, to provide for an increase of its capital from time to time as may be deemed expedient, subject to the limitations of this act; but no such increase shall be valid until the increased capital shall be paid in, and notice thereof shall have been transmitted to the comptroller of the currency, and his certificate obtained, specifying the amount of such increase of capital stock, and that the same has been duly paid to such association.

Capital stock, how may be increased.

Sec. 14. And be it further enacted, That it shall be lawful for any such association to purchase, hold, and convey real estate as follows:

First. Such as shall be necessary for its immediate accommodation in the transaction of its business.

Second. Such as shall be mortgaged to it in good faith by way of security for loans made by such association, or for moneys due thereto.

Third. Such as shall be conveyed to it in satisfaction of debts previously contracted in the course of its dealings.

Fourth. Such as it shall purchase at sales under judgments, decrees, or mortgage held by such association.

Such association shall not purchase or hold real estate in any other case or for any other purpose than as specified in this section.

Real estate of such association.

Sec. 15. And be it further enacted, That every association, after having complied with the provisions of this Act preliminary to the commencement of banking business under its provisions, shall transfer and deliver to the treasurer of the United States any United States bonds bearing interest to an amount not less than one third of the capital stock paid in; which bonds shall be deposited with the treasurer of the United States, and by him safely kept in his office until the same shall be otherwise disposed of, in pursuance of the provisions of this act.

Associations, before commencing banking business, to transfer to treasurer United States bonds,

Sec. 16. And be it further enacted, That upon the making of any such transfer and delivery, the association making the same shall be entitled and shall be entitled to receive ninety per cent. of their current value in circulating currency notes.

to receive from the comptroller of the currency circulating notes of different denominations, in blank, registered and countersigned as hereinafter provided, equal in amount to ninety per centum of the current market value of the United States bonds so transferred and delivered, but not exceeding the par value thereof, if bearing interest at the rate of six per centum, or of equivalent United States bonds bearing a less rate of interest; and at no time shall the total amount of such notes, issued to any such association, exceed the amount at such time actually paid in of its capital stock.

Issue of circulating notes under this act, not to exceed $300,000,000.

How to be apportioned.

Sec. 17. And be it further enacted, That the entire amount of circulating notes to be issued under this act shall not exceed three hundred millions of dollars. One hundred and fifty millions of which sum shall be apportioned to associations in the States, in the District of Columbia, and in the Territories, according to representative population, and the remainder shall be apportioned by the Secretary of the Treasury among associations formed in the several States, in the District of Columbia, and in the Territories, having due regard to the existing banking capital, resources, and business, of such States, District, and Territories.

Circulating notes, how to be prepared.

Notes to express what.

Sec. 18. And be it further enacted, That, in order to furnish suitable notes for circulation, the comptroller of the currency is hereby authorized and required, under the direction of the Secretary of the Treasury, to cause plates to be engraved in the best manner to guard against counterfeiting and fraudulent alterations, and to have printed therefrom, and numbered, such quantity of circulating notes, in blank, of the denominations of five dollars, ten dollars, twenty dollars, fifty dollars, one hundred dollars, five hundred dollars, and one thousand dollars, as may be required to supply, under this act, the associations entitled to receive the same; which notes shall express upon their face that they are secured by United States bonds, deposited with the treasurer of the United States, and issued under the provisions of this act, which statement shall be attested by the written or engraved signatures of the treasurer and register, and by the imprint of the seal of the treasury; and shall also express upon their face the promise of the association receiving the same, to pay on demand, attested by the signatures of the president, or vice-president, and cashier; and the said notes shall bear such devices and such other statements, and shall be in such form, as the Secretary of the Treasury shall, by regulation, direct.

Associations to have what amount of money on hand.

When not to make new loans, &c.

What may be deemed lawful money.

Sec. 41. And be it further enacted, That every such association shall at all times have on hand, in lawful money of the United States, an amount equal to at least twenty-five per centum of the aggregate amount of its outstanding notes of circulation and its deposits; and whenever the amount of its outstanding notes of circulation and its deposits shall exceed the above-named proportion for the space of twelve days, or whenever such lawful money of the United States shall at any time fall below the amount of twenty-five per centum of its circulation and deposits, such association shall not increase its liabilities by making any new loans or discounts otherwise than by discounting or purchasing bills of exchange, payable at sight, nor make any dividend of its profits, until the required proportion between the aggregate amount of its outstanding notes of circulation and its deposits and lawful money of the United States shall be restored: *Provided, however,* That clearing-house certificates, representing specie or lawful money specially deposited for the purpose of any clearing-house association, shall be deemed to be lawful money in the possession of any association belonging to such clearing-house holding and owning such certificates, and considered to be a part of the lawful money which such association is required to have, under the foregoing provisions of this section: *Provided, further,* That any balance due to any association organized under this act in other places from any association in the cities of Boston, Providence, New York, Philadelphia, Baltimore, Cincinnati, Chicago, St. Louis, or New Orleans, in good credit, subject to be drawn for at sight, and available to redeem their circulating notes and deposits, may be deemed to be a part of the lawful money which such association in other places than the cities of Boston, Providence, New York, Philadelphia, Baltimore, Cincinnati, Chicago, St.

Louis, and New Orleans, are required to have by the foregoing pro-visions of this section, to the extent of three fifths of the said amount of twenty-five per centum required. And it shall be competent for the comptroller of the currency to notify any such association whose lawful money reserve, as aforesaid, shall fall below said proportion of twenty-five per centum, to make good such reserve; and if such association shall fail for thirty days thereafter so to make good its reserve of lawful money of the United States, the comptroller may, with the concurrence of the Secretary of the Treasury, appoint a receiver to wind up the business of such association, as provided in this act.

The National Bank Act of 1864

An Act to provide a National Currency, secured by a Pledge of United States Bonds, and to provide for the Circulation and Redemption thereof.

June 3, 1864.
1865, ch. 78, §§ 6,7.
Post, p. 484.

Be it enacted by the Senate and House of Representatives of the United States of America in Congress assembled, That there shall be established in the treasury department a separate bureau, which shall be charged with the execution of this and all other laws that may be passed by congress respecting the issue and regulation of a national currency secured by United States bonds. The chief officer of the said bureau shall be deno-minated the comptroller of the currency, and shall be under the general direction of the Secretary of the Treasury. He shall be appointed by the President, on the recommendation of the Secretary of the Treasury, by and with the advice and consent of the Senate, and shall hold his office for the term of five years unless sooner removed by the President, upon reasons to be communicated by him to the Senate; he shall receive an annual salary of five thousand dollars; he shall have a competent deputy, appointed by the secretary, whose salary shall be two thousand five hundred dollars, and who shall possess the power and perform the duties attached by law to the office of comptroller during a vacancy in such office and during his absence or inability; he shall employ, from time to time, the necessary clerks to dis-charge such duties as he shall direct, which clerks shall be appointed and classified by the Secretary of the Treasury in the manner now provided by law. Within fifteen days from the time of notice of his appointment the comptroller shall take and subscribe the oath of office prescribed by the constitution and laws of the United States; and he shall give to the United States a bond in the penalty of one hundred thousand dollars, with not less than two responsible sureties, to be approved by the Secretary of the Treas-ury, conditioned for the faithful discharge of the duties of his office. The deputy-comptroller so appointed shall also take the oath of office prescribed by the constitution and laws of the United States, and shall give a like bond in the penalty of fifty thousand dollars. The comptroller and deputy-comp-troller shall not, either directly or indirectly, be interested in any association issuing national currency under the provisions of this act.

Currency bureau established.

Comptroller of the currency.

Appointment.

Term of office.

Salary.

Deputy comptroller.

Clerks.

Comptroller to take oath within what time.

Bond.

Oath and bond of deputy comptroller.

Not to be interested in any banking association.

Sec. 2. And be it further enacted, That the comptroller of the cur-rency, with the approval of the Secretary of the Treasury, shall devise a seal, with suitable inscriptions, for his office, a description of which, with a certificate of approval by the Secretary of the Treasury, shall be filed in the office of the Secretary of State with an impression thereof, which shall there-upon become the seal of office of the comptroller of the currency, and the same may be renewed when necessary. Every certificate, assignment, and conveyance executed by the comptroller, in pursuance of any authority con-ferred on him by law, and sealed with his seal of office, shall be received in evidence in all places and courts whatsoever; and all copies of papers in the office of the comptroller, certified by him and authenticated by the said seal, shall in all cases be evidence equally and in like manner as the original. An impression of such seal directly on the paper shall be as valid as if made on wax or wafer.

Seal of currency bureau,

and where to be kept.

Certain papers under such seal to be evidence.

Impression may be upon paper.

Sec. 3. And be it further enacted, That there shall be assigned to the comptroller of the currency by the Secretary of the Treasury suitable rooms in the treasury building for conducting the business of the currency bureau, in which shall be safe and secure fire-proof vaults, in which it shall be the duty of the comptroller to deposit and safely keep all the plates not neces-

Rooms for currency bureau.

Fire-proof vaults.

sarily in the possession of engravers or printers, and other valuable things belonging to his department; and the comptroller shall from time to time furnish the necessary furniture, stationery, fuel, lights, and other proper conveniences for the transaction of the said business.

Sec. 4. *And be it further enacted,* That the term "United States Bonds," as used in this act, shall be construed to mean all registered bonds now issued, or that may hereafter be issued, on the faith of the United States by the Secretary of the Treasury in pursuance of law.

Sec. 5. *And be it further enacted,* That associations for carrying on the business of banking may be formed by any number of persons, not less in any case than five, who shall enter into articles of association, which shall specify in general terms the object for which the association is formed, and may contain any other provisions, not inconsistent with the provisions of this act, which the association may see fit to adopt for the regulation of the business of the association and the conduct of its affairs, which said articles shall be signed by the persons uniting to form the association, and a copy of them forwarded to the comptroller of the currency, to be filed and preserved in his office.

Sec. 6. *And be it further enacted,* That the persons uniting to form such an association shall, under their hands, make an organization certificate, which shall specify—

First. The name assumed by such association, which name shall be subject to the approval of the comptroller.

Second. The place where its operations of discount and deposit are to be carried on, designating the state, territory, or district, and also the particular county and city, town, or village.

Third. The amount of its capital stock, and the number of shares into which the same shall be divided.

Fourth. The names and places of residence of the shareholders, and the number of shares held by each of them.

Fifth. A declaration that said certificate is made to enable such persons to avail themselves of the advantages of this act.

The said certificate shall be acknowledged before a judge of some court of record or a notary public, and such certificate, with the acknowledgement thereof authenticated by the seal of such court or notary, shall be transmitted to the comptroller of the currency, who shall record and carefully preserve the same in his office. Copies of such certificate, duly certified by the comptroller, and authenticated by his seal of office, shall be legal and sufficient evidence in all courts and places within the United States, or the jurisdiction of the government thereof, of the existence of such association, and of every other matter or thing which could be proved by the production of the original certificate.

Sec. 7. *And be it further enacted,* That no association shall be organized under this act, with a less capital than one hundred thousand dollars, nor in a city whose population exceeds fifty thousand persons, with a less capital than two hundred thousand dollars: **Provided,** That banks with a capital of not less than fifty thousand dollars may, with the approval of the Secretary of the Treasury, be organized in any place the population of which does not exceed six thousand inhabitants.

Sec. 8. *And be it further enacted,* That every association formed pursuant to the provisions of this act shall, from the date of the execution of its organization certificate, be a body corporate, but shall transact no business except such as may be incidental to its organization and necessarily preliminary, until authorized by the comptroller of the currency to commence the business of banking. Such association shall have power to adopt a corporate seal, and shall have succession by the name designated in its organization certificate, for the period of twenty years from its organization, unless sooner dissolved according to the provisions of its articles of association, or by the act of its shareholders owning two thirds of its stock, or unless the franchise shall be forfeited by a violation of this act; by such name it may make contracts, sue and be sued, complain and defend, in any court of law and equity as fully as natural persons; it may elect or appoint directors, and by its board of directors appoint a president, vice-president, cashier, and other officers, define their duties, require bonds of them and fix the penalty thereof, dismiss said officers or any of them at pleasure, and appoint others to fill their places, and exercise under this act all such incidental powers as shall be necessary to carry on the business of banking by discounting and negotiating promissory notes, drafts, bills of exchange, and other evidences of debt; by receiving deposits; by buying and selling exchange, coin, and bullion; by loaning money on personal security; by obtaining, issuing, and circulating notes according to the provisions of this act; and its board of directors shall also have power to define and regulate by by-laws, not inconsistent with the provisions of this act, the manner in which its stock shall be transferred, its directors elected or appointed, its officers appointed, its property transferred, its general business conducted, and all the privileges granted by this act to associations organized under it shall be exercised and enjoyed; and its usual business shall be transacted at an office or banking house located in the place specified in its organization certificate. **By-laws.**

Sec. 9. And be it further enacted, That the affairs of every association shall be managed by not less than five directors, one of whom shall be the president. Every director shall, during his whole term of service, be a citizen of the United States; and at least three fourths of the directors shall have resided in the state, territory, or district in which such association is located one year next preceding their election as directors, and be residents of the same during their continuance in office. Each director shall own, in his own right, at least ten shares of the capital stock of the association of which he is a director. Each director, when appointed or elected, shall take an oath that **Oath.** he will, so far as the duty devolves on him, diligently and honestly administer the affairs of such association, and will not knowingly violate, or willingly permit to be violated, any of the provisions of this act, and that he is the bona fide owner, in his own right, of the number of shares of stock required by this act, subscribed by him, or standing in his name on the books of the association, and that the same is not hypothecated, or in any way pledged, as security for any loan or debt; which oath, subscribed by himself, and certified by the officer before whom it is taken, shall be immediately transmitted to the comptroller of the currency, and by him filed and preserved in his office. **Directors; qualifications; one to be president.**

Sec. 10. And be it further enacted, That the directors of any association first elected or appointed shall hold their places until their successors shall be elected and qualified. All subsequent elections shall be held annually on such day in the month of January as may be specified in the articles of association; and the directors so elected shall hold their places for one year, and until their successors are elected and qualified. But any director ceasing to be the owner of the requisite amount of stock, or having in any other manner become disqualified, shall thereby vacate his place. Any vacancy in the board shall be filled by appointment by the remaining directors, and any director so appointed shall hold his place until the next election. If from any cause an election of directors shall not be made at the time appointed, the association shall not for that cause be dissolved, but an election may be held on any subsequent day, thirty days' notice thereof in all cases having been given in a newspaper published in the city, town, or county in which the association is located; and if no newspaper is published in such city, town, or county, such notice shall be published in a newspaper published nearest thereto. If the articles of association do not fix the day on which the election shall be held, or if the election should not be held on the day fixed, the day for the election shall be designated by the board of directors in their by-laws, or otherwise: **Provided,** That if the directors fail to fix the day, as aforesaid, shareholders representing two thirds of the shares may. **Term of office of directors. Elections. Vacancies, how filled.**

Sec. 11. And be it further enacted, That in all elections of directors, and in deciding all questions at meetings of shareholders, each shareholder shall be entitled to one vote on each share of stock held by him. Shareholders may vote by proxies duly authorized in writing; but no officer, clerk, teller, or book-keeper of such association shall act as proxy; and no shareholder whose liability is past due and unpaid shall be allowed to vote. **Voting and proxies.**

Sec. 12. And be it further enacted, That the capital stock of any association formed under this act shall be divided into shares of one hundred dollars each, and be deemed personal property and transferable on the books of the association in such manner as may be prescribed in the **Capital stock to be divided into shares.**

by-laws or articles of association; and every person becoming a shareholder by such transfer shall, in proportion to his shares, succeed to all the rights and liabilities of the prior holder of such shares, and no change shall be made in the articles of association by which the rights, remedies, or security of the existing creditors of the association shall be impaired. The shareholders of each association formed under the provisions of this act, and of each existing bank or banking association that may accept the provisions of this act, shall be held individually responsible, equally and ratably, and not one for another, for all contracts, debts, and engagements of such association to the extent of the amount of their stock therein at the par value thereof, in addition to the amount invested in such shares; except that the shareholders of any banking association now existing under state laws, having not less than five millions of dollars of capital actually paid in, and a surplus of twenty per centum on hand, both to be determined by the comptroller of the currency, shall be liable only to the amount invested in their shares; and such surplus of twenty per centum shall be kept undiminished, and be in addition to the surplus provided for in this act; and if at any time there shall be a deficiency in said surplus of twenty per centum, the said banking association shall not pay any dividends to its shareholders until such deficiency shall be made good; and in case of such deficiency, the comptroller of the currency may compel said banking association to close its business and wind up its affairs under the provisions of this act. And the comptroller shall have authority to withhold from an association his certificate authorizing the commencemement of business, whenever he shall have reason to suppose that the shareholders thereof have formed the same for any other than the legitimate objects contemplated by this act.

Sec. 13. And be it further enacted, That it shall be lawful for any association formed under this act, by its articles of association, to provide for an increase of its capital from time to time, as may be deemed expedient, subject to the limitations of this act: *Provided,* That the maximum of such increase in the articles of association shall be determined by the comptroller of the currency; and no increase of capital shall be valid until the whole amount of such increase shall be paid in, and notice thereof shall have been transmitted to the comptroller of the currency, and his certificate obtained specifying the amount of such increase of capital stock, with his approval thereof, and that it has been duly paid in as part of the capital of such association. And every association shall have power, by the vote of shareholders owning two thirds of its capital stock, to reduce the capital of such association to any sum not below the amount required by this act, in the formation of associations: *Provided,* That by no such reduction shall its capital be brought below the amount required by this act for its outstanding circulation, nor shall any such reduction be made until the amount of the proposed reduction has been reported to the comptroller of the currency and his approval thereof obtained.

Sec. 14. And be it further enacted, That at least fifty per centum of the capital stock of every association shall be paid in before it shall be authorized to commence business; and the remainder of the capital stock of such association shall be paid in instalments of at least ten per centum each on the whole amount of the capital as frequently as one instalment at the end of each succeeding month from the time it shall be authorized by the comptroller to commence business; and the payment of each instalment shall be certified to the comptroller, under oath, by the president or cashier of the association.

Sec. 15. And be it further enacted, That if any shareholder, or his assignee, shall fail to pay any instalment on the stock when the same is required by the foregoing section to be paid, the directors of such association may sell the stock of such delinquent shareholder at public auction, having given three weeks' previous notice thereof in a newspaper published and of general circulation in the city or county where the association is located, and if no newspaper is published in said city or county, then in a newspaper published nearest thereto, to any person who will pay the highest price therefor, and not less than the amount then due thereon, with the expenses of advertisement and sale; and the excess, if any, shall be paid to the delinquent shareholder. If no bidder can be found who will pay for such

Margin notes:
- Transfer.
- Rights of existing creditors not be impaired.
- Individual liability.
- When comptroller may withhold certificate.
- Increase of capital stock.
- Maximum.
- Minimum.
- Amount to be paid in before commencing business.
- Remainder, when to be paid.
- Proceedings, if shareholder fails to pay instalments.
- Stock of delinquent shareholders to be sold.

stock the amount due thereon to the association, and the cost of advertisement and sale, the amount previously paid shall be forfeited to the association, and such stock shall be sold as the directors may order, within six months from the time of such forfeiture, and if not sold it shall be cancelled and deducted from the capital stock of the association; and if such cancellation and reduction shall reduce the capital of the association below the minimum of capital required by this act, the capital stock shall, within thirty days from the date of such cancellation, be increased to the requirements of the act; in default of which a receiver may be appointed to close up the business of the association according to the provisions of the fiftieth section of this act.

Sec. 16. And be it further enacted, That every association, after having complied with the provisions of this act, preliminary to the commencement of banking business under its provisions, and before it shall be authorized to commence business, shall transfer and deliver to the treasurer of the United States any United States registered bonds bearing interest to an amount not less than thirty thousand dollars nor less than one third of the capital stock paid in, which bonds shall be deposited with the treasurer of the United States and by him safely kept in his office until the same shall be otherwise disposed of, in pursuance of the provisions of this act; and the Secretary of the Treasury is hereby authorized to receive and cancel any United States coupon bonds, and to issue in lieu thereof registered bonds of like amount, bearing a like rate of interest, and having the same time to run; and the deposit of bonds shall be, by every association, increased as its capital may be paid up or increased, so that every association shall at all times have on deposit with the treasurer registered United States bonds to the amount of at least one third of its capital stock actually paid in: *Provided,* That nothing in this section shall prevent an association that may desire to reduce its capital or to close up its business and dissolve its organization from taking up its bonds upon returning to the comptroller its circulating notes in the proportion hereinafter named in this act, nor from taking up any excess of bonds beyond one third of its capital stock and upon which no circulating notes have been delivered.

United States registered bonds to be deposited with treasurer to an amount equal to one third of the capital stock.

Deposit to be increased;

may be diminished.

Sec. 17. And be it further enacted, That whenever a certificate shall have been transmitted to the comptroller of the currency, as provided in this act, and the association transmitting the same shall notify the comptroller that at least fifty per centum of its capital stock has been paid in as aforesaid, and that such association has complied with all the provisions of this act as required to be complied with before such association shall be authorized to commence the business of banking, the comptroller shall examine into the condition of such association, ascertain especially the amount of money paid in on account of its capital, the name and place of residence of each of the directors of such association, and the amount of the capital stock of which each is the bona fide owner, and generally whether such association has complied with all the requirements of this act to entitle it to engage in the business of banking; and shall cause to be made and attested by the oaths of a majority of the directors and by the president or cashier of such association, a statement of all the facts necessary to enable the comptroller to determine whether such association is lawfully entitled to commence the business of banking under this act.

Comptroller to examine and determine if association can commence business.

Sec. 18. And be it further enacted, That if, upon a careful examination of the facts so reported and of any other facts which may come to the knowledge of the comptroller, whether by means of a special commission appointed by him for the purpose of inquiring into the condition of such association, or otherwise, it shall appear that such association is lawfully entitled to commence the business of banking, the comptroller shall give to such association a certificate, under his hand and official seal, that such association has complied with all the provisions of this act required to be complied with before being entitled to commence the business of banking under it, and that such association is authorized to commence said business accordingly; and it shall be the duty of the association to cause said certificate to be published in some newspaper published in the city or county where the association is located for at least sixty days next after the issuing thereof: *Provided,* That if no newspaper is published in such city or

When association is found entitled to commence business, comptroller to give certificate.

Certificate to be published.

county the certificate shall be published in a newspaper published nearest thereto.

Transfers of bonds by association, to be made to the treasurer in trust.

Sec. 19. And be it further enacted, That all transfers of United States bonds which shall be made by any association under the provisions of this act shall be made to the treasurer of the United States in trust for the association, with a memorandum written or printed on each bond, and signed by the cashier or some other officer of the association making the deposit, a receipt therefor to be given to said association, or by the comptroller of the currency, or by a clerk appointed by him for that purpose, stating that it is held in trust for the association on whose behalf such transfer is made, and as security for the redemption and payment of any circulating notes that have been or may be delivered to such association. No assignment or transfer of any such bonds by the treasurer shall be deemed valid or of binding force and effect unless countersigned by the comptroller of the currency. It shall be the duty of the comptroller of the currency to keep in his office a book in which shall be entered the name of every association from whose accounts such transfer of bonds is made by the treasurer, and the name of the party to whom such transfer is made; and the par value of the bonds so transferred shall be entered therein; and it shall be the duty of the comptroller, immediately upon countersigning and entering the same, to advise by mail the association from whose account such transfer was made of the kind and numerical designation of the bonds and the amount thereof so transferred.

How executed.

Comptroller to keep transfer book, &c.

Sec. 20. And be it further enacted, That it shall be the duty of the comptroller of the currency to countersign and enter in the book, in the manner aforesaid, every transfer or assignment of any bonds held by the treasurer presented for his signature; and the comptroller shall have at all times during office hours access to the books of the treasurer, for the purpose of ascertaining the correctness of the transfer or assignment presented to him to countersign; and the treasurer shall have the like access to the book above mentioned, kept by the comptroller, during office hours, to ascertain the correctness of the entries in the same; and the comptroller shall also at all times have access to the bonds on deposit with the treasurer, to ascertain their amount and condition.

Transfers to be countersigned and entered.

Books to be accessible.

Sec. 21. And be it further enacted, That upon the transfer and delivery of bonds to the treasurer, as provided in the foregoing section, the association making the same shall be entitled to receive from the comptroller of the currency circulating notes of different denominations, in blank, registered and countersigned as hereinafter provided, equal in amount to ninety per centum of the current market value of the United States bonds so transferred and delivered, but not exceeding ninety per centum of the amount of said bonds at the par value thereof, if bearing interest at a rate not less than five per centum per annum; and at no time shall the total amount of such notes, issued to any such association, exceed the amount at such time actually paid in of its capital stock.

Associations, after transfer, may receive circulating notes.

1865, ch. 82.
Post, p. 498.

Limit of amount.

Sec. 22. And be it further enacted, That the entire amount of notes for circulation to be issued under this act shall not exceed three hundred millions of dollars. In order to furnish suitable notes for circulation, the comptroller of the currency is hereby authorized and required, under the direction of the Secretary of the Treasury, to cause plates and dies to be engraved, in the best manner to guard against counterfeiting and fraudulent alterations, and to have printed therefrom, and numbered, such quantity of circulating notes, in blank, of the denominations of one dollar, two dollars, three dollars, five dollars, ten dollars, twenty dollars, fifty dollars, one hundred dollars, five hundred dollars, and one thousand dollars, as may be required to supply, under this act, the associations entitled to receive the same; which notes shall express upon their face that they are secured by United States bonds, deposited with the treasurer of the United States by the written or engraved signatures of the treasurer and register, and the imprint of the seal of the treasury; and shall also express upon their face the promise of the association receiving the same to pay on demand, attested by the signatures of the president or vice-president and cashier. And the said notes shall bear such devices and such other statements, and shall be in such form, as the Secretary of the Treasury shall, by regulation, direct: **Provided,** That not more than one sixth part of the notes furnished to an associa-

Entire circulation not to exceed $300,000,000.

Comptroller to prepare the notes.

Denominations.

Notes to express what.

Devices.

tion shall be of a less denomination than five dollars, and that after specie payments shall be resumed no association shall be furnished with notes of a less denomination than five dollars.

Sec. 23. And be it further enacted. That after any such association shall have caused its promise to pay such notes on demand to be signed by the president or vice-president and cashier thereof, in such manner as to make them obligatory promissory notes, payable on demand, at its place of business, such association is hereby authorized to issue and circulate the same as money; and the same shall be received at par in all parts of the United States in payment of taxes, excises, public lands, and all other dues to the United States, except for duties on imports; and also for all salaries and other debts and demands owing by the United States to individuals, corporations, and associations within the United States, except interest on the public debt, and in redemption of the national currency. And no such association shall issue post notes or any other notes to circulate as money than such as are authorized by the foregoing provisions of this act.

When notes may be circulated as money;

to be received for all dues, except, &c.

Post notes, &c., not to be issued.

Sec. 24. And be it further enacted, That it shall be the duty of the comptroller of the currency to receive worn-out or mutilated circulating notes issued by any such banking association, and also, on due proof of the destruction of any such circulating notes, to deliver in place thereof to such association other blank circulating notes to an equal amount. And such worn-out or mutilated notes, after a memorandum shall have been entered in the proper books, in accordance with such regulations as may be established by the comptroller as well as all circulating notes which shall have been paid or surrendered to be cancelled, shall be burned to ashes in presence of four persons, one to be appointed by the Secretary of the Treasury, one by the comptroller of the currency, one by the treasurer of the United States, and one by the association, under such regulations as the Secretary of the Treasury may prescribe. And a certificate of such burning, signed by the parties so appointed, shall be made in the books of the comptroller, and a duplicate thereof forwarded to the association whose notes are thus cancelled.

Worn-out and muti- lated notes.

Sec. 25. And be it further enacted, That it shall be the duty of every banking association having bonds deposited in the office of the treasurer of the United States, once or oftener in each fiscal year, and at such time or times during the ordinary business hours as said officer or officers may select, to examine and compare the bonds so pledged with the books of the comptroller and the accounts of the association, and, if found correct, to execute to the said treasurer a certificate setting forth the different kinds and the amounts thereof, and that the same are in the possession and custody of the treasurer at the date of such certificate. Such examination may be made by an officer or agent of such association, duly appointed in writing for that purpose, whose certificate before mentioned shall be of like force and validity as if executed by such president or cashier; and a duplicate signed by the treasurer shall be retained by the association.

Associations to ex- amine annually its bonds deposited, and make certificate.

Examination of associations.

Sec. 26. And be it further enacted, That the bonds transferred to and deposited with the treasurer of the United States, as hereinbefore provided, by any banking association for the security of its circulating notes, shall be held exclusively for that purpose, until such notes shall be redeemed, except as provided in this act; but the comptroller of the currency shall give to any such banking association powers of attorney to receive and appropriate to its own use the interest on the bonds which it shall have so transferred to the treasurer; but such powers shall become inoperative whenever such banking association shall fail to redeem its circulating notes as aforesaid. Whenever the market or cash value of any bonds deposited with the treasurer of the United States, as aforesaid, shall be reduced below the amount of the circulation issued for the same, the comptroller of the currency is hereby authorized to demand and receive the amount of such depreciation in other United States bonds at cash value, or in money, from the association receiving said bills, to be deposited with the treasurer of the United States as long as such depreciation continues. And said comptroller, upon the terms prescribed by the Secretary of the Treasury, may permit an exchange to be made of any of the bonds deposited with the treasurer by an association for other bonds of the United States authorized by this act to be received as security for circu-

Deposited bonds to be held exclusively to secure circula- tion.

Provision as to interest.

If bonds depreciate, security to be made good.

Bonds may be ex- changed, if, &c.;

lating notes, if he shall be of opinion that such an exchange can be made without prejudice to the United States, and he may direct the return of any of said bonds to the banking association which transferred the same, in sums of not less than one thousand dollars, upon the surrender to him and the cancellation of a proportionate amount of such circulating notes: *Provided,* That the remaining bonds which shall have been transferred by the banking association offering to surrender circulating notes shall be equal to the amount required for the circulating notes not surrendered by such banking association, and that the amount of bonds in the hands of the treasurer shall not be diminished below the amount required to be kept on deposit with him by this act: *And provided,* That there shall have been no failure by such association to redeem its circulating notes, and no other violation by such association of the provisions of this act, and that the market or cash value of the remaining bonds shall not be below the amount required for the circulation issued for the same.

Sec. 27. And be it further enacted, That it shall be unlawful for any officer acting under the provisions of this act to countersign or deliver to any association, or to any other company or person, any circulating notes contemplated by this act, except as hereinbefore provided, and in accordance with the true intent and meaning of this act. And any officer who shall violate the provisions of this section shall be deemed guilty of a high misdemeanor, and on conviction thereof shall be punished by fine not exceeding double the amount so countersigned and delivered, and imprisonment not less than one year and not exceeding fifteen years, at the discretion of the court in which he shall be tried.

Sec. 28. And be it further enacted, That it shall be lawful for any such association to purchase, hold, and convey real estate as follows:—

First. Such as shall be necessary for its immediate accommodation in the transaction of its business.

Second. Such as shall be mortgaged to it in good faith by way of security for debts previously contracted.

Third. Such as shall be conveyed to it in satisfaction of debts previously contracted in the course of its dealings.

Fourth. Such as it shall purchase at sales under judgments, decrees, or mortgages held by such association, or shall purchase to secure debts due to said association.

Such associations shall not purchase or hold real estate in any other case or for any other purpose than as specified in this section. Nor shall it hold the possession of any real estate under mortgage, or hold the title and possession of any real estate purchased to secure any debts due to it for a longer period than five years.

Sec. 29. And be it further enacted, That the total liabilities to any association, of any person, or of any company, corporation, or firm for money borrowed, including in the liabilities of a company or firm the liabilities of the several members thereof, shall at no time exceed one tenth part of the amount of the capital stock of such association actually paid in: *Provided,* That the discount of bona fide bills of exchange drawn against actually existing values, and the discount of commercial or business paper actually owned by the person or persons, corporation, or firm negotiating the same shall not be considered as money borrowed.

Sec. 30. And be it further enacted, That every association may take, receive, reserve, and charge on any loan or discount made, or upon any note, bill of exchange, or other evidences of debt, interest at the rate allowed by the laws of the state or territory where the bank is located, and no more, except that where by the laws of any state a different rate is limited for banks of issue organized under state laws, the rate so limited shall be allowed for associations organized in any such state under this act. And when no rate is fixed by the laws of the state or territory, the bank may take, receive, reserve, or charge a rate not exceeding seven per centum, and such interest may be taken in advance, reckoning the days for which the note, bill, or other evidence of debt has to run. And the knowingly taking, receiving, reserving, or charging a rate of interest greater than aforesaid shall be held and adjudged a forfeiture of the entire interest which the note, bill, or other evidence of debt carries with it, or which has been agreed to be

may be returned upon cancellation of circulating notes.

Proviso.

The countersigning and delivery of circulating notes, except as permitted by this act, made unlawful.

Penalty.

Associations may hold, &c., certain real estate.

Real estate.

No person, &c., to be liable to association for more than, &c.

Certain discounts not to be included.

Rate of interest.

Penalty for taking greater interest.

paid thereon. And in case a greater rate of interest has been paid, the person or persons paying the same, or their legal representatives, may recover back, in any action of debt, twice the amount of the interest thus paid from the association taking or receiving the same: *Provided,* That such action is commenced within two years from the time the usurious transaction occurred. But the purchase, discount, or sale of a bona fide bill of exchange, payable at another place than the place of such purchase, discount, or sale, at not more than the current rate of exchange for sight drafts in addition to the interest, shall not be considered as taking or receiving a greater rate of interest.

Sec. 31. And be it further enacted, That every association in the cities hereinafter named shall, at all times, have on hand, in lawful money of the United States, an amount equal to at least twenty-five per centum of the aggregate amount of its notes in circulation and its deposits; and every other association shall, at all times, have on hand, in lawful money of the United States, an amount equal to at least fifteen per centum of the aggregate amount of its notes in circulation, and of its deposits. And whenever the lawful money of any association in any of the cities hereinafter named shall be below the amount of twenty-five per centum of its circulation and deposits, and whenever the lawful money of any other association shall be below fifteen per centum of its circulation and deposits, such associations shall not increase its liabilities by making any new loans or discounts otherwise than by discounting or purchasing bills of exchange payable at sight, nor make any dividend of its profits until the required proportion between the aggregate amount of its outstanding notes of circulation and deposits and its lawful money of the United States shall be restored: *Provided,* That three fifths of said fifteen per centum may consist of balances due to an association available for the redemption of its circulating notes from associations approved by the comptroller of the currency, organized under this act, in the cities of Saint Louis, Louisville, Chicago, Detroit, Milwaukie, New Orleans, Cincinnati, Cleveland, Pittsburg, Baltimore, Philadelphia, Boston, New York, Albany, Leavenworth, San Francisco, and Washington City: *Provided, also,* That clearing-house certificates, representing specie or lawful money specially deposited for the purpose of any clearing-house association, shall be deemed to be lawful money in the possession of any association belonging to such clearing-house holding and owning such certificate, and shall be considered to be a part of the lawful money which such association is required to have under the foregoing provisions of this section: *Provided,* That the cities of Charleston and Richmond may be added to the list of cities in the national associations of which other associations may keep three fifths of their lawful money, whenever, in the opinion of the comptroller of the currency, the condition of the southern states will warrant it. And it shall be competent for the comptroller of the currency to notify any association, whose lawful money reserve as aforesaid shall be below the amount to be kept on hand as aforesaid, to make good such reserve; and if such association shall fail for thirty days thereafter so to make good its reserve of lawful money of the United States, the comptroller may, with the concurrence of the Secretary of the Treasury, appoint a receiver to wind up the business of such association, as provided in this act.

Sec. 32. And be it further enacted, That each association organized in any of the cities named in the foregoing section shall select, subject to the approval of the comptroller of the currency, an association in the city of New York, at which it will redeem its circulating notes at par. And each of such associations may keep one half of its lawful money reserve in cash deposits in the city of New York. And each association not organized within the cities named in the preceding section shall select, subject to the approval of the comptroller of the currency, an association in either of the cities named in the preceding section at which it will redeem its circulating notes at par, and the comptroller shall give public notice of the names of the associations so selected at which redemptions are to be made by the respective associations, and of any change that may be made of the association at which the notes of any association are redeemed. If any association shall fail either to make the selection or to redeem its notes as aforesaid, the comptroller of the currency may, upon receiving satisfactory evidence thereof, appoint a receiver, in the manner provided for in this act, to wind up its affairs: *Provided,* That nothing in this section shall relieve any association from its liability to redeem its circulating notes at its own counter, at par, in lawful money, on demand: *And provided, further,* That every association formed or existing under the provisions of this act shall take and receive at par, for any debt or liability to said association, any and all notes or bills issued by any association existing under and by virtue of this act.

Each association to take notes of other associations.

Dividends.

Sec. 33. And be it further enacted, That the directors of any association may, semi-annually, each year, declare a dividend of so much of the net profits of the association as they shall judge expedient; but each association shall, before the declaration of a dividend, carry one tenth part of its net profits of the preceding half year to its surplus fund until the same shall amount to twenty per centum of its capital stock.

Surplus funds.

Sec. 34. And be it further enacted, That every association shall make to the comptroller of the currency a report, according to the form which may be prescribed by him, verified by the oath or affirmation of the president or cashier of such association; which report shall exhibit in detail, and under appropriate heads, the resources and liabilities of the association before the commencement of business on the morning of the first Monday of the months of January, April, July, and October of each year, and shall transmit the same to the comptroller within five days thereafter. And any bank failing to make and transmit such report shall be subject to a penalty of one hundred dollars for each day after five days that such report is delayed beyond that time. And the comptroller shall publish abstracts of said reports in a newspaper to be designated by him for that purpose in the city of Washington, and the separate report of each association shall be published in a newspaper in the place where such association is established, or if there be no newspaper at such place, then in a newspaper published at the nearest place thereto, at the expense of the association making such report. In addition to the quarterly reports required by this section, every association shall, on the first Tuesday of each month, make to the comptroller of the currency a statement, under the oath of the president or cashier, showing the condition of the association making such statement, on the morning of the day next preceding the date of such statement, in respect to the following items and particulars, to wit: average amount of loans and discounts, specie, and other lawful money belonging to the association, deposits, and circulation. And associations in other places than those cities named in the thirty-first section of this act shall also return the amount due them available for the redemption of their circulation.

Associations to report to comptroller quarterly.

Contents of report.

Penalty for failing to report.

Comptroller to publish abstracts.

Monthly statements.

Sec. 35. And be it further enacted, That no association shall make any loan or discount on the security of the shares of its own capital stock, nor be the purchaser or holder of any such shares, unless such security or purchase shall be necessary to prevent loss upon a debt previously contracted in good faith; and stock so purchased or acquired shall, within six months from the time of its purchase, be sold or disposed of at public or private sale, in default of which a receiver may be appointed to close up the business of the association, according to the provisions of this act.

Associations not to make loans, &c., on the security of their own stock, &c.

Sec. 36. And be it further enacted, That no association shall at any time be indebted, or in any way liable, to an amount exceeding the amount of its capital stock at such time actually paid in and remaining undiminished by losses or otherwise, except on the following accounts, that is to say:—

First. On account of its notes of circulation.

Second. On account of moneys deposited with, or collected by, such association.

Third. On account of bills of exchange or drafts drawn against money actually on deposit to the credit of such association, or due thereto.

Fourth. On account of liabilities to its stockholders for dividends and reserved profits.

Indebtedness not to exceed capital stock, except, &c.

Sec. 37. And be it further enacted, That no association shall, either directly or indirectly, pledge or hypothecate any of its notes of circulation, for the purpose of procuring money to be paid in on its capital stock, or to be used in its banking operations, or otherwise; nor shall any association use

Associations not to hypothecate circulating notes, for, &c.;

its circulating notes, or any part thereof, in any manner or form, to create or increase its capital stock.

Sec. 38. And be it further enacted, That no association, or any member thereof, shall, during the time it shall continue its banking operations, withdraw, or permit to be withdrawn, either in form of dividends or otherwise, any portion of its capital. And if losses shall at any time have been sustained by any such association equal to or exceeding its undivided profits then on hand, no dividend shall be made; and no dividend shall ever be made by any association, while it shall continue its banking operations, to an amount greater than its net profits then on hand, deducting therefrom its losses and bad debts. And all debts due to any association, on which interest is past due and unpaid for a period of six months, unless the same shall be well secured, and shall be in process of collection, shall be considered bad debts within the meaning of this act: *Provided,* That nothing in this section shall prevent the reduction of the capital stock of the association under the thirteenth section of this act.

Sec. 39. And be it further enacted, That no association shall at any time pay out on loans or discounts, or in purchasing drafts or bills of exchange, or in payment of deposits, or in any other mode pay or put in circulation the notes of any bank or banking association which shall not, at any such time, be receivable, at par, on deposit and in payment of debts by the association so paying out or circulating such notes; nor shall it knowingly pay out or put in circulation any notes issued by any bank or banking association which at the time of such paying out or putting in circulation is not redeeming its circulating notes in lawful money of the United States.

Sec. 40. And be it further enacted, That the president and cashier of every such association shall cause to be kept at all times a full and correct list of the names and residences of all the shareholders in the association, and the number of shares held by each, in the office where its business is transacted; and such list shall be subject to the inspection of all the shareholders and creditors of the association, and the officers authorized to assess taxes under state authority, during business hours of each day in which business may be legally transacted; and a copy of such list, on the first Monday of July in each year, verified by the oath of such president or cashier, shall be transmitted to the comptroller of the currency.

Sec. 41. And be it further enacted, That the plates and special dies to be procured by the comptroller of the currency for the printing of such circulating notes shall remain under his control and direction, and the expenses necessarily incurred in executing the provisions of this act respecting the procuring of such notes, and all other expenses of the bureau, shall be paid out of the proceeds of the taxes or duties now or hereafter to be assessed on the circulation, and collected from associations organized under this act. And in lieu of all existing taxes, every association shall pay to the treasurer of the United States, in the months of January and July, a duty of one half of one per centum each half year from and after the first day of January, eighteen hundred and sixty-four, upon the average amount of its notes in circulation, and a duty of one quarter of one per centum each half year upon the average amount of its deposits, and a duty of one quarter of one per centum each half year, as aforesaid, on the average amount of its capital stock beyond the amount invested in United States bonds; and in case of default in the payment thereof by any association, the duties aforesaid may be collected in the manner provided for the collection of United States duties of other corporations, or the treasurer may reserve the amount of said duties out of the interest, as it may become due, on the bonds deposited with him by such defaulting association. And it shall be the duty of each association, within ten days from the first days of January and July of each year, to make a return, under the oath of its president or cashier, to the treasurer of the United States, in such form as he may prescribe, of the average amount of its notes in circulation, and of the average amount of its deposits, and of the average amount of its capital stock, beyond the amount invested in United States bonds, for the six months next preceding said first days of January and July as aforesaid, and in default of such return, and for each default thereof, each defaulting association shall forfeit and pay to the United States the sum of two hundred dollars, to be collected either out of the interest as it may become due such association on the bonds deposited with the treasurer, or, at his option, in the manner in which penalties are to be collected of other corporations under the laws of the United States; and in case of such default the amount of the duties to be paid by such association shall be assessed upon the amount of notes delivered to such association by the comptroller of the currency, and upon the highest amount of its deposits and capital stock, to be ascertained in such other manner as the treasurer may deem best: *Provided,* That nothing in this act shall be construed to prevent all the shares in any of the said associations, held by any person or body corporate, from being included in the valuation of the personal property of such person or corporation in the assessment of taxes imposed by or under state authority at the place where such bank is located, and not elsewhere, but not at a greater rate than is assessed upon other moneyed capital in the hands of individual citizens of such state: *Provided, further,* That the tax so imposed under the laws of any state upon the shares of any of the associations authorized by this act shall not exceed the rate imposed upon the shares in any of the banks organized under authority of the state where such association is located: *Provided, also,* That nothing in this act shall exempt the real estate of associations from either state, county, or municipal taxes to the same extent, according to its value, as other real estate is taxed.

Shares not hereby exempted from taxation by state authority.

Limit of state tax.

Real estate to be taxed.

Sec. 42. And be it further enacted, That any association may go into liquidation and be closed by the vote of its shareholders owning two thirds of its stock. And whenever such vote shall be taken it shall be the duty of the board of directors to cause notice of this fact to be certified, under the seal of the association, by its president or cashier, to the comptroller of the currency, and publication thereof to be made for a period of two months in a newspaper published in the city of New York, and also in a newspaper published in a city or town in which the association is located, and if no newspaper be there published, then in the newspaper published nearest thereto, that said association is closing up its affairs, and notifying the holders of its notes and other creditors to present the notes and other claims against the association for payment. And at any time after the expiration of one year from the time of the publication of such notice as aforesaid, the said association may pay over to the treasurer of the United States the amount of its outstanding notes in the lawful money of the United States, and take up the bonds which said association has on deposit with the treasurer for the security of its circulating notes; which bonds shall be assigned to the bank in the manner specified in the nineteenth section of this act, and from that time the outstanding notes of said association shall be redeemed at the treasury of the United States, and the said association and the shareholders thereof shall be discharged from all liabilities therefor.

How associations may be closed.

Proceedings.

Sec. 43. And be it further enacted, That the treasurer, on receiving from an association lawful money for the payment and redemption of its outstanding notes, as provided for in the preceding section of this act, shall execute duplicate receipts therefor, one to the association and the other to the comptroller of the currency, stating the amount received by him, and the purpose for which it has been received, which amount shall be paid into the treasury of the United States, and placed to the credit of such association upon redemption account. And it shall be the duty of the treasurer, whenever he shall redeem any of the notes of said association, to cause the same to be mutilated, and charged to the redemption account of said association; and all notes so redeemed by the treasurer shall, every three months, be certified to and burned in the manner prescribed in the twenty-fourth section of this act.

Treasurer to execute duplicate receipts.

Redeemed notes to be mutilated, &c.

Sec. 44. And be it further enacted, That any bank incorporated by special law, or any banking institution organized under a general law of any state, may, by authority of this act, become a national association under its provisions, by the name prescribed in its organization certificate; and in such case the articles of association and the organization certificate required by this act may be executed by a majority of the directors of the bank or banking institution; and said certificate shall declare that the owners of two thirds of the capital stock have authorized the directors to make such certificate and to change and convert the said bank or banking institution

State banks may become national associations.

into a national association under this act. And a majority of the directors, after executing said articles of association and organization certificate, shall have power to execute all other papers, and to do whatever may be required to make its organization perfect and complete as a national association. The shares of any such bank may continue to be for the same amount each as they were before said conversion, and the directors aforesaid may be the directors of the association until others are elected or appointed in accordance with the provisions of this act; and any state bank which is a stockholder in any other bank, by authority of state laws, may continue to hold its stock, although either bank, or both, may be organized under and have accepted the provisions of this act. When the comptroller shall give to such association a certificate, under his hand and official seal, that the provisions of this act have been complied with, and that it is authorized to commence the business of banking under it, the association shall have the same powers and privileges, and shall be subject to the same duties, responsibilities, and rules, in all respects as are prescribed in this act for other associations organized under it, and shall be held and regarded as an association under this act: *Provided, however,* That no such association shall have a less capital than the amount prescribed for banking associations under this act.

Sec. 45. And be it further enacted, That all associations under this act, when designated for that purpose by the Secretary of the Treasury, shall be depositaries of public money, except receipts from customs, under such regulations as may be prescribed by the Secretary; and they may also be employed as financial agents of the government; and they shall perform all such reasonable duties, as depositaries of public moneys and financial agents of the government, as may be required of them. And the Secretary of the Treasury shall require of the associations thus designated satisfactory security, by the deposit of United States bonds and otherwise, for the safe-keeping and prompt payment of the public money deposited with them, and for the faithful performance of their duties as financial agents of the government: *Provided,* That every association which shall be selected and designated as receiver or depositary of the public money shall take and receive at par all of the national currency bills, by whatever association issued, which have been paid in to the government for internal revenue, or for loans or stocks.

Sec. 46. And be it further enacted, That if any such association shall at any time fail to redeem, in the lawful money of the United States, any of its circulating notes, when payment thereof shall be lawfully demanded, during the usual hours of business, at the office of such association, or at its place of redemption aforesaid, the holder may cause the same to be protested, in one package, by a notary-public, unless the president or cashier of the association whose notes are presented for payment, or the president or cashier of the association at the place at which they are redeemable, shall offer to waive demand and notice of the protest, and shall, in pursuance of such offer, make, sign, and deliver to the party making such demand an admission in writing, stating the time of the demand, the amount demanded, and the fact of the non-payment thereof; and such notary-public, on making such protest, or upon receiving such admission, shall forthwith forward such admission or notice of protest to the comptroller of the currency, retaining a copy thereof. And after such default, on examination of the facts by the comptroller, and notice by him to the association, it shall not be lawful for the association suffering the same to pay out any of its notes, discount any notes or bills, or otherwise prosecute the business of banking, except to receive and safely keep money belonging to it, and to deliver special deposits: *Provided,* That if satisfactory proof be produced to such notary-public that the payment of any such notes is restrained by order of any court of competent jurisdiction, such notary-public shall not protest the same; and when the holder of such notes shall cause more than one note or package to be protested on the same day, he shall not receive pay for more than one protest.

Sec. 47. And be it further enacted, That on receiving notice that any such association has failed to redeem any of its circulating notes, as specified in the next preceding section, the comptroller of the currency, with the concurrence of the Secretary of the Treasury, may appoint a special agent (of whose appointment immediate notice shall be given to such association) who shall immediately proceed to ascertain whether such association has

Mode of procedure.

Association, when so designated, may be depositaries of public moneys, except, &c.;

may be financial agents.

Designated depositaries to pay promptly;

to receive national currency bills at par.

If associations fail to redeem their circulation, the notes may be protested, unless, &c.

Notice of protest, &c., to be forwarded to comptroller.

Association not to do business further, except, &c.

Notes not to be protested in certain cases.

Fees of notary. Upon notice of failure to redeem circulation, comptroller to send special agent to ascertain facts, refused to pay its circulating notes in the lawful money of the United States, when demanded as aforesaid, and report to the comptroller the fact so ascertained; and if, from such protest or the report so made, the comptroller shall be satisfied that such association has refused to pay its circulating notes as aforesaid and is in default, he shall, within thirty days after he shall have received notice of such failure, declare the United States bonds and securities pledged by such association forfeited to the United States, and the same shall thereupon be forfeited accordingly. And thereupon the comptroller shall immediately give notice in such manner as the Secretary of the Treasury shall, by general rules or otherwise, direct, to the holders of the circulating notes of such association to present them for payment at the treasury of the United States, and the same shall be paid as presented in lawful money of the United States; whereupon said comptroller may, in his discretion, cancel an amount of bonds pledged by such association equal at current market rates, not exceeding par, to the notes paid. And it shall be lawful for the Secretary of the Treasury, from time to time, to make such regulations respecting the disposition to be made of such circulating notes after presentation thereof for payment as aforesaid, and respecting the perpetuation of the evidence of the payment thereof as may seem to him proper; but all such notes, on being paid, shall be cancelled. And for any deficiency in the proceeds of the bonds pledged by such association, when disposed of as hereinafter specified, to reimburse to the United States the amount so expended in paying the circulating notes of such association, the United States shall have a first and paramount lien upon all the assets of such association; and such deficiency shall be made good out of such assets in preference to any and all other claims whatsoever, except the necessary costs and expenses of administering the same.

Sec. 48. And be it further enacted, That whenever the comptroller shall become satisfied, as in the last preceding section specified, that any association has refused to pay its circulating notes as therein mentioned, he may, instead of cancelling the United States bonds pledged by such association, as provided in the next preceding section, cause so much of them as may be necessary to redeem the outstanding circulating notes of such association to be sold at public auction in the city of New York, after giving thirty days' notice of such sale to such association.

Sec. 49. And be it further enacted, That the comptroller of the currency may, if he shall be of opinion that the interests of the United States will be best promoted thereby, sell at private sale any of the bonds pledged by such association, and receive therefor either money or the circulating notes of such failing association: *Provided,* That no such bonds shall be sold by private sale for less than par, nor less than the market value thereof at the time of sale: *And provided, further,* That no sales of any such bonds, either public or private, shall be complete until the transfer thereof shall have been made with the formalities prescribed in this act.

Sec. 50. And be it further enacted, That on becoming satisfied, as specified in this act, that any association has refused to pay its circulating notes as therein mentioned, and is in default, the comptroller of the currency may forthwith appoint a receiver, and require of him such bond and security as he shall deem proper, who, under the direction of the comptroller, shall take possession of the books, records, and assets of every description of such association, collect all debts, dues, and claims belonging to such association, and, upon the order of a court of record of competent jurisdiction, may sell or compound all bad or doubtful debts, and, on a like order, sell all the real and personal property of such association, on such terms as the court shall direct; and may, if necessary to pay the debts of such association, enforce the individual liability of the stockholders provided for by the twelfth section of this act; and such receiver shall pay over all money so made to the treasurer of the United States, subject to the order of the comptroller of the currency, and also make report to the comptroller of the currency of all his acts and proceedings. The comptroller shall thereupon cause notice to be given, by advertisement in such newspapers as he may direct, for three consecutive months, calling on all persons who may have claims against such association to present the same, and to make legal proof thereof. And from time to time the comptroller, after full provision shall

---

Side notes (left margin):

when to declare securities forfeited,

to notify holders of notes to present them for payment,

to pay notes and cancel bonds.

The United States to have priority of lien upon assets for any deficiency in redemption of circulation.

Bonds pledged as security may be sold at auction;

or at private sale.

Proviso.

Comptroller may appoint a receiver to close affairs of defaulting association.

Bond and duties of receiver, &c.

have been first made for refunding to the United States any such deficiency in redeeming the notes of such association as is mentioned in this act, shall make a ratable dividend of the money so paid over to him by such receiver on all such claims as may have been proved to his satisfaction or adjudicated in a court of competent jurisdiction; and from time to time, as the proceeds of the assets of such association shall be paid over to him, he shall make further dividends, as aforesaid, on all claims previously proved or adjudicated; and the remainder of such proceeds, if any, shall be paid over to the shareholders of such association, or their legal representatives, in proportion to the stock by them respectively held: *Provided, however,* That if such association against which proceedings have been so instituted, on account of any alleged refusal to redeem its circulating notes as aforesaid, shall deny having failed to do so, such association may, at any time within ten days after such association shall have been notified of the appointment of an agent, as provided in this act, apply to the nearest circuit, or district, or territorial court of the United States, to enjoin further proceedings in the premises; and such court, after citing the comptroller of the currency to show cause why further proceedings should not be enjoined, and after the decision of the court or finding of a jury that such association has not refused to redeem its circulating notes, when legally presented, in the lawful money of the United States, shall make an order enjoining the comptroller, and any receiver acting under his direction, from all further proceedings on account of such alleged refusal.

If association denies that it has failed to redeem its notes, it may apply to the courts for an injunction.

Proceedings.

Sec. 51. And be it further enacted, That all fees for protesting the notes issued by any such banking association shall be paid by the person procuring the protest to be made, and such banking association shall be liable therefor; but no part of the bonds pledged by such banking association, as aforesaid, shall be applied to the payment of such fees. And all expenses of any preliminary or other examinations into the condition of any association shall be paid by such association; and all expenses of any receivership shall be paid out of the assets of such association before distribution of the proceeds thereof.

Fees for protest and other expenses, how to be paid.

Sec. 52. And be it further enacted, That all transfer of the notes, bonds, bills of exchange, and other evidences of debt owing to any association, or of deposits to its credit; all assignments of mortgages, sureties on real estate, or of judgments or decrees in its favor; all deposits of money, bullion, or other valuable thing for its use, or for the use of any of its shareholders or creditors; and all payments of money to either, made after the commission of an act of insolvency, or in contemplation thereof, with a view to prevent the application of its assets in the manner prescribed by this act, or with a view to the preference of one creditor to another, except in payment of its circulating notes, shall be utterly null and void.

Transfers, assignments, &c., in contemplation of insolvency, &c., to be void.

Sec. 53. And be it further enacted, That if the directors of any association shall knowingly violate, or knowingly permit any of the officers, agents, or servants of the association to violate any of the provisions of this act, all the rights, privileges, and franchises of the association derived from this act shall be thereby forfeited. Such violation shall, however, be determined and adjudged by a proper circuit, district, or territorial court of the United States, in a suit brought for that purpose by the comptroller of the currency, in his own name, before the association shall be declared dissolved. And in cases of such violation, every director who participated in or assented to the same shall be held liable in his personal and individual capacity for all damages which the association, its shareholders, or any other person, shall have sustained in consequence of such violation.

Penalty upon directors for violations of this act.

Violation, how to be determined.

Personal liability.

Sec. 54. And be it further enacted, That the comptroller of the currency, with the approbation of the Secretary of the Treasury, as often as shall be deemed necessary or proper, shall appoint a suitable person or persons to make an examination of the affairs of every banking association, which person shall not be a director or other officer in any association whose affairs he shall be appointed to examine, and who shall have power to make a thorough examination into all the affairs of the association, and, in doing so, to examine any of the officers and agents thereof on oath; and shall make a full and detailed report of the condition of the association to the comptroller. And the association shall not be subject to any other visitorial

Comptroller may appoint person to examine the affairs of any association.

Duty of such examiner.

powers than such as are authorized by this act, except such as are vested in the several courts of law and chancery. And every person appointed to make such examination shall receive for his services at the rate of five dollars for each day by him employed in such examination, and two dollars for every twenty-five miles he shall necessarily travel in the performance of his duty, which shall be paid by the association by him examined.

Pay.

Sec. 55. *And be it further enacted,* That every president, director, cashier, teller, clerk, or agent of any association, who shall embezzle, abstract, or wilfully misapply any of the moneys, funds, or credits of the association, or shall, without authority from the directors, issue or put in circulation any of the notes of the association, or shall, without such authority, issue or put forth any certificate of deposit, draw any order or bill of exchange, make any acceptance, assign any note, bond, draft, bill of exchange, mortgage, judgment, or decree, or shall make any false entry in any book, report, or statement of the association, with intent, in either case, to injure or defraud the association or any other company, body politic or corporate, or any individual person, or to deceive any officer of the association, or any agent appointed to examine the affairs of any such association, shall be deemed guilty of a misdemeanor, and upon conviction thereof shall be punished by imprisonment not less than five nor more than ten years.

Penalty upon officers, &c., of association for embezzlement, &c., of funds.

Sec. 56. *And be it further enacted,* That all suits and proceedings arising out of the provisions of this act, in which the United States or its officers or agents shall be parties, shall be conducted by the district attorneys of the several districts, under the direction and supervision of the solicitor of the treasury.

District attorneys to conduct certain suits.

Sec. 57. *And be it further enacted.* That suits, actions, and proceedings, against any association under this act, may be had in any circuit, district, or territorial court of the United States held within the district in which such association may be established; or in any state, county, or municipal court in the county or city in which said association is located, having jurisdiction in similar cases: *Provided, however,* That all proceedings to enjoin the comptroller under this act shall be had in a circuit, district, or territorial court of the United States, held in the district in which the association is located.

In what courts, suits, &c., under this act may be prosecuted.

Proceedings for injunctions to be in what courts.

Sec. 58. *And be it further enacted,* That every person who shall mutilate, cut, deface, disfigure, or perforate with holes, or shall unite or cement together, or do any other thing to any bank bill, draft, note, or other evidence of debt, issued by any such association, or shall cause or procure the same to be done, with intent to render such bank bill, draft, note, or other evidence of debt unfit to be reissued by said association, shall, upon conviction, forfeit fifty dollars to the association who shall be injured thereby, to be recovered by action in any court having jurisdiction.

Penalty for mutilating notes to make them unfit for reissue.

Sec. 59. *And be it further enacted,* That if any person shall falsely make, forge, or counterfeit, or cause or procure to be made, forged, or counterfeited, or willingly aid or assist in falsely making, forging, or counterfeiting, any note in imitation of, or purporting to be in imitation of, the circulating notes issued under the provisions of this act, or shall pass, utter, or publish, or attempt to pass, utter, or publish, any false, forged, or counterfeited note, purporting to be issued by any association doing a banking business under the provisions of this act, knowing the same to be falsely made, forged, or counterfeited, or shall falsely alter, or cause or procure to be falsely altered, or willingly aid or assist in falsely altering, any such circulating notes, issued as aforesaid, or shall pass, utter, or publish, or attempt to pass, utter, or publish, as true, any falsely altered or spurious circulating note issued, or purporting to have been issued, as aforesaid, knowing the same to be falsely altered or spurious, every such person shall be deemed and adjudged guilty of felony, and being thereof convicted by due course of law shall be sentenced to be imprisoned and kept at hard labor for a period of not less than five years, nor more than fifteen years, and fined in a sum not exceeding one thousand dollars.

Penalty for counterfeiting notes,

for knowingly uttering, &c.,

Sec. 60. *And be it further enacted,* That if any person shall make or engrave, or cause or procure to be made or engraved, or shall have in his custody or possession any plate, die, or block after the similitude of any plate, die or block from which any circulating notes issued as aforesaid shall

for engraving, &c., plates for forging notes, &c.,

have been prepared or printed, with intent to use such plate, die, or block, or cause or suffer the same to be used, in forging or counterfeiting any of the notes issued as aforesaid, or shall have in his custody or possession any blank note or notes engraved and printed after the similitude of any notes issued as aforesaid, with intent to use such blanks, or cause or suffer the same to be used, in forging or counterfeiting any of the notes issued as aforesaid, or shall have in his custody or possession any paper adapted to the making of such notes, and similar to the paper upon which any such notes shall have been issued, with intent to use such paper, or cause or suffer the same to be used, in forging or counterfeiting any of the notes issued as aforesaid, every such person, being thereof convicted by due course of law, shall be sentenced to be imprisoned and kept to hard labor for a term not less than five or more than fifteen years, and fined in a sum not exceeding one thousand dollars.

for having blank notes, &c., with intent,

for having paper, &c.

Sec. 61. And be it further enacted, That it shall be the duty of the comptroller of the currency to report annually to congress at the commencement of its session—

Comptroller to report annually to congress.

First. A summary of the state and condition of every association from whom reports have been received the preceding year, at the several dates to which such reports refer, with an abstract of the whole amount of banking capital returned by them, of the whole amount of their debts and liabilities, the amount of circulating notes outstanding, and the total amount of means and resources, specifying the amount of lawful money held by them at the times of their several returns, and such other information in relation to said associations as, in his judgment, may be useful.

Contents of report.

Contents of comptroller's report to congress.

Second. A statement of the associations whose business has been closed during the year, with the amount of their circulation redeemed and the amount outstanding.

Third. Any amendment to the laws relative to banking by which the system may be improved, and the security of the holders of its notes and other creditors may be increased.

Fourth. The names and compensation of the clerks employed by him, and the whole amount of the expenses of the banking department during the year. And such report shall be made by or before the first day of December in each year, and the usual number of copies for the use of the senate and house, and one thousand copies for the use of the department, shall be printed by the public printer and in readiness for distribution at the first meeting of congress.

Sec. 62. And be it further enacted, That the act entitled "An act to provide a national currency, secured by a pledge of United States stocks, and to provide for the circulation and redemption thereof," approved February twenty-fifth, eighteen hundred and sixty-three, is hereby repealed: *Provided,* That such repeal shall not affect any appointments made, acts done, or proceedings had, or the organization, acts, or proceedings of any association organized or in the process of organization under the act aforesaid: *And provided, also,* That all such associations so organized or in process of organization shall enjoy all the rights and privileges granted, and be subject to all the duties, liabilities, and restrictions imposed by this act, and with the approval of the comptroller of the currency, in lieu of the name specified in their respective organization certificates, may take any other name preferred by them and duly certified to the comptroller, without prejudice to any right acquired under this act, or under the act hereby repealed; but no such change shall be made after six months from the passage of this act: *Provided, also,* That the circulation issued or to be issued by such association shall be considered as a part of the circulation provided for in this act.

Repeal of act of 1863, ch. 58.
Vol. xii. p. 665.

Saving clauses.

Sec. 63. And be it further enacted, That persons holding stock as executors, administrators, guardians, and trustees, shall not be personally subject to any liabilities as stockholders; but the estates and funds in their hands shall be liable in like manner and to the same extent as the testator, intestate, ward, or person interested in said trust-funds would be if they were respectively living and competent to act and hold the stock in their own names.

Executors, trustees, &c., holding stock, not to be personally liable.

Sec. 64. *And be it further enacted,* That congress may at any time amend, alter, or repeal this act.

Approved, June 3, 1864.

The Redistribution Act of 1874

An Act fixing the amount of United States notes, providing for a redistribution of the national-bank currency, and for other purposes.

Be it enacted by the Senate and House of Representatives of the United States of America in Congress assembled, That the act entitled "An act to provide a national currency secured by a pledge of United States bonds, and to provide for the circulation and redemption thereof," approved June third, eighteen hundred and sixty-four, shall hereafter be known as "the national-bank act."

Sec. 2. That section thirty-one of the "the national-bank act" be so amended that the several associations therein provided for shall not hereafter be required to keep on hand any amount of money whatever, by reason of the amount of their respective circulations; but the moneys required by said section to be kept at all times on hand shall be determined by the amount of deposits in all respects, as provided for in the said section.

Release of reserves
on circulation.
Reserves on deposits
retained.
Five per cent. on
circulation to be
deposited in treasury
for redemption of
circulation.

Sec. 3. That every association organized, or to be organized, under the provisions of the said act, and of the several acts amendatory thereof, shall at all times keep and have on deposit in the treasury of the United States, in lawful money of the United States, a sum equal to five per centum of its circulation, to be held and used for the redemption of such circulation; which sum shall be counted as a part of its lawful reserve, as provided in section two of this act; and when the circulating-notes of any such associations, assorted or unassorted, shall be presented for redemption, in sums of one thousand dollars, or any multiple thereof, to the Treasurer of the United States, the same shall be redeemed in United States notes. All notes so redeemed shall be charged by the Treasurer of the United States to the respective associations issuing the same, and he shall notify them severally, on the first day of each month, or oftener, at his discretion, of the amount of such redemptions; and whenever such redemptions for any association shall amount to the sum of five hundred dollars, such association so notified shall forthwith deposit with the Treasurer of the United States a sum in United States notes equal to the amount of its circulating-notes so redeemed. And all notes of national banks worn, defaced, mutilated, or otherwise unfit for circulation shall, when received by any assistant treasurer, or at any designated depository of the United States, be forwarded to the Treasurer of the United States for redemption as provided herein. And when such redemptions have been so re-imbursed, the circulating-notes so redeemed shall be forwarded to the respective associations by which they were issued; but if any of such notes are worn, mutilated, defaced, or rendered otherwise unfit for use, they shall be forwarded to the Comptroller of the Currency and destroyed and replaced as now provided by law: *Provided,* That each of said associations shall re-imburse to the Treasury the charges for transportation, and the costs for assorting such notes; and the associations hereafter organized shall also severally re-imburse to the Treasury the cost of engraving such plates as shall be ordered by each association respectively; and the amount assessed upon each association shall be in proportion to the circulation redeemed, and be charged to the fund on deposit with the Treasurer: *And provided further,* That so much of section thirty-two of said national-bank act requiring or permitting the redemption of its circulating-notes elsewhere than at its own counter except as provided for in this section, is hereby repealed.

To be counted as
part of reserve.
Notes to be re-
deemed on presenta-
tion to Treasurer.
To be charged to
respective associa-
tions.
Monthly notice of
redemptions.
Deposit with Treas-
urer amount equal to
notes redeemed,
when.
Assistant treasurer
and depositaries to
forward mutilated
notes to Treasurer
for redemption.
Notes redeemed to
be forwarded to
associations.
Associations to pay
cost of transporting
and assorting.
Associations here-
after organized to
pay cost of engrav-
ing plates.
Proportionate as-
sessment of charges.
Repeal of part of §
32, ch. 106, vol.
xiii, p. 109. No re-
demption elsewhere
than as herein pro-
vided for.

Sec. 4. That any association organized under this act, or any of the acts of which this is an amendment, desiring to withdraw its circulation-notes, in whole or in part, may, upon the deposit of lawful money with the Treasurer of the United States in sums of not less than nine thousand dollars, take up the bonds which said association has on deposit with the treasurer for the security of such circulating-notes; which bonds shall be assigned to the bank in the manner specified in the nineteenth section of the national-bank act; and the outstanding notes of said association, to an amount equal to the legal-tender notes deposited, shall be redeemed at the Treasury of the United States, and destroyed as now provided by law: *Provided,* That the amount of the bonds on deposit for circulation shall not be reduced below fifty thousand dollars.

Sec. 19, ch. 106, vol. xiii, p. 105. Redemption and destruction of outstanding notes. Limit to reduction of bonds on deposit.

Sec. 5. That the Comptroller of the Currency shall, under such rules and regulations as the Secretary of the Treasury may prescribe, cause the charter-numbers of the association to be printed upon all national-bank notes which may be hereafter issued by him.

Charter numbers of associations to be printed on national-bank notes.

Sec. 6. That the amount of United States notes outstanding and to be used as a part of the circulating-medium, shall not exceed the sum of three hundred and eighty-two million dollars, which said sum shall appear in each monthly statement of the public debt, and no part thereof shall be held or used as a reserve.

Limit to amount of outstanding United States notes.

No part to be held as reserve.

Sec. 7. That so much of the act entitled "An act to provide for the redemption of the three per centum temporary loan certificates, and for an increase of national bank notes" as provides that no circulation shall be withdrawn under the provisions of section six of said act, until after the fifty-four millions granted in section one of said act shall have been taken up, is hereby repealed; and it shall be the duty of the Comptroller of the Currency, under the direction of the Secretary of the Treasury, to proceed forthwith, and he is hereby authorized and required, from time to time, as applications shall be duly made therefor, and until the full amount of fifty-five million dollars shall be withdrawn, to make requisitions upon each of the national banks described in said section, and in the manner therein provided, organized in States having an excess of circulation, to withdraw and return so much of their circulation as by said act may be apportioned to be withdrawn from them, or, in lieu thereof, to deposit in the Treasury of the United States lawful money sufficient to redeem such circulation, and upon the return of the circulation required, or the deposit of lawful money, as herein provided, a proportionate amount of the bonds held to secure the circulation of such association as shall make such return or deposit shall be surrendered to it.

Repeal of part of ch. 252, vol. xvi, p. 251.

Withdrawal of currency to secure equitable distribution.

Sec. 8. That upon the failure of the national banks upon which requisition for circulation shall be made, or of any of them, to return the amount required, or to deposit in the Treasury lawful money to redeem the circulation required, within thirty days, the Comptroller of the Currency shall at once sell, as provided in section forty-nine of the national-currency act approved June third, eighteen hundred and sixty-four, bonds held to secure the redemption of the circulation of the association or associations which shall so fail, to an amount sufficient to redeem the circulation required of such association or associations, and with the proceeds, which shall be deposited in the Treasury of the United States, so much of the circulation of such association or associations shall be redeemed as will equal the amount required and not returned and if there be any excess of proceeds over the amount required for such redemption, it shall be returned to the association or associations whose bonds shall have been sold. And it shall be the duty of the Treasurer, assistant treasurers, designated depositaries, and national bank depositaries of the United States, who shall be kept informed by the Comptroller of the Currency of such associations as shall fail to return circulation as required, to assort and return to the Treasury for redemption the notes of such associations as shall come into their hands until the amount required shall be redeemed, and in like manner to assort and return to the Treasury, for redemption, the notes of such national banks as have failed, or gone into voluntary liquidation for the purpose of winding up their affairs, and of such as shall hereafter so fail or go into liquidation.

When national banks fail to comply with requisitions, duty of Comptroller.

Sec. 49, ch. 106, vol. xiii, p. 114.

Duty of treasurer, assistants, and depositaries.

Redemption of notes of banks in liquidation.

Sec. 9. That from and after the passage of this act it shall be lawful for the Comptroller of the Currency, and he is hereby required, to issue circulating-notes without delay, as applications therefor are made, not to exceed the sum of fifty-five million dollars, to associations organized, or to be organized, in those States and Territories having less than their proportion of circulation, under an apportionment made on the basis of population and

Redistribution of currency withdrawn.

of wealth, as shown by the returns of the census of eighteen hundred and seventy; and every association hereafter organized shall be subject to, and be governed by, the rules, restrictions, and limitations, and possess the rights, privileges, and franchises, now or hereafter to be prescribed by law as to national banking associations, with the same power to amend, alter, and repeal provided by "the national-bank act:" *Provided,* That the whole

Limit to withdrawal. amount of circulation withdrawn and redeemed from banks transacting business shall not exceed fifty-five million dollars, and that such circulation shall be withdrawn and redeemed as it shall be necessary to supply the circulation previously issued to the banks in those States having less than their apportionment: *And provided further,* That not more than thirty million dollars

Proviso. tionment: *And provided further,* That not more than thirty million dollars shall be withdrawn and redeemed as herein contemplated during the fiscal year ending June thirtieth, eighteen hundred and seventy-five.

APPROVED, June 20, 1874.

The McFadden Act of 1927

February 25, 1927.
[H. R. 2.]
[Public, No. 639.]

An Act to further amend the national banking laws and the Federal Reserve Act, and for other purposes.

National banking associations.
Vol. 40, p. 1044, amended.

Be it enacted by the Senate and House of Representatives of the United States of America in Congress assembled, That the Act entitled "An Act to provide for the consolidation of the national banking associations," approved November 7, 1918, be amended by adding at the end thereof a new section to read as follows:

Consolidation of State, etc., banks with national, allowed.

"*Sec. 3.* That any bank incorporated under the laws of any State, or any bank incorporated in the District of Columbia, may be consolidated with a national banking association located in the same county, city, town, or village under the charter of such national banking association on such terms and conditions as may be lawfully agreed upon by a majority of the board of directors of each association or bank proposing to consolidate, and which

Agreement of shareholders necessary.

agreement shall be ratified and confirmed by the affirmative vote of the shareholders of each such association or bank owning at least two-thirds of its capital stock outstanding, or by a greater proportion of such capital stock in the case of such State bank if the laws of the State where the same is

Publication in newspapers of notice of meeting.

organized so require, at a meeting to be held on the call of the directors after publishing notice of the time, place, and object of the meeting for four consecutive weeks in some newspaper of general circulation published in the place where the said association or bank is situated, and in the legal newspaper for the publication of legal notices or advertisements, if any such paper has been designated by the rules of a court in the county where such association or bank is situated, and if no newspaper is published in the place, then in a paper of general circulation published nearest thereto, unless such notice of meeting is waived in writing by all stockholders of any such association or bank, and after sending such notice to each shareholder of record by registered mail at least ten days prior to said meeting, but any additional notice shall be given to the shareholders of such State bank which may be required by the laws of the State where the same is organized. The

Capital stock requirement.

capital stock of such consolidated association shall not be less than that required under existing law for the organization of a national banking association in the place in which such consolidated association is located; and

All property rights, franchises, etc., transferred.

all the rights, franchises, and interests of such State or District bank so consolidated with a national banking association in and to every species of property, real, personal, and mixed, and choses in action thereto belonging, shall be deemed to be transferred to and vested in such national banking association into which it is consolidated without any deed or other transfer, and the said consolidated national banking association shall hold and enjoy the same and all rights of property, franchises, and interests including the

Fiduciary rights.

right of succession as trustee, executor, or in any other fiduciary capacity in the same manner and to the same extent as was held and enjoyed by such State or District bank so consolidated with such national banking association.

Dissenting shareholders to be paid for holdings.

When such consolidation shall have been effected and approved by the comptroller any shareholder of either the association or of the State or District bank so consolidated, who has not voted for such consolidation, may give notice to the directors of the consolidated association within twenty days

214   **Appendices**

from the date of the certificate of approval of the comptroller that he dissents from the plan of consolidation as adopted and approved, whereupon he shall be entitled to receive the value of the shares so held by him, to be ascertained by an appraisal made by a committee of three persons, one to be selected by the shareholder, one by the directors of the consolidated association, and the third by the two so chosen; and in case the value so fixed shall not be satisfactory to such shareholder he may within five days after being notified of the appraisal appeal to the Comptroller of the Currency, who shall cause a reappraisal to be made, which shall be final and binding; and the consolidated association shall pay the expenses of reappraisal, and the value as ascertained by such appraisal or reappraisal shall be deemed to be a debt due and shall be forthwith paid to said shareholder by said consolidated association, and the shares so paid for shall be surrendered and, after due notice, sold at public auction within thirty days after the final appraisement provided for in this Act; and if the shares so sold at public auction shall be sold at a price greater than the final appraised value, the excess in such sale price shall be paid to the said shareholder; and the consolidated association shall have the right to purchase such shares at public auction, if it is the highest bidder therefor, for the purpose of reselling such shares within thirty days thereafter to such person or persons and at such price as its board of directors by resolution may determine. The liquidation of such shares of stock in any State bank shall be determined in the manner prescribed by the law of the State in such cases if such provision is made in the State law; otherwise as hereinbefore provided. No such consolidation shall be in contravention of the law of the State under which such bank is incorporated.

"The words 'State bank,' 'State banks,' 'bank,' or 'banks,' as used in this section, shall be held to include trust companies, savings banks, or other such corporations or institutions carrying on the banking business under the authority of State laws."

Sec. 2. (a) That section 5136 of the Revised Statutes of the United States, subsection "second" thereof as amended, be amended to read as follows:

"Second. To have succession from the date of the approval of this Act, or from the date of its organization if organized after such date of approval until such time as it be dissolved by the act of its shareholders owning two-thirds of its stock, or until its franchise becomes forfeited by reason of violation of law, or until terminated by either a general or a special Act of Congress or until its affairs be placed in the hands of a receiver and finally wound up by him."

(b) That section 5136 of the Revised Statutes of the United States, subsection "seventh" thereof, be further amended by adding at the end of the first paragraph thereof the following:

"*Provided,* That the business of buying and selling investment securities shall hereafter be limited to buying and selling without recourse marketable obligations evidencing indebtedness of any person, copartnership, association, or corporation, in the form of bonds, notes and/or debentures, commonly known as investment securities, under such further definition of the term 'investment securities' as may by regulation be prescribed by the Comptroller of the Currency, and the total amount of such investment securities of any one obligor or maker held by such association shall at no time exceed 25 per centum of the amount of the capital stock of such association actually paid in and unimpaired and 25 per centum of its unimpaired surplus fund, but this limitation as to total amount shall not apply to obligations of the United States, or general obligations of any State or of any political subdivision thereof, or obligations issued under authority of the Federal Farm Loan Act: *And provided further,* That in carrying on the business commonly known as the safe-deposit business no such association shall invest in the capital stock of a corporation organized under the law of any State to conduct a safe-deposit business in an amount in excess of 15 per centum of the capital stock of such association actually paid in and unimpaired and 15 per centum of its unimpaired surplus," so that the subsection as amended shall read as follows:

"Seventh. To exercise by its board of directors, or duly authorized officers

Appraisal of value thereof.

Reappraisal by Comptroller if value not satisfactory.

Expenses of.

Sale of surrendered shares.

Liquidation of stock under State laws, etc.

No consolidation contravening laws of the State.

Inclusion of trust companies, etc., as banks.

Corporate powers. R.S., sec. 5136, p.993, amended.

Succession continued until dissolved by shareholders. Vol. 42, p.767, amended.

General banking business. R.S., sec. 5136, p. 993, amended.

Matter inserted.

Amended section.

or agents, subject to law, all such incidental powers as shall be necessary to carry on the business of banking; by discounting and negotiating promissory notes, drafts, bills of exchange, and other evidences of debt; by receiving deposits; by buying and selling exchange, coin, and bullion; by loaning money on personal security; and by obtaining, issuing, and circulating notes according to the provisions of this title: *Provided,* That the business of buying and selling investment securities shall hereafter be limited to buying and selling without recourse marketable obligations evidencing indebtedness of any person, copartnership, association, or corporation, in the form of bonds, notes and/or debentures, commonly known as investment securities, under such further definition of the term 'investment securities' as may by regulation be prescribed by the Comptroller of the Currency, and the total amount of such investment securities of any one obligor or maker held by such association shall at no time exceed 25 per centum of the amount of the capital stock of such association actually paid in and unimpaired and 25 per centum of its unimpaired surplus fund, but this limitation as to total amount shall not apply to obligations of the United States, or general obligations of any State or of any political subdivision thereof, or obligations issued under authority of the Federal Farm Loan Act: *And provided further,* That in carrying on the business commonly known as the safe deposit business no such association shall invest in the capital stock of a corporation organized under the law of any State to conduct a safe deposit business in an amount in excess of 15 per centum of the capital stock of such association actually paid in and unimpaired and 15 per centum of its unimpaired surplus.

"But no association shall transact any business except such as is incidental and necessarily preliminary to its organization, until it has been authorized by the Comptroller of the Currency to commence the business of banking."

Sec. 3. That section 5137 of the Revised Statutes of the United States, subsection "First" thereof, be amended to read as follows:

"First. Such as shall be necessary for its accommodation in the transaction of its business."

Sec. 4. That section 5138 of the Revised Statutes of the United States, as amended, be amended to read as follows:

"SEC. 5138. No national banking association shall be organized with a less capital than $100,000, except that such associations with a capital of not less than $50,000 may, with the approval of the Secretary of the Treasury, be organized in any place the population of which does not exceed six thousand inhabitants, and except that such associations with a capital of not less than $25,000 may, with the sanction of the Secretary of the Treasury, be organized in any place the population of which does not exceed three thousand inhabitants. No such association shall be organized in a city the population of which exceeds fifty thousand persons with a capital of less than $200,000, except that in the outlying districts of such a city where the State laws permit the organization of State banks with a capital of $100,000 or less, national banking associations now organized or hereafter organized may, with the approval of the Comptroller of the Currency, have a capital of not less than $100,000."

Sec. 5. That section 5142 of the Revised Statutes of the United States, as amended, be amended to read as follows:

"SEC. 5142. Any national banking association may, with the approval of the Comptroller of the Currency, and by a vote of shareholders owning two-thirds of the stock of such associations, increase its capital stock to any sum approved by the said comptroller, but no increase in capital shall be valid until the whole amount of such increase is paid in and notice thereof, duly acknowledged before a notary public by the president, vice president, or cashier of said association, has been transmitted to the Comptroller of the Currency and his certificate obtained specifying the amount of such increase in capital stock and his approval thereof, and that it has been duly paid in as part of the capital of such association: *Provided, however,* That a national banking association may, with the approval of the Comptroller of the Currency, and by the vote of shareholders owning two-thirds of the stock of such association, increase its capital stock by the declaration of a stock dividend, provided that the surplus of said association, after the approval of the increase, shall be at least equal to 20 per centum of the capital stock as increased. Such increase shall not be effective until a certificate certifying to such declaration of dividend, signed by the president, vice president, or cashier of said association and duly acknowledged before a notary public, shall have been forwarded to the Comptroller of the Currency and his certificate obtained specifying the amount of such increase of capital stock by stock dividend, and his approval thereof."

Effective on approval of Comptroller.

Sec. 6. That section 5150 of the Revised Statutes of the United States be amended to read as follows:

Board of directors. R.S., sec. 5150, p. 995, amended. Chairman thereof.

"Sec. 5150. The president of the bank shall be a member of the board and shall be the chairman thereof, but the board may designate a director in lieu of the president to be chairman of the board, who shall perform such duties as may be designated by the board."

Sec. 7. That section 5155 of the Revised Statutes of the United States be amended to read as follows:

Branches allowed. R.S., sec. 5155, p. 996, amended. Conditions.

"Sec. 5155. The conditions upon which a national banking association may retain or establish and operate a branch or branches are the following:

" (a) A national banking association may retain and operate such branch or branches as it may have in lawful operation at the date of the approval of this Act, and any national banking association which has continuously maintained and operated not more than one branch for a period of more than twenty-five years immediately preceding the approval of this Act may continue to maintain and operate such branch.

Branches allowed to continue.

If maintained for preceding 25 years.

" (b) If a State bank is hereafter converted into or consolidated with a national banking association, or if two or more national banking associations are consolidated, such converted or consolidated association may, with respect to any of such banks, retain and operate any of their branches which may have been in lawful operation by any bank at the date of the approval of the Act.

By State banks converted into nationals.

" (c) A national banking association may, after the date of the approval of this Act, establish and operate new branches within the limits of the city, town, or village in which said association is situated if such establishment and operation are at the time permitted to State banks by the law of the State in question.

Establishing, if permitted by State laws.

" (d) No branch shall be established after the date of the approval of this Act within the limits of any city, town, or village of which the population by the last decennial census was less than twenty-five thousand. No more than one such branch may be thus established where the population, so determined, of such municipal unit does not exceed fifty thousand; and not more than two such branches where the population does not exceed one hundred thousand. In any such municipal unit where the population exceeds one hundred thousand the determination of the number of branches shall be within the discretion of the Comptroller of the Currency.

Conditions permitting.

Population limitations.

" (e) No branch of any national banking association shall be established or moved from one location to another without first obtaining the consent and approval of the Comptroller of the Currency.

Consent of Comptroller required.

" (f) The term 'branch' as used in this section shall be held to include any branch bank, branch office, branch agency, additional office, or any branch place of business located in any State or Territory of the United States or in the District of Columbia at which deposits are received, or checks paid, or money lent.

"Branch" defined.

" (g) This section shall not be construed to amend or repeal section 25 of the Federal Reserve Act, as amended, authorizing the establishment by national banking associations of branches in foreign countries, or dependencies, or insular possessions of the United States.

Foreign branches not affected. Vol. 42, p. 28.

" (h) The words 'State bank,' 'State banks,' 'bank,' or 'banks,' as used in this section, shall be held to include trust companies, savings banks, or other such corporations or institutions carrying on the banking business under the authority of State laws."

Trust companies, etc., included as banks.

Sec. 8. That section 5190 of the Revised Statutes of the United States be amended to read as follows:

Banking office. R. S., sec. 5190, p. 1003, amended.

Sec. 5190. The general business of each national banking association shall be transacted in the place specified in its organization certificate and in the branch or branches, if any, established or maintained by it in accordance with the provisions of section 5155 of the Revised Statutes, as amended by this Act."

Sec. 9. That the first paragraph of section 9 of the Federal Reserve Act, as amended, be amended so as to read as follows:

"SEC. 9. Any bank incorporated by special law of any State, or organized under the general laws of any State or of the United States, desiring to become a member of the Federal reserve system, may make application to the Federal Reserve Board, under such rules and regulations as it may prescribe, for the right to subscribe to the stock of the Federal reserve bank organized within the district in which the applying bank is located. Such application shall be for the same amount of stock that the applying bank would be required to subscribe to as a national bank. The Federal Reserve Board, subject to the provisions of this Act and to such conditions as it may prescribe pursuant thereto may permit the applying bank to become a stockholder of such Federal reserve bank.

"Any such State bank which, at the date of the approval of this Act, has established and is operating a branch or branches in conformity with the State law, may retain and operate the same while remaining or upon becoming a stockholder of such Federal reserve bank; but no such State bank may retain or acquire stock in a Federal reserve bank except upon relinquishment of any branch or branches established after the date of the approval of this Act beyond the limits of the city, town, or village in which the parent bank is situated."

Sec. 10. That section 5200 of the Revised Statutes of the United States, as amended, be amended to read as follows:

"SEC. 5200. The total obligations to any national banking association of any person, copartnership, association, or corporation shall at no time exceed 10 per centum of the amount of the capital stock of such association actually paid in and unimpaired and 10 per centum of its unimpaired surplus fund. The term 'obligations' shall mean the direct liability of the maker or acceptor of paper discounted with or sold to such association and the liability of the indorser, drawer, or guarantor who obtains a loan from or discounts paper with or sells paper under his guaranty to such association and shall include in the case of obligations of a copartnership or association the obligations of the several members thereof. Such limitation of 10 per centum shall be subject to the following exceptions:

" (1) Obligations in the form of drafts or bills of exchange drawn in good faith against actually existing values shall not be subject under this section to any limitation based upon such capital and surplus.

" (2) Obligations arising out of the discount of commercial or business paper actually owned by the person, copartnership, association, or corporation negotiating the same shall not be subject under this section to any limitation based upon such capital and surplus.

" (3) Obligations drawn in good faith against actually existing values and secured by goods or commodities in process of shipment shall not be subject under this section to any limitation based upon such capital and surplus.

" (4) Obligations as indorser or guarantor of notes, other than commercial or business paper excepted under (2) hereof, having a maturity of not more than six months, and owned by the person, corporation, association, or copartnership indorsing and negotiating the same, shall be subject under this section to a limitation of 15 per centum of such capital and surplus in addition to such 10 per centum of such capital and surplus.

" (5) Obligations in the form of banker's acceptances of other banks of the kind described in section 13 of the Federal Reserve Act shall not be subject under this section to any limitation based upon such capital and surplus.

" (6) Obligations of any person, copartnership, association, or corporation, in the form of notes or drafts secured by shipping documents, warehouse receipts or other such documents transferring or securing title covering readily marketable nonperishable staples when such property is fully covered by insurance, if it is customary to insure such staples, shall be subject under this section to a limitation of 15 per centum of such capital and surplus in addition to such 10 per centum of such capital and surplus when the market

---

Margin notes (left column):

In place where organized, and in branches. **Ante,** p. 1228.

State, etc., banks. Vol. 40, p. 232, amended. Applications of, to become Federal Reserve member banks.

Stock to be subscribed.
Permission from Reserve Board.

Retention of established branches.

Branches outside municipal limits to be relinquished.

National banks. R.S., sec. 5200, p. 1005. Limit of loans by, to any person. Vol. 40, p. 967. Vol. 41, p. 296, amended. Meaning of "obligations."

Exceptions.

Drafts, etc., secured by existing values.

Discounted business paper.

Secured by goods in transit.

Discounts of other than business paper maturing within six months. Amounts extended.

Rediscounts of acceptances of other banks. Vol. 39, p. 752; Vol. 42, pp. 1478, 1479. Covered by shipping documents, etc., of nonperishable staples, etc. Amount extended.

value of such staples securing such obligation is not at any time less than 115 per centum of the face amount of such obligation, and to an additional increase of limitation of 5 per centum of such capital and surplus in addition to such 25 per centum of such capital and surplus when the market value of such staples securing such additional obligation is not at any time less than 120 per centum of the face amount of such additional obligation, and to a further additional increase of limitation of 5 per centum of such capital and surplus in addition to such 30 per centum of such capital and surplus when the market value of such staples securing such additional obligation is not at any time less than 125 per centum of the face amount of such additional obligation, and to a further additional increase of limitation of 5 per centum of such capital and surplus in addition to such 35 per centum of such capital and surplus when the market value of such staples securing such additional obligation is not at any time less than 130 per centum of the face amount of such additional obligation, and to a further additional increase of limitation of 5 per centum of such capital and surplus in addition to such 40 per centum of such capital and surplus when the market value of such staples securing such additional obligation is not at any time less than 135 per centum of the face amount of such additional obligation, and to a further additional increase of limitation of 5 per centum of such capital and surplus in addition to such 45 per centum of such capital and surplus when the market value of such staples securing such additional obligation is not at any time less than 140 per centum of the face amount of such additional obligation, but this exception shall not apply to obligations of any one person, copartnership, association or corporation arising from the same transactions and/or secured upon the identical staples for more than ten months.

Market values of security required.

Time limitation of paper.

" (7) Obligations of any person, copartnership, association, or corporation in the form of notes or drafts secured by shipping documents or instruments transferring or securing title covering livestock or giving a lien on livestock when the market value of the livestock securing the obligation is not at any time less than 115 per centum of the face amount of the notes covered by such documents shall be subject under this section to a limitation of 15 per centum of such capital and surplus in addition to such 10 per centum of such capital and surplus.

Secured by livestock. Amount extended.

" (8) Obligations of any person, copartnership, association, or corporation in the form of notes secured by not less than a like amount of bonds or notes of the United States issued since April 24, 1917, or certificates of indebtedness of the United States, shall (except to the extent permitted by rules and regulations prescribed by the Comptroller of the Currency, with the approval of the Secretary of the Treasury) be subject under this section to a limitation of 15 per centum of such capital and surplus in addition to such 10 per centum of such capital and surplus."

Federal securities as collateral. Amount extended.

Sec. 11. That section 5202 of the Revised Statutes of the United States as amended be amended by adding at the end thereof a new paragraph to read as follows:

"Eight. Liabilities incurred under the provisions of section 202 of Title II of the Federal Farm Loan Act, approved July 17, 1916, as amended by the Agricultural Credits Act of 1923."

Indebtedness of national banks, exceptions.
R. S., sec. 5202, p. 1006, amended.
Intermediate credit banks, paper added.
Vol. 42, p. 1481.

Sec. 12. That section 5208 of the Revised Statutes of the United States as amended be amended by striking out the words "or who shall certify a check before the amount thereof shall have been regularly entered to the credit of the drawer upon the books of the bank," and in lieu thereof inserting the following: "or who shall certify a check before the amount thereof shall have been regularly deposited in the bank by the drawer thereof," so that the section as amended shall read as follows:

False certifying of checks.
R. S., sec. 5208, p. 1007, amended.
Matter stricken out.
Matter inserted.
Amended section.

"SEC. 5208. It shall be unlawful for any officer, director, agent, or employee of any Federal reserve bank, or any member bank as defined in the Act of December 23, 1913, known as the Federal Reserve Act, to certify any check drawn upon such Federal reserve bank or member bank unless the person, firm, or corporation drawing the check has on deposit with such Federal reserve bank or member bank, at the time such check is certified, an amount of money not less than the amount specified in such check. Any check so certified by a duly authorized officer, director, agent, or employee shall be a

Falsely certifying checks by officials of reserve or member banks, unlawful.
Vol. 40, p. 972, amended.

Responsibility of bank.

Penalty for violations.

Vol. 38, p. 262.
If a national bank.

R. S., sec. 5234, p. 1012.
Other banks.
Vol. 38, p. 260.
Punishment for violations by bank officers, etc.

Certifying, before actual deposit.

good and valid obligation against such Federal reserve bank or member bank; but the act of any officer, director, agent, or employee of any such Federal reserve bank or member bank in violation of this section shall, in the discretion of the Federal Reserve Board, subject such Federal reserve bank to the penalties imposed by section 11, subsection (h) of the Federal Reserve Act, and shall subject such member bank, if a national bank, to the liabilities and proceedings on the part of the Comptroller of the Currency provided for in section 5234, Revised Statutes, and shall, in the discretion of the Federal Reserve Board, subject any other member bank to the penalties imposed by section 9 of said Federal Reserve Act for the violation of any of the provisions of said Act. Any officer, director, agent, or employee of any Federal reserve bank or member bank who shall willfully violate the provisions of this section, or who shall resort to any device, or receive any fictitious obligation, directly or collaterally, in order to evade the provisions thereof, or who shall certify a check before the amount thereof shall have been regularly deposited in the bank by the drawer thereof, shall be deemed guilty of a misdemeanor and shall, on conviction thereof in any district court of the United States, be fined not more than $5,000, or shall be imprisoned for not more than five years, or both, in the discretion of the court."

R. S., sec. 5211, p. 1007, amended.

National banks to make three reports each year to the Comptroller.
Verification, etc.
Vol. 42, p. 1007, amended.

Sec. 13. That section 5211 of the Revised Statutes of the United States as amended be amended to read as follows:

"Sec. 5211. Every association shall make to the Comptroller of the Currency not less than three reports during each year, according to the form which may be prescribed by him, verified by the oath or affirmation of the president, or of the cashier, or of a vice president, or of an assistant cashier of the association designated by its board of directors to verify such reports in the absence of the president and cashier, taken before a notary public properly authorized and commissioned by the State in which notary resides and the association is located, or any other officer having an official seal, authorized in such State to administer oaths, and attested by the signature of

at least three of the directors. Each such report shall exhibit, in detail and under appropriate heads, the resources and liabilities of the association at the close of business on any past day by him specified, and shall be transmitted to the comptroller within five days after the receipt of a request or requisition therefor from him; and the statement of resources and liabilities,

together with acknowledgment and attestation in the same form in which it is made to the comptroller, shall be published in a newspaper published in the place where such association is established, or if there is no newspaper in the place, then in the one published nearest thereto in the same county, at the expense of the association; and such proof of publication shall be fur-

nished as may be required by the comptroller. The comptroller shall also have power to call for special reports from any particular association whenever in his judgment the same are necessary in order to obtain a full and complete knowledge of its condition."

Sec. 14. That section 22 of the Federal Reserve Act, subsection (a), paragraph 2 thereof, be amended to read as follows:

" (a) No member bank and no officer, director, or employee thereof shall hereafter make any loan or grant any gratuity to any bank examiner. Any bank officer, director, or employee violating this provision shall be deemed guilty of a misdemeanor and shall be imprisoned not exceeding one year, or fined not more than $5,000, or both, and may be fined a further sum equal to the money so loaned or gratuity given.

"Any examiner or assistant examiner who shall accept a loan or gratuity from any bank examined by him, or from an officer, director, or employee thereof, or who shall steal, or unlawfully take, or unlawfully conceal any money, note, draft, bond, or security or any other property of value in the possession of any member bank or from any safe deposit box in or adjacent to the premises of such bank, shall be deemed guilty of a misdemeanor and shall, upon conviction thereof in any district court of the United States, be imprisoned for not exceeding one year, or fined not more than $5,000, or both, and may be fined a further sum equal to the money so loaned, gratuity given, or property stolen, and shall forever thereafter be disqualified from holding office as a national bank examiner."

Sec. 15. That section 24 of the Federal Reserve Act be amended to read as follows:

"SEC. 24. Any national banking association may make loans secured by first lien upon improved real estate, including improved farm land, situated within its Federal reserve district or within a radius of one hundred miles of the place in which such bank is located, irrespective of district lines. A loan secured by real estate within the meaning of this section shall be in the form of an obligation or obligations secured by mortgage, trust deed, or other such instrument upon real estate when the entire amount of such obligation or obligations is made or is sold to such association. The amount of any such loan shall not exceed 50 per centum of the actual value of the real estate offered for security, but no such loan upon such security shall be made for a longer term than five years. Any such bank may make such loans in an aggregate sum including in such aggregate any such loans on which it is liable as indorser or guarantor or otherwise equal to 25 per centum of the amount of the capital stock of such association actually paid in and unimpaired and 25 per centum of its unimpaired surplus fund, or to one-half of its savings deposits, at the election of the association, subject to the general limitation contained in section 5200 of the Revised Statutes of the United States. Such banks may continue hereafter as heretofore to receive time and savings deposits and to pay interest on the same, but the rate of interest which such banks may pay upon such time deposits or upon savings or other deposits shall not exceed the maximum rate authorized by law to be paid upon such deposits by State banks or trust companies organized under the laws of the State wherein such national banking association is located."

Sec. 16. That section 5139 of the Revised Statutes of the United States be amended by inserting in the first sentence thereof the following words: "or into shares of such less amount as may be provided in the articles of association" so that the section as amended shall read as follows:

"SEC. 5139. The capital stock of each association shall be divided into shares of $100 each, or into shares of such less amount as may be provided in the articles of association, and be deemed personal property, and transferable on the books of the association in such manner as may be prescribed in the by-laws or articles of association. Every person becoming a shareholder by such transfer shall, in proportion to his shares, succeed to all rights and liabilities of the prior holder of such shares; and no change shall be made in the articles of association by which the rights, remedies, or security of the existing creditors of the association shall be impaired.

Sec. 17. That section 5146 of the Revised Statutes of the United States as amended be amended by inserting in lieu of the second sentence thereof the following: "Every director must own in his own right shares of the capital stock of the association of which he is a director the aggregate par value of which shall not be less than $1,000, unless the capital of the bank shall not exceed $25,000 in which case he must own in his own right shares of such capital stock the aggregate value of which shall not be less than $500," so that the section as amended shall read as follows:

"SEC. 5146. Every director must during his whole term of service, be a citizen of the United States, and at least three-fourths of the directors must have resided in the State, Territory, or District in which the association is located, or within fifty miles of the location of the office of the association, for at least one year immediately preceding their election, and must be residents of such State or within a fifty-mile territory of the location of the association during their continuance in office. Every director must own in his own right shares of the capital stock of the association of which he is a director the aggregate par value of which shall not be less than $1,000, unless the capital of the bank shall not exceed $25,000 in which case he must own in his own right shares of such capital stock the aggregate par value of which shall not be less than $500. Any director who ceases to be the owner of the required number of shares of the stock, or who becomes in any other manner disqualified, shall thereby vacate his place."

Sec. 18. That the second subdivision of the fourth paragraph of section 4 of the Federal Reserve Act be amended to read as follows:

Vol. 30, p.754, amended.

Real estate loans by national banks allowed, farm land included.

Form of security.

Permissible amounts.

Aggregate sum.

Ante, p. 1229.
Time and savings deposits allowed.

Interest limitation.

Capital of national banks.
R. S., sec. 5130, p. 903, amended.

Capital stock shares of $100 each or less amount.

Rights transferred to new holder.

National bank directors.
R. S., sec. 5146, p. 995, amended.
Vol. 41, p. 1199.
New matter.

Amended section.

Directors.
Citizenship and residence required.

Stock ownership modified.

Place vacated if ownership ceases, etc.

Reserve banks.
Vol. 38, p. 254.
Continuance of succession.

"Second. To have succession after the approval of this Act until dissolved by Act of Congress or until forfeiture of franchise for violation of law."

Sec. 19. That section 3 of the Federal Reserve Act, as amended, is further amended by adding at the end thereof the following:

"The Federal Reserve Board may at any time require any Federal Reserve Bank to discontinue any branch of such Federal Reserve Bank established under this section. The Federal Reserve Bank shall thereupon proceed to wind up the business of such branch bank, subject to such rules and regulations as the Federal Reserve Board may prescribe."

APPROVED, February 25, 1927.

Banking Act of 1933 (excerpts)

An Act to provide for the safer and more effective use of the assets of banks, to regulate interbank control, to prevent the undue diversion of funds into speculative operations, and for other purposes.

Be it enacted by the Senate and House of Representatives of the United States of America in Congress assembled, That the short title of this Act shall be the "Banking Act of 1933."

"SEC. 12B. (a) There is hereby created a Federal Deposit Insurance Corporation (hereinafter referred to as the 'Corporation') , whose duty it shall be to purchase, hold, and liquidate, as hereinafter provided, the assets of national banks which have been closed by action of the Comptroller of the Currency, or by vote of their directors, and the assets of State member banks which have been closed by action of the appropriate State authorities, or by vote of their directors; and to insure, as hereinafter provided, the deposits of all banks which are entitled to the benefits of insurance under this section.

" (b) The management of the Corporation shall be vested in a board of directors consisting of three members, one of whom shall be the Comptroller of the Currency, and two of whom shall be citizens of the United States to be appointed by the President, by and with the advice and consent of the Senate. One of the appointive members shall be the chairman of the board of directors of the Corporation and not more than two of the members of such board of directors shall be members of the same political party. Each such appointive member shall hold office for a term of six years and shall receive compensation at the rate of $10,000 per annum, payable monthly out of the funds of the Corporation, but the Comptroller of the Currency shall not receive additional compensation for his services as such member.

" (c) There is hereby authorized to be appropriated, out of any money in the Treasury not otherwise appropriated, the sum of $150,000,000, which shall be available for payment by the Secretary of the Treasury for capital stock of the Corporation in an equal amount, which shall be subscribed for by him on behalf of the United States. Payments upon such subscription shall be subject to call in whole or in part by the board of directors of the Corporation. Such stock shall be in addition to the amount of capital stock required to be subscribed for by Federal reserve banks and member and nonmember banks as hereinafter provided, and the United States shall be entitled to the payment of dividends on such stock to the same extent as member and nonmember banks are entitled to such payment on the class A stock of the Corporation held by them. Receipts for payments by the United States for or on account of such stock shall be issued by the Corporation to the Secretary of the Treasury and shall be evidence of the stock ownership of the United States.

" (d) The capital stock of the Corporation shall be divided into shares of $100 each. Certificates of stock of the Corporation shall be of two classes— class A and class B. Class A stock shall be held by member and nonmember banks as hereinafter provided and they shall be entitled to payment of dividends out of net earnings at the rate of 6 per centum per annum on the capital stock paid in by them, which dividends shall be cumulative, or to the extent of 30 per centum of such net earnings in any one year, whichever amount shall be the greater, but such stock shall have no vote at meetings of stockholders. Class B stock shall be held by Federal reserve banks only and shall not be entitled to the payment of dividends. Every Federal reserve bank shall subscribe to shares of class B stock in the Corporation to an

---

Side notes (left margin):

Branches of Federal reserve banks.

Discontinuance by Federal Reserve Board at any time. Vol. 40, p. 232, amended.

June 16, 1933. [H. R. 5661.] [Public, No. 66.]

Banking Act of 1933. Post, p. 888.

Federal Deposit Insurance Corporation; created. Duty to liquidate, etc., closed national and State member banks. Post, pp. 279, 969. Insurance of deposits. Management of Corporation.

Directors, appointment.

Terms of office; compensation.

Appropriation authorized, payment for Corporation capital stock. Post, p. 279. Payments subject to call. To be additional.

Dividend payments to United States.

Receipts for payments.

Capital stock, divided into shares of $100 each. Stock certificates, classes. Class A, by which banks to be held. Dividend payments, amount.

Class B, held by Reserve bank. Subscription for.

amount equal to one half of the surplus of such bank on January 1, 1933, and its subscriptions shall be accompanied by a certified check payable to the Corporation in an amount equal to one half of such subscription. The remainder of such subscription shall be subject to call from time to time by the board of directors upon ninety days' notice.

Payments.

" (e) Every bank which is or which becomes a member of the Federal Reserve System on or before July 1, 1934, shall take all steps necessary to enable it to become a class A stockholder of the Corporation on or before July 1, 1934; and thereafter no State bank or trust company or mutual savings bank shall be admitted to membership in the Federal Reserve System until it becomes a class A stockholder of the Corporation, no national bank in the continental United States shall be granted a certificate by the Comptroller of the Currency authorizing it to commence the business of banking until it becomes a member of the Federal Reserve System and a class A stockholder of the Corporation, and no national bank in the continental United States for which a receiver or conservator has been appointed shall be permitted to resume the transaction of its banking business until it becomes a class A stockholder of the Corporation. Every member bank shall apply to the Corporation for class A stock of the Corporation in an amount equal to one half of 1 per centum of its total deposit liabilities as computed in accordance with regulations prescribed by the Federal Reserve Board; except that in the case of a member bank organized after the date this section takes effect, the amount of such class A stock applied for by such member bank during the first twelve months after its organization shall equal 5 per centum of its paid-up capital and surplus, and beginning after the expiration of such twelve months' period the amount of such class A stock of such member bank shall be adjusted annually in the same manner as in the case of other member banks. Upon receipt of such application the Corporation shall request the Federal Reserve Board, in the case of a State member bank, or the Comptroller of the Currency, in the case of a national bank, to certify upon the basis of a thorough examination of such bank whether or not the assets of the applying bank are adequate to enable it to meet all of its liabilities to depositors and other creditors as shown by the books of the bank; and the Federal Reserve Board or the Comptroller of the Currency shall make such certification as soon as practicable. If such certification be in the affirmative, the Corporation shall grant such application and the applying bank shall pay one half of its subscription in full and shall thereupon become a class A stockholder of the Corporation: *Provided,* That no member bank shall be required to make such payment or become a class A stockholder of the Corporation before July 1, 1934. The remainder of such subscription shall be subject to call from time to time by the board of directors of the Corporation. If such certification be in the negative, the Corporation shall deny such application. If any national bank shall not have become a class A stockholder of the Corporation on or before July 1, 1934, the Comptroller of the Currency shall appoint a receiver or conservator therefor in accordance with the provisions of existing law. Except as provided in subsection (g) of this section, if any State member bank shall not have become a class A stockholder of the Corporation on or before July 1, 1934, the Federal Reserve Board shall terminate its membership in the Federal Reserve System in accordance with the provisions of section 9 of this Act.

Subscriptions for class A on or before July 1, 1934.
Post, p. 969.
Admission to membership thereafter; subscription required.
National banks.
Certificate to commence or resume banking business denied unless member and class A stockholder.

Application for class A.
Amount.

Exception; member bank hereafter organized.

Amount.

Certification respecting sufficiency of applying bank's assets.

Payment if certification affirmative; amount.

Proviso.
Not required before July 1, 1934.
Payment of remainder subject to call.
Denial of application if certification negative.
Receiver or conservator; appointment.
Termination of membership, State member bank not subscribing class A on or before July 1, 1934
Post, p. 180.

" (f) Any State bank or trust company or mutual savings bank which applies for membership in the Federal Reserve System or for conversion into a national banking association on or after July 1, 1936, may, with the consent of the Corporation, obtain the benefits of this section, pending action on such application, by subscribing and paying for the same amount of stock of the Corporation as it would be required to subscribe and pay for upon becoming a member bank. Thereupon the provisions of this section applicable to member banks shall be applicable to such State bank or trust company or mutual savings bank to the same extent as if it were already a member bank: *Provided,* That if the application of such State bank or trust company or mutual savings bank for membership in the Federal Reserve System or for conversion into a national banking association be approved and it shall not complete its membership in the Federal Reserve System or its conversion into a national banking association within a reasonable time,

Applications for membership on or before July 1, 1936.

Benefits to accrue during pendency of.

Provisions thereafter applicable.

Proviso.
Repayment if membership application not completed or disapproved, etc.

or if such application shall be disapproved, then the amount paid by such State bank or trust company or mutual savings bank on account of its subscription to the capital stock of the Corporation shall be repaid to it and it shall no longer be subject to the provisions or entitled to the privileges of this section.

Deposit by State bank with membership application, when stock purchase unlawful under State laws.

" (g) If any State bank or trust company, or mutual savings bank (referred to in this subsection as 'State bank') which is or which becomes a member of the Federal Reserve System is not permitted by the laws under which it was organized to purchase stock in the Corporation, it shall apply to the Corporation for admission to the benefits of this section and, if such application be granted after appropriate certification in accordance with this section, it shall deposit with the Corporation an amount equal to the amount which it would have been required to pay in on account of a subscription to capital stock of the Corporation. . . . Such deposit shall be

Conditions subject to.

Interest payments.

subject to the same conditions with respect to repayment as amounts paid on subscriptions to class A stock by other member banks and the Corporation shall pay interest thereon at the same rate as dividends are actually paid on outstanding shares of class A stock. . . . If the laws under which such State bank was organized be amended so as to authorize State banks to subscribe for class A stock of the Corporation, such State bank shall within six months thereafter subscribe for an appropriate amount of such class A stock and the deposit hereinafter provided for in lieu of payment upon class A stock shall be applied upon such subscription. If the law under which such State bank was organized be not amended at the next session of the State legislature following the admission of such State bank to the benefits of this section so as to authorize State banks to purchase such class A stock, or if the law be so amended and such State bank shall fail within six months thereafter to purchase such class A stock, the deposit previously made with the Corporation shall be returned to such State bank and it shall no longer be entitled to the benefits of this section, unless it shall have been closed in the meantime on account of inability to meet the demands of its depositors.

Application of deposit to subscription, if subscription hereafter legalized.

Termination of State bank to rights of membership.

When right to subscribe not granted.

When granted and failure to purchase stock.

" (l) Effective on and after July 1, 1934 (thus affording ample time for examination and preparation), unless the President shall by proclamation fix an earlier date, the Corporation shall insure as hereinafter provided the deposits of all member banks, and on and after such date and until July 1, 1936, of all nonmember banks, which are class A stockholders of the Corporation. Notwithstanding any other provision of law, whenever any national bank which is a class A stockholder of the Corporation shall have been closed by action of its board of directors or by the Comptroller of the Currency, as the case may be, on account of inability to meet the demands of its depositors, the Comptroller of the Currency shall appoint the Corporation receiver for such bank. As soon as possible thereafter the Corporation shall organize a new national bank to assume the insured deposit liabilities of such closed bank, to receive new deposits and otherwise to perform temporarily the functions provided for it in this paragraph. For the purposes of this subsection, the term 'insured deposit liability' shall mean with respect to the owner of any claim arising out of a deposit liability of such closed bank the following percentages of the net amount due to such owner by such closed bank on account of deposit liabilities: 100 per centum of such net amount not exceeding $10,000; and 75 per centum of the amount, if any, by which set net amount exceeds $10,000 but does not exceed $50,000; and 50 per centum of the amount, if any, by which such net amount exceeds $50,000: *Provided,* That, in determining the amount due to such owner for the purpose of fixing such percentage, there shall be added together all net amounts due to such owner in the same capacity or the same right, on account of deposits, regardless of whether such deposits be maintained in his name or in the names of others for his benefit. For the purposes of this subsection, the term 'insured deposit liabilities' shall mean the aggregate amount of all such insured deposit liabilities of such closed bank. The Corporation shall determine as expeditiously as possible the net amounts due to depositors of the closed bank and shall make available to the new bank an amount equal to the insured deposit liabilities of such closed bank, whereupon such new bank shall assume the insured deposit liability of such closed bank to each of its

Insurance of deposits, member banks; effective July 1, 1934.
Post, pp. 969, 970.
President may fix earlier date.
Nonmember banks.

Corporation as receiver of closed national bank.

Organization of new national bank.

"Insured deposit liability," construed.

Percentages.

Proviso.
Determination of amounts for fixing percentages.

"Insured deposit liabilities," construed.

Determination of amounts due depositors.

Amounts made available.

depositors, and the Corporation shall be subrogated to all rights against the closed bank of the owners of such deposits and shall be entitled to receive the same dividends from the proceeds of the assets of such closed bank as would have been payable to each such depositor until such dividends shall equal the insured deposit liability to such depositor assumed by the new bank, whereupon all further dividends shall be payable to such depositor. Of the amount thus made available by the Corporation to the new bank, such portion shall be paid to it in cash as may be necessary to enable it to meet immediate cash demands and the remainder shall be credited to it on the books of the Corporation subject to withdrawal on demand and shall bear interest at the rate of 3 per centum per annum until withdrawn. The new bank may, with the approval of the Corporation, accept new deposits, which, together with all amounts made available to the new bank by the Corporation, shall be kept on hand in cash, invested in direct obligations of the United States, or deposited with the Corporation or with a Federal reserve bank. Such new bank shall maintain on deposit with the Federal reserve bank of its district the reserves required by law of member banks but shall not be required to subscribe for stock of the Federal reserve bank until its own capital stock has been subscribed and paid for in the manner hereinafter provided. The articles of association and organization certificate of such new bank may be executed by such representatives of the Corporation as it may designate; the new bank shall not be required to have any directors at the time of its organization, but shall be managed by an executive officer to be designated by the Corporation; and no capital stock need be paid in by the Corporation; but in other respects such bank shall be organized in accordance with the existing provisions of law relating to the organization of national banks; and, until the requisite amount of capital stock for such bank has been subscribed and paid for in the manner hereinafter provided, such bank shall transact no business except that authorized by this subsection and such business as may be incidental to its organization. When in the judgment of the Corporation it is desirable to do so, the Corporation shall offer capital stock of the new bank for sale on such terms and conditions as the Corporation shall deem advisable, in an amount sufficient in the opinion of the Corporation to make possible the conduct of the business of the new bank on a sound basis, but in no event less than that required by section 5138 of the Revised Statutes, as amended (U.S.C., title 12, sec. 51), for the organization of a national bank in the place where such new bank is located, giving the stockholders of the closed bank the first opportunity to purchase such stock. Upon proof that an adequate amount of capital stock of the new bank has been subscribed and paid for in cash by subscribers satisfactory to the Comptroller of the Currency, he shall issue to such bank a certificate of authority to commence business and thereafter it shall be managed by directors elected by its own shareholders and may exercise all of the powers granted by law to national banking associations. If an adequate amount of capital for such new bank is not subscribed and paid in, the Corporation may offer to transfer its business to any other banking institution in the same place which will take over its assets, assume its liabilities, and pay to the Corporation for such business such amount as the Corporation may deem adequate. Unless the capital stock of the new bank is sold or its assets acquired and its liabilities assumed by another banking institution, in the manner herein prescribed, within two years from the date of its organization, the Corporation shall place the new bank in voluntary liquidation and wind up its affairs. The Corporation shall open on its books a deposit insurance account and, as soon as possible after taking possession of any closed national bank, the Corporation shall make an estimate of the amount which will be available from all sources for application in satisfaction of the portion of the claims of depositors to which it has been subrogated and shall debit to such deposit insurance account the excess, if any, of the amount made available by the Corporation to the new bank for depositors over and above the amount of such estimate. It shall be the duty of the Corporation to realize upon the assets of such closed bank, having due regard to the condition of credit in the district in which such closed bank is located; to enforce the individual liability of the stockholders and directors thereof; and to wind up the affairs of such closed bank in conformity with the provisions of

Corporation subrogated to rights against closed bank. Entitlement to dividends.

Payments to be made in cash.

Credits.

Interest rate.

Acceptance of new deposits.

Investments authorized.

Maintenance of reserve with reserve bank.

Subscription for stock not required.

Articles of association and organization.

Management of new bank.

Capital stock payments by Corporation.

Transaction of business.

Officers of capital stock of new bank.

Amount.

R. S., sec. 5138, p. 993. U.S.C., p. 261.

Preemption right of stockholders.

Certificate to commence business; when to issue.

Management thereafter.

Transfer of business, when stock subscription inadequate.

Voluntary liquidation of new bank when not transferred.

Deposit insurance account.

Duty of Corporation to open.

Debits to.

Additional duties of Corporation; liquidation of closed bank.

law relating to the liquidation of closed national banks, except as herein otherwise provided, retaining for its own account such portion of the amount realized from such liquidation as it shall be entitled to receive on account of its subrogation to the claims of depositors and paying to depositors and other creditors the amount available for distribution to them, after deducting therefrom their share of the costs of the liquidation of the closed bank. If the total amount realized by the Corporation on account of its subrogation to the claims of depositors be less than the amount of the estimate hereinabove provided for, the deposit insurance account shall be charged with the deficiency and, if the total amount so realized shall exceed the amount of such estimate, such account shall be credited with such excess. With respect to such closed national banks, the Corporation shall have all the rights, powers, and privileges now possessed by or hereafter given receivers of insolvent national banks and shall be subject to the obligations and penalties not inconsistent with the provisions of this paragraph to which such receivers are now or may hereafter become subject.

Powers and rights of Corporation as receiver.

Closed State member banks.

"Whenever any State member bank which is a class A stockholder of the Corporation shall have been closed by action of its board of directors or by the appropriate State authority, as the case may be, on account of inability to meet the demands of its depositors, the Corporation shall accept appointment as receiver thereof, if such appointment be tendered by the appropriate State authority and be authorized or permitted by State law. Thereupon the Corporation shall organize a new national bank, in accordance with the provisions of this subsection, to assume the insured deposit liabilities of such closed State member bank, to receive new deposits and otherwise to perform temporarily the functions provided for in this subsection. Upon satisfactory recognition of the right of the Corporation to receive dividends on the same basis as in the case of a closed national bank under this subsection, such recognition being accorded by State law, by allowance of claims by the appropriate State authority, by assignment of claims by depositors, or by any other effective method, the Corporation shall make available to such new national bank, in the manner prescribed by this subsection, an amount equal to the insured deposit liabilities of such closed State member bank; and the Corporation and such new national bank shall perform all of the functions and duties and shall have all the rights and privileges with respect to such State member bank and the depositors thereof which are prescribed by this subsection with respect to closed national banks holding class A stock in the Corporation: *Provided*, That the rights of depositors and other creditors of such State member bank shall be determined in accordance with the applicable provisions of State law: *And provided further,* That, with respect to such State member bank, the Corporation shall possess the powers and privileges provided by State law with respect to a receiver of such State member bank, except in so far as the same are in conflict with the provisions of this subsection.

Corporation as receiver of.

Organization of new bank.

Purpose.

Funds to cover insured deposit liabilities made available by Corporation when right to dividends recognized.

Management of new bank.

Provisos.
Determination of rights of depositors, etc.

Powers, etc., of Corporation under State law.

"Whenever any State member bank which is a class A stockholder of the Corporation shall have been closed by action of its board of directors or by the appropriate State authority, as the case may be, on account of inability to meet the demands of its depositors, and the applicable State law does not permit the appointment of the Corporation as receiver of such bank, the Corporation shall organize a new national bank, in accordance with the provisions of this subsection, to assume the insured deposit liabilities of such closed State member bank, to receive new deposits, and otherwise to perform temporarily the functions provided for in this subsection. Upon satisfactory recognition of the right of the Corporation to receive dividends on the same basis as in the case of a closed national bank under this subsection, such recognition being accorded by State law, by allowance of claims by the appropriate State authority, by assignment of claims by depositors, or by any other effective method, the Corporation shall make available to such new bank, in accordance with the provisions of this subsection, the amount of insured deposit liabilities as to which such recognition has been accorded; and such new bank shall assume such insured deposit liabilities and shall in other respects comply with the provisions of this subsection respecting new banks organized to assume insured deposit liabilities of closed national banks. In so far as possible in view of the applicable provisions of State law,

Organization of new bank, when appointment of Corporation as receiver unlawful.

Functions.

Funds to be made available when right of Corporation to receive dividends recognized.

Assumption of insured deposit liabilities.

the Corporation shall proceed with respect to the receiver of such closed bank and with respect to the new bank organized to assume its insured deposit liabilities in the manner prescribed by this subsection with respect to closed national banks and new banks organized to assume their insured deposit liabilities; except that the Corporation shall have none of the powers, duties, or responsibilities of a receiver with respect to the winding up of affairs of such closed State member bank. The Corporation, in its discretion, however, may purchase and liquidate any or all of the assets of such bank.

Sec. 11. (b) Such section 19 of the Federal Reserve Act, as amended, is further amended by adding at the end thereof the following new paragraphs:

Vol. 38, p. 270.

"No member bank shall, directly or indirectly by any device whatsoever, pay any interest on any deposit which is payable on demand: *Provided,* That nothing herein contained shall be construed as prohibiting the payment of interest in accordance with the terms of any certificate of deposit or other contract heretofore entered into in good faith which is in force on the date of the enactment of this paragraph; but no such certificate of deposit or other contract shall be renewed or extended unless it shall be modified to conform to this paragraph, and every member bank shall take such action as may be necessary to conform to this paragraph as soon as possible consistently with its contractual obligations: *Provided, however,* That this paragraph shall not apply to any deposit of such bank which is payable only at an office thereof located in a foreign country, and shall not apply to any deposit made by a mutual savings bank, nor to any deposit of public funds made by or on behalf of any State, country, school district, or other subdivision or municipality, with respect to which payment of interest is required under State law.

Interest payments on demand deposits prohibited.
Provisos.
Prior contracts.

Application to deposit payable in foreign country.

Public funds.

"The Federal Reserve Board shall from time to time limit by regulation the rate of interest which may be paid by member banks on time deposits, and may prescribe different rates for such payment on time and savings deposits having different maturities or subject to different conditions respecting withdrawal or repayment or subject to different conditions by reason of different locations. No member bank shall pay any time deposit before its maturity, or waive any requirement of notice before payment of any savings deposit except as to all savings deposits having the same requirement."

Regulation of interest rate, time deposits.

Payment before maturity prohibited.

Sec. 13. The Federal Reserve Act, as amended, is amended by inserting between sections 23 and 24 thereof (U.S.C., title 12, secs. 64 and 371; Supp. VI, title 12, sec. 371) the following new section:

Vol. 38, p. 273.
U.S.C., pp. 263, 283;
Supp. VI, p. 137.

"SEC. 23A. No member bank shall (1) make any loan or any extension of credit to, or purchase securities under repurchase agreement from, any of its affiliates, or (2) invest any of its funds in the capital stock, bonds, debentures, or other such obligations of any such affiliate, or (3) accept the capital stock, bonds, debentures, or other such obligations of any such affiliate as collateral security for advances made to any person, partnership, association, or corporation, if, in the case of any such affiliate, the aggregate amount of such loans, extensions of credit, repurchase agreements, investments, and advances against such collateral security will exceed 10 per centum of the capital stock and surplus of such member bank, or if, in the case of all such affiliates, the aggregate amount of such loans, extensions of credits, repurchase agreements, investments, and advances against such collateral security will exceed 20 per centum of the capital stock and surplus of such member bank.

Loans, investments, etc., prohibited by member banks to affiliates.

Percentage permitted.

"Within the foregoing limitations, each loan or extension of credit of any kind or character to an affiliate shall be secured by collateral in the form of stocks, bonds, debentures, or other such obligations having a market value at the time of making the loan or extension of credit of at least 20 per centum more than the amount of the loan or extension of credit, or of at least 10 per centum more than the amount of the loan or extension of credit if it is secured by obligations of any State, or of any political subdivision or agency thereof: *Provided,* That the provisions of this paragraph shall not apply to loans or extensions of credit secured by obligations of the United States Government, the Federal intermediate credit banks, the Federal land banks, the Federal Home Loan Banks, or the Home Owners' Loan Corporation, or

Security.

Proviso.
United States obligations, etc.

by such notes, drafts, bills of exchange, or bankers' acceptances as are eligible for rediscount or for purchase by Federal reserve banks. A loan or extension of credit to a director, officer, clerk, or other employee or any representative of any such affiliate shall be deemed a loan to the affiliate to the extent that the proceeds of such loan are used for the benefit of, or transferred to, the affiliate.

Loans to officers of affiliate.

"For the purposes of this section the term 'affiliate' shall include holding company affiliates as well as other affiliates, and the provisions of this section shall not apply to any affiliate (1) engaged solely in holding the bank premises of the member bank with which it is affiliated, (2) engaged solely in conducting a safe-deposit business or the business of an agricultural credit corporation or livestock loan company, (3) in the capital stock of which a national banking association is authorized to invest pursuant to section 25 of the Federal Reserve Act, as amended, (4) organized under section 25 (a) of the Federal Reserve Act, as amended, or (5) engaged solely in holding obligations of the United States Government, the Federal intermediate credit banks, the Federal land banks, the Federal Home Loan Banks, or the Home Owners' Loan Corporation; but as to any such affiliate, member banks shall continue to be subject to other provisions of law applicable to loans by such banks and investments by such banks in stocks, bonds, debentures, or other such obligations."

"Affiliate," construed.
Affiliates not included.

Vol. 38, p. 273.
U.S.C., p. 292.

Sec. 23. Paragraph (c) of section 5155 of the Revised Statutes, as amended (U.S.C., title 12, sec. 36), is amended to read as follows:

R.S., sec. 5155, p. 996. U.S.C., p. 261.
Branches.
Establishment by association, upon approval.

" (c) A national banking association may, with the approval of the Comptroller of the Currency, establish and operate new branches: (1) Within the limits of the city, town or village in which said association is situated, if such establishment and operation are at the time expressly authorized to State banks by the law of the State in question; and (2) at any point within the State in which said association is situated, if such establishment and operation are at the time authorized to State banks by the statute law of the State in question by language specifically granting such authority affirmatively and not merely by implication or recognition, and subject to the restrictions as to location imposed by the law of the State on State banks. No such association shall establish a branch outside of the city, town, or village in which it is situated unless it has a paid-in and unimpaired capital stock of not less than $500,000: *Provided,* That in States with a population of less than one million, and which have no cities located therein with a population exceeding one hundred thousand, the capital shall be not less than $250,000: *Provided,* That in States with a population of less than one-half million, and which have no cities located therein with a population exceeding fifty thousand, the capital shall not be less than $100,000."

Branch outside of city, etc.

Provisos.
States having population of less than one million.
Less than one half million.

Paragraph (d) of section 5155 of the Revised Statutes, as amended (U.S.C., title 12, sec. 36), is amended to read as follows:

R.S., sec. 5155, p. 996. U.S.C., p. 261.
Aggregate capital of association; amount.

" (d) The aggregate capital of every national banking association and its branches shall at no time be less than the aggregate minimum capital required by law for the establishment of an equal number of national banking associations situated in the various places where such association and its branches are situated."

Related Legislation

The Trust Powers Act of 1962

An Act to place authority over the trust powers of national banks in the Comptroller of the Currency.

September 28, 1962
[H. R. 12577]

Be it enacted by the Senate and House of Representatives of the United States of America in Congress assembled, That (a) the Comptroller of the Currency shall be authorized and empowered to grant by special permit to national banks applying therefor, when not in contravention of State or local law, the right to act as trustee, executor, administrator, registrar of stocks and bonds, guardian of estates, assignee, receiver, committee of estates of lunatics, or in any other fiduciary capacity in which State banks, trust companies, or other corporations which come into competition with national banks are permitted to act under the laws of the State in which the national bank is located.

National banks.
Trust powers.

(b) Whenever the laws of such State authorize or permit the exercise of any or all of the foregoing powers by State banks, trust companies, or other corporations which compete with national banks, the granting to and the exercise of such powers by national banks shall not be deemed to be in contravention of State or local law within the meaning of this Act.

(c) National banks exercising any or all of the powers enumerating in this section shall segregate all assets held in any fiduciary capacity from the general assets of the bank and shall keep a separate set of books and records showing in proper detail all transactions engaged in under authority of this section. The State banking authorities may have access to reports of examination made by the Comptroller of the Currency insofar as such reports relate to the trust department of such bank, but nothing in this Act shall be construed as authorizing the State banking authorities to examine the books, records, and assets of such bank.

(d) No national bank shall receive in its trust department deposits of current funds subject to check or the deposit of checks, drafts, bills of exchange, or other items for collection or exchange purposes. Funds deposited or held in trust by the bank awaiting investment shall be carried in a separate account and shall not be used by the bank in the conduct of its business unless it shall first set aside in the trust department United States bonds or other securities approved by the Comptroller of the Currency.

(e) In the event of the failure of such bank the owners of the funds held in trust for investment shall have a lien on the bonds or other securities so set apart in addition to their claim against the estate of the bank.

(f) Whenever the laws of a State require corporations acting in a fiduciary capacity to deposit securities with the State authorities for the protection of private or court trusts, national banks so acting shall be required to make similar deposits and securities so deposited shall be held for the protection of private or court trusts, as provided by the State law. National banks in such cases shall not be required to execute the bond usually required of individuals if State corporations under similar circumstances are exempt from this requirement. National banks shall have power to execute such bond when so required by the laws of the State.

(g) In any case in which the laws of a State require that a corporation acting as trustee, executor, administrator, or in any capacity specified in this section, shall take an oath or make an affidavit, the president, vice president, cashier, or trust officer of such national bank may take the necessary oath or execute the necessary affidavit.

(h) It shall be unlawful for any national banking association to lend any officer, director, or employee any funds held in trust under the powers conferred by this section. Any officer, director, or employee making such loan, or to whom such loan is made, may be fined not more than $5,000, or imprisoned not more than five years, or may be both fined and imprisoned, in the discretion of the court.

Penalty.

(i) In passing upon applications for permission to exercise the powers enumerated in this section, the Comptroller of the Currency may take into consideration the amount of capital and surplus of the applying bank, whether or not such capital and surplus is sufficient under the circumstances of the case, the needs of the community to be served, and any other facts and circumstances that seem to him proper, and may grant or refuse the application accordingly: *Provided,* That no permit shall be issued to any national banking association having a capital and surplus less than the capital and surplus required by State law of State banks, trust companies, and corporations exercising such powers.

(j) Any national banking association desiring to surrender its right to exercise the powers granted under this section, in order to relieve itself of the necessity of complying with the requirements of this section, or to have returned to it any securities which it may have deposited with the State authorities for the protection of private or court trusts, or for any other purpose, may file with the Comptroller of the Currency a certified copy of a resolution of its board of directors signifying such desire. Upon receipt of such resolution, the Comptroller of the Currency, after satisfying himself that such bank has been relieved in accordance with State law of all duties as trustee, executory, administrator, registrar of stocks and bonds, guardian of estates, assignee, receiver, committee of estates of lunatics or other fiduciary, under court, private, or other appointments previously accepted under authority of this section, may, in his discretion, issue to such bank a certificate certifying that such bank is no longer authorized to exercise the powers granted by this section. Upon the issuance of such a certificate by the Comptroller of the Currency, such banks (1) shall no longer be subject to the provisions of this section or the regulations of the Comptroller of the Currency made pursuant thereto, (2) shall be entitled to have returned to it any securities which it may have deposited with the State authorities for the protection of private or court trusts, and (3) shall not exercise thereafter any of the powers granted by this section without first applying for and obtaining a new permit to exercise such powers pursuant to the provisions of this section. The Comptroller of the Currency is authorized and empowered to promulgate such regulations as he may deem necessary to enforce compliance with the provisions of this section and the proper exercise of the powers granted therein.

Savings provisions.

Sec. 2. Nothing contained in this Act shall be deemed to affect or curtail the right of any national bank to act in fiduciary capacities under a permit granted before the date of enactment of this Act by the Board of Governors of the Federal Reserve System, nor to affect the validity of any transactions entered into at any time by any national bank pursuant to such permit. On and after the date of enactment of this Act the exercise of fiduciary powers by national banks shall be subject to the provisions of this Act and the requirements of regulations issued by the Comptroller of the Currency pursuant to the authority granted by this Act.

Repeal.
38 Stat. 262.

Sec. 3. Subsection (k) of section 11 of the Federal Reserve Act (12 U.S.C. 248 (k)) is repealed.

68A Stat. 203.

Sec. 4. Paragraph (2) of subsection (a) of section 584 of the Internal Revenue Code of 1954 is amended by inserting "or the Comptroller of the Currency" immediately after "the Board of Governors of the Federal Reserve System".

Sec. 5. Section 581 of the Internal Revenue Code of 1954 is amended by striking out "section 11 (k) of the Federal Reserve Act (38 Stat. 262; 12 U.S.C. 248 (k)) ", and inserting in lieu thereof "authority of the Comptroller of the Currency".

APPROVED, September 28, 1962.

The Sherman Act of 1890

July 2, 1890.

An Act to protect trade and commerce against unlawful restraints and monopolies.

Be it enacted by the Senate and House of Representative of the United States of America in Congress assembled,

Trusts, etc., in the States, in restraint of trade, etc., illegal.
Persons combining, guilty of misdemeanor.
Penalty.

Sec. 1. Every contract, combination in the form of trust or otherwise, or conspiracy, in restraint of trade or commerce among the several States, or with foreign nations, is hereby declared to be illegal. Every person who shall make any such contract or engage in any such combination or conspiracy, shall be deemed guilty of a misdemeanor, and, on conviction thereof, shall be punished by fine not exceeding five thousand dollars, or by imprisonment not exceeding one year, or by both said punishments, in the discretion of the court.

Persons attempting to monopolize, etc., guilty of misdemeanor.
Penalty.

Sec. 2. Every person who shall monopolize, or attempt to monopolize, or combine or conspire with any other person or persons, to monopolize any part of the trade or commerce among the several States, or with foreign nations, shall be deemed guilty of a misdemeanor, and, on conviction thereof, shall be punished by fine not exceeding five thousand dollars, or by imprisonment not exceeding one year, or by both said punishments, in the discretion of the court.

Trusts, etc., in Territories or District of Columbia illegal.

Persons engaged therein guilty of misdemeanor.

Sec. 3. Every contract, combination in form of trust or otherwise, or conspiracy, in restraint of trade or commerce in any Territory of the United States or of the District of Columbia, or in restraint of trade or commerce between any such Territory and another, or between any such Territory or Territories and any State or States or the District of Columbia, or with foreign nations, or between the District of Columbia and any State or States or foreign nations, is hereby declared illegal. Every person who shall make any such contract or engage in any such combination or conspiracy, shall be deemed guilty of a misdemeanor, and, on conviction thereof, shall be punished by fine not exceeding five thousand dollars, or by imprisonment not exceeding one year, or by both said punishments, in the discretion of the court.

Sec. 4. The several circuit courts of the United States are hereby invested with jurisdiction to prevent and restrain violations of this act; and it shall be the duty of the several district attorneys of the United States, in their respective districts, under the direction of the Attorney-General, to institute proceedings in equity to prevent and restrain such violations. Such proceedings may be by way of petition setting forth the case and praying that such violations shall be enjoined or otherwise prohibited. When the parties complained of shall have been duly notified of such petition the court shall proceed, as soon as may be, to the hearing and determination of the case; and pending such petition and before final decree, the court may at any time make such temporary restraining order or prohibition as shall be deemed just in the premises.

Sec. 5. Whenever it shall appear to the court before which any proceeding under section four of this act may be pending, that the ends of justice require that other parties should be brought before the court, the court may cause them to be summoned, whether they reside in the district in which the court is held or not; and subpoenas to that end may be served in any district by the marshal thereof.

Sec. 6. Any property owned under any contract or by any combination, or pursuant to any conspiracy (and being the subject thereof) mentioned in section one of this act, and being in the course of transportation from one State to another, or to a foreign country, shall be forfeited to the United States, and may be seized and condemned by like proceedings as those provided by law for the forfeiture, seizure, and condemnation of property imported into the United States contrary to law.

Sec. 7. Any person who shall be injured in his business or property by any other person or corporation by reason of anything forbidden or declared to be unlawful by this act may sue therefor in any circuit court of the United States in the district in which the defendant resides or is found, without respect to the amount in controversy, and shall recover three fold the damages by him sustained, and the costs of suit, including a reasonable attorney's fee.

Sec. 8. That the word "person," or "persons," wherever used in this act shall be deemed to include corporations and associations existing under or authorized by the laws of either the United States, the laws of any of the Territories, the laws of any State, or the laws of any foreign country.
APPROVED, July 2, 1890.

The Clayton Act of 1914 (excerpts)

An Act to supplement existing laws against unlawful restraints and monopolies, and for other purposes.

Be it enacted by the Senate and House of Representatives of the United States of America in Congress assembled, That "antitrust laws," as used herein, includes the Act entitled "An Act to protect trade and commerce against unlawful restraints and monopolies," approved July second, eighteen hundred and ninety; sections seventy-three to seventy-seven, inclusive, of an Act entitled "An Act to reduce taxation, to provide revenue for the Government, and for other purposes," of August twenty-seventh, eighteen hundred and ninety-four; an Act entitles "An Act to amend sections seventy-three and seventy-six of the Act of August twenty-seventh, eighteen hundred and ninety-four, entitled 'An Act to reduce taxation, to provide revenue for the Government, and for other purposes,'" approved February twelfth, nineteen hundred and thirteen; and also this Act.

"Commerce," as used herein, means trade or commerce among the several States and with foreign nations, or between the District of Columbia or any Territory of the United States and any State, Territory, or foreign nation, or between any insular possessions or other places under the jurisdiction of the United States, or between any such possession or place and any State or

Penalty

Jurisdiction of United States circuit courts.
Prosecuting officers.

Procedure.

Hearing, etc.

Temporary restraining order, etc.

Process.

Trust, etc., property in transit.
Ante, p. 209.
Forfeiture, seizure, and condemnation.

Damages.

Litigation.

Recovery.

"Person," or "persons," defined.

October 15, 1914.
[H. R. 15657.]
[Public, No. 212.]

Antitrust Act, 1914.
Laws included in this Act.
Vol. 26, p. 209.
Vol. 28, p. 570.

Vol. 37, p. 667.

Meaning of terms.
"Commerce."

Insular possessions included.

Territory of the United States or the District of Columbia or any foreign nation, or within the District of Columbia or any Territory or any insular possession or other place under the jurisdiction of the United States: *Provided,* That nothing in this Act contained shall apply to the Philippine Islands.

The word "person" or "persons" whenever used in this Act shall be deemed to include corporations and associations existing under or authorized by the laws of either the United States, the laws of any of the Territories, the laws of any State, or the laws of any foreign country.

Sec. 7. That no corporation engaged in commerce shall acquire, directly or indirectly, the whole or any part of the stock or other share capital of another corporation engaged also in commerce, where the effect of such acquisition may be to substantially lessen competition between the corporation whose stock is so acquired and the corporation making the acquisition, or to restrain such commerce in any section or community, or tend to create a monopoly of any line of commerce.

No corporation shall acquire, directly or indirectly, the whole or any part of the stock or other share capital of two or more corporations engaged in commerce where the effect of such acquisition, or the use of such stock by the voting or granting of proxies or otherwise, may be to substantially lessen competition between such corporations, or any of them, whose stock or other share capital is so acquired, or to restrain such commerce in any section or community, or tend to create a monopoly of any line of commerce.

This section shall not apply to corporations purchasing such stock solely for investment and not using the same by voting or otherwise to bring about, or in attempting to bring about, the substantial lessening of competition. Nor shall anything contained in this section prevent a corporation engaged in commerce from causing the formation of subsidiary corporations for the actual carrying on of their immediate lawful business, or the natural and legitimate branches or extensions thereof, or from owning and holding all or a part of the stock of such subsidiary corporations, when the effect of such formation is not to substantially lessen competition.

Nor shall anything herein contained be construed to prohibit any common carrier subject to the laws to regulate commerce from aiding in the construction of branches or short lines so located as to become feeders to the main line of the company so aiding in such construction or from acquiring or owning all or any part of the stock of such branch lines, nor to prevent any such common carrier from acquiring and owning all or any part of the stock of a branch or short line constructed by an independent company where there is no substantial competition between the company owning the branch line so constructed and the company owning the main line acquiring the property or an interest therein, nor to prevent such common carrier from extending any of its lines through the medium of the acquisition of stock or otherwise of any other such common carrier where there is no substantial competition between the company extending its lines and the company whose stock, property, or an interest therein is so acquired.

Nothing contained in this section shall be held to affect or impair any right heretofore legally acquired: *Provided,* That nothing in this section shall be held or construed to authorize or make lawful anything heretofore prohibited or made illegal by the antitrust laws, nor to exempt any person from the penal provisions thereof or the civil remedies therein provided.

Sec. 8. That from and after two years from the date of the approval of this Act no person shall at the same time be a director or other officer or employee of more than one bank, banking association or trust company, organized or operating under the laws of the United States, either of which has deposits, capital, surplus, and undivided profits aggregating more than $5,000,000; and no private banker or person who is a director in any bank or trust company, organized and operating under the laws of a State, having deposits, capital, surplus, and undivided profits aggregating more than $5,000,000, shall be eligible to be a director in any bank or banking association organized or operating under the laws of the United States. The eligibility of a director, officer, or employee under the foregoing provisions shall be determined by the average amount of deposits, capital, surplus, and undivided profits as shown in the official statements of such bank, banking association, or trust company filed as provided by law during the fiscal year next preceding the date set for the annual election of directors, and when a director, officer, or employee has been elected or selected in accordance with the provisions of this Act it shall be lawful for him to continue as such for one year thereafter under said election or employment.

Temporary continuance.

No bank, banking association or trust company, organized or operating under the laws of the United States, in any city or incorporated town or village of more than two hundred thousand inhabitants, as shown by the last preceding decennial census of the United States, shall have as a director or other officer or employee any private banker or any director or other officer or employee of any other bank, banking association or trust company located in the same place: *Provided,* That nothing in this section shall apply to mutual savings banks not having a capital stock represented by shares: *Provided further,* That a director or other officer or employee of such bank, banking association, or trust company may be a director or other officer or employee of not more than one other bank or trust company organized under the laws of the United States or any State where the entire capital stock of one is owned by stockholders in the other: *And provided further,* That nothing contained in this section shall forbid a director of class A of a Federal reserve bank, as defined in the Federal Reserve Act, from being an officer or director or both an officer and director in one member bank.

Large municipalities.
Service as officers, etc., in United States and private banks, forbidden.

Provisos.
Mutual savings banks excepted.
Permitted if stock owned by stockholders of the other.

Federal reserve banks.
Ante, p. 225.

That from and after two years from the date of the approval of this Act no person at the same time shall be a director in any two or more corporations, any one of which has capital, surplus, and undivided profits aggregating more than $1,000,000, engaged in whole or in part in commerce, other than banks, banking associations, trust companies and common carriers subject to the Act to regulate commerce, approved February fourth, eighteen hundred and eighty-seven, if such corporations are or shall have been theretofore, by virtue of their business and location of operation, competitors, so that the elimination of competition by agreement between them would constitute a violation of any of the provisions of any of the antitrust laws. The eligibility of a director under the foregoing provision shall be determined by the aggregate amount of the capital, surplus, and undivided profits, exclusive of dividends declared but not paid to stockholders, at the end of the fiscal year of said corporation next preceding the election of directors, and when a director has been elected in accordance with the provisions of this Act it shall be lawful for him to continue as such for one year thereafter.

Restriction on service as director in two or more competing corporations.

Not applicable to banks or carriers.
Vol. 24, p. 379.

Determination of eligibility.

Temporary continuance.

When any person elected or chosen as a director or officer or selected as an employee of any bank or other corporation subject to the provisions of this Act is eligible at the time of his election or selection to act for such bank or other corporation in such capacity his eligibility to act in such capacity shall not be affected and he shall not become or be deemed amenable to any of the provisions hereof by reason of any change in the affairs of such bank or other corporation from whatsoever cause, whether specifically excepted by any of the provisions hereof or not, until the expiration of one year from the date of his election or employment.

Service allowed for one year after eligibility ceases.

Sec. 11. That authority to enforce compliance with sections two, three, seven and eight of this Act by the persons respectively subject thereto is hereby vested: in the Interstate Commerce Commission where applicable to common carriers, in the Federal Reserve Board where applicable to banks, banking associations and trust companies, and in the Federal Trade Commission where applicable to all other character of commerce, to be exercised as follows:

Enforcement of Act.

Interstate Commerce Commission.
Federal Reserve Board.
Federal Trade Commission.

Whenever the commission or board vested with jurisdiction thereof shall have reason to believe that any person is violating or has violated any of the provisions of sections two, three, seven and eight of this Act, it shall issue and serve upon such person a complaint stating its charges in that respect, and containing a notice of a hearing upon a day and at a place therein fixed at least thirty days after the service of said complaint. The person so complained of shall have the right to appear at the place and time so fixed and show cause why an order should not be entered by the commission or board requiring such person to cease and desist from the violation of the law so charged in said complaint. Any person may make application, and upon

Procedure.
Service of complaints alleging violations.

Appearance of accused.

good cause shown may be allowed by the commission or board, to intervene and appear in said proceeding by counsel or in person. The testimony in any such proceeding shall be reduced to writing and filed in the office of the commission or board. If upon such hearing the commission or board, as the case may be, shall be of the opinion that any of the provisions of said sections have been or are being violated, it shall make a report in writing in which it shall state its findings as to the facts, and shall issue and cause to be served on such person an order requiring such person to cease and desist from such violations, and divest itself of the stock held or rid itself of the directors chosen contrary to the provisions of sections seven and eight of this Act, if any there be, in the manner and within the time fixed by said order. Until a transcript of the record in such hearing shall have been filed in a circuit court of appeals of the United States, as hereinafter provided, the commission or board may at any time, upon such notice and in such manner as it shall deem proper, modify or set aside, in whole or in part, any report or any order made or issued by it under this section.
Other parties may intervene.

Statement of findings and issue of order to cease violations.

Modification of report or order.

If such person fails or neglects to obey such order of the commission or board while the same is in effect, the commission or board may apply to the circuit court of appeals of the United States, within any circuit where the violation complained of was or is being committed or where such person resides or carries on business, for the enforcement of its order, and shall certify and file with its application a transcript of the entire record in the proceeding, including all the testimony taken and the report and order of the commission or board. Upon such filing of the application and transcript the court shall cause notice thereof to be served upon such person and thereupon shall have jurisdiction of the proceeding and of the question determined therein, and shall have power to make and enter upon the pleadings, testimony, and proceedings set forth in such transcript a decree affirming, modifying, or setting aside the order of the commission or board. The findings of the commission or board as to the facts, if supported by testimony, shall be conclusive. If either party shall apply to the court for leave to adduce additional evidence, and shall show to the satisfaction of the court that such additional evidence is material and that there were reasonable grounds for the failure to adduce such evidence in the proceeding before the commission or board, the court may order such additional evidence to be taken before the commission or board and to be adduced upon the hearing in such manner and upon such terms and conditions as to the court may seem proper. The commission or board may modify its findings as to the facts, or make new findings, by reason of the additional evidence so taken, and it shall file such modified or new findings, which, if supported by testimony, shall be conclusive, and its recommendation, if any, for the modification or setting aside of its original order, with the return of such additional evidence. The judgment and decree of the court shall be final, except that the same shall be subject to review by the Supreme Court upon certiorari as provided in section two hundred and forty of the Judicial Code.

Circuit court of appeals to enforce order.
Application, etc.

Jurisdiction of court, etc.

Findings conclusive of facts.
Production of additional evidence.

Modification, etc., of findings.

Judgment final.
Review by Supreme Court.
Vol. 36, p. 1157.

Any party required by such order of the commission or board to cease and desist from a violation charged may obtain a review of such order in said circuit court of appeals by filing in the court a written petition praying that the order of the commission or board be set aside. A copy of such petition shall be forthwith served upon the commission or board, and thereupon the commission or board forthwith shall certify and file in the court a transcript of the record as hereinbefore provided. Upon the filing of the transcript the court shall have the same jurisdiction to affirm, set aside, or modify the order of the commission or board as in the case of an application by the commission or board for the enforcement of its order, and the findings of the commission or board as to the facts, if supported by testimony, shall in like manner be conclusive.

Applications to set aside orders.

Procedure, etc.

The jurisdiction of the circuit court of appeals of the United States to enforce, set aside, or modify orders of the commission or board shall be exclusive.

Exclusive jurisdiction of court.

Such proceedings in the circuit court of appeals shall be given precedence over other cases pending therein, and shall be in every way expedited. No order of the commission or board or the judgment of the court to enforce

Precedence and expediting.
No antitrust liability impaired.

234   **Appendices**

the same shall in any wise relieve or absolve any person from any liability under the antitrust Acts.

Complaints, orders, and other processes of the commission or board under this section may be served by anyone duly authorized by the commission or board, either (a) by delivering a copy thereof to the person to be served, or to a member of the partnership to be served, or to the president, secretary, or other executive officer or a director of the corporation to be served; or (b) by leaving a copy thereof at the principal office or place of business of such person; or (c) by registering and mailing a copy thereof addressed to such person at his principal office or place of business. The verified return by the person so serving said complaint, order, or other process setting forth the manner of said service shall be proof of the same, and the return post-office receipt for said complaint, order, or other process registered and mailed as aforesaid shall be proof of the service of the same.

Service of process.

Personal.

At place of business.
By registered mail.

Proof of return.

The Celler-Kefauver Amendment to the Clayton Act

An Act to amend an Act entitled "An Act to supplement existing laws against unlawful restraints and monopolies, and for other purposes," approved October 15, 1914 (38 Stat. 730), as amended.

December 20, 1950
(H. R. 2734)
[Public Law 899]

Be it enacted by the Senate and House of Representatives of the United States of America in Congress assembled, That: sections 7 and 11 of an Act entitled "An Act to supplement existing laws against unlawful restraints and monopolies, and for other purposes," approved October 15, 1914, as amended (U.S.C., title 15, secs. 18 and 21), are hereby amended to read as follows:

Monopolies, etc.

38 Stat. 731, 734.

"*Sec. 7.* That no corporation engaged in commerce shall acquire, directly or indirectly, the whole or any part of the stock or other share capital and no corporation subject to the jurisdiction of the Federal Trade Commission shall acquire the whole or any part of the assets of another corporation engaged also in commerce, where in any line of commerce in any section of the country, the effect of such acquisition may be substantially to lessen competition, or to tend to create a monopoly.

Restrictions on acquisition of certain stock, etc.

"No corporation shall acquire, directly or indirectly, the whole or any part of the stock or other share capital and no corporation subject to the jurisdiction of the Federal Trade Commission shall acquire the whole or any part of the assets of one or more corporations engaged in commerce, where in any line of commerce in any section of the country, the effect of such acquisition, of such stocks or assets, or of the use of such stock by the voting or granting of proxies or otherwise, may be substantially to lessen competition, or to tend to create a monopoly.

"This section shall not apply to corporations purchasing such stock solely for investment and not using the same by voting or otherwise to bring about, or in attempting to bring about, the substantial lessening of competition. Nor shall anything contained in this section prevent a corporation engaged in commerce from causing the formation of subsidiary corporations for the actual carrying on of their immediate lawful business, or the natural and legitimate branches or extensions thereof, or from owning and holding all or a part of the stock of such subsidiary corporations, when the effect of such formation is not to substantially lessen competition.

Exceptions.

"Nor shall anything herein contained be construed to prohibit any common carrier subject to the laws to regulate commerce from aiding in the construction of branches or short lines so located as to become feeders to the main line of the company so aiding in such construction or from acquiring or owning all or any part of the stock of such branch lines, nor to prevent any such common carrier from acquiring and owning all or any part of the stock of a branch or short line constructed by an independent company where there is no substantial competition between the company owning the branch line so constructed and the company owning the main line acquiring the property or an interest therein, nor to prevent such common carrier from extending any of its lines through the medium of the acquisition of stock or otherwise of any other common carrier where there is no substantial competition between the company extending its lines and the company whose stock, property, or an interest therein is so acquired.

"Nothing contained in this section shall be held to affect or impair any right heretofore legally acquired: *Provided,* That nothing in this section shall be held or construed to authorize or make lawful anything heretofore prohibited or made illegal by the antitrust laws, nor to exempt any person from the penal provisions thereof or the civil remedies therein provided.

"Nothing contained in this section shall apply to transactions duly consummated pursuant to authority given by the Civil Aeronautics Board, Federal Communications Commission, Federal Power Commission, Interstate Commerce Commission, the Securities and Exchange Commission in the exercise of its jurisdiction under section 10 of the Public Utility Holding Company Act of 1935, the United States Maritime Commission, or the Secretary of Agriculture under any statutory provision vesting such power in such Commission, Secretary, or Board.

"Sec. 11. That authority to enforce compliance with sections 2, 3, 7, and 8 of this Act by the persons respectively subject thereto is hereby vested in the Interstate Commerce Commission where applicable to common carriers subject to the Interstate Commerce Act, as amended; in the Federal Communications Commission where applicable to common carriers engaged in wire or radio communication or radio transmission of energy; in the Civil Aeronautics Board where applicable to air carriers and foreign air carriers subject to the Civil Aeronautics Act of 1938; in the Federal Reserve Board where applicable to banks, banking associations, and trust companies; and in the Federal Trade Commission where applicable to all other character of commerce to be exercised as follows:

"Whenever the Commission or Board vested with jurisdiction thereof shall have reason to believe that any person is violating or has violated any of the provisions of sections 2, 3, 7, and 8 of this Act, it shall issue and serve upon such person and the Attorney General a complaint stating its charges in that respect, and containing a notice of a hearing upon a day and at a place therein fixed at least thirty days after the service of said complaint. The person so complained of shall have the right to appear at the place and time so fixed and show cause why an order should not be entered by the Commission or Board requiring such person to cease and desist from the violation of the law so charged in said complaint. The Attorney General shall have the right to intervene and appear in said proceeding and any person may make application, and upon good cause shown may be allowed by the Commission or Board, to intervene and appear in said proceeding by counsel or in person. The testimony in any such proceeding shall be reduced to writing and filed in the office of the Commission or Board. If upon such hearing the Commission or Board, as the case may be, shall be of the opinion that any of the provisions of said sections have been or are being violated, it shall make a report in writing, in which it shall state its findings as to the facts, and shall issue and cause to be served on such person an order requiring such person to cease and desist from such violations, and divest itself of the stock, or other share capital, or assets, held or rid itself of the directors chosen contrary to the provisions of sections 7 and 8 of this Act, if any there be, in the manner and within the time fixed by said order. Until a transcript of the record in such hearing shall have been filed in a United States court of appeals, as hereinafter provided, the Commission or Board may at any time, upon such notice, and in such manner as it shall deem proper, modify or set aside, in whole or in part, any report or any order made or issued by it under this section.

"If such person fails or neglects to obey such order of the Commission or Board while the same is in effect, the Commission or Board may apply to the United States court of appeals, within any circuit where the violation complained of was or is being committed or where such person resides or carries on business, for the enforcement of its order, and shall certify and file with its application a transcript of the entire record in the proceeding, including all the testimony taken and the report and order of the Commission or Board. Upon such filing of the application and transcript the court shall cause notice thereof to be served upon such person, and thereupon shall have jurisdiction of the proceeding and of the question determined therein, and shall have power to make and enter upon the pleadings, testimony, and proceedings set forth in such transcript a decree affirming, modi-

---

Margin notes (left column):

49 Stat. 818.
15 U. S. C. § 79j.

Compliance.
38 Stat. 730, 731, 732. 15 U. S. C. §§ 13, 14, 18, 19.
Ante, p. 1125.
24 Stat. 379.
49 U. S. C. note prec. § 1; Sup. III, § 1 **et seq.**
52 Stat. 973.
49 U. S. C. §§ 401-682, Sup. III, § 401 **et seq.**
Ante, pp. 395, 417.
Complaint.
Notice of hearing.

38 Stat. 730, 731, 732. 15 U. S. C. §§ 13, 14, 18, 19.
Ante, p. 1125.

Testimony.

Issuance of order.

Failure to obey order.

Jurisdiction of U. S. court of appeals.

fying, or setting aside the order of the Commission or Board. The findings of the Commission or Board as to the facts, if supported by substantial evidence, shall be conclusive. If either party shall apply to the court for leave to adduce additional evidence, and shall show to the satisfaction of the court that such additional evidence is material and that there were reasonable grounds for the failure to adduce such evidence in the proceeding before the Commission or Board, the court may order such additional evidence to be taken before the Commission or Board and to be adduced upon the hearing in such manner and upon such terms and conditions as to the court may seem proper. The Commission or Board may modify its findings as to the facts, or make new findings, by reason of the additional evidence so taken, and it shall file such modified or new findings, which, if supported by substantial evidence, shall be conclusive, and its recommendations, if any, for the modification or setting aside of its original order, with the return of such additional evidence. The judgment and decree of the court shall be final, except that the same shall be subject to review by the Supreme Court upon certiorari as provided in section 1254 of title 28, United States Code.

Additional evidence.

62 Stat. 928.
28 U. S. C., Sup.
III, § 1254.
Review.

"Any party required by such order of the Commission or Board to cease and desist from a violation charged may obtain a review of such order in said United States court of appeals by filing in the court a written petition praying that the order of the Commission or Board be set aside. A copy of such petition shall be forthwith served upon the Commission or Board, and thereupon the Commission or Board forthwith shall certify and file in the court a transcript of the record as hereinbefore provided. Upon the filing of the transcript the court shall have the same jurisdiction to affirm, set aside, or modify the order of the Commission or Board as in the case of an application by the Commission or Board for the enforcement of its order, and the findings of the Commission or Board as to the facts, if supported by substantial evidence, shall in like manner be conclusive.

"The jurisdiction of the United States court of appeals to enforce, set aside, or modify orders of the Commission or Board shall be exclusive.

"Such proceedings in the United States court of appeals shall be given precedence over cases pending therein, and shall be in every way expedited. No order of the Commission or Board or the judgment of the court to enforce the same shall in anywise relieve or absolve any person from any liability under the antitrust Acts.

Precedence of proceedings.

Service of processes, etc.

"Complaints, orders, and other processes of the Commission or Board under this section may be served by anyone duly authorized by the Commission or Board, either (a) by delivering a copy thereof to the person to be served, or to a member of the partnership to be served, or to the president, secretary, or other executive officer or a director of the corporation to be served; or (b) by leaving a copy thereof at the principal office or place of business of such person; or (c) by registering and mailing a copy thereof addressed to such person at his principal office or place of business. The verified return by the person so serving said complaint, order, or other process setting forth the manner of said service shall be proof of the same, and the return post-office receipt for said complaint, order, or other process registered and mailed as aforesaid shall be proof of the service of the same."

APPROVED, December 29, 1950.

The Bank Holding Company Act of 1956 (excerpts)

An Act to define bank holding companies, control their future expansion, and require divestment of their nonbanking interests.

May 9, 1956
[H. R. 6227]

Be it enacted by the Senate and House of Representatives of the United States of America in Congress assembled, That this Act may be cited as the "Bank Holding Company Act of 1956."

Bank Holding Company Act of 1956.

Definitions

Sec. 2. (a) "Bank holding company" means any company (1) which directly or indirectly owns, controls, or holds with power to vote, 25 per centum or more of the voting shares of each of two or more banks or of a company which is or becomes a bank holding company by virtue of this Act, or (2) which controls in any manner the election of a majority of the directors of each of two or more banks, or (3) for the benefit of whose shareholders or members 25 per centum or more of the voting shares of each of two or more banks or a bank holding company is held by trustees; and for the purposes of this Act, any successor to any such company shall be deemed to be a bank holding company from the date as of which such predecessor company became a bank holding company. Notwithstanding the foregoing (A) no bank shall be a bank holding company by virtue of its ownership or control of shares in a fiduciary capacity, except where such shares are held for the benefit of the shareholders of such bank, (B) no company shall be a bank holding company which is registered under the Investment Company Act of 1940, and was so registered prior to May 15, 1955 (or which is affiliated with any such company in such manner as to constitute an affiliated company within the meaning of such Act), unless such company (or such affiliated company), as the case may be, directly owns 25 per centum or more of the voting shares of each of two or more banks, (C) no company shall be a bank holding company by virtue of its ownership or control of shares acquired by it in connection with its underwriting of securities and which are held only for such period of time as will permit the sale thereof upon a reasonable basis, (D) no company formed for the sole purpose of participating in a proxy solicitation shall be a bank holding company by virtue of its control of voting rights of shares acquired in the course of such solicitation, and (E) no company shall be a bank holding company if at least 80 per centum of its total assets are composed of holdings in the field of agriculture.

54 Stat. 789.
15 USC 80a-51.

(b) "Company" means any corporation, business trust, association, or similar organization, but shall not include (1) any corporation the majority of the shares of which are owned by the United States or by any State, or (2) any corporation or community chest, fund, or foundation, organized and operated exclusively for religious, charitable, or educational purposes, no part of the net earnings of which inures to the benefit of any private shareholder or individual, and no substantial part of the activities of which is carrying propaganda, or otherwise attempting to influence legislation, or (3) any partnership.

(c) "Bank" means any national banking association or any State bank, savings bank, or trust company, but shall not include any organization operating under section 25 (a) of the Federal Reserve Act, or any organization which does not do business within the United States. "State member bank" means any State bank which is a member of the Federal Reserve System. "District bank" means any State bank organized or operating under the Code of Law for the District of Columbia.

41 Stat. 378.
12 USC 611, 612.

"State member bank."
"District bank."

(d) "Subsidiary," with respect to a specified bank holding company, means (1) any company 25 per centum or more of whose voting shares (excluding shares owned by the United States or by any company wholly owned by the United States) is owned or controlled by such bank holding company; or (2) any company the election of a majority of whose directors is controlled in any manner by such bank holding company; (3) any company 25 per centum or more of whose voting shares are held by trustees for the benefit of the shareholders or members of such bank holding company.

(e) The term "successor" shall include any company which acquires directly or indirectly from a bank holding company shares of any bank, when and if the relationship between such company and the bank holding company is such that the transaction effects no substantial change in the control of the bank or beneficial ownership of such shares of such bank. The Board may, by regulation, further define the term "successor" to the extent necessary to prevent evasion of the purposes of this Act.

(f) "Board" means the Board of Governors of the Federal Reserve System.

(g) "Agriculture," as used in section 2 (a), includes farming in all its branches including fruitgrowing, dairying, the raising of livestock, bees, furbearing animals, or poultry, forestry or lumbering operations, and the production of naval stores, and operations directly related thereto.

Acquisition of Bank Shares or Assets

Sec. 3. (a) It shall be unlawful except with the prior approval of the Board (1) for any action to be taken which results in a company becoming a bank holding company under section 2 (a) of this Act; (2) for any bank holding company to acquire direct or indirect ownership or control of any voting shares of any bank if, after such acquisition, such company will directly or indirectly own or control more than 5 per centum of the voting shares of such bank; (3) for any bank holding company or subsidiary thereof, other than a bank, to acquire all or substantially all of the assets of a bank; or (4) for any bank holding company to merge or consolidate with any other bank holding company. Notwithstanding the foregoing this prohibition shall not apply to (A) shares acquired by a bank, (i) in good faith in a fiduciary capacity, except where such shares are held for the benefit of the shareholders of such bank, or (ii) in the regular course of securing or collecting a debt previously contracted in good faith, but any shares acquired after the date of enactment of this Act in securing or collecting any such previously contracted debt shall be disposed of within a period of two years from the date on which they were acquired; or (B) additional shares acquired by a bank holding company in a bank in which such bank holding company owned or controlled a majority of the voting shares prior to such acquisition.

(b) Upon receiving from a company any application for approval under this section, the Board shall give notice to the Comptroller of the Currency, if the applicant company or any bank the voting shares or assets of which are sought to be acquired is a national banking association or a District bank, or to the appropriate supervisory authority of the interested State, if the applicant company or any bank the voting shares or assets of which are sought to be acquired is a State bank, and shall allow thirty days within which the views and recommendations of the Comptroller of the Currency or the State supervisory authority, as the case may be, may be submitted. If the Comptroller of the Currency or the State supervisory authority so notified by the Board disapproves the application in writing within said thirty days, the Board shall forthwith give written notice of that fact to the applicant. Within three days after giving such notice to the applicant, the Board shall notify in writing the applicant and the disapproving authority of the date for commencement of a hearing by it on such application. Any such hearing shall be commenced not less than ten nor more than thirty days after the Board has given written notice to the applicant of the action of the disapproving authority. The length of any such hearing shall be determined by the Board, but it shall afford all interested parties a reasonable opportunity to testify at such hearing. At the conclusion thereof, the Board shall by order grant or deny the application on the basis of the record made at such hearing.

(c) In determining whether or not to approve any acquisition or merger or consolidation under this section, the Board shall take into consideration the following factors: (1) the financial history and condition of the company or companies and the banks concerned; (2) their prospects; (3) the character of their management; (4) the convenience, needs, and welfare of the communities and the area concerned; and (5) whether or not the effect of such acquisition or merger or consolidation would be to expand the size or extent of the bank holding company system involved beyond limits consistent with adequate and sound banking, the public interest, and the preservation of competition in the field of banking.

(d) Notwithstanding any other provision of this section, no application shall be approved under this section which will permit any bank holding company or any subsidiary thereof to acquire, directly or indirectly, any voting shares of, interest in, or all or substantially all of the assets of any additional bank located outside of the State in which such bank holding company maintains its principal office and place of business or in which it conducts its principal operations unless the acquisition of such shares or assets of a State bank by an out-of-State bank holding company is specifically authorized by the statute laws of the State in which such bank is located, by language to that effect and not merely by implication.

Interests in Nonbanking Organizations

Sec. 4. (a) Except as otherwise provided in this Act, no bank holding company shall—

(1) after the date of enactment of this Act acquire direct or indirect ownership or control of any voting shares of any company which is not a bank, or

(2) after two years from the date of enactment of this Act or from the date as of which it becomes a bank holding company, whichever is later, retain direct or indirect ownership or control of any voting shares of any company which is not a bank or a bank holding company or engage in any business other than that of banking or of managing or controlling banks or of furnishing services to or performing services for any bank of which it owns or controls 25 per centum or more of the voting shares.

The Board is authorized, upon application by a bank holding company, to extend the period referred to in paragraph (2) above from time to time as to such bank holding company for not more than one year at a time if, in its judgment, such an extension would not be detrimental to the public interest, but no such extension shall extend beyond a date five years after the date of enactment of this Act or five years after the date as of which a company becomes a bank holding company, whichever is later.

(b) After two years from the date of enactment of this Act, no certificate evidencing shares of any bank holding company shall bear any statement purporting to represent shares of any other company except a bank or a bank holding company, nor shall the ownership, sale, or transfer of shares of any bank holding company be conditioned in any manner whatsoever upon the ownership, sale, or transfer of shares of any other company except a bank or a bank holding company.

Nonapplicability of prohibitions.

(c) The prohibitions in this section shall not apply—

(1) to shares owned or acquired by a bank holding company in any company engaged solely in holding or operating properties used wholly or substantially by any bank with respect to which it is a bank holding company in its operations or acquired for such future use or engaged solely in conducting a safe deposit business, or solely in the business of furnishing services to or performing services for such holding company and banks with respect to which it is a bank holding company, or in liquidating assets acquired from such bank holding company and such banks;

(2) to shares acquired by a bank company holding which is a bank, or by any banking subsidiary of a bank holding company, in satisfaction of a debt previously contracted in good faith, but such bank holding company or such subsidiaries shall dispose of such shares within a period of two years from the date on which they were acquired or from the date of enactment of this Act, whichever is later;

(3) to shares acquired by a bank holding company from any of its subsidiaries which subsidiary has been requested to dispose of such shares by any Federal or State authority having statutory power to examine such subsidiary, but such bank holding company shall dispose of such shares within a period of two years from the date on which they were acquired or from the date of enactment of this Act, whichever is later;

(4) to shares which are held or acquired by a bank holding company which is a bank or by any banking subsidiary of a bank holding company, in good faith in a fiduciary capacity, except where such shares are held for the benefit of the shareholders of such bank holding company or any of its subsidiaries, or to shares which are of the kinds and amounts eligible for investment by National banking associations under the provisions of section 5136 of the Revised Statutes, or to shares lawfully acquired and owned prior to the date of enactment of this Act by a bank which is a bank holding company, or by any of its wholly owned subsidiaries;

12 USC 24.

(5) to shares of any company which are held or acquired by a bank holding company which do not include more than 5 per centum of the outstanding voting securities of such company, and do not have a value greater than 5 per centum of the value of the total assets of the bank holding company, or to the ownership by a bank holding company of shares, securities, or obligations of an investment company which is not

a bank holding company and which is not engaged in any business other than investing in securities, which securities do not include more than 5 per centum of the outstanding voting securities of any company and do not include any single asset having a value greater than 5 per centum of the value of the total assets of the bank holding company;

(6) to shares of any company all the activities of which are of a financial, fiduciary, or insurance nature and which the Board after due notice and hearing, and on the basis of the record made at such hearing, by order has determined to be so closely related to the business of banking or of managing or controlling banks as to be a proper incident thereto and as to make it unnecessary for the prohibitions of this section to apply in order to carry out the purposes of this Act;

(7) to any bank holding company which is a labor, agricultural, or horticultural organization and which is exempt from taxation under section 501 of the Internal Revenue Code of 1954; or

68A Stat. 163.
26 USC 501.

(8) to shares held or acquired by a bank holding company in any company which is organized under the laws of a foreign country and which is engaged principally in the banking business outside the United States.

Administration

Sec. 5. (a) Within one hundred and eighty days after the date of enactment of this Act, or within one hundred and eighty days after becoming a bank holding company, whichever is later, each bank holding company shall register with the Board on forms prescribed by the Board, which shall include such information with respect to the financial condition and operations, management, and intercompany relationships of the bank holding company and its subsidiaries, and related matters, as the Board may deem necessary or appropriate to carry out the purposes of this Act. The Board may, in its discretion, extend the time within which a bank holding company shall register and file the requisite information.

(b) The Board is authorized to issue such regulations and orders as may be necessary to enable it to administer and carry out the purposes of this Act and prevent evasions thereof.

(c) The Board from time to time may require reports under oath to keep it informed as to whether the provisions of this Act and such regulations and orders issued thereunder have been complied with; and the Board may make examinations of each bank holding company and each subsidiary thereof, the cost of which shall be assessed against, and paid by, such holding company. The Board shall, as far as possible use the reports of examinations made by the Comptroller of the Currency, the Federal Deposit Insurance Corporation, or the appropriate State bank supervisory authority for the purposes of this section.

(d) Before the expiration of two years following the date of enactment of this Act, and each year thereafter in the Board's annual report to the Congress, the Board shall report to the Congress the results of the administration of this Act, stating what, if any, substantial difficulties have been encountered in carrying out the purposes of this Act, and any recommendations as to changes in the law which in the opinion of the Board would be desirable.

Report to Congress.

Borrowing by Bank Holding Company or Its Subsidiaries

Sec. 6. (a) From and after the date of enactment of this Act, it shall be unlawful for a bank—

(1) to invest any of its funds in the capital stock, bonds, debentures, or other obligations of a bank holding company of which it is a subsidiary, or of any other subsidiary of such bank holding company;

(2) to accept the capital stock, bonds, debentures, or other obligations of a bank holding company of which it is a subsidiary or any other subsidiary of such bank holding company, as collateral security for ad-

vances made to any person or company: *Provided, however,* That any bank may accept such capital stock, bonds, debentures, or other obligations as security for debts previously contracted, but such collateral shall not be held for a period of over two years;

(3) to purchase securities, other assets or obligations under repurchase agreement from a bank holding company of which it is a subsidiary or any other subsidiary of such bank holding company; and

(4) to make any loan, discount or extension of credit to a bank holding company of which it is a subsidiary or to any other subsidiary of such bank holding company.

Non-interest-bearing deposits to the credit of a bank shall not be deemed to be a loan or advance to the bank of deposit, nor shall the giving of immediate credit to a bank upon uncollected items received in the ordinary course of business be deemed to be a loan or advance to the depositing bank.

(b) The provisions of this section shall not apply (1) to the capital stock, bonds, debentures, or other obligations of any company described in section 4 (c) (1) of this Act, or (2) to any company whose subsidiary status has arisen out of a bona fide debt to the bank contracted prior to the date of the creation of such status, or (3) to any company whose subsidiary status exists by reason of the ownership or control of voting shares thereof by the bank as executor, administrator, trustee, receiver, agent, or depositary, or in any other fiduciary capacity, except where such shares are held for the benefit of all or a majority of the stockholders of such bank.

Ante, p. 136.

Reservation of Rights to States

Sec. 7. The enactment by the Congress of the Bank Holding Company Act of 1956 shall not be construed as preventing any State from exercising such powers and jurisdiction which it now has or may hereafter have with respect to banks, bank holding companies, and subsidiaries thereof.

Penalties

Sec. 8. Any company which willfully violates any provision of this Act, or any regulation or order issued by the Board pursuant thereto, shall upon conviction be fined not more than $1,000 for each day during which the violation continues. Any individual who willfully participates in a violation of any provision of this Act shall upon conviction be fined not more than $10,000 or imprisoned not more than one year, or both. Every officer, director, agent, and employee of a bank holding company shall be subject to the same penalties for false entries in any book, report, or statement of such bank holding company as are applicable to officers, directors, agents, and employees of member banks for false entries in any books, reports, or statements of member banks under section 1005 of title 18, United States Code.

62 Stat. 750.

Judicial Review

Sec. 9. Any party aggrieved by an order of the Board under this Act may obtain a review of such order in the United States Court of Appeals within any circuit wherein such party has its principal place of business, or in the Court of Appeals in the District of Columbia, by filing in the court, within sixty days after the entry of the Board's order, a petition praying that the order of the Board be set aside. A copy of such petition shall be forthwith served upon the Board, and thereupon the Board shall certify and file in the court a transcript of the record made before the Board. Upon the filing of the transcript the court shall have jurisdiction to affirm, set aside, or modify the order of the Board and to require the Board to take such action with regard to the matter under review as the court deems proper. The findings of the Board as to the facts, if supported by substantial evidence, shall be conclusive.

The Bank Merger Act of 1960

May 13, 1960
[S. 1062]

An Act to amend the Federal Deposit Insurance Act to require Federal approval for mergers and consolidations of insured banks.

Be it enacted by the Senate and House of Representatives of the United States of America in Congress assembled. That subsection (c) of section 18 of the Federal Deposit Insurance Act is amended by striking out the third sentence and inserting in lieu thereof the following: "No insured bank shall merge or consolidate with any other insured bank or, either directly or indirectly, acquire the assets of, or assume liability to pay any deposits made in, any other insured bank without the prior written consent (i) of the Comptroller of the Currency if the acquiring, assuming, or resulting bank is to be a national bank or a District bank, or (ii) of the Board of Governors of the Federal Reserve System if the acquiring, assuming, or resulting bank is to be a State member bank (except a District bank), or (iii) of the Corporation if the acquiring, assuming, or resulting bank is to be a nonmember insured bank (except a District bank). Notice of any proposed merger, consolidation, acquisition of assets, or assumption of liabilities, in a form approved by the Comptroller, the Board, or the Corporation, as the case may be, shall (except in a case where the furnishing of reports under the seventh sentence of this subsection is not required) be published, at appropriate intervals during a period (prior to the approval or disapproval of the transaction) at least as long as the period allowed under such sentence for furnishing such reports, in a newspaper of general circulation in the community or communities where the main offices of the banks involved are located (or, if there is no such newspaper in any such community, then in the newspaper of general circulation published nearest thereto). In granting or withholding consent under this subsection, the Comptroller, the Board, or the Corporation, as the case may be, shall consider the financial history and condition of each of the banks involved, the adequacy of its capital structure, its future earnings prospects, the general character of its management, the convenience and needs of the community to be served, and whether or not its corporate powers are consistent with the purposes of this Act. In the case of a merger, consolidation, acquisition of assets, or assumption of liabilities, the appropriate agency shall also take into consideration the effect of the transaction on competition (including any tendency toward monopoly), and shall not approve the transaction unless, after considering all of such factors, it finds the transaction to be in the public interest. In the interests of uniform standards, before acting on a merger, consolidation, acquisition of assets, or assumption of liabilities under this subsection, the agency (unless it finds that it must act immediately in order to prevent the probable failure of one of the banks involved) shall request a report on the competitive factors involved from the Attorney General and the other two banking agencies referred to in this subsection (which report shall be furnished within thirty calendar days of the date on which it is requested, or within ten calendar days of such date if the requesting agency advises the Attorney General and the other two banking agencies that an emergency exists requiring expeditious action). The Comptroller, the Board, and the Corporation shall each include in its annual report to the Congress a description of each merger, consolidation, acquisition of assets, or assumption of liabilities approved by it during the period covered by the report, along with the following information: the name and total resources of each bank involved; whether a report has been submitted by the Attorney General hereunder, and, if so, a summary by the Attorney General of the substance of such report; and a statement by the Comptroller, the Board, or the Corporation, as the case may be, of the basis for its approval."

APPROVED, May 13, 1960.

Federal Deposit Insurance Act, amendment.
64 Stat. 892.
12 USC 1828
Mergers and consolidations.

Publications of notice.

Report by Attorney General.

Report to Congress.

The Bank Merger Act of 1966

February 21, 1966
[S. 1698]

An Act to establish a procedure for the review of proposed bank mergers so as to eliminate the necessity for the dissolution of merged banks, and for other purposes.

Bank mergers.
64 Stat. 892.

Be it enacted by the Senate and House of Representatives of the United States of America in Congress assembled, That (a) section 18 (c) of the Federal Deposit Insurance Act (12 U.S.C. 1828 (c)) is amended to read:

"(c) (1) Except with the prior written approval of the responsible agency, which shall in every case referred to in this paragraph be the Corporation, no insured bank shall—

"(A) merge or consolidate with any noninsured bank or institution;

"(B) assume liability to pay any deposits made in, or similiar liabilities of, any noninsured bank or institution;

"(C) transfer assets to any noninsured bank or institution in consideration of the assumption of liabilities for any portion of the deposits made in such insured bank.

"(2) No insured bank shall merge or consolidate with any other insured bank or, either directly or indirectly, acquire the assets of, or assume liability to pay any deposits made in, any other insured bank except with the prior written approval of the responsible agency, which shall be—

"(A) the Comptroller of the Currency if the acquiring, assuming, or resulting bank is to be a national bank or a District bank;

"(B) the Board of Governors of the Federal Reserve System if the acquiring, assuming, or resulting bank is to be a State member bank (except a District bank);

"(C) the Corporation if the acquiring, assuming, or resulting bank is to be a nonmember insured bank (except a District bank).

Notice of proposed merger transactions.

"(3) Notice of any proposed transaction for which approval is required under paragraph (1) or (2) (referred to hereafter in this subsection as a 'merger transaction') shall, unless the responsible agency finds that it must act immediately in order to prevent the probable failure of one of the banks involved, be published—

"(A) prior to the granting of approval of such transaction,

"(B) in a form approved by the responsible agency,

"(C) at appropriate intervals during a period at least as long as the period allowed for furnishing reports under paragraph (4) of this subsection, and

"(D) in a newspaper of general circulation in the community or communities where the main offices of the banks involved are located, or, if there is no such newspaper in any such community, then in the newspaper of general circulation published nearest thereto.

Attorney General.
Reports on competitive factors.

"(4) In the interests of uniform standards, before acting on any application for approval of a merger transaction, the responsible agency, unless it finds that it must act immediately in order to prevent the probable failure of one of the banks involved, shall request reports on the competitive factors involved from the Attorney General and the other two banking agencies referred to in this subsection. The reports shall be furnished within thirty calendar days of the date on which they are requested, or within ten calendar days of such date if the requesting agency advises the Attorney General and the other two banking agencies that an emergency exists requiring expeditious action.

"(5) The responsible agency shall not approve—

"(A) any proposed merger transaction which would result in a monopoly, or which would be in furtherance of any combination or conspiracy to monopolize or to attempt to monopolize the business of banking in any part of the United States, or

"(B) any other proposed merger transaction whose effect in any section of the country may be substantially to lessen competition, or to tend to create a monopoly, or which in any other manner would be in restraint of trade, unless it finds that the anticompetitive effects of the proposed transaction are clearly outweighed in the public interest by the probable effect of the transaction in meeting the convenience and needs of the community to be served.

In every case, the responsible agency shall take into consideration the financial and managerial resources and future prospects of the existing and proposed institutions, and the convenience and needs of the community to be served.

" (6) The responsible agency shall immediately notify the Attorney General of any approval by it pursuant to this subsection of a proposed merger transaction. If the agency has found that it must act immediately to prevent the probable failure of one of the banks involved and reports on the competitive factors have been dispensed with, the transaction may be consummated immediately upon approval by the agency. If the agency has advised the Attorney General and the other two banking agencies of the existence of an emergency requiring expeditious action and has requested reports on the competitive factors within ten days, the transaction may not be consummated before the fifth calendar day after the date of approval by the agency. In all other cases, the transaction may not be consummated before the thirtieth calendar day after the date of approval by the agency.

" (7) (A) Any action brought under the antitrust laws arising out of a merger transaction shall be commenced prior to the earliest time under paragraph (6) at which a merger transaction approved under paragraph (5) might be consummated. The commencement of such an action shall stay the effectiveness of the agency's approval unless the court shall otherwise specifically order. In any such action, the court shall review de novo the issues presented.

" (B) In any judicial proceeding attacking a merger transaction approved under paragraph (5) on the ground that the merger transaction alone and of itself constituted a violation of any antitrust laws other than section 2 of the Act of July 2, 1890; (section 2 of the Sherman Antitrust Act, 15 U.S.C. 2), the standards applied by the court shall be identical with those that the banking agencies are directed to apply under paragraph (5).

26 Stat. 209.

" (C) Upon the consummation of a merger transaction in compliance with this subsection and after the termination of any antitrust litigation commenced within the period prescribed in this paragraph, or upon the termination of such period if no such litigation is commenced therein, the transaction may not thereafter be attacked in any judicial proceeding on the ground that it alone and of itself constituted a violation of any antitrust laws other than section 2 of the Act of July 2, 1890 (section 2 of the Sherman Antitrust Act, 15 U.S.C. 2), but nothing in this subsection shall exempt any bank resulting from a merger transaction from complying with the antitrust laws after the consummation of such transaction.

" (D) In any action brought under the antitrust laws arising out of a merger transaction approved by a Federal supervisory agency pursuant to this subsection, such agency, and any State banking supervisory agency having jurisdiction within the State involved, may appear as a party of its own motion and as of right, and be represented by its counsel.

" (8) For the purposes of this subsection, the term 'antitrust laws' means the Act of July 2, 1890 (the Sherman Antitrust Act, 15 U.S.C. 1–7), the Act of October 15, 1914 (the Clayton Act, 15 U.S.C. 12–27), and any other Acts in pari materia.

" (9) Each of the responsible agencies shall include in its annual report to the Congress a description of each merger transaction approved by it during the period covered by the report, along with the following information:

" (A) the name and total resources of each bank involved;

" (B) whether a report was submitted by the Attorney General under paragraph (4), and, if so, a summary by the Attorney General of the substance of such report; and

" (C) a statement by the responsible agency of the basis for its approval."

(b) Section 18 of such Act is further amended by adding at the end thereof the following new subsection:

" (i) (1) No insured State nonmember bank (except a District bank) shall, without the prior consent of the Corporation, reduce the amount or retire any part of its common or preferred capital stock, or retire any part of its capital notes or debentures.

" (2) No insured bank shall convert into an insured State bank if its capital stock or its surplus will be less than the capital stock or surplus, respectively, of the converting bank at the time of the shareholder's meeting approving such conversion, without the prior written consent of—

"(A) the Comptroller of the Currency if the resulting bank is to be a District bank;

"(B) the Board of Governors of the Federal Reserve System if the resulting bank is to be a State member bank (except a District bank);

"(C) the Corporation if the resulting bank is to be a State non-member insured bank (except a District bank).

"(3) Without the prior written consent of the Corporation, no insured bank shall convert into a noninsured bank or institution.

"(4) In granting or withholding consent under this subsection, the responsible agency shall consider—

"(A) the financial history and condition of the bank,

"(B) the adequacy of its capital structure,

"(C) its future earnings prospects,

"(D) the general character of its management,

"(E) the convenience and needs of the community to be served, and

"(F) whether or not its corporate powers are consistent with the purposes of this Act."

Prior mergers. *Sec. 2.* (a) Any merger, consolidation, acquisition of assets, or assumption of liabilities involving an insured bank which was consummated prior to June 17, 1963, the bank resulting from which has not been dissolved or divided and has not effected a sale or distribution of assets and has not taken any other similar action pursuant to a final judgment under the antitrust laws prior to the enactment of this Act, shall be conclusively presumed to have not been in violation of any antitrust laws other than section 2 of the Act of July 2, 1890 (section 2 of the Sherman Antitrust Act, 15 U.S.C. 2).

(b) No merger, consolidation, acquisition of assets, or assumption of liabilities involving an insured bank which was consummated after June 16, 1963, and prior to the date of enactment of this Act and as to which no litigation was initiated by the Attorney General prior to the date of enactment of this Act may be attacked after such date in any judicial proceeding on the ground that it alone and of itself constituted a violation of any

26 Stat. 209. antitrust laws other than section 2 of the Act of July 2, 1890 (section 2 of the Sherman Antitrust Act, 15 U.S.C. 2).

(c) Any court having pending before it on or after the date of enactment of this Act any litigation initiated under the antitrust laws by the Attorney General after June 16, 1963, with respect to the merger, consolidation, acquisition of assets, or assumption of liabilities of an insured bank consummated after June 16, 1963, shall apply the substantive rule of law set forth in section 18(c)(5) of the Federal Deposit Insurance Act, as amended by this Act.

"Antitrust laws." (d) For the purposes of this section, the term "antitrust laws" means the **38 Stat. 730.** Act of July 2, 1890 (the Sherman Antitrust Act, 15 U.S.C. 1–7), the Act of October 15, 1914 (the Clayton Act, 15 U.S.C. 12–27), and any other Acts in pari materia.

12 USC 1828. *Sec. 3.* Any application for approval of a merger transaction (as the term "merger transaction" is used in section 18(c) of the Federal Deposit Insurance Act) which was made before the date of enactment of this Act, but was withdrawn or abandoned as a result of any objections made or any suit brought by the Attorney General, may be reinstituted and shall be acted upon in accordance with the provisions of this Act without prejudice by such withdrawal, abandonment, objections, or judicial proceedings.

Approved, February 21, 1966.

Bibliography

A. Manuscripts

Board of Governors of the Federal Reserve System. Records, minutes and opinions, Federal Reserve Archives.

Boutwell, George. Papers, Library of Congress.

Chase, Salmon Portland. Papers, Library of Congress.

_____. Papers, Pennsylvania Historical Society.

Cooke, Jay. Memoirs, Baker Library, Harvard University.

_____. Papers, Pennsylvania Historical Society.

Cushing, Caleb. Papers, Library of Congress.

Ewing, Thomas. Papers, Library of Congress.

Fessenden, William Pitt. Papers, Library of Congress.

Forgan, James B. Papers, The First National Bank of Chicago.

Gage, Lyman Judson. Papers, Library of Congress.

Grant, Ulysses S. Papers, Library of Congress.

Johnson, Andrew. Papers, Library of Congress.

Lincoln, Abraham. Papers, Library of Congress.

McCulloch, Hugh. Papers, Library of Congress.

_____. Papers, Lilly Library, Indiana University.

_____. Notebooks, United States Treasury Archives.

McKinley, William. Papers, Library of Congress.

Sherman, John. Papers, Library of Congress.

Trenholm, William L. Papers, Library of Congress.

United States Comptroller of the Currency. Letters and forms, National Archives.

United States Treasury. Letters and circulars, National Archives.

Walker, Robert J. Papers, Library of Congress.

Washington, George. Papers, Library of Congress.

Wolcott, Oliver. Papers, Library of Congress.

B. Government Publications

Board of Governors of the Federal Reserve System. *Annual Reports for 1914-1967.*

_____. *Federal Reserve Bulletin, various issues from 1914 to 1967.*

Continental Congress. *Journals,* XX, 1781.

Federal Deposit Insurance Corporation. *Annual Reports for 1952, 1953.*

United States Bureau of the Census. *Historical Statistics of the United States, Colonial Times to 1957.*

United States Comptroller of the Currency, Advisory Committee on Banking. *National Banks and the Future.* Washington, 1962.

_____. *Annual Reports for 1863-1966.*

_____. *Instructions and Suggestions of the Comptroller of the Currency.* Washington, 1864.

_____. *Instructions in Regard to the Organization, Extension, and Management of National Banks, 1884.*

_____. *Instructions Relative to the Organization and Management of National Banks, 1891.*

_____. *Instructions and Suggestions of the Comptroller of the Currency Relative to the Organization and Management of National Banks for 1893, 1900, 1902-1905, 1907, 1909.*

_____. *Instructions of the Comptroller of the Currency Relative to the Organization and Management of National Banks for 1911, 1912, 1914, 1918.*

_____. *Instructions of the Comptroller of the Currency Relative to the Organization and Powers of National Banks for 1919, 1920, 1923, 1928.*

_____. *Instructions to National Bank Examiners.* Washington, 1912, 1917, 1951.

_____. *Consolidations of the National Banks.* Washington, 1928.

_____. *Digest of Opinions, Relating to Operations and Powers of National Banks.* Washington, 1960.

United States Congress, Joint Committee on the Economic Report. *Subcommittee on General Credit Control and Debt Management (Monetary Policy and the Management of the Public Debt—Replies to Questions and Other Materials).* Parts 1 and 2, 1952.

United States *Congressional Globe.* 25 Congress, 2 session, 1837-1838; 37 Congress, 2 and 3 sessions, 1861-1863; 38 Congress, 1 and 2 sessions, 1863-1865.

United States *Congressional Record.* 48 Congress, 2 session, 1884-1885; 63 Congress, 2 session, 1913-1914; 64 Congress, 1 session, 1915-1916; 65 Congress, 3 session, 1918-1919; 66 Congress, 1 session, 1919; 67 Congress, 1 and 2 sessions, 1921-1922.

United States House of Representatives. *Journal.* 15 Congress, 2 session, 1818-1819.

————. *Report No. 2111 (Power of the Comptroller of the Currency Over National Banks).* 72 Congress, 2 session.

————. *Banking and Currency Committee (Hearings on an Amendment to Abolish the Office of the Comptroller of the Currency).* 67 Congress, 1 session.

————. *Banking and Currency Committee (Hearings on the Extension of a Temporary Plan for Deposit Insurance.)* 73 Congress, 2 session.

————. *Banking and Currency Committee (Hearings on the Banking Act of 1935).* 74 Congress, 1 session.

————. *Banking and Currency Committee (Hearings on the Financial Institutions Act of 1957).* Parts 1 and 2. 85 Congress, 1 session.

————. *Banking and Currency Committee (Hearings on the Conflict of Federal and State Banking Laws).* 88 Congress, 1 session.

————. *Banking and Currency Committee (Hearings to Eliminate Unsound Competition for Savings and Time Deposits).* 89 Congress, 2 session.

————. *Banking and Currency Committee, Subcommittee on Domestic Finance (Hearings to Amend the Bank Merger Act of 1960).* 89 Congress, 1 session.

————. *Banking and Currency Committee (Subcommittee hearings on Legislation to Provide a Guaranty Fund for Depositors in Banks).* 72 Congress, 1 session.

————. *Banking and Currency Committee and Subcommittee on Bank Supervision and Insurance (Hearings on the Consolidation of Bank Examining and Supervisory Functions).* 89 Congress, 1 session.

United States Senate. *Document No. 186 (Administrative Procedure in Government Agencies).* Parts 9 and 13. 76 Congress, 3 session.

————. *Banking and Currency Committee (Hearings on the Nomination of John Skelton Williams).* Parts 1-3. 65 Congress, 3 session.

————. *Banking and Currency Committee (Hearings on Operation of the National and Federal Reserve Banking Systems).* Parts 1-5, 71 Congress, 3 session; Parts 1 and 2, 72 Congress, 1 session.

————. *Summary of the Financial Institutions Act of 1957.* 85 Congress, 1 session.

United States Treasury. *Annual Reports for 1790-1828, 1860-1863, 1897-1898, 1901, 1935-1936.*

————. *Documents and Statements Pertaining to the Banking Emergency.* Part 1. Washington, 1933.

United States Statutes at Large. *The Statutes at Large, Treaties, and Proclamations of the United States of America.* 37 Congress, 1861-1863; 38 Congress, 1863-1865; 39 Congress, 1865-1867; 41 Congress, 1869-1871; 43 Congress, 1873-1875; 45 Congress, 1877-1879; 49 Congress, 1885-1887; 56 Congress, 1899-1901; 73 Congress, 1933-1934.

C. Newspapers and Periodicals

American Banker.
The Atlantic Monthly.
The Bankers Magazine.
Banking.
Bicknall's Counterfeit Detector and Bank Note List.
The Board of Trade Journal and Commercial Gazette.
The Weekly Bond Buyer.
Building and Loan Annals.
Business Week.
Chicago Daily Tribune.
The Commercial and Financial Chronicle.
Current History.
Daily National Intelligencer.
De Bow's Review.
Dun's Review.
The Economist.
The Fortnightly.
Fortune.
Harper's Weekly.
Indianapolis Sun.
The Merchants' Magazine and Commercial Review (Hunt's).
New York Daily Tribune.
New York Evening Post.
The New York Herald.
The New York Times.
The New Yorker.
New York World.
North American Review.
The Saturday Evening Post.
Thompson's Bank Note and Commercial Reporter.
The Wall Street Journal.
The Washington Evening Star.
The Washington Post.

D. Proceedings

American Academy of Political Science. *Proceedings, January 1911.*
American Bankers Association. *The Commercial and Financial Chronicle, Supplement, November 22, 1902.*
American Economic Association. *American Economic Review, March 1936.*
National Association of Supervisors of State Banks. *Proceedings of the Thirty-Seventh Annual Convention, 1938.*

The Monetary Commission. *Report of the Proceedings of the Monetary Commission* of the Indianapolis Convention, 1897 and 1898.

E. Articles, Pamphlets, and Printed Speeches

Anderson, George E. "The Experiment in Supervision." *Banking,* 31, August 1938.
———. "Uniform Bank Supervision." *Banking,* 31, July 1938.

Anonymous. "The National Banks: Down with the Banks—Greenbacks Forever." Reprinted from *Hines Quarterly,* April 1869.

———. *A Reply to the Report of a Committee of the New York Clearing House Association on the Currency Act.* 1864.

———. *An Examination into the Prospective Effects of the National Banks upon the Public Welfare.* New York, 1863.

Baird, Henry Carey. *Pamphlets on Money, Banks and Finance.* Philadelphia: Henry Carey Baird & Co., 1873, 1875.

Breckenridge, R. M. "Notes: The Comptroller's Objections to Currency Reform." *The Journal of Political Economy,* VII, March 1899.

Cagle, Caroline H. and Kolb, Raymond C. "New Commercial Banking Offices, 1936-1947." *Federal Reserve Bulletin,* 34, May 1948.

Cleveland, F. A. "The Financial Reports of National Banks as a Means of Public Control." *The Annals of the American Academy of Political and Social Science,* XXIV, July 1904.

Dunne, Gerald T. "A Christmas Present for the President." *Business Horizons,* 6, Winter 1963.

———. "President Grant and Chief Justice Chase: A Footnote to the Legal Tender Cases." *Saint Louis University Law Journal,* 5, Fall 1959.

Flint, Waldo. *Some Strictures on an Act to Provide a National Currency, Secured by a Pledge of United States Stocks; and To Provide for the Circulation and Redemption Thereof.* Boston, 1863.

Gallatin, James. *Letters on the Proposed United States Banking System, and Further Issues of Legal Tender.* New York, 1863.

Goldenweiser, E. A. "Pritchard on the Federal Reserve Bank Note: Comment." *The Journal of Political Economy,* LV, August 1947.

Golembe, Carter H. "The Deposit Insurance Legislation of 1933." *Political Science Quarterly,* LXXV, June 1960.

Hammond, Bray. "Long and Short Term Credit in Early American Banking." *The Quarterly Journal of Economics,* XLIX, November 1934.

———. "The North's Empty Purse, 1861-1862." *The American Historical Review,* LXVII, October 1961.

Head, J. M. "Are National Banks Doomed?" *The Bankers Magazine,* CXI, September 1925.

Hilkert, Robert N. "The Muddle in Bank Supervision." *Business Review,* Federal Reserve Bank of Philadelphia, June 1964.

Jones, Homer. "An Appraisal of the Rules and Procedures of Bank Supervision, 1929-39." *The Journal of Political Economy,* XLVIII, April 1940.

Kinsella, Thomas. *National Banks: What Shall Be Substituted For Them? (An Address on Currency Reform).* Brooklyn, 1882.

Leong, Y. S. "An Estimate of the Volume of Deposit Currency in the United States." *The Journal of Political Economy,* XXXVII, October 1929.

Lord, Eleazar. *A Letter on National Currency Addressed to the Secretary of the Treasury.* New York, 1861.

———. *Six Letters on the Necessity and Practicability of a National Currency, and the Principles and Measures Essential to It.* New York, 1862.

Martin, Warwick. *National Banks and Legal-Tender Notes: Ten Letters Published in the American Sentry.* Washington, D. C., 1881.

McCulloch, Hugh. *Answers of the Comptroller of the Currency.* Cooke Papers, Pennsylvania Historical Society, July 1863.

Mortimer, Frank C. "National Banks and the Federal Reserve System." *Speech delivered at the Annual Convention of the American Institute of Banking, San Francisco, California, August 19, 1915.*

Murphy, George A. "The Challenge of Change in Banking." *Speech delivered at Stonier Graduate School of Banking, Rutgers University, New Brunswick, New Jersey, June 17, 1966.*

Norris, Frank L. "National Bank Examination." *Paper read at Brighton Beach, New York, July 8, 1912.*

O'Connor, J. F. T. *Address before the Dallas Clearing House Association.* Washington, D. C., 1933.

Patman, Wright. "The Truth About the Bank Merger Bill." *Speech before the House of Representatives, October 22, 1965.*

Pole, J. W. "Extent of Federal Supervision of Banking Today." *Congressional Digest,* 10, December 1931.

———; Dawes, Henry M.; Adams, Elmer E.; and Fleming, Robert V. "Would Extension of the Branch Banking System

Be Beneficial?" *Congressional Digest,* 10, December 1931.

Pritchard, Leland J. "The Federal Reserve Bank Note." *The Journal of Political Economy,* LV, April 1947.

———. "A Reply." *The Journal of Political Economy,* LV, August 1947.

Ridgely, William Barret. "Government Control of Banks and Trust Companies." *The Annals of the American Academy of Political and Social Science,* XXIV, July 1904.

Saxon, James J. "The Antitrust Laws and the Public Welfare." *Remarks before the Illinois State Chamber of Commerce, Chicago, Illinois, October 21, 1966.*

———. "Banks and Community Progress." *Remarks before the Florida Bankers Association, Miami Beach, Florida, March 22, 1963.*

———. "The Future of Banking Progress." *Speech before the National Bank Division of the American Bankers Association, San Francisco, California, October 24, 1966.*

———. "The Role of Deposit Insurance in Bank Regulation." *Remarks before the Seventh District Texas Bankers Association, Fort Worth, Texas, February 22, 1963.*

———. "The Specter of Over-Regulation." *Remarks before the National Bank Divi-* sion, American Bankers Association, Chicago, Illinois, October 4, 1965.

Schwartz, Anna Jacobson. "The Beginning of Competitive Banking in Philadelphia, 1782-1809," *The Journal of Political Economy,* LV, October 1947.

Scudder, Moses Lewis, Jr. *National Banking: A Discussion of the Merits of the Present System.* New York: G. P. Putnam's Sons, 1879.

Spaulding, Elbridge Gerry. "One Hundred Years of Progress in the Business of Banking." *Speech at the Meeting of the Bankers' Association at the International Exposition, Philadelphia, Pennsylvania, May 30, 1876.*

Warburg, Paul. "Political Pressure and the Future of the Federal Reserve System." *The Annals of the American Academy of Political and Social Science,* XCIX, January 1922.

Wettereau, James O. "New Light on the First Bank of the United States." *The Pennsylvania Magazine of History and Biography,* LXI, July 1937.

Wilkeson, Samuel. *How Our National Debt May Be A National Blessing.* Philadelphia, 1865.

Williams, John E. and Everitt, John L. *Report on the National Bank Currency Act, its Defects and its Effects.* New York, 1863.

Wilson, George, Jr. *How To Abolish the National Bank System.* St. Louis, 1879.

F. Books, Monographs, and Doctoral Dissertations

American Bankers Association, Economic Policy Commission. *Banking After the Crisis.* New York: American Bankers Association. 1934.

———. *The Bank Chartering History and Policies of the United States.* New York: American Bankers Association, 1935.

American Institute of Banking. *Contemporary Legislative and Banking Problems.* New York: American Institute of Banking, 1934.

Anderson, George Laverne. "The National Banking System, 1865-1875: A Sectional Institution." Urbana: University of Illinois, 1933.

Anderson, Thomas Joel. *Federal and State Control of Banking.* New York: The Bankers Publishing Company, 1934.

Bach, G. L. *Federal Reserve Policy-Making.* New York: Alfred A. Knopf, 1950.

Barger, Harold. *The Management of Money: A Survey of American Experience.* Chicago: Rand McNally and Company, 1964.

Barnett, George E. *State Banks and Trust Companies Since the Passage of the National-Bank Act.* Washington, D. C.: National Monetary Commission, 1911.

Bayley, Rafael A. *The National Loans of the United States, from July 4, 1776, to June 30, 1880.* Washington, D. C.: Government Printing Office, 1882.

Burgess, Warren Randolph. *The Reserve Banks and the Money Market.* New York and London: Harper and Brothers, 1936.

Caldwell, Lynton K. *The Administrative Theories of Hamilton and Jefferson.* Chicago: University of Chicago Press, 1944.

Carson, Deane, (ed.). *Banking and Monetary Studies.* Homewood, Illinois: Richard D. Irwin, Inc., 1963.

Cartinhour, Gaines Thomson. *Branch, Group and Chain Banking.* New York: The Macmillan Company, 1931.

Chapman, John M. and Westerfield, Ray B. *Branch Banking.* New York and London: Harper and Brothers, 1942.

Charlton, Joseph William. "The History of Banking in Illinois Since 1863." The University of Chicago Libraries, 1939.

Chittenden, L. E. *Personal Reminiscences 1840-1890.* New York: Richmond, Croscup and Company, 1893.

Clarke, M. St. Clair and Hall, D. A. *Legislative and Documentary History* of the Bank of the United States. Washington, D. C.: Gales and Seaton, 1832.

Collins, Charles Wallace. The Branch Banking Question. New York: The Macmillan Company, 1926.

Davis, Andrew MacFarland. The National Banking System: The Origin of the National Banking System. Washington, D. C.: National Monetary Commission, 1910.

Dewey, Davis Rich. Banking in the United States Before the Civil War: The Second United States Bank. Washington, D. C.: National Monetary Commission, 1910.

_____. Financial History of the United States. New York, London, Toronto: Longmans, Green and Co., 1939.

Donald, David (ed.). Inside Lincoln's Cabinet: The Civil War Diaries of Salmon P. Chase. New York: Longmans, Green and Co., 1954.

Dorfman, Joseph. The Economic Mind in American Civilization, 1606-1865. New York: The Viking Press, 1946.

Dunne, Gerald T. Monetary Decisions of the Supreme Court. New Brunswick: Rutgers University Press, 1960.

Eccles, Marriner S. Beckoning Frontiers. New York: Alfred A. Knopf, 1951.

Fischer, Gerald C. American Banking Structure: Its Evolution and Regulation. New York: Columbia University Press, 1967.

_____. Bank Holding Companies. New York: Columbia University Press, 1961.

Forgan, James B. Recollections of a Busy Life. New York: The Bankers Publishing Company, 1924.

Fox, Guy. "Supervision of Banking by the Comptroller of the Currency." Reprinted in Emmette S. Redford, Public Administration and Policy Formation. Austin: University of Texas Press, 1956.

Gage, Lyman Judson. Memoirs of Lyman J. Gage. New York: House of Field, Inc., 1937.

Gallatin, Albert. The Writings of Albert Gallatin. Henry Adams, (ed.). Philadelphia: J. B. Lippincott and Co., 1879.

Glass, Carter. An Adventure in Constructive Finance. Garden City: Doubleday, Page and Co., 1927.

Golembe, Carter H. and Warburton, Clark. Insurance of Bank Obligations in Six States During the Period 1829-1866. (Unpublished.) Washington, D. C.: Federal Deposit Insurance Corporation, 1958.

Gouge, William M. A Short History of Paper Money and Banking in the United States. Philadelphia: T. W. Ustick, 1833.

Grayson, Theodore J. Leaders and Periods of American Finance. New York: John Wiley and Sons, Inc., 1932.

Griffiths, William H. The Story of American Bank Note Company. New York: American Bank Note Company, 1959.

Hacker, Louis M. Alexander Hamilton in the American Tradition. New York: McGraw-Hill Book Company, Inc., 1957.

Hamilton, Alexander. The Works of Alexander Hamilton. Henry Cabot Lodge, (ed.). New York and London: G. P. Putnam's Sons, 1904.

Hammond, Bray. Banks and Politics in America from the Revolution to the Civil War. Princeton: Princeton University Press, 1957.

Harding, W. P. G. The Formative Period of the Federal Reserve System. Boston and New York: Houghton Mifflin Company, 1925.

Heinberg, John Gilbert. The Office of the Comptroller of the Currency. Baltimore: The Johns Hopkins Press, 1926.

Helderman, Leonard C. National and State Banks: A Study of Their Origins. Boston and New York: Houghton Mifflin Company, 1931.

Hepburn, A. Barton. A History of Currency in the United States. New York: The Macmillan Company, 1924.

Holdsworth, John Thom. Banking in the United States Before the Civil War: The First Bank of the United States. Washington. D. C.: National Monetary Commission, 1910.

James, F. Cyril. The Growth of Chicago Banks. New York and London: Harper and Brothers, 1938.

James, Marquis. Life of Andrew Jackson: Portrait of a President. Indianapolis: The Bobbs-Merrill Company, 1937.

Kane, Thomas P. The Romance and Tragedy of Banking: Problems and Incidents of Governmental Supervision of National Banks. New York: The Bankers Publishing Co., 1930.

Kinley, David. The Independent Treasury of the United States and Its Relations to the Banks of the Country. Washington, D. C.: National Monetary Commission, 1910.

Kirwan, Albert D. John J. Crittenden: The Struggle for the Union. Lexington: University of Kentucky Press, 1962.

Knox, John Jay. A History of Banking in the United States. New York: Bradford Rhodes and Company, 1900.

Larson, Henrietta Malia. Jay Cooke, Private Banker. Cambridge: Harvard University Press, 1936.

Laughlin, James Laurence. The Federal Reserve Act: Its Origin and Problems. New York: The Macmillan Company, 1933.

Lewis, Lawrence, Jr. A History of the Bank of North America: The First Bank Chartered in the United States. Philadelphia: J. B. Lippincott and Co., 1882.

Link, Arthur S. Wilson: The New Freedom. Princeton: Princeton University Press, 1956.

Malburn, William P. What Happened to

Our Banks. Indianapolis: The Bobbs-Merrill Company, 1934.

McCulloch, Hugh. *Men and Measures of Half a Century.* New York: Charles Scribner's Sons, 1889.

Mitchell, Broadus. *Heritage from Hamilton.* New York: Columbia University Press, 1957.

Morris, Henry C. *The History of The First National Bank of Chicago.* Chicago: R. R. Donnelley and Sons Company, 1902.

Morse, John T., Jr. *The Life of Alexander Hamilton.* Boston: Little, Brown, and Company, 1876.

Newcomb, Simon. *A Critical Examination of Our Financial Policy during the Southern Rebellion.* New York: D. Appleton and Company, 1865.

North, Douglass C. *The Economic Growth of the United States, 1790-1860.* Englewood Cliffs: Prentice-Hall, 1961.

Oberholtzer, Ellis Paxson. *Jay Cooke: Financier of the Civil War.* Philadelphia: George W. Jacobs and Company, 1907.

O'Connor, J. F. T. *The Banking Crisis and Recovery Under the Roosevelt Administration.* Chicago: Callaghan and Company, 1938.

Parton, James. *Life of Andrew Jackson.* Volume III. New York: Mason Brothers, 1860.

Pollard, James E. *The Journal of Jay Cooke or The Gibraltar Records.* Columbus: The Ohio State University Press, 1935.

Prescott, Frederick, C. *Alexander Hamilton and Thomas Jefferson.* New York: American Book Company, 1934.

Robertson, Ross M. *History of the American Economy.* New York: Harcourt, Brace and World, Inc., 1964.

Schlesinger, Arthur, Jr. *The Age of Jackson.* Boston: Little, Brown and Company, 1946.

Schuckers, J. W. *The Life and Public Services of Salmon Portland Chase.* New York: D. Appleton and Company, 1874.

Scroggs, William O. *A Century of Banking Progress.* Garden City: Doubleday, Page and Company, 1924.

Seager, Robert. *And Tyler Too: A Biography of John and Julia G. Tyler.* New York: McGraw-Hill Book Company, 1963.

Sherman, John. *Recollections of Forty Years in The House, Senate and Cabinet.* New York: The Werner Company, 1895.

Staff, Board of Governors of the Federal Reserve System. *Banking Studies.* Baltimore: Waverly Press, 1941.

Stilwell, Silas M. *Private History of the Origin and Purpose of The National Banking Law and System of Organized Credits for The United States.* New York: Trow's Printing and Bookbinding Co., 1879.

_____. *A System of National Finance: Notes Explanatory of Mr. Chase's Plan of National Finance.* Washington, D. C.: Government Printing Office, 1861.

Studenski, Paul and Krooss, Herman E. *Financial History of the United States.* New York, Toronto, London: McGraw-Hill Book Company, Inc., 1952.

_____. *Financial History of the United States.* New York, San Francisco, London: McGraw-Hill Book Company, Inc., 1963.

Sumner, William Graham. *A History of Banking in the United States.* New York: The Journal of Commerce and Commercial Bulletin, 1896.

Swanson, William Walker. "The Establishment of the National Banking System." University of Chicago, 1910.

Sweedlun, Verne S. "The Establishment of the National Banking System." University of Kansas, 1929.

Thompson, Thomas William. *Checks and Balances: A Study of the Dual Banking System in America.* Washington: National Association of Supervisors of State Banks, 1962.

Trescott, Paul B. *Money, Banking, and Economic Welfare.* New York: McGraw-Hill Book Company, Inc., 1960.

Trowbridge, J. T. *The Ferry-Boy and the Financier.* Boston: Walker, Wise, and Company, 1864.

Unger, Irwin. *The Greeback Era.* Princeton: Princeton University Press, 1964.

Upham, Cyril B. and Lamke, Edwin. *Closed and Distressed Banks.* Washington, D. C.: The Brookings Institution, 1934.

Van Deusen, Glyndon Garlock. *The Life of Henry Clay.* Boston: Little, Brown and Company, 1937.

Warden, Robert B. *An Account of the Private Life and Public Services of Salmon Portland Chase.* Cincinnati: Wilstach, Baldwin and Co., 1874.

Watkins, Leonard L. *Commercial Banking Reform in the United States.* Ann Arbor: University of Michigan, School of Business Administration, 1938.

White, Horace. *Money and Banking.* New York: Ginn and Company, 1936.

White, Leonard D. *The Federalists.* New York: The Macmillan Company, 1948.

_____. *The Jacksonians.* New York: The Macmillan Company, 1954.

_____. *The Jeffersonians.* New York: The Macmillan Company, 1951.

Wilburn, Jean Alexander. *Biddle's Bank: The Crucial Years.* New York: Columbia University Press, 1967.

Williams, Ralph D. "Historical Development and Administrative Role of the Comptroller of the Currency in the National Banking System of the United States." New York University, 1963.

Willis, Henry Parker. *The Federal Reserve System.* New York: The Ronald Press Company, 1923.

Woodworth, G. Walter. *The Money Market and Monetary Management.* New York, Evanston, and London: Harper and Row, 1965.

G. Miscellaneous

Board of Governors of the Federal Reserve System, Committee on Branch, Group and Chain Banking. "Branch Banking in the United States." (Unpublished.) 1932.

Continental-Illinois Bank and Trust Company. General archives.

The First National Bank of Chicago. General archives and organization papers. Minutes (from 1863-1865).

The First Pennsylvania Banking and Trust Company. General archives and organization papers. Minutes (from 1863-1865).

The Philadelphia National Bank. General archives.

Index

Administrative Assistant to the Comptroller, position of, 174, 177; from 1961 to the present, listing, 190

Advisory Committee on Banking, 149, 150, 155

agencies regulating banks, bank-examination cooperation among, 134-37; friction among, 107-16; listed, 1-9; move to unite in one single agency, 163; and stabilization policy, 141; supervisory jurisdiction of each, *table*, 2; supervisory policies set by, 163-64. *See also* Comptroller of the Currency, Federal Deposit Insurance Corporation, Federal Reserve System

Aldrich, Nelson, 88_n

Aldrich Bill, 88-90

allocation of banking resources, 153, 167-71

American Bankers Association, and bank regulation, 7-8; and branch banking, 101, 132; and central bank, 89; and condition reports, 81; Currency Commission of, 89-91; urges simplification and codification of banking law, 147

American colonies, banking in, 11-12; paper money in, 12-13

Analectic Magazine, 36

anti-trust legislation, Bank Holding Company Act of 1956, 237-42; Bank Merger Act of 1960, 243; Bank Merger Act of 1966, 243-46; bank mergers inhibited by, 154-56, 159; Celler-Kefauver Amendment to Clayton Act, 235-37; Clayton Act of 1914, 231-35; effects of, summarized, 186-87; Sherman Act of 1890, 230-31; Trust Powers Act of 1962, 228-30

auditing of Comptroller's Office, 177-78

Bank chartering, application form for, *photo*, 174; bond-secured currency as requirement for, 23; charter certificate, *photo*, 179; and circulation limitation, 57-59; Comptroller's role in, 59-61, 95; constraints on entry, 57-61; and conversions of state banks to national, 57-59; excesses in, 126; Federal Reserve's influence on, 95; and free-banking, 23, 61, 66-69; from 1860s to 1914, 57-69; from 1931 to 1955, 125-31; from 1935 to the present, 153-54; under National Bank Act of 1864, 49-54; of national banks, 57-69; of new banks versus conversion of old, 57-58; political aspects of, 21-22; post-depression policy on, 125-31; by special legislative acts, 21-22; of state banks under federal supervision, 126-31; of state banks, resurgence of, 64-66; of state banks versus national banks, 2, 61; supervisory officials' rulings on, 168-69

bank examination, beginnings of, 24-25; by Chief National Bank Examiner, 175-77, 180-81; Comptrollers' views on, 71-79;

conceptual role of, 165-67; cooperation among federal agencies on, 134-37; examiners' reports, *photos* 164, 166; federal, 25, 71-81; Federal Reserve Act's provisions for, 106-7; fee system for, 74, 76-79; fees for in 1875, *table*, 78; of foreign branches of national banks, 181; in foreign countries, 165; friction between federal agencies over, 107-16, 134-35; and loan evaluation problems in post-depression era, 134-35; loan classifications for, 135; as mandatory under national charter, 52; novel philosophy of, 136-37; and security valuation by new investment standards, 135-37; staff for, 176-77; by states, 24-25, 69-71

bank failures, during depression, 120-22, 125; effects of, 7; in rural areas, 99, 105

Bank Holding Company Act of 1956, 237-42

bank holidays, 122

Bank Merger Act of 1960, 156, 243

Bank Merger Act of 1966, 159, 178, 186-87, 243-46

bank mergers, and anti-trust legislation, 154-56, 159, 168, 178, 186-87; and issue of interlocking directorates, 155-56; from 1921 to 1931, *table*, 97; of national and state to permit branching, 101-2; of national and state from 1946 to 1966, *table*, 157

bank notes, of Bank of North America, *photo*, 14; of Bank of the United States, 19; bond-secured, 23, 37; circulation of, 63; in Colonial America, 14-16, *photo*, 14; counterfeiting of, 29-31; decline in profitability of issue, 62-64; depreciation of, 36; of Federal Reserve Bank, 180, *photos* 91, 109; limitations on national-bank issue of, 57-58; of national banks, 51, *photos* 52, 62, 119; pre-Civil War, 29; redemption and discounting of, 2; retirement of, 91, 119; securities for, *table*, 63; of state banks, 16, 36, *photo*, 22

Bank of Maryland, 13

Bank of Missouri, 28

Bank of New York, 13

Bank of North America, 13, 14

Bank of Pennsylvania, 13

Bank of the United States, branches of, 28; as central bank, 19; effect on economy of, 19-20; first, 18-19; recharter failures of, 20-22, 36; second, 19-20, *photo*, 20; statements of condition of, 23-24; third, 20-21, 36

bank regulation, and allocation of banking resources, 153, 167-71; before 1863, 11-32; beginnings of, 5-9, 17-20; and chartering, 21-23, 57-69, 125-31; and examination, 24-25, 69-81, 107-16; federal, first half century of, 55-86; federal agencies responsible for, 1-9; of multi-offices and multi-units, 81-86; and no-bank movement, 22; opposition to, 17; of state versus national banks, 2, 20-21; and supervision of operations, 23-27, 69-81

bank supervision, and allocation of banking resources, 153, 167-71; and bank-obliga-

tion of, 35-36; issuance of 35; and Legal Tender Act, 41; redemption of, 55-59
group banking, depression's effect on, 133-34; origin of, 85-86

Hamilton, Alexander, and Bank of the United States, 18-19; objection to branching, 28; portrait of, 18
Hamilton, John, quoted, 92
Hamlin, Charles, 109
Hannah, Adam, 85
Harding, William P. G., and condition reports, 110; quoted on abolishing Comptroller's Office, 115; and examination reports, 109
Hepburn, A. Barton, and banker opposition to Glass-Owen Bill, 91; and currency reform, 90
Hilkert, Robert N., quoted, 160-61
Hodge's Bank Note Safeguard, 31
holidays, banking, 122
Holmes, Oliver Wendell, 3
Hooper, Samuel, and Currency Act of 1863, 39, 41, 44
Hoover, Herbert, and national-bank branching, 105; and National Credit Corporation, 120
"Hooverville," photo, 125
Hugo, Victor, 188
Hulburd, Hiland R., and bank examination, 72, 77; and chartering, 61; and condition reports, 79-81; mentioned, 58

Incorporation laws, and bank chartering, 21-23
Independent Bankers Association, 149
Independent Treasury System, 21
inflation, during Revolutionary War, 12; post-World War II, 140-41
Insolvent National Bank Division, 180
Instructions in Regard to the Organization . . . of National Banks, see Manual of Instructions
insurance, see deposit insurance
Internal Revenue Act of March 3, 1865, and tax on state-bank notes, 57
investment banking, 15, 150
investments, of banks in the U.S., 1914-1930, table, 99; valuation of a bank's by examiners, 135-37

Jackson, Andrew, and no-bank movement, 22; opposition to central bank, 20, 32
Jefferson, Thomas, chose dollar as monetary unit, 12; opposition to first Bank of the United States, 19
Joint Economic Committee of Congress, 131
Jordan, Edward, and Currency Act of 1863, 37, 41, 44
Justice Department, anti-trust litigation to prevent bank mergers, 155-56, 159, 186-87

Kane, Thomas P., 108
Kefauver, Estes, and bank-acquisition legislation, 156
Kennedy, John F., economic policy of, 141-42; mentioned, 147
Knox, John J., and bank examination, 72; and chartering, 61, 67; mentioned, 173; and national currency, 40; portrait of, 62

Lacey, Edward, and bank supervision, 73, 75; and chartering, 67; and condition reports, 81
land banks, 11
Legal Division, 178
Legal Tender Act of 1862, 34-35, 41
legislation, historic banking, 191-246
lending, see loans
Lincoln, Abraham, signature on National Bank Act of 1864, photo, 46; support of National Currency Act of 1863, 42
liquidation, 180
liquidity ratio, of commercial banks, 147
"loan bills," Colonial, 11
loans, classification for bank-examining purposes, 134-35; increased volume of in post-World War II era, 143; liberalization of national bank rules on, 149-53; real estate, 65-66, 150-53; in U.S. from 1914 to 1930, table, 99
Lord, Eleazar, 37

McAdoo, William, and currency reform, 90; and Federal Reserve friction with Comptroller, 110
McCulloch, Hugh, and bank examination, 42, 71; and branching, 82; and chartering, 59-61; and condition reports, 79; and conversion of state banks, 52-53, 57; as first Comptroller, 47; monetary contraction policy of, 56; and National Bank Act of 1864, 51; portrait of, 48; Currency Act of 1863 revised by, 49-50
McFadden, Louis T., attempts to abolish Office of Comptroller, 113-15; urges investigation of Comptroller Williams, 115
McFadden Act, branching restrictions of, 105; effect on national banks, 98; text of, 214-22
McIntosh, Joseph W., concern over national banks' decline, 96-97; and Federal Reserve System, 116; mentioned, 173; quoted on chartering, 95-96; portrait of, 96
McKinney, Frank E., 149
McLean, George P., 116
McVickar, John, 36
Mann, Abijah, 23
Manual of Instructions, 59-60, 67-68, photo, 60

Massachusetts Bank, 13
Medill, Joseph, 36, 39
mergers, *see* bank mergers
Messersmith, George R., 40
Michigan Free Bank Act of 1837, 23
Miller, Adolf, 107
Missouri, litigation on branching, 104
money supply, banks' role in creating, 6;
Constitution's provisions for, 12; Contraction Act of 1866, 56; pre-1860, 29-32; and stabilization policy of 1961 to 1967, 141
Morse-Heinz banking chain, 85
multi-office banking, branch banking, 27-29, 81-85, 101-5, 131-34; chain banking, 85-86; group banking, 85-86; in post-depression period, 131-34
Murray, Lawrence, and bank examination, 79; and bank supervision, 75; and branching, 101; chartering policy of, 68; portrait of, 176

Nash, Simeon, 40
National Bank Act of 1864, and bank supervision, 71; and branching, 81-82, 101; and chartering, 68; name changed from National Banking Act, 81; passage of, 49; passages of, *photo*, 46; provisions of, 49, 51; real-estate loan provisions of, 65-66; reserves requirements of, 64; text of, 195-212
National Bank Consolidation Act of 1918, 101
National Banking Review, The, 148ₙ, 179
national banks, assessed to finance Comptroller's Office, 177-78; bond-secured circulation of, 90; branching of, 81-86, 101-5; chartering of, 95-96; circulation limitations on, 57-59; as foundation of Federal Reserve System, 95-96; lending rules of, 149, 152-53; liberalization of restraints on under Saxon's Comptrollership, 149-53; McFadden Act's effect on, 98; membership in Federal Reserve, 91-93; mergers of, from 1946 to 1966, *table*, 157; names and titles of, 49; National Currency Act of 1863 creates system of, 36-50; notes of, *photos* 52, 62, 119; remaining today of the first fifty, 190; re-opening of after 1933 suspension, 123, retrogression of system, 95-100; versus state banks, 2, 64-66, 95-100; state banks' reluctance to become, 47-49, 52-54; supervision of, 69-81; tax differential forces state banks to convert to, 53-54
National Banks and the Future, 149
National Credit Corporation, 120
National Currency Act of 1863, authorship of, 44-45; and branching, 81; circulation limitations of, 57; and Comptroller's staff, 173; Currency Bureau established by, 45-47; excerpts from, 191-95; lobbying for, 43-44; mentioned, 69, 71; passage of, 44-45; revised by National Bank Act of 1864, 49-50

National Currency Commission, proposal for, 90
National Monetary Commission, 88
National Reserve Association, 88
National Reserve Bank, 90
National Reserve Board, 90
Nevada, bank holidays in, 122
New York banks, country's cash reserves pooled in, 87-88
New York Free-Bank Law of 1838, 23, 82
New York Subtreasury, *photo*, 56
no-bank legislation, 22, 23
nonbank intermediaries, competition with commercial banks, 144-46, 152
notes, *see* bank notes

O'Connor, J.F.T., friction with Crowley of FDIC, 134; mentioned, 173; portrait of, 127; quoted on chartering, 128
Office of the Comptroller of the Currency, *see* Comptroller of the Currency, Office of
Olcott, Thomas W., 47
"Operation Twist," 141
Oregon, bank holidays in, 122
Organization Division, 179-80
"overbanking," 126, 131
Owen, Robert L., 90
Owen-Glass Bill, *see* Glass-Owen Bill

Panic of 1873, 68
paper money, Chase's advocacy of, 36; in Colonial era, 11-12; greenbacks, 35-36, 41, 55-59. *See also* currency
Parliamentary Currency Act of 1751, 13
Parliamentary Currency Act of 1764, 13
Patman, Wright, Saxon hearings held by, 160
Patterson, Joseph, 47
Perrin, John, 91-92
Pole, John W., and branching, 105, 132; concern over national banking system, 96-97; and Federal Reserve System, 116; mentioned, 173; portrait of, 106; quoted on bank examination, 112; quoted on bank failures, 99; quoted on chartering, 96
Potter, Orlando Bronson, 37, 44
printing tester, *photo*, 145
Proclamation of March 6, 1933, 122-23
Proclamation of March 9, 1933, 123
Proclamation of March 18, 1933, 124
promissory notes, Colonial, 11
Pujo Committee, 88

Raleigh, Sir Walter, 52
Randolph, Edmund, and first Bank of the United States, 19
real-estate loans, 65-66, 150, 152-53
receiverships, during depression, 123-24
recessions, of 1948, 140; of 1953-54, 140; of 1960, 141. *See also* depressions

banks after depression, 122-25; Secretary's relationship with Comptroller, 171; stabilization policy of, 141

Treasury-Federal Reserve Accord of 1951, 141, 143

Trenholm, William L., and bank examination, 78; and bank supervision, 73-75; and chartering, 67

Trust Powers Act of 1962, 228-30

Tyler, John, 21

Union Investment Company, 85

unit banking vs. branch banking, 27-29, 154

United States agencies, *see* name of agency, i.e. Treasury Department

United States economy, *see* economy of the United States

unsecured promissory notes, 151-52

Van Buren, Martin, 20

Walker, Amasa, 39

Walker, Robert, 39

Wall Street, "Black Thursday" panic scene on, *photo*, 120

Washington County Bank, Williamsport, Md., 82

Weeks, John M., 113

Western states, circulation limitations in, 59

White, Horace, 63

Wickersham, George W., 101

Wiener, Norbert, 161

wildcatting, 29

Williams, John Skelton, character, 113; and chartering, 69; friction with Congress, 113-15; friction with Federal Reserve Board, 107-10, 113-15; and Glass-Owen Bill, 90; mentioned, 149, 173; portrait of, 114

Willis, H. Parker, 89-90

Wilson, Woodrow, and currency reform proposals, 89; and idea of Federal Reserve Board, 89; quoted, *photo*, 94; signs Federal Reserve Act, 93; support of Glass-Owen Bill, 90

"windowdressing," 81

Woods, Noah, quoted, 77